MW00809774

Renegotiat.

Rising powers often seek to reshape the world order, triggering con-
frontations with those who seek to defend the status quo. In recent
years, as international institutions have grown in prevalence and influence, they have increasingly become central arenas for international
contestation. Phillip Lipscy examines how international institutions
evolve as countries seek to renegotiate the international order. He offers
a new theory of institutional change and explains why some institutions
change flexibly while others successfully resist or fall to the wayside.
The book uses a wealth of quantitative and qualitative empirical evidence to evaluate the theory from international organizations such as
the International Monetary Fund, World Bank, European Union,
League of Nations, United Nations, the International Telecommunications Satellite Organization, and Internet Corporation for Assigned
Names and Numbers. The book will also be of particular interest to
scholars interested in the historical and contemporary diplomacy of the
United States, Japan, and China.

PHILLIP Y. LIPSCY (Stanford University) is Assistant Professor of
Political Science and The Thomas Rohlen Center Fellow at the Freeman
Spogli Institute for International Studies. His fields of research include
international relations, international organizations, international and
comparative political economy, and the politics of East Asia, particularly Japan. Lipscy obtained his PhD in political science at Harvard
University and MA in international policy studies and BA in economics
and political science at Stanford University.

Renegotiating the World Order

Institutional Change in International Relations

PHILLIP Y. LIPSCY

Stanford University

CAMBRIDGE
UNIVERSITY PRESS

CAMBRIDGE
UNIVERSITY PRESS

University Printing House, Cambridge CB2 8BS, United Kingdom

One Liberty Plaza, 20th Floor, New York, NY 10006, USA

477 Williamstown Road, Port Melbourne, VIC 3207, Australia

314-321, 3rd Floor, Plot 3, Splendor Forum, Jasola District Centre, New Delhi - 110025, India

79 Anson Road, #06-04/06, Singapore 079906

Cambridge University Press is part of the University of Cambridge.

It furthers the University's mission by disseminating knowledge in the pursuit of education, learning and research at the highest international levels of excellence.

www.cambridge.org
Information on this title: www.cambridge.org/9781316604281

© Cambridge University Press 2017

First published 2017
First paperback edition 2018

A catalogue record for this publication is available from the British Library

Library of Congress Cataloging in Publication data
NAMES: Lipscy, Phillip Y., author.
TITLE: Renegotiating the world order : institutional change in international relations / Phillip Y. Lipscy.
DESCRIPTION: Cambridge : Cambridge University Press, 2016. | Includes bibliographical references and index.
IDENTIFIERS: LCCN 2016035545 | ISBN 9781107149762 (hardback)
SUBJECTS: LCSH: International agencies. | International organization. | Regionalism (International organization) | International relations. |
BISAC: POLITICAL SCIENCE / International Relations / General.
CLASSIFICATION: LCC JZ4839 .L56 2016 | DDC 341.2–dc23 LC record available at https://lccn.loc.gov/2016035545

ISBN 978-1-107-14976-2 Hardback
ISBN 978-1-316-60428-1 Paperback

To Rie, Sora, and Mari

Contents

Figures

Tables

Acknowledgments

This book has benefited from the guidance, criticism, and support of so many wonderful people and organizations. The book was developed from a dissertation project at the Department of Government at Harvard University. My dissertation committee, Lisa Martin (Chair), Jeffry Frieden, Andy Kydd, Susan Pharr, and Beth Simmons gave me the impetus for this project and spent countless hours helping me refine the theoretical and empirical approach. I could not have done it without them. I would also like to give special thanks to the participants in my book conference at Stanford University – Lawrence Broz, Jim Fearon, Judy Goldstein, David Lake, Ken Scheve, Ken Schultz, Mike Tomz, and Erik Voeten – who provided extremely valuable advice and critique as I worked toward finalizing the book. The two anonymous reviewers also gave me excellent suggestions. I would also like to express my gratitude to Daniel Okimoto, my dear friend and mentor, who took the risk of admitting me into his graduate seminar on Japanese politics at Stanford, despite me being a sophomore with oddly bleached hair. I probably would not have chosen this career were it not for that rather stunning decision. Thank you.

I received invaluable feedback and insights from many scholars at various stages of this project, among them Jim Alt, Jennifer Amyx, Bob Bates, Jonathan Bendor, Lisa Blaydes, Bear Braumoeller, Lawrence Broz, Amy Catalinac, Seok-ju Cho, Keith Darden, Jorge Dominguez, Asif Efrat, Margarita Estevez-Abe, Jim Fearon, Martha Finnemore, Jeffry Frieden, Judy Goldstein, Michael Green, Avner Greif, Bill Grimes, Steph Haggard, Koichi Hamada, Michael Hiscox, Nobuhiro Hiwatari, Dan Hopkins, Takeo Hoshi, Llewelyn Hughes, Karen Jusko, Miles Kahler, Saori Katada, Junko Kato, Steven Kelts, Rie Kijima, Yevgeniy Kirpichevsky,

Masaru Kohno, Barbara Koremenos, Kenji Kushida, Andy Kydd, David Laitin, David Lake, Olivia Lau, Stan Markus, Isabela Mares, Nikolay Marinov, Lisa Martin, Terry Moe, Colin Moore, Andrew Moravcsik, Kimberly Morgan, Isaac Nakhimovsky, Rebecca Nelson, Thomas Oatley, Daniel Okimoto, Sonal Pandya, Louis Pauly, Maggie Penn, Susan Pharr, Alison Post, Andrew Reeves, Jonathan Rodden, Stephen Rosen, Frances Rosenbluth, Ryo Sahashi, Holger Schmidt, Ken Scheve, Ken Schultz, Sandra Sequeira, Ian Shapiro, Ken Shepsle, Kay Shimizu, Gi-Wook Shin, Beth Simmons, Peter Swenson, Hitoshi Tanaka, Strom Thacker, Mike Tomz, Erik Voeten, and Barry Weingast. I would also like to thank the participants of various seminars and workshops at George Washington, Harvard, Princeton, Stanford, and Yale, as well as participants at the annual meetings of AAS, APSA, IPES, ISA, and MPSA. Additional thanks to my many colleagues and friends for their excellent suggestions, feedback, and moral support. I would also like to express particular appreciation to Meiko Kotani, Jackie Sargent, Huma Shaikh, Eliana Vasquez, Thom Wall, and Debbie Warren for their friendship and support throughout the process.

I received absolutely excellent research assistance from Andrea Da Motta Calvo, Laura Conigliaro, Alison Ge, Alejandro Gramaglia, Lonjezo Hamisi, Trevor Incerti, Azusa Katagiri, Zvisinei Sandi, and Angela Zhang. Lizhi Liu and Zheng Wu deserve special mention for being willing to participate in my book conference and compile over fifty pages of notes!

This project was made possible by the generous support of several organizations. I am thankful for the financial support I received from the Graduate School of Arts and Sciences, the Program on U.S.-Japan Relations, the Reischauer Institute of Japanese Studies, and the Weatherhead Center for International Affairs at Harvard University, as well as the Department of Political Science, Freeman Spogli Institute for International Studies, and Walter H. Shorenstein Asia-Pacific Research Center at Stanford University. My appreciation also goes to the Institute for Global and International Studies at The George Washington University, the Center for Strategic and International Studies, and the Institute of Social Science at Tokyo University for hosting me during my field research. I would also like to express my sincere gratitude to the many government officials in China, Europe, Japan, Taiwan, and the United States, as well as the European Union, IMF, United Nations, and World Bank, for their generosity with their time and resources. I am particularly indebted to Chris Allen, Mitsuru Kitano, Jerry Liu, and Hirofumi Takinami.

My gratitude also goes to William G. Jacoby and four anonymous reviewers of the *American Journal of Political Science*. The material in Chapter 3 is adapted and extended with permission from a 2015 article published by the author in that journal entitled, "Explaining Institutional Change: Policy Areas, Outside Options, and the Bretton Woods Institutions."

Finally, I would like to thank my family, without whom I could not have completed this project. Masae Serizawa, my mother, and Motoko Serizawa, my grandmother, sacrificed immensely for me in my youth and essentially made everything in my life possible. My father and mother-in-law, Ben and Miyoko Lipscy, developed my intellectual curiosity and discipline from an early stage, and I doubt I would have otherwise become an academic. Last but not least, I would like to thank my dearest wife Rie and my vivacious daughters, Sora and Mari, for putting up with me throughout this project and bringing so much joy to my life every day. This book is dedicated to them.

I

Introduction

In June 1926, Brazil and Spain announced that they would withdraw from the League of Nations. At issue was the League's proposal to grant Germany a permanent seat on the League's Council, while denying similar status for other aspiring countries. Spain still fancied itself a Great Power, despite losing the vast majority of its colonial possessions in the nineteenth century. Brazil was the preeminent state in Latin America, and it asserted that the Council was unbalanced:

It must be recognized how odious becomes the exclusion of America from representation by one of its States, in the permanent framework of the Council, in view of the fact that the privilege of such a representation is accorded to the other continents.[1]

The permanent members of the League Council rejected these demands, but a compromise was proposed: "semi-permanent" seats, which would give states like Brazil and Spain the opportunity to remain on the Council indefinitely, contingent on election by the Assembly. Both countries found this compromise unacceptable. Spain eventually rescinded its decision to withdraw, but Brazil left and never returned to the League.

In 1984, the United States threatened to withdraw from the United Nations Educational, Scientific and Cultural Organization (UNESCO). US representatives criticized UNESCO programs and personnel as answering "to an agenda that is often inimical to US interests" and adopting a policy stance that "too frequently coincides with that of the Soviet Union."[2] UNESCO operated under one-country-one-vote rules,

[1] Edwards 1929, 144.   [2] US Department of State 1984, 3.

I

and the United States was frequently outvoted by countries sympathetic to the Eastern Bloc. The US government found it unacceptable that it was obligated to contribute the largest share of the budget to an organization that so poorly reflected its own interests:

> The representative principle of one nation one vote is not inappropriate to UNESCO. But it should be understood that the UNESCO decision-making system can ... establish cumulative trends antithetical to the position of the geographic group that contributes to an overwhelmingly large part of the budget.[3]

The United States proposed several reforms that would increase its voice in the organization, most importantly modifications to the decision rules to require support from major financial contributors to the agency. When these demands were denied, the United States formally withdrew from the organization. Gregory J. Newell, assistant secretary of state for international organization affairs, asserted that the threat of US withdrawal would put pressure on the organization and speed up the pace of reform.[4] However, serious reform only came in 1999 with the appointment of Koichiro Matsuura as Director General, and the United States would remain absent from the organization for nearly twenty years.

In the early 1980s, Japanese policymakers initiated a campaign for greater representation and voice in the Bretton Woods institutions: the International Monetary Fund (IMF) and the World Bank. Japanese representatives declared that the status quo failed to reflect their country's emergence as the second largest economy in the world.[5] Japan pushed for voting rights commensurate with the size of its economy, greater representation of its nationals as employees, and ideological recognition for its developmental principles. Japanese officials adopted an aggressive bargaining strategy, threatening to withhold financial contributions if its goals were not met. As I will show in Chapter 4, Japanese objectives were achieved much more rapidly in the World Bank than in the IMF.

These anecdotes illustrate the basic dynamic that lies at the heart of this book. Policymakers frequently create institutions to facilitate and manage

---

[3] The Honorable Gregory Newell, letter to Mr. A. M'Bow. Presented by US Permanent Representative, Jean Gerard, July 13, 1984, 2.

[4] David R. Francis, "UNESCO Faces up to US Pullout, Shrinking Budget," *Christian Science Monitor*, December 17, 1984 .

[5] For example, Statement by Haruo Mayekawa (Alternative Governor of the Fund and the Bank of Japan), *Summary Proceedings of the IMF-World Bank Annual Meetings*, 1981, 59; Statement by Michio Watanabe (Governor of the Fund and the Bank of Japan), *Summary Proceedings of the IMF-World Bank Annual Meetings*, 1982, 59.

international cooperation. However, member countries often grow dissatisfied with their representation or influence over such arrangements. The source of dissatisfaction varies: domination by a single country can breed resentment; wealthy states may perceive that their influence is not commensurate to their financial contributions; rapidly rising states may feel that existing arrangements do not sufficiently reflect their newfound power.

Some institutions change swiftly to accommodate dissatisfied participants. Others decline or collapse as members exit. Yet some others resist change, but nonetheless remain robust. Why? What are the implications of this variation in institutional change for our understanding of international relations and the nature of political institutions? Will newly rising states – such as Brazil, China, and India – encounter accommodation or resistance as they seek to establish themselves in positions of influence in the contemporary world order? These are the puzzles this book seeks to answer.

This book proposes and evaluates a novel theory of institutional change in international relations, drawing insights from the economics literature on industrial organization. The core insight is that political institutions are affected by the underlying characteristics of their policy areas, much like firms are affected by markets. However, there is a crucial difference in how competition affects firms and institutions: whereas competition among firms primarily affects pricing and quality incentives, competition among international institutions affects the context of interstate bargaining among members, shaping the trajectory of institutional change.

I will argue that policy areas vary in their propensity for competition, both among institutions and from bilateral, unilateral, and private sources. For example, while development aid can be distributed effectively by many types of donors – private, public, small, large, unilateral, multilateral – there are compelling reasons to concentrate functions in a single, universalistic institution for managing international financial crises – the need for global surveillance and coverage over financial institutions, sufficient availability of funding on short notice, and political cover for imposing controversial conditions on countries in crisis. In turn, institutional members are confronted with very different bargaining contexts across policy areas. In institutions situated in competitive policy areas, outside options are attractive: dissatisfied members have plenty of alternative mechanisms through which to pursue their objectives. Hence, dissatisfied members can credibly threaten exit from an institution if their demands are not met. In contrast, in policy areas where outside options are unavailable or unattractive, such leverage cannot be brought to bear. Hence, competition disciplines institutions: competitive institutions must adjust frequently and flexibly or risk irrelevance as members move on to more satisfactory arrangements. Rigidity in the face of widespread dissatisfaction, or path dependence, is sustainable only for institutions that are able to limit competition and hence the attractiveness of outside options. As this book will illustrate, this theory provides a powerful explanation for institutional change across a wide range of policy issues, such as international finance, collective security, and internet governance.

WHY COUNTRIES BARGAIN OVER INTERNATIONAL INSTITUTIONS

Why should we care about institutional change in international relations, and how it varies across policy areas? What motivates countries to pursue institutional change? One important reason why policymakers across the globe care about their status in international institutions is prestige.[6] A permanent seat on the UN Security Council is widely seen as an indicator of contemporary great power status. Recognition as a great power was a major foreign policy objective for many countries, such as Germany, Japan, and Russia, prior to World War II, and it remains an important issue for aspiring countries today. Similarly, voting shares in major economic institutions are often seen as indicative of a country's standing in the world economy.[7] Countries often celebrate the placement of their citizens as leaders in international organizations as a mark of recognition and national achievement.[8]

---

[6] For the role of prestige and status in international relations, see Dore 1975; Gilpin 1981; Kang 2003; Lebow 2008; Paul, Larson, and Wohlforth 2014.

[7] A *New York Times* article published on the verge of the establishment of the IMF noted that: "Much more important than the precise amount of foreign exchange which becomes available to member nations under the quotas to be agreed upon in connection with the international monetary fund is the matter of national prestige in the ranking of one country against another in the new scale of relative national economic importance being fashioned here." (John H. Crider, "Fund Quotas Show Race for Prestige," *The New York Times*, July 10, 1944.)

[8] For example, the presidential office of South Korea commented that Ban Ki-moon's appointment as Secretary General of the United Nations "is a significant and proud occasion that constitutes a testimony to the heightened status of (South) Korea in the world." ("Asia Heralds Pick of South Korea's Ban as U.N. Secretary-General," *Asia Post*, October 14, 2006). In 1999, the Thai candidacy of Supachai Panitchpakdi for Director General of the WTO was described as a "matter of national prestige," and Thai Deputy

However, bargaining over international institutions is not only a matter of status or prestige. As I will illustrate in subsequent chapters, influence over international institutions brings important, tangible benefits. A large body of recent scholarship shows that countries such as the United States often exercise asymmetrical, informal influence over the operation of major international institutions, biasing policy outcomes in their favor.[9] For example, US influence over the IMF means greater support for US allies during economic crises and less risk for US economic interests abroad. Japanese diplomats note that Japan's lack of permanent representation on the UN Security Council has proven costly on several occasions, depriving them of access to internal deliberations and the ability to shape the agenda on resolutions such as those vis-à-vis North Korea.[10] Lack of employee representation diminishes the ability of member states to make use of informal networks to acquire information and shape the policy output of an organization. Factors such as the location of an institution's headquarters can also affect the ideological leanings of an international organization and consequent policymaking. In the 1990s, the economic orthodoxy espousing sound macro and liberal market policies as a prerequisite to economic growth acquired the location-specific appellation: "The Washington Consensus," reflecting the headquarter locations of the US Treasury and the Bretton Woods institutions.

Contestation over international institutions has grown increasingly salient since the end of World War II, as the United States and its allies established and expanded an international architecture centered around international institutions such as the United Nations, Bretton Woods Institutions, and General Agreement on Tariffs and Trade (GATT)/World Trade Organization (WTO).[11] International institutions have proliferated and expanded dramatically over the past seven decades, and they now routinely occupy central functions across a wide range of issues areas that were traditionally managed through unilateral or bilateral means. It is no surprise that rising powers such as Germany and Japan, and more recently China and India, have placed high priority on securing greater

---

Foreign Minister Suhumbhand noted that "Thai public sentiment towards [the US] could be severely damaged if Washington snubbed Supachai." ("Thai Pride at Stake in Race for Job," *AFP*, March 30, 1999).

[9] See among others, Thacker 1999; Broz and Hawes 2006; Fleck and Kilby 2006; Stone 2011; Lim and Vreeland 2013.

[10] Personal Interview, Japanese Representative to the United Nations, 2005.

[11] See, among others, Krasner 1983; Keohane 1984; Ikenberry 2000.

influence in the international institutional architecture, either by seeking reforms or proposing new institutions more favorably disposed to their interests. I will return to this topic in the concluding chapter, where I discuss the broader implications of this book.

Contemporary foreign policymakers clearly place immense importance in securing adequate representation and voice in international institutions. British MEP Charles Tannock explained the value of a UN Security Council seat as follows:

It's essential, as a defining characteristic of a nation's foreign policy, to have the ability to speak, when they want to, in their national interest. And clearly, the seat in the UN is one of the most important things that we can have as a nuclear power, as a founding member of the Security Council.[12]

Indian Prime Minister Manmohan Singh, campaigning to obtain a permanent seat for his own country, criticized the Security Council for a "democratic deficit," and remarked that:

Until the UN becomes more representative of the contemporary world and more relevant to our concerns and aspirations, its ability to deliver on . . . its own charter obligations will remain limited[13]

Bank of Japan Governor Toshihiko Fukui expressed similar sentiments about the distribution of quotas in the IMF, which determine voting shares, by noting that "It is important to recognize that the current distribution of IMF quotas represents another form of unsustainable global imbalance."[14] Malaysian Foreign Ministry representative Tan Seng Sung noted that "Reforms are therefore needed to the decision-making structures and processes in the [international financial institutions]. This will balance the current leanings towards free market principles against issues facing emerging markets, taking into cognizance the need to accommodate the different interests and circumstances of individual countries that are at different stages of development."[15]

Similarly, commenting on perceived US domination of the Internet Corporation for Assigned Names and Numbers (ICANN), the organization that manages the assignment of internet domain names, UN

---

[12] "EU to ask for UN Security Council Seat," *RT*, May 5, 2011.
[13] "India, South Africa Demand UN Reform," *BBC News*, September 9, 2005.
[14] "Statement by the Honorable Toshihiko Fukui Governor of the Bank of Japan and Alternate Governor of the IMF for Japan at Twelfth Meeting of the International Monetary and Financial Committee Washington, D.C.," September 24, 2005.
[15] Martin Khor, "Reform the IMF Quota and Decision-making System," *Third World Network*, August 3, 2000.

Secretary General Kofi Anan asserted that, "developing countries find it difficult to follow all these processes and feel left out of Internet governance structures ... For historical reasons, the United States has the ultimate authority over some of the Internet's core resources. It is an authority that many say should be shared with the international community."[16] The empirical chapters of this book contain numerous examples that illustrate the same point. Asymmetrical representation and influence over international institutions is not only a compelling topic for academic reasons: it is a top priority for policymakers across the globe.

INSTITUTIONAL CHANGE IN INTERNATIONAL RELATIONS

How do institutions change in response to international bargaining? Scholars have long recognized the tendency for institutions to "lock in" initial conditions, even after considerable shifts in underlying realities.[17] This tendency has also been observed in international institutions, particularly in reference to the extension of the stabilizing effects of hegemony beyond the apex of a dominant state's power.[18] Such institutional rigidity, or path dependence, can be helpful for maintaining continuity and stability in the international system. However, it can also produce glaring discrepancies between a state's perception of its place in the international order and its ability to obtain preferred outcomes.

Historically, a particularly contentious form of institutional rigidity has concerned distributional outcomes – the distribution of national representation and influence among member states in an international institution. Rapidly growing states have often expressed frustration at what they see as the excruciatingly slow pace of change in institutional features such as voting shares and other forms of formal representation, composition of personnel, and influence and agenda-setting power. This has been a central issue for high-growth states that were poorly represented at the initial bargaining phase of major post–World War II international organizations. Among these states are Japan, Germany, and Italy, the Axis Powers of World War II, as well as many developing states that were either dependencies or too weak to play a major role in the

---

[16] Kofi Annan, "The U.N. Isn't a Threat to the Net," *The New York Times*, November 5, 2005.
[17] David 1985; Goldstone 1988; Arthur 1994; Pierson 2000.
[18] Krasner 1976; Keohane 1984; Ikenberry 2001.

initial bargaining process. While such states have increased their relative geopolitical and economic weight in the international system, recognition of their newfound status in international organizations has not been automatic.

Easily quantifiable measures point to a striking lack of change in distributional attributes of some of the most prominent international organizations. The most conspicuous of these is what can be described as the World War II effect, the tendency for contemporary institutions to reflect the outcome of a war fought over seventy years ago. The five permanent members of the UN Security Council – China, France, Russia, the United Kingdom, and the United States – incorporated the principal Allied Powers of World War II, and membership has remained static since inception despite considerable shifts in underlying geopolitical conditions. While it is difficult to construct a single measure that captures the geopolitical weight of a state in the international system, a strong case can be made for accepting new members. According to one widely cited measure, the Composite Index of National Capability collected by the Correlates of War project,[19] Japan has outranked France and the United Kingdom since roughly the 1970s and has been about on par with Russia since the collapse of the Soviet Union. A similar argument could be made for the inclusion of Germany and India, two countries that have also been active participants in UN peacekeeping operations. In terms of overall contributions to the regular budget of the UN, as of 2010, Japan and Germany were the second and third largest contributors, together accounting for about 20 percent of the total budget, far outstripping the contributions of permanent members China (3.2 percent) and Russia (1.6 percent).[20] Nonetheless, reforming the Security Council has proved difficult despite repeated attempts.

The voting shares of the IMF have also exhibited a tendency to overrepresent inception members and underrepresent members who joined later.[21] Figure 1.1 separates G7 states into Allied and Axis powers according to their affiliation during World War II and plots shares of IMF voting power as a proportion of shares of world gross domestic product (GDP) – the most straightforward measure of a country's weight

---

[19] Singer, Bremer, and Stuckey 1972 (v. 3.02).
[20] Secretariat of the United Nations, "Status of Contributions as at 31 December 2010," ST/ADM/SER.B/828.
[21] Rapkin, Elston, and Strand 1997.

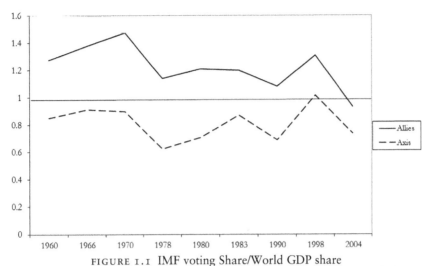

FIGURE I.I IMF voting Share/World GDP share
Note: Allies include Canada, France, United Kingdom, and United States. Axis includes Germany, Italy, and Japan. GDP is nominal. Data from IMF, Economics Intelligence Unit, and Rapkin et al. (1997).

in the global economy. By this measure, the wartime Axis powers (Germany, Italy, Japan) have lagged behind their actual place in the world economy despite the passing of over half a century and dramatic shifts in economic realities.[22]

Similarly, employment in international organizations has tended to favor nationals from the victors of World War II at the expense of the defeated powers. The Union of International Associations compiles data on the high-ranking officers in international organizations by country of nationality and educational background. According to this data, among the G7 countries, the former Allied powers of World War II have on average about twice as many prominent officers per country compared to Axis powers. As of 2012, France (337) had considerably more high-ranking officers than Germany (260), and Japan (49) had fewer than much smaller states such as Australia (101) and Canada (161).[23] Similarly, employees of international organizations educated in the entire city

---

[22] The IMF quota formulas incorporate measures besides GDP, including share of world trade and reserves. However, the quota formulas themselves have been historically subject to negotiation among major quota holders and actual quota shares do not necessarily reflect outcomes of the quota formulas. See Chapters 3 and 4.

[23] Union of International Associations 2014, figure 8.3.

of Tokyo are only a fraction of those educated in single academic institutions such as Harvard or Yale University.[24] The picture is much the
same for developing countries that were not well-represented at the
inception of many postwar institutions, such as Korea, India, and communist China. The selection of top level executives also remains stable by
convention in a range of institutions – most notably the norm that assigns
a European national as the Managing Director of the International Monetary Fund and a US national as the President of the World Bank.

This discrepancy in personnel has multiple causes – for example, due to
limited labor market mobility and language barriers, East Asian nationals
have traditionally faced greater obstacles and risk in pursuing full-time
employment at international organizations. However, there are several
institutional factors that tend to make employment static. Most notably,
the distribution of institutional headquarters tilts toward countries such as
France and the United States, which played important roles in institution
building in the postwar period. The presence of an institutional headquarters can facilitate the employment of host-country nationals for a variety of
reasons, among them: 1. Reducing hardship for nationals who can continue to reside in their home country. 2. Greater visibility and opportunities
to establish contacts with current employees. 3. The tendency for current
employees to prefer new hires with similar training or backgrounds.

In sharp contrast to these examples of path dependence, or the stubborn persistence of initial conditions, some international institutions have
responded flexibly and rapidly to shifts in international realities. The
substantive chapters of this book will highlight many instances of flexible
adjustment among international institutions. For example, some institutions, such as Intelsat during its later years, utilize mechanical voting rules
designed to adjust seamlessly to the ebb and flow of power. Unlike the
IMF, the voting rules of the Council of the European Union have
exhibited no bias in favor of inception members. Development lending
institutions, such as the World Bank, often distribute voting rights and
informal influence in ways that closely mirror underlying economic power
and financial contributions.

Perceived imbalances in distributional features of international institutions are a politically salient issue for member states. Diplomatic cam-
paigns to bring about redistributive change are ubiquitous. Nonetheless,
there is striking variation in the degree of change that materializes. Some

---

[24] Union of International Associations 2005, figure 6.2.2.

institutions successfully resist change for decades at a time. Other institutions adapt rapidly. Yet some others collapse as dissatisfied members pursue exit. These outcomes have important implications for the evolution of international cooperation and how the international system accommodates rising powers.

INSTITUTIONAL RENEGOTIATION

Despite the development of a large body of literature in recent decades on international institutions, regimes, and organizations, detailed examinations of institutional change have been relatively scarce. One leading cause for this scarcity is that scholars have often approached the question of institutional change and persistence in dichotomous terms, asking questions such as: do institutions matter?; are institutions persistent, or are they malleable to underlying power and interests?; do institutions lock in and magnify initial conditions, or do they respond dynamically to the outcomes of rational interactions among members?

In the 1980s–1990s, scholars of institutions split sharply along paradigmatic lines. The neorealist-neoliberal debate focused scholarly attention on whether or not international institutions "matter." More specifically, are international institutions epiphenomenal to underlying state interests and capabilities (the neorealist position),[25] or do they have an independent impact on the outcome of international politics (the neoliberal position)?[26] In the former case, institutional change is simply a reflection of underlying interstate dynamics and unworthy of independent examination. In the latter case, institutions have some independent staying power and therefore deserve special attention.[27]

The neorealist-neoliberal debate split scholars into opposing camps and focused attention on the dichotomous questions of whether international institutions mattered, whether they exerted an independent effect, and whether the policy output of institutions was purely epiphenomenal to underlying state interests. Much of the subsequent work in the neoliberal tradition has responded to this debate by demonstrating that international institutions do indeed exert a powerful influence on international relations in a wide range of empirical applications.[28]

---

[25] Mearsheimer 1994; Gruber 2000; Glennon 2003.
[26] Among others, see Gilpin 1981; Keohane 1984; Pierson 1996; Glennon 2003.
[27] See, for example, Krasner 1976.
[28] Among others, see Martin and Simmons 1998; Lake 2001; Gilligan and Johns 2012.

The dichotomous nature of the neorealist-neoliberal debate left the literature largely devoid of generalizable, rationalist theories about *variations* in the proclivity for institutions to change.[29] Specifically, what variables might explain differences in the tendency for international institutions to resist or accept change? When are we likely to observe institutions that will rapidly mirror underlying shifts in preferences and power, and under what conditions will we find institutions that remain robust in the presence of such shifts?

Historical institutionalism provides one theoretical framework to analyze how path dependence and lock-in can lead to the persistence of initial conditions over time in international institutions. The key insight concerns the existence of increasing returns processes that tend to push systems to extreme conditions. In neoclassical economics, decreasing returns are usually assumed as conditions conducive to the attainment of stable equilibria. Increasing returns can produce autocatalytic positive feedback loops under conditions such as network externalities or disproportionately large sunk costs.[30] However, in applications to politics, historical institutionalists have generally focused not on variations in institutional change, but instead on using increasing returns processes to justify paying greater attention to history, initial conditions, and the impact of critical junctures on subsequent policymaking. This has led to a focus on contextual variables such as unintended consequences and accidents arising from issue complexity and short time-horizons.[31] While such factors surely matter, and they can be magnified in the presence of increasing returns processes, this focus has limited the utility of the theoretical framework for explaining variation in institutional persistence and change. As Peters, Pierre, and King argue: "the [historical institutionalist] theory unfortunately has less to offer in terms of explanation, let alone prediction, for [institutional] changes. Further, historical institutionalism has no way of dealing adequately with the more gradual transformations we have demonstrated."[32]

Unfortunately, rationalist approaches toward international institutions, which have evolved from the neoliberal tradition, have also failed to generate a compelling theoretical framework through which to analyze institutional change. As Jupille, Mattli, and Snidal argue, an important

---

[29] Powell 1994; Martin 1997.   [30] Goldstone 1988; David 1994; Pierson 2000.
[31] Pierson 1996.
[32] Peters, Pierre, and King 2005, 1296. Important exceptions in the domestic political context include Thelen 2004; Mahoney and Thelen 2009.

limitation of rationalist approaches toward institutions is that they generally predict "relatively frictionless movement from new problem to optimal institutional solution."[33] More specifically, scholars in the rationalist tradition have primarily focused their attention on explaining how various features of issue areas and strategic settings affect the patterns and forms of international cooperation,[34] while paying less attention to the sources and cause of variation in institutional change and persistence. Hence, one implicit implication of most rationalist theories is that institutional change should closely follow shifts in underlying features of the strategic setting, such as interests, power, and the nature of problems being confronted.

An important contribution of this book is to show that variations in institutional change and persistence can be explained by a fundamentally rationalist framework. It is not the case that rational choice necessarily implies optimal design or adaptation. Variation in the tendency for institutions to change or persist can also arise as outcomes of rational, redistributive conflict. Institutions embody specific mechanisms to aggregate the preferences of members, and these mechanisms have important distributive consequences. Institutional change is often a contentious affair, in which a subset of states prefers maintenance of the status quo, while another subset prefers reform or the creation of alternative arrangements. What my theory shows is that such distributive conflict resolves in strikingly different ways according to underlying characteristics of policy areas, resulting in varying patterns of institutional change. The theory can explain both the stubborn persistence of some institutional arrangements and the rapid adjustment of others. The theory also provides an explanation for the proliferation of seemingly ineffectual international institutions: policymakers face strong incentives to propose alternative institutions – even if they are redundant or ultimately ineffective – in order to escape dissatisfactory distributive outcomes and to apply leverage vis-à-vis status quo institutions.

This book synthesizes important concepts from the rational and historical institutionalist schools of international relations. The theory incorporates network effects – a key concept from the economic literature of path dependence – as a variable within a rationalist, strategic choice

---

[33] Jupille, Mattli, and Snidal 2013, 15.

[34] For example, see Oye 1985; Martin 1992; Abbott and Snidal 1998; Koremenos, Lipson, and Snidal 2001; Rosendorff and Milner 2001; Magee and Morelli 2003; Koremenos 2005; Johns 2007.

approach toward institutions[35] in order to generate generalizable predictions about institutional change that can be evaluated against empirical evidence. The theory moves beyond previous dichotomous debates by explaining variation in institutional change and persistence: what kind of institutions are persistent or path dependent, and what kind of institutions adjust flexibly in accordance with underlying power? The theory generates testable empirical predictions that are not foreshadowed by any existing theories or debates.

Ex Ante vs. Ex Post Bargaining

One elegant solution to the neorealist-neoliberal debate of the 1980s and 1990s was proposed by James Fearon.[36] Fearon argued that many features of international cooperation can be captured by a simple model that separates cooperation into an initial bargaining phase, which is zero-sum and determines the terms of cooperation, and an enforcement phase, in which ongoing cooperation is maintained. This formulization of international cooperation has spawned a rich literature that focuses on institutional design and bargaining at the initial stages of cooperation.[37] However, an important shortcoming of this approach is that it does not provide much leverage over an important and common feature of international bargaining: renegotiation of distributive arrangements in the presence of a preexisting institution.

Redistributive institutional change can be conceptualized as a bargaining problem. In an anarchic international system with no higher authority, states dissatisfied with existing distributional outcomes must bargain with other states for a revision of the status quo. If such bargaining is successful, a new distributive arrangement will emerge and institutional change will be observed. However, because existing scholarship on international institutions has focused on bargaining at the initial stages of cooperation,[38] it is not very helpful when contemplating renegotiation and institutional change.

The type of ex post renegotiation I analyze in this book is distinct from ex ante bargaining over institutional design features[39] such as escape

---

[35] Lake and Powell 1999.   [36] Fearon 1998.

[37] Abbott and Snidal 1998; Koremenos, Lipson, and Snidal 2001; Rosendorff and Milner 2001; Thompson 2005; Mitchell 2006.

[38] For example, Fearon 1998; Drezner 2000; Blaydes 2004.

[39] Koremenos, Lipson, and Snidal 2001.

clauses[40] or provisions for flexibility.[41] Empirically, international institutions and associated rules are often created by a different set of actors operating under vastly different conditions than those who subsequently seek redistributive change. For example, the UN Charter was negotiated initially in 1942–1945 primarily among the United States, USSR, and Great Britain with some input from the fifty initial signatory members. About two-thirds of UN membership is now comprised of states that had no role in negotiating the Charter, a document that specifies the composition of the Security Council as well as specific procedures for reform. The UN Charter is not subject to renegotiation on each occasion a new member is admitted to the institution. For member states such as Germany and Japan, institutional rules have been effectively exogenous. In more extreme cases, such as governance over the internet, status quo institutional arrangements have been established unilaterally, essentially without an initial bargaining phase. This is a common feature of international institutions: institutional design and renegotiation are fundamentally distinct processes.

ARGUMENT AND LAYOUT OF THE BOOK

The central argument of the book is that political institutions are affected by characteristics of their policy areas, much like private firms are affected by markets. While markets affect firm behavior primarily through price and production incentives, policy areas affect the context under which institutions are renegotiated. In policy areas where it is easy to pursue similar ends through unilateral, bilateral, or multilateral alternatives, institutions are disciplined by competition: they must adjust flexibly or face irrelevance. On the other hand, when the nature of a policy area makes it costly to pursue outside options, institutions can survive despite inflexibility and distorted representation among its members.

The theoretical premises of the book will be laid out in Chapter 2. While some policy problems can be resolved effectively using a variety of forms – unilateral measures, bilateral cooperation, multilateral institutions – others are more effectively managed through institutional solutions that inherently limit alternatives. In effect, policy areas vary in their propensity for competition, both among institutions and from bilateral, unilateral, and private sources. In turn, institutions differ in the

---

[40] Rosendorff and Milner 2001.   [41] Koremenos 2001.

attractiveness of available outside options for members. Where outside
options are attractive, members can utilize the threat of exit to push for
distributional change in line with their actual capabilities. In policy areas
where outside options are unavailable or unattractive, such leverage is
difficult to bring to bear. I develop a formal model of institutional renegotiation to illustrate how unattractive outside options can lead to distributive rigidity. The theory predicts that institutions operating in competitive
policy areas will change flexibly or diminish as they lose members and
resources to alternatives. The ability of a competitive institution to adapt
hinges on the nature of internal rules, which affect the incentives of
dissatisfied states to challenge the status quo or leave.[42] Institutions that
face limited competition are better able to resist change, effectively trap-
ping   dissatisfied   states   despite   maintaining   skewed   distributive
outcomes.[43]

The empirical chapters of the book examine a wide range of institutions to evaluate the predictive power of the theory. Existing research
on international institutions has often relied on case study comparisons or
quantitative analysis of outcomes associated with single institutions. This
stems from a basic challenge of causal inference: it is difficult to isolate
independent variables of interest across diverse institutional settings, in
which a multitude of factors vary simultaneously. The WTO and Organization of the Petroleum Exporting Countries (OPEC) not only facilitate
cooperation in different policy areas, but they also have different membership, time periods of existence, formal rules, and headquarter locations. This poses a crucial challenge to the comparative study of
international institutions.

Chapter 3 overcomes this problem of causal inference by exploiting
common features of the IMF and World Bank (the Bretton Woods Institutions). Several features of the Bretton Woods institutions make it possible to isolate the effect of policy area characteristics on institutional
change. Because the IMF and World Bank are sister institutions, they have
essentially identical membership and institutional rules governing the
redistribution of voting rights. However, the de facto determination of

---

[42] This can be thought of as analogous to the choice between Exit and Voice in Hirschman
1970.
[43] One might think of this as analogous to the economics literature on the chain store
paradox and efforts by monopolists to deter entry (Selten 1978; Kreps and Wilson 1982):
just as monopolists can retain greater rents when the cost of entry is high for competitors,
overrepresented states can retain a greater share of the distributive pie in institutions
where the cost of creating or moving to competing institutions is high.

voting shares has occurred through a highly politicized bargaining process, resulting in a significant divergence between the two institutions. Through quantitative analysis of voting shares, I show that the World Bank, which faces relatively more competition from other development institutions and bilateral aid donors, has changed more flexibly in response to demands from underrepresented countries. While share distributions in the World Bank tend to reflect contemporaneous distributions of GDP, share distributions in the IMF are primarily determined by share distributions in previous time periods. Despite identical membership and rules, the World Bank closely reflects underlying shifts in power, while the IMF is remarkably path dependent.

In Chapter 4, I supplement the quantitative analysis of aggregate voting shares in the Bretton Woods institutions by examining Japan's efforts to secure greater influence over the IMF and World Bank since the 1980s. Japan is a useful case study because the country grew rapidly from the ravages of war to become the second largest economy in the world by the late twentieth century. Hence, it is useful to examine how quickly each institution responded to Japan's growing economic weight. As the theory predicts, Japan achieved much more rapid success in the World Bank compared to IMF. This is illustrated using three separate indicators: voting shares, qualitative evidence based on ideological influence Japan sought to exercise, and quantitative analysis of Japanese influence over lending outcomes in each institution. Japan's experience also validates the proposed causal mechanisms: a primary bargaining strategy of Japanese policymakers was to threaten disengagement from the institutions, but the credibility of this threat was considerably greater vis-à-vis the World Bank.

The chapter also illustrates how institutional distortions can have significant consequences that go beyond issues of prestige or narrow national interests. Although East Asian states now account for about a third of global economic activity, formal and informal representation in the IMF has lagged far behind. Using quantitative and qualitative evidence, I show that this political distortion has likely exacerbated economic distortions, such as the so-called global imbalances exemplified by rapid accumulation of reserves in East Asia and current account deficits in the United States. Hence, bargaining over institutional change is not simply a matter of ego or prestige, but outcomes can have important consequences for the substantive operation of the world order.

In Chapter 5, I examine an observable implication of my theory, which I call "policy area discipline." In competitive policy areas, the theory predicts that members of institutions will tend to eschew institutions with rigid internal rules: rigid institutions will either be reformed in the direction of greater flexibility, or members and resources will be lost to more flexible institutions. Hence, over time, we should be able to observe a relative decline in cooperation facilitated by rigid institutions, much as competition in private markets weeds out uncompetitive firms. To evaluate this prediction, I examine distributive conflict in institutions that operate in two policy areas: development aid and regional integration. As discussed in Chapter 3, development institutions confront widespread competition from a multitude of global, regional, bilateral, and private sources of development aid. Nonetheless, some development institutions have adopted inherently rigid governance rules, such as one-country-one-vote arrangements, that make it difficult to accommodate underlying shifts in economic power. I show that, over time, development aid resources have shifted from institutions with inflexible governance structures to those that allow for greater flexibility. In institutions with inflexible rules, such as the UN Development Programme, states have circumvented formal procedures by entering into co-funded or earmarked projects, in which the role of the institution is reduced to a subcontractor of the member state. I also examine the experience of the International Fund for Agricultural Development (IFAD), an organization that modified its internal decision rules in response to competitive pressures. IFAD came into existence with institutional rules that were inflexible and quickly became unbalanced: one third of voting rights were permanently allocated to each of the Organisation for Economic Co-operation and Development (OECD), OPEC, and developing countries. IFAD was also characterized by attractive outside options as a development lending institution focusing on agriculture. In the 1980s, OPEC's high voting share became a point of contention, leading to dysfunction as OECD countries curtailed their participation and contributions. This was resolved when a change in the voting rules was adopted, bringing share distributions in line with global economic weights. I show both quantitatively and qualitatively how the exercise of outside options undermined IFAD under the original rules, and how this was remedied after reform.

Like development institutions, regional integration projects are characterized by attractive outside options, at least during initial phases of cooperation. Regional integration projects are circumscribed geographically by definition and therefore exhibit no tendency toward universality. Member countries always have the option of forming alternative regional groupings or pursuing cooperation through other venues. I will present several pieces of evidence consistent with the operation of policy area discipline among regional integration projects. First, integration projects that have adopted inflexible decision-rules have generally failed, been superseded by other organizations, or achieved minimal political and economic integration. Second, I examine the European Union and show that voting shares in the Council, despite being determined in a highly politicized bargaining process, exhibit no bias against new members and have been distributed consistently and predictably according to the population size of each member state. This outcome contrasts sharply with path dependent institutions such as the IMF and UN Security Council, and suggests that members seeking to join the European Union (EU) have historically exercised nontrivial leverage over representational outcomes. However, regional integration projects may become more rigid as cooperation deepens and incorporates institutional forms that reduce the credibility of outside options. I will focus in particular on the role of monetary union, which is by its nature exclusive – for a variety of reasons, it is undesirable to maintain multiple currencies within a single country – and highly costly to exit. Hence, countries that have joined the European Monetary Union face a very different bargaining context from historical EU members or those that have opted out.

The Bretton Woods institutions are useful because they offer cross-institutional variation in policy area characteristics while holding other variables constant. In Chapter 6, I examine a different form of exogenous variation in policy area characteristics: over-time variation due to technological change. The International Telecommunications Satellite Organization (Intelsat) was created in 1964 as an institution to coordinate the use of global communications satellites, when the relevant technology and capacity was largely monopolized by the United States. Over time, technological diffusion lowered the cost of launching and maintaining communications satellites, increasing competition and eroding Intelsat's dominant position in its policy area. Using quantitative data on voting shares and declassified archival material on US bargaining strategies vis-à-vis other members of the organization, I show how this shift in the characteristics of the policy area led to increasing flexibility of representation and influence over Intelsat. I also test the validity of outside options as a causal mechanism by exploiting variation in the timing of communications satellite launches: consistent with the proposed causal mechanism, states that launched satellites early on saw their voting shares in Intelsat increase relatively more rapidly.

Chapter 7 examines ICANN, an institution that shares many similarities with Intelsat, but differs in one fundamental respect: due to high network externalities, outside options remain highly unattractive. ICANN is the organization that oversees the assignment of internet domain names. Despite its legal status as a nonprofit organization with non-government representatives from across the globe, ICANN has fallen under the direct jurisdiction of the US government. In particular, changes to the root zone file of the Domain Name System (DNS) by ICANN have been subject to authorization by the National Telecommunications and Information Agency of the US Department of Commerce. In comparison, the regulatory influence of other governments has been severely constrained. ICANN bylaws limit the participation of government representatives in the institution's administration, and government input is restricted to providing advice through the toothless Government Advisory Committee. In practice, ICANN has largely operated under the leadership of private sector actors under the loose guidance of US government agencies. This status quo has led to calls for greater internationalization of governance over the internet, centering on proposals to shift ICANN's authority to UN agencies. However, the United States has been able to repeatedly thwart attempts by other countries to exert greater influence over ICANN due to network effects, which make it prohibitively costly to develop an alternative assignment system. This has deprived other countries of credible outside options, and the institution has maintained a distributive arrangement closely reflecting US preferences – leadership by the private sector and limited meddling by foreign governments – despite the global proliferation of the internet.

Chapter 8 applies the theory to the League of Nations and UN Security Council. The first section examines conflicts within the League, which resulted in a wide range of countries, such as Costa Rica, Spain, Brazil, Japan, Germany, and Italy formally exercising their outside options. I show that the League suffered from a basic mismatch between rules and policy area characteristics. As a collective security organization, the League sought to displace traditional security arrangements such as the balance of power and bilateral alliances. This meant that the League faced formidable competition in its policy area from well-established structures designed to safeguard national security. At the same time, the internal rules of the League were inflexible and biased against the strongest military powers of the era. Not only did the most powerful states in the League have a limited share of formal voting power, but they were classified as "interested parties" and lost their voting rights entirely on issues of the greatest concern to them. The League also alienated developing countries, such as Costa Rica, by imposing membership dues without offering clear benefits in return. The consequences of unbalanced representation in an institution with attractive outside options led to abstention, outright exit, and the ultimate irrelevance of the institution.

The UN Security Council has also failed as a collective security institution in the literal sense. However, the Security Council has been able to draw on the universality of UN membership and representation among the most powerful members of the international system to facilitate cooperation in a more limited capacity: legitimating and authorizing the uses of international force. Collective international legitimization clearly benefits from universality and the diversity of interests represented on the Security Council. As sources of legitimacy, limited-membership multilateral security arrangements, such as NATO, are clearly second-best options, limiting the attractiveness of outright exit from the institution. Stable membership has also been facilitated by internal rules crafted by the architects of the UN, who explicitly sought to remedy the failures of the League. UN membership was tied to various multilateral aid and assistance programs, enticing developing countries to remain members. The UN Security Council was designed to more adequately safeguard the interests of powerful states. As predicted by the theory, less attractive outside options and a closer correspondence between underlying power and institutional representation has made the Security Council more resistant to change in comparison to the League. I will also discuss how policy paralysis in the UN Security Council during the Cold War and US efforts to elevate the General Assembly as a credible alternative facilitated the only episode of Security Council reform since its creation.

Chapter 9 examines China–Taiwan competition over institutional representation. Since 1949, China and Taiwan have competed over representation in international organizations. The nature of China–Taiwan contestation offers a unique opportunity to examine interstate bargaining over institutions where outside options are irrelevant by construction – that is, a "placebo test" for my theoretical predictions. This is for two reasons: 1. the subject of negotiation was the entry/exit of each country, and therefore threats to exit were moot; 2. any systemic variation in outside options attributable to policy areas are controlled for by the fact that the exit of one country was balanced by entry of another within equivalent policy areas. It would be troubling if China–Taiwan competition demonstrated variation consistent with my theory – for example, competitive institutions responding more quickly to China's demands – as it would indicate that alternative mechanisms are likely at work. For example, institutional change might be more likely in certain types of policy areas due to factors such as norms, individual leadership, or US willingness to accommodate rising powers. Consistent with the premises of my theory, the evidence in this chapter demonstrates that China's success in replacing Taiwan was not associated with policy area variation observed in the rest of the book.

Finally, Chapter 10 summarizes the key findings of the book. I will discuss how the evidence presented in the book relates to alternative explanations of institutional change. A discussion of broader implications will follow, touching on applications to domestic political institutions and what the theory tells us about institutions and how to study them. Finally, I will discuss policy implications, focusing on strategies for more effective institutional design and reform as well as how to think about China's rise and its policy toward international organizations.

2

A Theory of Institutional Change

In this chapter, I will present a theoretical framework that explains variations in distributive institutional change based on policy area characteristics. I will argue that some policy problems are amenable to a variety of solutions, such as unilateral, bilateral, or limited multilateral mechanisms, while others are more effectively managed through specific forms that limit the viability of alternative policy instruments. In turn, the resultant pattern of international cooperation affects outside options and bargaining leverage available to member states. Competitive institutions face strong pressures to change flexibly in order to accommodate disgruntled members: there are few reasons to remain within a dissatisfactory arrangement if attractive alternatives are readily available. On the other hand, institutions in policy areas with unattractive alternatives can sustain skewed distributions among members.

The first section of this chapter develops a theory of institutional competition in international relations and how specific policy area features affect patterns of cooperation and the availability of outside options for member states. The second section develops a formal model to consider how the availability of outside options affects bargaining outcomes and the tendency for international institutions to change. Finally, I will outline the empirical predictions that emerge from the theory and discuss the empirical strategy that motivates the subsequent chapters.

INSTITUTIONS AND POLICY AREAS

Since the nineteenth century, economists going back to Cournot have examined how market characteristics impact firm behavior, leading to a fruitful literature on industrial organization. Oft cited characteristics are increasing returns, network externalities, product differentiation, barriers to entry, inter-firm principal-agent problems, market size, and rules of the game such as prohibitions against collusion or other forms of regulation.[1] For example, scale economies tend to create natural monopolies[2] and holdup problems facilitate vertical integration.[3] The basic premise of my theory is that international institutions are analogously and generalizably affected by characteristics of their policy areas.

While sometimes phrased in different terms, scholars of international relations have investigated various features of institutional policy areas and their impact on institutionalization. In formal models of interstate cooperation, the strategic setting is often assumed to affect the form of cooperation characterizing an institution that emerges. For example, whereas collaboration problems (prisoner's dilemma payoffs) involve enforcement problems and therefore might necessitate mechanisms to monitor and extend the shadow of the future, coordination problems (stag hunt payoffs) only require initial mechanisms for states to settle upon a mutually preferable equilibrium.[4] The rational design project[5] develops numerous conjectures on how states might rationally design institutions based on variation in distribution problems, enforcement problems, the number of actors and the asymmetries among them, and levels of uncertainty. All of these variables will be influenced by the particular policy area in which cooperation is taking place. Scholars have also explored the strategic conditions that influence membership and voting rules[6] as well as escape clauses.[7] Existing work also indicates when we might observe the presence of formal international organizations, which are usually defined as having greater centralization and agency.[8] In particular, the presence of enforcement problems and uncertainty over behavior or the state of the world will tend to lead to the creation of formal international organizations to provide monitoring and enforcement functions.[9] In turn, formal international organizations are characterized by bureaucratic autonomy that might lead to unintended consequences or mission expansion.[10] However, theorizing about the

---

[1] For a general overview, see Tirole 1988.   [2] For an early survey, see Hicks 1935.
[3] Among others, see Williamson 1971.   [4] Oye 1985; Martin 1992.
[5] Koremenos, Lipson, and Snidal 2001.   [6] Magee and Morelli 2003.
[7] Rosendorff and Milner 2001.   [8] Abbott and Snidal 1998.
[9] Martin 1992; Abbott and Snidal 1998; Koremenos 2001.
[10] Barnett and Finnemore 1999.

effects of policy area features on institutional change remains comparatively limited.[11]

The Effect of Competition on Political Institutions

At the outset, it is helpful to consider some important differences between firms and political institutions, which form the basis for my theoretical propositions. There are some theoretical concepts that travel well between the two: for example, transaction costs[12] and the principal-agent relationship.[13] However, other insights do not readily transfer. Theories of monopoly pricing and monopoly profits are not directly relevant to political institutions, which are not generally designed for profit-maximization. On the flipside, political institutions can be impacted by policy area features in ways that are distinct from firms and therefore neglected by scholars of industrial organization. My theory focuses on one such feature: the effect of policy area characteristics on redistributive bargaining among members.

Shareholders of private firms are primarily concerned about maximization of risk-adjusted returns, and publicly-traded shares are priced based on the views of diverse market participants about the future prospects of a firm. These factors tend to mitigate the salience of firm-specific factors for private shareholders. For example, suppose a firm, such as Standard Oil or Microsoft, is able to establish a monopoly in a given market and therefore earn abnormal profits. In an efficient market, the price of the firm's stock will be bid up accordingly to a level where future, risk-adjusted returns are comparable to other securities.[14] As a result, shareholders do not have strong incentives to focus their attention on monopolies or highly profitable firms. In fact, historically, the highest equity market returns have come not from highly profitable, large firms, but from small, out of favor securities.[15] The pricing mechanism for shares largely eliminates the possibility that shareholders will face unattractive outside options when considering an ownership stake in a firm. There is no link between the market concentration of a firm and the ability of shareholders to pursue exit. A shareholder who grows dissatisfied with corporate performance or leadership can easily reallocate capital to more

[11] Powell 1994; Martin 1997.
[12] Keohane 1984; Lake 1996; Abbott and Snidal 1998; Lake 2009.
[13] Hawkins et al. 2006.   [14] See Malkiel and Fama 1970; Malkiel 2003 for overviews.
[15] Fama and French 1993.

attractive opportunities or, alternatively, attempt to obtain a controlling stake through the purchase of additional shares.

In contrast, there are several features of political institutions that elevate the importance of policy area variation for member states. First, members seek decision-making shares and influence over political institutions for the sake of obtaining preferred policy outcomes rather than returns on capital or residual claimancy. Although issue linkage is always possible, there is no common currency or motive, akin to profit-maximization, that translates the value of a favorable position on the United Nations Security Council to greater voting rights in the International Monetary Fund (IMF).

Second, members generally cannot trade their claims on institutions with other entities.[16] There is no equivalent of the hostile takeover: dissatisfied members cannot seize control of decision-making procedures by seeking to buy out the ownership rights of other parties. As a more limited tactic, countries can utilize foreign aid as a means to secure support from other countries in international forums such as the UN Security Council and International Whaling Commission.[17] However, vote buying through foreign aid is only effective vis-à-vis developing countries, and decision-making authority ultimately continues to rest with the targeted party.

Third, since ownership rights over international institutions are not easily transacted, there is no price mechanism to even out attractiveness across institutional settings. If an institution dominates an important policy area, members cannot expect to obtain equal value by participating in another institution in an unrelated field. If a private investor feels slighted by her lack of voice over the corporate affairs of Microsoft, she can move on with ease to a completely distinct business such as McDonalds or US Steel. To state the obvious, it would be absurd for Germany to consider substituting the North Atlantic Treaty Organization (NATO) with the North Atlantic Salmon Conservation Organization (NASCO).

In combination, these factors mean that a dissatisfied member seeking change in a political institution must generally rely on one of two mechanisms:

1. reform based on formal institutional rules or
2. informal bargaining with other member states.

---

[16] An interesting exception to this was the Bank for International Settlements prior to 2001, which allowed shareholding by both national governments and private entities.
[17] Kuziemko and Werker 2006; Miller and Dolsak 2007.

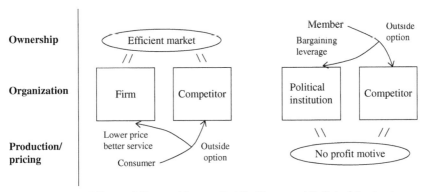

FIGURE 2.1: Effects of Competition on Public Firms and Political Institutions

The premise of my theory is that such bargaining is affected by the propensity of institutions to face competition.

These points are depicted in Figure 2.1. For firms, the effects of competition primarily manifest in production and pricing incentives: a monopolist facing newfound competition will attempt to retain consumers by cutting prices or improving the quality of service. Market efficiency in the pricing of ownership shares mitigates the effect of competition on shareholders. The impact of competition on political institutions is a mirror image of that for firms. Competition in an institution's policy area will not directly impact an institution's production and pricing incentives: since, for the most part, international institutions are not designed for profit maximization and the cooperation they produce is not explicitly priced, there is no clear relationship between greater competition and production. On the other hand, competition has a direct effect on the bargaining dynamics among institution members. The next section considers what specific policy area features affect competitive dynamics for international institutions.

Policy Area Features Affecting Competition

My argument rests on the premise that policy areas vary in their propensity for competition, and that this affects the bargaining leverage available to members states. Specifically, some policy problems can be adequately resolved through a variety of mechanisms such as unilateral, bilateral, regional, or non-state arrangements. In such policy areas, institutions face credible competition – explicit or implicit – from numerous alternative mechanisms. On the other hand, some policy problems give rise to patterns of cooperation, such as universalism, that make competition difficult or costly. In turn, the resultant pattern of institutionalization impacts the outside options and bargaining leverage of member states.

What underlying variables affect the likelihood that institutions will face competition within their policy areas? Two variables are particularly relevant. First, *network effects* arise when the marginal utility of joining an activity increases with the total number of participating actors.[18] International policy areas exhibit varying degrees of network effects. On the lower end, military alliances do not necessarily benefit from the inclusion of ever more states due to problems such as free riding, force integration, and commonality of strategic interests.[19] Development aid can also be pursued reasonably effectively without universalistic cooperation – agencies with limited capacity can focus on small-scale initiatives and often compete with each other to secure access to funding and projects.[20] On the higher end, agreement on international standards such as the technical protocols for internet domain names benefits greatly from universal cooperation: a country attempting to implement an alternative scheme unilaterally would find itself cut off from the rest of the network.[21] However, other aspects of the internet, such as content regulation, do not feature the same network effects and are handled more diffusely.[22] The potential for cross-national spillover also affects potential network effects: financial contagion often spreads unpredictably and globally, necessitating greater participation and universal cooperation, whereas similar effects may be less salient in areas such as foreign direct investment and security cooperation. High network effects provide incentives for states to cooperate through universalistic, monopolistic international organizations. Once such organizations are formed, the costs of pursuing alternative forms of cooperation are high, and states face strong incentives to remain within the existing framework.

Second, *barriers to entry* represent hindrances to alternative forms of cooperation.[23] Scholars of international relations have often pointed to high initial costs of institution-building.[24] However, some institutions are

---

[18] For example, Katz and Shapiro 1985; Liebowitz and Margolis 1995; Milner 2006.
[19] For example, Sandler 1993.   [20] For example, see discussion in Bush 2011.
[21] Drezner 2004.   [22] Drezner 2007, 95–101.
[23] The economics and legal literature on barriers to entry generally infers that such barriers exist when firms achieve high levels of concentration or abnormally high and sustained returns on capital. For example, Bain 1956; Demsetz 1968; Stigler 1968; Demsetz 1982.
[24] For example, Keohane 1984.

more costly to build than others. Institutions requiring highly specialized legal, scientific, or policy-specific expertise and bureaucratic formalization are more difficult to replicate than informal institutions or institutions requiring only administrative functions, such as G8 and G20 meetings. By nature, some policy areas involve the sharing of sensitive strategic or economic information that may hinder the creation of alternative arrangements: for example, intelligence, information related to nuclear programs, or information about sensitive economic data during crises. Commodity cartel institutions, such as the Organization of the Petroleum Exporting Countries (OPEC) and the International Coffee Organization, are difficult to replicate if the international production profile of a particular commodity is highly concentrated.

Another important barrier to entry is exclusivity. Competition among institutions is more likely to arise if members can pursue simultaneous cooperation through multiple avenues. For example, in development aid, a country that is a member of the World Bank can simultaneously provide aid bilaterally or join other aid institutions, such as regional development banks or UN-affiliated aid agencies. This means institutions facilitating similar types of cooperation can coexist alongside one another, and states can experiment freely with alternatives without jeopardizing their position in existing institutions. Military alliances are characterized by moderately higher degrees of exclusivity due to geopolitical realities: for example, membership in the Warsaw Pact was incompatible with simultaneous membership in NATO, though not necessarily all other alliance relationships. At the high end of exclusivity, it is generally impractical to pursue membership in more than one monetary union at a time due to the transaction costs associated with multiple currencies and monetary policy regimes. Exclusivity tends to reduce the availability of alternative options, as fewer configurations of institutions are possible without overlapping membership. In addition, exclusivity raises the cost and risk associated with exit, as it limits the ability of states to experiment with alternatives and gradually reallocate resources away from existing arrangements.

Some institutions may involve scale economies in the traditional, financial sense. The salience of this factor for international institutions is mitigated by the lack of a profit motive and the fact that most international institutions involve fiscal outlays that pale in comparison to domestic public agencies, at least in developed economies. However, on the margin, high initial financial costs will reduce the attractiveness of exit for all members, and it may serve as an important deterrent to exit for states with limited economic resources.

Member states of an existing institution may also attempt to erect artificial barriers to entry, for example, by creating rules that prohibit the establishment of competing institutions, linking extraneous benefits to continuing participation in an institution, or by threatening punitive action against states that seek to exit. The feasibility of these artificial barriers will vary in direct proportion to the "natural" network effects and barriers present in a policy area. In a policy area where incentives to cooperate under universalistic arrangements are strong and the costs of constructing alternative institutions are high, a state interested in maintaining the status quo will not need to offer lucrative inducements or threaten severe punishment to deter exit. On the other hand, in a policy area where exit is inherently attractive, defending the status quo will be costly: a larger number of members will need to be bought off or deterred, and more resources will need to be committed to make recalcitrant members indifferent between remaining and leaving. In addition, status quo states will have fewer incentives to aggressively defend an institution that is subject to strong, centrifugal forces. The logic of attractive exit also applies to status quo states: it is not worth expending a king's ransom defending an institutional arrangement where alternative means of cooperation will produce comparable benefits.[25]

Network effects create incentives to pursue cooperation under a single cooperative arrangement. Barriers to entry affect the viability of alternatives. I predict that the presence of high network effects and high barriers to entry will be associated with the least competitive configuration: a single institution with low viability of alternative arrangements. On the other hand, low network effects and low barriers to entry will be associated with the greatest degree of competition: multiple institutions and/or the widely recognized feasibility of regional, bilateral, or private sector alternatives. The combination of high network effects and low barriers to entry will be characterized by a dominant, universalistic institution, but efforts to supplant the existing institution may occur with some frequency, as is the case in private sector competition over products such as computer operating systems, browsers, and search engines. A policy area with low network effects but high barriers will not necessarily

---

[25] For sure, in some extreme cases, such as where fundamental national security interests are at stake, states may conclude that the costs are worth bearing: one example might be the 1968 Soviet invasion of Czechoslovakia, which was in part an effort to forestall exit from the Warsaw Pact.

produce universalistic institutions, but the high costs of building or joining alternatives will place some limitations on competition.

Defining Policy Areas

When defining policy areas, some ambiguity is inevitable. Some institutions, such as the International Criminal Court (ICC) and OPEC, specialize relatively narrowly in easily defined tasks – respectively, the persecution of crimes of international concern and coordination of production and pricing among petroleum producers. On the other hand, an institution like the Organisation for Economic Co-operation and Development (OECD) does not have a well-defined mandate and promotes cooperation across a range of areas, such as setting of international standards, international testing, and collection of economic data.

Despite ambiguities, it is possible to theorize about and make empirical observations about competition among international institutions. In international development, a wide range of international institutions compete with each other and with private organizations and bilateral donors over funding and access to aid projects.[26] Similarly, myriad regional integration projects facilitate cooperation among different configurations of oftentimes the same member states, competing on different conceptions of regional identity. International standardized testing of educational achievement resembles a duopoly between the Programme for International Student Assessment (PISA), administered by the OECD, and Trends in International Mathematics and Science Study (TIMSS), administered by the International Association for the Evaluation of Educational Achievement.[27] Barriers to entry were high when the International Telecommunications Satellite Organization (Intelsat) was originally created due to the high technological sophistication and outlays required to produce communications satellites, resulting in monopolization.[28] However, this barrier eroded with time as technological diffusion allowed most states, and subsequently private firms, to launch their own satellites.

It is also worth emphasizing that analogous ambiguity is widespread in private markets: firms often produce multiple products with a range

[26] For example, see Bush 2011.   [27] For example, see Kijima 2010.   [28] Krasner 1991.

of functions, making it difficult to precisely define market boundaries. For example, does Whole Foods compete in the natural foods market, in which case it might constitute a monopoly, or the broader groceries market, in which it is a small player?[29] Does Microsoft possess a monopoly over operating systems because it controls over 90 percent of market share, or does the possibility of rapid disruption based on technological developments in areas such as browsers indicate healthy competition?[30] Conglomerate firms that compete in many markets, such as Berkshire Hathaway or General Electric, are analogous to the OECD or UN. This challenge of precisely defining market boundaries has not hindered scholars of industrial organization or the commonplace application of antitrust law. It should not be considered an obstacle to analogous theoretical development concerning political institutions.

For illustrative purposes, Table 2.1 categorizes several policy areas according to propensity for competition and provides several examples of associated international organizations. Many of these policy areas will be discussed in greater detail in subsequent chapters. In policy areas where there are minimal network effects and barriers to entry, competition is expected to be intense. For example, some international institutions replicate functions that are commonly performed by private sector entities and individual governments, such as scientific research, the provision of telecommunication services, and development assistance. On the other end of the spectrum are policy areas subject to network effects and high barriers to entry. These features are commonly associated with technical standard setting organizations, which require the accumulation of expertise and benefit from universality for the purposes of coordination. As I will discuss in Chapter 8, international legitimation and universality are mutually self-reinforcing, placing limits on competition from alternatives. Some policy areas fall into a middling range. International trade benefits from common standards and enforcement procedures, and most favored nation (MFN) rules generate network effects: agreements become more valuable as

---

[29] See related documents available at: US District Court for the District of Columbia, "*Federal Trade Commission, Plaintiff,* v. *Whole Foods Market,* Inc., and Wild Oats Markets, Inc.," Civ. No. 07-cv-01021-PLF, FTC File No. 071 0114, www.ftc.gov/os/caselist/0710114/0710114.shtm.

[30] Summary documents available at: Department of Justice, "*United States* v. *Microsoft,*" www.usdoj.gov/atr/cases/ms_index.htm.

TABLE 2.1 *Propensity for Competition by Policy Area*

Propensity for Competition	Policy Area	Examples
	Academic / Scientific Research	The World Vegetable Center
Higher	Consultation and Dialogue	G7; G20; Asian and Pacific Council
	Telecommunication Services (technology widely available)	Intelsat (later years); Eutelsat
	Security Guarantees	League of Nations; North Atlantic Treaty Organization
	Development Aid	World Bank; Asian Development Bank
	Regional Integration Projects (early phase)	European Economic Community; Mercosur
	Trade	World Trade Organization; North American Free Trade Agreement
	Commodity Management	Organization of the Petroleum Exporting Countries; International Cotton Advisory Committee
	Sports Federations	International Olympic Committee; Fédération Internationale de Football Association
	Currency Union	European Monetary Union
	Collective Legitimization	United Nations Security Council
Lower	Telecommunication Services (technology restricted)	Intelsat (early years)
	Management of Financial Crises	International Monetary Fund; Chiang Mai Initiative
	Management of Standards; Regulation of Network Infrastructure	Internet Corporation for Assigned Names and Numbers; International Organization for Standardization

more members join and strike agreements. However, MFN rules are essentially an artificial construct: there is no fundamental or natural barrier to non-universal trade agreements, and these have proliferated in recent years. Organizations that specialize in the management of commodities are often associated with high barriers to entry due to the uneven global distribution of natural resources, and there is a compelling rationale to expand membership to all producing countries for the purposes of managing production and prices. However, these organizations are not subject to network effects due to incentives to free ride: if a cartel is successfully formed, exit becomes more, not less, attractive for members. Sports federations also benefit from universality: contests such as the Olympics are more compelling if national athletes test their skills against competitors drawn from all corners of the world. However, barriers to entry are modest, and lower-level competitions may be equally or more attractive in some circumstances due to factors such as familiarity, local rivalries, and the distribution of talent.

Table 2.1 is presented for illustrative purposes, not as a definitive classification of policy areas. However, it should be useful in clarifying the theoretical premises of this book as well as offering guidelines for future, derivative research. In the empirical chapters that follow, policy areas will be characterized more carefully through reference to theoretical expectations, secondary literature, and empirical evidence.

INSTITUTIONAL RENEGOTIATION

Policy area characteristics of international institutions have an important effect on the availability of outside options for member states. In this subsection, I develop a formal model to examine how variation in outside options and institutional rules interact to determine how flexibly institutions respond to redistributive bargaining. Redistributive institutional change can be conceptualized as a bargaining problem. The existing literature on international institutions has focused almost exclusively on bargaining at the initial stages of cooperation, and subsequent cooperation is generally characterized as an enforcement problem.[31] This characterization of institutional bargaining is elegant and helpful for analyzing a wide range of empirical variation. However, it does not provide much leverage over an important and common feature of

---

[31] Fearon 1998; Drezner 2000; Blaydes 2004.

international bargaining: renegotiation of distributive arrangements in the presence of a preexisting institution. Existing work that analyzes the use of outside options has generally focused on unilateral action by hegemonic states.[32] In contrast, I examine how outside options across policy areas can affect the bargaining leverage of institutional member states regardless of their relative power positions.

I will develop two main arguments about redistributive institutional change. First, the magnitude and frequency of change should be correlated with the general attractiveness of outside options available to states. Attractive outside options constrain the bargaining range and make extreme distributive outcomes unsustainable in equilibrium. International institutions in policy areas with attractive outside options will tend to experience change that is comparatively more responsive to shifts in relative underlying power. In other words, institutions where member states have favorable alternatives will approximate the epiphenomenal institutions of the traditional neorealist perspective. In policy areas where outside options are unattractive, distributive arrangements can deviate considerably from underlying power distributions without precipitating institutional change. In such cases, seemingly glaring imbalances can persist, leaving states to grudgingly accept arrangements that they might perceive as fundamentally unfair or biased.

Second, internal rules governing the ease of institutional reform will interact with the attractiveness of outside options to affect how institutions evolve in response to underlying shifts in member state power or capabilities. Some institutions are designed with internal rules providing for considerable flexibility in the renegotiation of distributional outcomes. Such rules make it less costly for dissatisfied states to initiate renegotiation. As such, challenges and renegotiation will tend to occur frequently. On the other hand, some institutional designs set a high bar for renegotiation, for example requiring a large majority or unanimity support for a proposal to be considered or providing no formal procedures for challenging the status quo. In such cases, even states with attractive outside options may not be able to successfully challenge an unacceptable status quo. Such institutions will therefore more likely encounter bargaining failure and exit. Hence, the interaction of the external environment and internal rules shapes the trajectory of distributive institutional change.

---

[32] Oatley and Nabors 1998; Gruber 2000; Voeten 2001.

A Formal Model of Ex Post Renegotiation

I will consider a model in which two states bargain over the fruits of cooperation in the presence of a pre-existing agreement. The strategic setting is akin to the standard Rubinstein bargaining model,[33] with several added features to reflect the stylized facts. The two-player version of the model can be interpreted as bargaining by two states or two groups of states acting as coherent units. The main findings are not dependent on the two-player assumption – I will discuss extensions to the n-player case in the subsequent subsection. As in standard bargaining models, the two states bargain over cooperative gains that are assumed to be unattainable unilaterally. I also allow for outside options,[34] that is, the possibility that players can choose to strategically opt out of the bargaining game.

Unlike conventional games of bargaining over international institutions, which generally assume negotiation from scratch, I incorporate a pre-existing and exogenous distribution of cooperative payoffs. Hence, I am modeling *renegotiation* of agreements or institutional arrangements that are already in existence. As an empirical matter, ex ante institutional rules are often handed down in the form of charters, treaties, agreements, or norms from bargaining outcomes or unilateral decisions reflecting a different set of actors, interests, and strategic settings. The model allows for the examination of bargaining in the shadow of such ex ante rules.

There are two players, 1 and 2, that bargain over potential cooperative agreements in a policy area. Each player makes a contribution to the cooperative arrangement, x_i (i = 1,2) ($x_i > 0$), which is also the maximum payoff the player can receive if it chooses not to pursue cooperation with the other player. One can think of x_i as an indicator of each player's material resources or power – a high x implies that a player brings a large contribution to the cooperative arrangement but also has the ability to obtain a fairly large payoff from opting out and going it alone. I assume non-negative and non-zero gains from cooperation, such that the total payoff from cooperation is defined as $x_1 + x_2 + g = \pi_o$, where $g > 0$ represents the gains from cooperation and π_o represents the total payoff from cooperation. An agreement on partition α_i is defined as

[33] Rubinstein 1982.
[34] Binmore, Shaked, and Sutton 1989; Muthoo 1999; Voeten 2001; Johns 2007.

a division of the total payoff from cooperation such that player i receives payoff α_i. In the two player game, player j (i $\neq$ j) will receive the total payoff from cooperation remaining after α_i is subtracted. Any α in the game is greater than or equal to zero and less than or equal to π_o.

At the first stage of the game, the two players are operating under a pre-existing cooperative arrangement that partitions π_o according to exogenously given weight α_{1SQ}, where α_{1SQ} represents the share of total cooperative payoffs received by player 1 and $\alpha_{2SQ} = \pi_o - \alpha_{1SQ}$ represents the payoff received by player 2.[35] Player 1 is potentially dissatisfied with the status quo. I define dissatisfaction as a status quo partition such that $\alpha_{1SQ}/\alpha_{2SQ} < x_1/x_2$, or $\alpha_{1SQ} < x_1$. That is, player 1 is dissatisfied if the status quo partition gives player 1 a smaller proportion of total gains than its proportion of contributions to the cooperative arrangement or if the status quo partition gives player 1 a smaller payoff than it can obtain by opting out. Only one of the two players can be dissatisfied by design, and I assume player 1 is the only potentially dissatisfied player.[36]

In the initial stage of the game, 1 can choose to abide by the status quo (SQ), initiate a challenge (CH) to renegotiate the existing partition, or pursue exit (X). If 1 chooses to abide by the status quo, the game ends and the players receive the status quo payoffs $(\alpha_{1SQ}, \pi_o - \alpha_{1SQ})$. If 1 chooses to exit, the game ends and the players receive their outside option payoffs, (x_1, x_2). If 1 chooses to challenge, 2 has an opportunity to opt out or make a new offer. If 2 chooses to make an offer, the game continues to the next stage, which is modeled as an alternating-offers Rubinstein bargaining game with outside options.

I assume that initiating a challenge entails some cost, c (c $\geq$ 0), such that in subsequent stages, the total payoff from cooperation is reduced to

---

[35] One way to interpret αSQ is an equilibrium outcome of this game in a prior time period when some parameter, such as the relative x's, were of a different value.

[36] Note that both states cannot be dissatisfied simultaneously by assumption. There are four possible cases of mutual dissatisfaction:

1. If α1SQ < x1 and α2SQ < x2, x1+ x2+ g > πo (i.e. x1 + x2 + g $\neq$ πo, which is a violation of an assumption) since g > 0.
2. If α1SQ/α2SQ < x1/x2, α2SQ/α1SQ > x2/x1, i.e. both states cannot be dissatisfied with their proportions simultaneously.
3. If α1SQ < x1 and α2SQ/α1SQ < x2/x1, x1α2SQ < x2α1SQ, which implies α2SQ < x2, which is a violation of assumptions as in the first case.
4. If α2SQ < x2 and α1SQ/α2SQ < x1/x2, x2α1SQ < x1α2SQ, which implies α1SQ < x1, which is a violation of assumptions as in the first case.

$\pi = \pi_0 - c$. One can interpret c as any costs incurred as the result of bringing a challenge to the status quo. Such costs might include lobbying or bribing efforts if a challenge requires approval of third parties in order to be placed on the agenda, bureaucratic and diplomatic costs involved in gathering and disseminating relevant information, and the resources expended on coordinating a challenge if the players represent a group of states acting as a unit. We can also think of the cost of challenge as being higher in institutions where the internal rules governing change are designed to be inflexible. For example, initiating a challenge is not costly in an institution that has clearly defined criteria for distributional out-comes – such as voting shares, board assignments, or allocation of resources – and formal mechanisms for periodic review. In comparison, an institution that has no criteria or formal procedures for revising distributional outcomes and sets a high bar for changes, such as unanim-ity rule, will involve higher costs of challenge as dissatisfied states must develop, justify, and build support for new mechanisms to initiate change.

Assuming 1 has initiated a challenge and 2 has chosen not to exit, 2 responds by proposing a new partition α_2.[37] 1 can respond by accepting 2's proposal (A), in which case the payoffs are $(\pi - \alpha_2, \alpha_2)$. 1 can also choose to exit at this stage, in which case both players receive their outside option payoffs, (x_1, x_2). Finally, 1 can reject 2's proposal and make a counteroffer (CO), in which case the game moves to the next stage.

---

[37] As in the standard Rubinstein bargaining model, the initial proposer will have a bargain-ing advantage in equilibrium. The main substantive conclusions do not change if 1 were able to offer the initial proposal, although challenges are more likely and 1 is much less likely to remain dissatisfied in equilibrium. Modeling 2 as the initial proposer produces equilibrium outcomes more easily reconciled with empirical facts. First, from a casual survey of the evidence, it appears much more common for institutional renegotiation to result in dissatisfied states remaining dissatisfied rather than previously satisfied states becoming dissatisfied with the new outcome, which is a likely equilibrium outcome if 1 proposes. Second, allowing 2 to make initial proposals is attractive for the sake of stability of outcomes, which is a common feature characterizing redistributive outcomes in international institutions. When 2 proposes first, 2 never finishes the game as a dissatisfied state in equilibrium. If the game were to be replayed with the equilibrium partition as the new status quo partition, and all parameters remained the same, 1 will abide the status quo. Hence, the equilibrium partition is stable to a repeated challenge by 1 in the meta-game in the absence of an exogenous shock such as a change in x_i. This does not necessarily hold if 1 is the initial proposer. When 1 is the initial proposer, 2 may finish the game dissatisfied. If 2 were then able to initiate a challenge as the dissatisfied state and make a proposal, a new equilibrium may be possible in which 1 is dissatisfied even given the same parameters, and so on. Such frequent challenge–counterchallenge cycles are not a common feature of institutional renegotiation.

If 1 chooses to make a counteroffer, it will offer a new partition, α_1. 2's choices are akin to 1's in the previous stage. Payoffs are discounted by the player-specific discount factor δ_i ($0 < \delta < 1$) in this stage, by δ^2_i in the subsequent stage, by δ^3_i in the subsequent stage, and so on.

Analysis

Equilibria are derived using subgame perfection and stationarity and are available in the chapter Appendix. Once a challenge occurs, there are four types of possible equilibrium outcomes depending on the relative magnitude of each player's outside options. Intuitively, if both players have attractive outside options, 1 will receive and accept an offer equivalent to its outside option, and 2 will receive the remaining cooperative payoff. The outcome is analogous if only 1 has an attractive outside option. If only 2 has an attractive outside option, 1 will receive a payoff decreasing in 2's outside option and increasing in 1's discount factor, and 2 will receive the remainder. Finally, if both have unattractive outside options, the equilibrium solution is equivalent to the standard Rubinstein bargaining model – payoffs will depend on relative discount factors, with the more patient player tending to receive a greater share of total payoffs.

The structure of payoffs gives rise to the following proposition:

Proposition 1: Consider the unique subgame perfect equilibrium of the game in which a challenge occurs and a new partition is accepted. In this equilibrium, ceteris paribus:

1. Equilibrium payoffs are not a function of outside options when outside options are small compared to total cooperative payoffs, such that $x_1/\pi \leq \delta_1\mu_1$ and $x_2/\pi \leq \delta_2\mu_2$.
2. Payoffs are a function of the outside options of one of the players when outside options are large as a proportion of total cooperative payoffs, such that $x_1/\pi > \delta_1\mu_1$ and $x2/\pi > \delta_2\mu_2$.
3. If $c = 0$, as the gains from cooperation, g, approach zero, the equilibrium partition α_1/α_2 approaches x_1/x_2.

Proof: See the Appendix

If a challenge to redistribute shares is successful, the degree to which the new shares reflect outside options is contingent on the overall attractiveness of outside options. In other words, in cooperative settings where attractive outside options are available, those outside options will have a direct effect on the ex post distribution of cooperative payoffs.

On the other hand, in settings where outside options are unattractive, redistributive outcomes will be determined by relative patience rather than outside options. From a substantive perspective, major redistributions favoring dissatisfied states based on relative patience appear unlikely. In practice, renegotiation of international institutions often occurs while the status quo distribution is still in place and some form of the status quo is expected to continue if renegotiation fails. For example, the UN Security Council has largely remained operative in its present form despite several failed attempts at expansion and reform. As such, under most circumstances, satisfied states are more likely to exhibit greater patience than dissatisfied states as renegotiation takes place.[38]

The third condition of Proposition 1 shows that large disparities between relative power (as expressed by x_1/x_2) and relative distributions of cooperative payoffs cannot be sustained when outside options are generally attractive. In other words, such disparities should only be possible when outside options are unattractive in a particular policy area compared to gains obtainable from cooperation.

It is reasonable to assume that relative attractiveness of outside options will generally correlate with a country's material capabilities or geopolitical/economic power in a particular policy area. As such, Proposition 1 implies that successful redistributive challenges in policy areas with attractive outside options will tend to occur in response to and tend to closely reflect shifts in relative power. On the other hand, successful challenges in policy areas where outside options are unattractive will not be correlated with shifts in relative power and should produce outcomes unrelated to relative power.

The equilibrium conditions under which 1 challenges give rise to the following proposition:

Proposition 2: Higher costs of challenge will tend to make challenges less likely. In particular:

1. When outside options are attractive, a high cost of challenge will tend to produce exit.
2. When outside options are unattractive, a high cost of challenge will tend to result in maintenance of the status quo (path dependence).

---

[38] Another way to model this is to explicitly assign the status quo partition as the reversion points for each player. This would make redistribution through relative patience impossible in equilibrium, as the satisfied player will not accept $\alpha_2 < \alpha_2 SQ$.

Proof: See the Appendix

In general, a high cost of challenge reduces the likelihood of a success-ful redistributive outcome. The alternative outcome depends on the attractiveness of outside options. If outside options are generally attract-ive, the outcome will be exit. Rather than choosing to accept an unpalat-able status quo within the institution, the dissatisfied state will opt out and pursue its attractive outside option. On the other hand, if outside options are unattractive, the status quo can be maintained even in the presence of highly dissatisfactory conditions for 1. In this case, player 1 has no appealing choice: it has minimal bargaining leverage and bar-gaining is too costly for a more favorable distribution to be renegotiated. However, opting out will result in an unattractive payoff. Hence, even if it is highly dissatisfied, 1 will choose to abide by the equilibrium under these conditions.

Extension to n-players

Unlike the bilateral case, applications of the Rubinstein bargaining setup to multilateral bargaining generally suffer from multiple equilibrium problems.[39] In particular, Herrero[40] has shown that virtually any equilib-rium distribution of payoffs can be supported in a multilateral version of the Rubinstein bargaining game. In addition, even when extensive form games are designed such that a unique subgame perfect equilibrium exists, small changes to the sequencing and structure of offers can considerably alter the distribution of equilibrium payoffs.[41]

Therefore, rather than deriving equilibria for a specific n-player exten-sive form game, I demonstrate that the propositions from the preceding subsection carry over in a somewhat modified form the n-player case regardless of the specific assumptions one makes about the extensive form. The propositions and proofs are provided in the Appendix. Sub-stantively, because outside options set the boundaries on the bargaining range, a wider range of outcomes can be supported when outside options are unattractive. As such, outcomes in which more states are dissatisfied by greater magnitudes are possible with unattractive outside options. Conversely, when outside options are attractive, large deviations between distributional outcomes and relative power cannot be sustained. As in the

[39] Herrero 1985; Sutton 1986; Osborne and Rubinstein 1990.   [40] Herrero 1985.
[41] Krishna and Serrano 1996; Muthoo 1999; Suh and Wen 2003.

Policy Area Effects

	Attractive outside options	Unattractive outside options
High cost of challenge	Exit	Path dependence of status quo
Low cost of challenge	Frequent renegotiation, outcomes correspond to relative power	Renegotiation possible, but outcomes do not necessarily correspond to relative power

Effect of Internal Rules

FIGURE 2.2: Effects of Outside Options and Costs of Renegotiation on Institutional Change

two player game, high costs will make a renegotiated outcome less likely and exit or status quo maintenance more likely.

EMPIRICAL IMPLICATIONS

Figure 2.2 presents a substantive representation of the predictions from the formal model. The figure provides predictions about likely institutional outcomes through renegotiation assuming an exogenous shift in relative power that leaves a state dissatisfied.[42] This might encompass factors such as rapid development in an economic institution, buildup of military capabilities in a security institution, or technological changes that alter the balance of power in a given policy area.

As indicated in Proposition 2, the likelihood of renegotiation in equilibrium is a decreasing function of the costs of initiating a challenge. Hence, renegotiation should be more frequent in institutions where costs of challenge are low. However, bargaining outcomes are also a function of outside options. If outside options are attractive while costs of challenge are high, the dissatisfied state is likely to opt out of the institution and pursue its outside option. It is not unusual for states to renounce their membership in an international organization entirely, as subsequent sections will illustrate, but a more common response is the reallocation

---

[42] The state might have been dissatisfied ex ante or become dissatisfied as a result of the shock. I am simply assuming that at the beginning of the game, player 1 is dissatisfied.

of diplomatic and financial resources to bilateral initiatives or other multilateral fora. In international trade, for example, stasis caused by expanding membership and unanimity rules within the World Trade Organization (WTO) has encouraged more and more states to pursue regional preferential trading agreements.[43] This includes countries such as Japan, which have traditionally viewed such regional agreements with skepticism and tended to prioritize progress at the multilateral level.

If outside options are unattractive while costs of challenge are high, the likely outcome is maintenance of the status quo. Although dissatisfied states may be deeply frustrated about the status quo distributive outcome, they have very little bargaining leverage to bring about change. This will be particularly true for institutional settings in which renegotiation takes place while the institution remains operative and bargaining failure is likely to result in reversion to the status quo.[44]

If challenge costs are low and outside options are attractive, redistributive bargaining can be expected to occur frequently. In such cases, shifts in relative power will be quickly reflected in redistributive bargains, and the overall distributional outcomes should closely approximate underlying power relationships. Institutions with low challenge costs and attractive outside options should therefore be most malleable to redistributive institutional change and least susceptible to path dependence. In this sense, this type of institution conforms most closely to the traditional neorealist view of international institutions as largely epiphenomenal to state power.

Finally, if challenge costs are low but outside options are unattractive, redistributive bargaining will not be responsive to underlying shifts in relative power. Holding all else constant, increases in relative power should result in no change in redistributive outcomes. However, renegotiation of status quo distributions may occur due to fluctuations in relative patience. Hence, while renegotiation in these types of institutions may occur with some frequency, outcomes should not mirror underlying changes in geopolitical or economic power.

Another way to illustrate these theoretical predictions is to depict graphically how institutional change occurs in response to a shift in relative power. Figure 2.3 depicts the bargaining range between player 1

---

[43] Mansfield and Reinhardt 2003.
[44] If an institution is established with a specific time frame for expiration or the challenge is highly disruptive for the normal functioning of the institution, a revision of the status quo based on relative discount factors is possible. However, such revisions will not be affected by shifts in relative power.

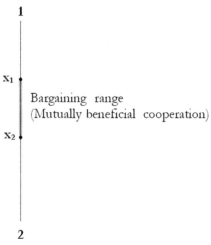

FIGURE 2.3: The Bargaining Range

and player 2. 1's utility is increasing downward, while 2's utility is increasing upward. x_1 and x_2 are the outside options of each player. The area bounded by the outside options is the bargaining range: mutually beneficial cooperation is possible as long as distributional outcomes fall within this range. Should they not, one or the other player would prefer exit to cooperation.

Figures 2.4 and 2.5 depict a set of equilibrium outcomes from the formal model developed in the previous subsection, assuming there is an ongoing shift in relative power over time and the game is played at each point in time based on the partition adopted in the previous time period. The curved, horizontal lines depict a relative shift in power in favor of player 1. Over time, 1's outside option is becoming more attractive compared to 2's outside option. This might correspond to relative economic growth or a military buildup in the context of an alliance. Using the security analogy, as 1 increases its military capabilities over time, exiting the alliance becomes more plausible, since unilateral defense is a more acceptable option. On the flipside, 1's military buildup makes exit less attractive for 2, as it stands to lose a more valuable ally. α corresponds to the status quo distributive arrangement that prevails for the institution before the relative shift takes place.

Figure 2.4 depicts an institution in a policy area with attractive outside options. For both participants, modest gains are possible beyond what is obtainable from exit, but the bargaining range is small because of the

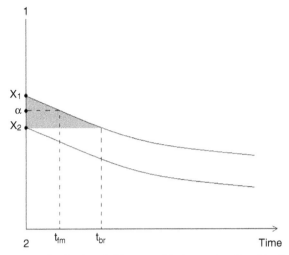

FIGURE 2.4: Institutional Change with Attractive Outside Options

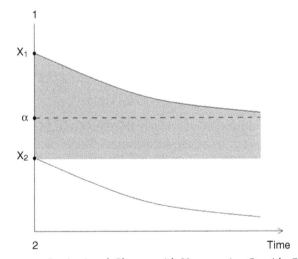

FIGURE 2.5: Institutional Change with Unattractive Outside Options

attractiveness of outside options. The figure shows two points at which the distributive arrangement defined by α would be unsustainable. The first point, t_{fm}, corresponds to the point at which the status quo would be unsustainable in the Rubinstein bargaining model presented in the previous section. At this point, 1 prefers exit to accepting the status quo. If the cost of challenge is high, 1 will exit the institution, and if the cost of challenge is low, 1 will challenge, and 2 will propose and achieve a redistribution that makes 1 indifferent between exiting and remaining in the institution. The second point, t_{br}, corresponds to the point at which no status quo distribution, that is, any α, is sustainable in light of the relative shift that has taken place. Beyond this point, even a distribution that had been maximally favorable to 1 at the outset will no longer be acceptable to 1.

Figure 2.5 depicts a situation where outside options are unattractive. This opens up the bargaining range and allows for a much wider range of distributive outcomes to be sustainable over time. In the figure, the status quo α is depicted as lying in a range where it is sustainable despite the power shift that has taken place. The figure illustrates how unattractive outside options make it possible for institutions to remain stable for a longer time given a specific shift in relative power. In the context of the formal model, Figure 2.5 corresponds to the condition where equilibrium distributions are determined by relative patience rather than outside options. Hence, any redistribution that does take place will not necessarily conform to the ongoing power shift. As with Figure 2.4, the gray region depicts status quo partitions that are sustainable over time. As the figure shows, a wider range of status quo distributions are sustainable over time under unattractive outside options.

EMPIRICAL STRATEGY

In the following chapters, I will evaluate the theoretical framework empirically by taking advantage of various features of international institutions that provide opportunities for causal inference. The first test of the theory will exploit unique features of the IMF and World Bank, two institutions that have identical membership and de jure rules but operate in distinct policy areas with varying outside options. The theoretical prediction is that distributive conflict in the World Bank will resemble Figure 2.4, while that in the IMF will resemble Figure 2.5. Attractive outside options in the policy area of development lending make it impossible to sustain highly skewed distributive arrangements for the World Bank, while the difficulty of creating alternatives to the IMF make status quo distributions more sticky and unresponsive to power shifts over time. As I will discuss in Chapter 7, the Internet Corporation for Assigned Names and Numbers (ICANN) is another institution with unattractive outside options stemming from network effects, and the institution has exhibited a strong tendency to resist change.

In comparison to the IMF and World Bank, which have relatively flexible internal rules concerning redistribution, the League of Nations and UN are characterized by relatively rigid rules and hence greater costs of initiating challenge. As I will argue in Chapter 8, the attractiveness of alternatives to the League, combined with unbalanced rules that inherently disadvantaged powerful states, facilitated recurrent brinksmanship and exit from the institution. The UN remedied the League's distributional imbalances by shifting formal power in the direction of powerful states, and the institution has established itself as the primary source of legitimacy for the authorization of international uses of force, placing relative limits on the attractiveness of outside options. As predicted by the theory, this has made distributive outcomes in the UN more stable compared to the League.

In Chapter 6, I examine variation in outside options created by technological change in the policy area of satellite telecommunications. When Intelsat was established, the United States held a monopoly on the technologies and capabilities to launch communications satellites into orbit. This made exit extremely unattractive for other member states, resulting in a path dependent institution dominated by the United States. However, the diffusion of relevant technologies and development of launch capabilities increased the attractiveness of outside options for other states over time. These stylized facts are depicted in Figure 2.6. Over time, as outside options become more attractive for 1, the bargaining range narrows,

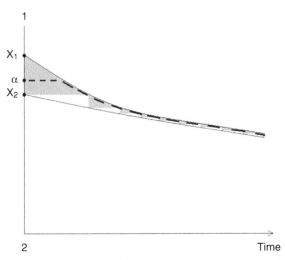

FIGURE 2.6: An Institution with Increasingly Attractive Outside Options

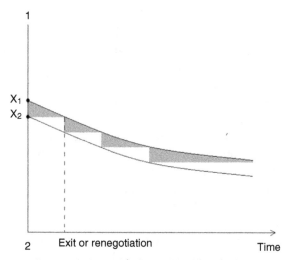

FIGURE 2.7: Renegotiation with Attractive Outside Options over Time

limiting the scope for unbalanced distributional outcomes. The dotted line depicts the predicted outcome according to the Rubinstein bargaining model. As shown, unattractive outside options initially create room for a stable partition, but as the outside options for 1 become more attractive over time, frequent redistribution becomes necessary to sustain the institution. As I will show, the history of Intelsat largely conforms to this prediction.

In Chapter 5, I will consider international cooperation in policy areas characterized by high degrees of competition and hence attractive outside options: development aid and early-phase regional integration projects. As depicted in Figure 2.7, in these policy areas, successful, ongoing cooperation requires frequent redistribution in line with underlying shifts in power. Institutions in these policy areas that do not adjust quickly will be beset with the exercise of outside options: empirically, such institutions will either lose members outright or wither as resources are allocated in the direction of more flexible institutions or bilateral/unilateral initiatives. Through this process, competitive policy areas should come to be dominated by institutions characterized by flexible internal rules. I call this tendency "policy area discipline."

The theory also generates additional observable implications that will be examined in the empirical chapters. First, the causal mechanisms specified by the theory imply that threats to exit will be an important feature of redistributive bargaining in international institutions, at least in cases where outside options are attractive. We should be able to observe dissatisfied states making such threats, and, depending on the institutional context, these threats should be effective in securing concessions from other member states. Second, policymakers should be cognizant of institutional competition and its potential effects on redistributive outcomes. We should observe countries satisfied with status quo arrangements in an institution discouraging the creation of competing arrangements in order to maintain their position. Similarly, we should observe dissatisfied countries threatening or pursuing the creation of competing institutions as a means of obtaining leverage in existing institutions. Aside from observing the outcomes of distributional conflicts, it will be important to confirm that the causal mechanisms outlined in this chapter correspond closely to observed processes of international renegotiation.

Formal and Informal Change

In subsequent chapters, I will often focus on formal institutional change, that is, shifts in easily observable indicators, particularly voting shares. There are several important advantages in doing so. First, formal indicators are easily quantifiable and therefore amenable to large-n statistical analysis. Second, voting shares are assigned to all members, making it possible to incorporate a large number of member states in the analysis without detailed qualitative study of each country. Third, countries clearly care about their voting shares in international institutions, as I will repeatedly demonstrate, and the shares are frequently among the primary issues contested in institutional bargaining. Fourth, voting shares, supplemented by an analysis of actual voting power, closely approximate the role of partitions posited in the formal model, dividing authority over the institution's decision-making structures.

However, the theoretical predictions developed in this chapter should also be applicable to more informal distributional outcomes in international institutions. These may include influence exercised through ideology, placement of own-country nationals within the institution, close relations between domestic government officials and employees of the institution, and agenda-setting norms. Insofar as these informal features of the institution are subject to negotiation, they should be susceptible to revision through threats of exit. For example, as I show in Chapter 4, even a seemingly impervious source of influence such as ideology may be subject to change through the appointment of personnel, the commissioning of studies, and other measures that challenge existing norms and beliefs within an institution. Although informal outcomes are generally less amenable to quantification, I will provide a quantitative test of my predictions regarding the Bretton Woods institutions in Chapter 4, and examine how redistributive bargaining affects both formal and informal outcomes wherever possible in the empirical analysis.

Exit: Observed and Implicit

In the empirical section, I will attempt to derive the characteristics of policy areas from theoretical first principles where possible.[45] This approach is based on a potential selection problem that emerges from the formal model. In policy areas where exit is attractive but institutional rules governing change are flexible, threats of exit will be credible, but exit will not necessarily be observed. Hence, attempting to surmise the intensity of competition in a policy area based on direct observation could lead to incorrect inferences. The absence of competition does not necessarily imply unattractive outside options. This is analogous to the concept of contestable markets in economics, in which the concentration of production in the hands of a small number of firms may not necessarily imply pricing power so long as market entry remains credible.[46]

As a practical matter, the seriousness of this potential concern is mitigated by several factors. The formal model generates useful insights about international bargaining, but reality is obviously more complex, and alternative institutions are generated for a wide variety of reasons that are orthogonal to the modeling assumptions. For legacy and bureaucratic reasons, politicians and foreign affairs officials often attempt to leave their mark by proposing new institutional frameworks. Competing institutions may also be proposed in order to meet orthogonal policy objectives such as confidence building or the expansion of authority and new positions for bureaucrats. In the real world, policymakers also make mistakes, attempting to create competing institutions in policy areas where they prove unviable. These factors mean that in essentially all policy areas examined, it is possible to observe "off-the-equilibrium path" efforts to establish institutional competition. This is true even in policy areas that have relatively unattractive outside options: the Conference of New Emerging Forces vs. the UN Security Council, the Asian Monetary Fund vs. the IMF, and various alternative domain assignment schemes vs. ICANN.

---

[45] Frieden 1999.   [46] Baumol 1982; Baumol, Panzar, and Willig 1982.

These failed efforts allow us to directly examine how network effects and barriers to entry stymie efforts to establish alternative institutions in policy areas that are not conducive to competition.

The potential for mistakes introduces another potential concern: policymakers seeking to defend the status quo in an institution may misread the credibility of outside options and concede more ground than necessary, or policymakers seeking change may not make full use of a credible outside option. This almost certainly happens on occasion. It is unrealistic to assume that policymakers will be able to consistently and precisely calibrate concessions to achieve exact indifference. As with other applications of formal theory to social scientific questions, the model generates useful predictions based on idealized assumptions. Reality is more messy. We can say, however, that if these problems are ubiquitous, the direction of bias is such that we should observe a weaker association between the attractiveness of outside options and institutional change. If the model is a reasonable approximation of actual institutional renegotiation, its predictions should be consistent with the empirical evidence.

ALTERNATIVE SOURCES OF VARIATION IN INSTITUTIONAL CHANGE

The theory developed in this chapter does not purport to explain all forms and manners of institutional change. What it does is offer a generalizable framework for predicting institutional change and patterns of institutionalized cooperation. A major advantage of the theory is that it applies in equal measure to diverse institutions such as the League of Nations, the IMF, and Intelsat. It also offers clear, testable predictions about substantively important political outcomes. However, there are several alternative potential sources of institutional change that need to be considered as the theory is evaluated empirically. In most cases, these alternative theories have some validity and are not mutually exclusive with the predictions posited here. In other cases, the alternative theories produce contrary expectations that are amenable to empirical tests. I will revisit these alterative explanations in the conclusion, but it is useful to articulate their main characteristics at the outset.

Power and Material Interests

Perhaps the simplest explanation for institutional change is that it is driven by the interests of powerful states. This perspective draws from

the neorealist tradition, which views institutions as being largely epiphenomenal to state interests.[47] If this is correct, institutional change should
happen when it is desired by powerful states, while change should be
foreclosed if powerful states resist it. Without a doubt, there is an element
of truth to this perspective. The largest, most powerful states in the
international system have important tools to influence or coerce other
states, and this is likely to give them greater influence over the trajectory
of international institutions.

One limitation of power-based theories is that they do not provide
much leverage to explain variations in institutional change. In particular,
the persistence of imbalances in institutions despite large relative shifts in
power runs counter to the notion that institutions consistently and
unproblematically reflect the interests of the most powerful states. To
put it differently, power-based theories do not sit well with the stubborn
persistence of initial conditions in institutional settings where the distribution of power has changed drastically. This book highlights several
examples of such institutions.

If power-based theories are correct, powerful states should generally
get their way in international institutions. This leads to a prediction that
differs from the theoretical framework presented in this chapter.
According to my theory, institutional change need not reflect underlying
power distributions, particularly in cases where outside options are
unattractive. In addition, it is possible for the interests of weaker states
to prevail over those of powerful states. For example, in an institution
with attractive outside options, dissatisfied weak states should be able to
use the threat of exit to secure change as effectively as powerful states. In
most power-based explanations of institutional change, "go it alone"
power is assumed, either explicitly or implicitly, to be a prerogative of
the most powerful countries such as the United States.[48] A central premise
of my theory is that whether or not countries can go it alone is a function
of policy area characteristics, and weak countries are just as capable of
exercising and threatening the use of outside options.

It is possible to reconcile my theory with power-based explanations by
defining the contribution of this book as clarifying what constitutes
"power" in institutionalized international cooperation. The theoretical
framework allows us to identify how underlying measures of state capabilities, such as economic size or military strength, translate into

---

[47] Mearsheimer 1994; Glennon 2003.   [48] Oatley and Nabors 1998; Gruber 2000.

influence over outcomes in institutions. Insofar as influence over out-comes is synonymous with power, we can think of competition as a factor that weakens the power of formally overrepresented states in institutions at the expense of underrepresented states.

Efficient Design

An alternative view of institutional change can be derived from more conventional rationalist theories of international institutions, which place heavy emphasis on rational design at the initial stages of institutional formation.[49] If states are generally correct in their assessments of the likelihood of credible distributional challenges, they should anticipate this at the design phase and establish institutional rules that will be able to effectively accommodate future challenges. This will reduce any potential mismatch between institutional rules and the nature of outside options in a particular policy area. This is not an alternative explanation for insti-tutional change per se, but it suggests that a more simplified theoretical framework may be appropriate: since institutional rules will be rationally designed to conform to policy area characteristics, mismatch between rules and outside options is unlikely. In effect, the upper left and lower right quadrants in Figure 2.2 should not be observed empirically: in policy areas where exit is attractive, flexible rules will be used by design, while states will seek to lock in positions of advantage by elevating the cost of challenge in policy areas where exit is unattractive.

The distinction between these two perspectives on institutional change comes down to the predictive insights of institution builders. Rational anticipation may be plausible in some circumstances, such as when policy area characteristics are well known due to the operational record of existing institutions. Policymakers do exhibit remarkable foresight on occasion, such as when US President Franklin Roosevelt opted to include China as a permanent member of the UN Security Council, calculating that the country would naturally take its place among the great powers.[50]

In other circumstances, designers may have less ability to design insti-tutions that accord with underlying policy area characteristics. It is more likely that policymakers will make mistakes in designing institutions to manage new policy issues with unknown characteristics, such as oppor-tunities for cooperation opened up by the development of new

---

[49] Fearon 1998; Koremenos, Lipson, and Snidal 2001.   [50] Hilderbrand 1990.

technologies. Designers may also face strong normative pressures to adopt particular principles, such as one-country-one-vote rules, even if these are unlikely to adequately reflect underlying distributions of power. Finally, intentional, inefficient design is a possibility. This is the international analogue of domestic bureaucratic design, in which opponents of agencies such as the Environmental Protection Agency undertake measures to make the bureaucracy as ineffectual as possible.[51] A member state may push for rules that make an institution unlikely to function effectively if they prefer other means of cooperation in a particular policy area, foresee the institution posing competition vis-à-vis a preferred arrangement, or disagree with the objectives of the institution.

If rational design theories are correct, institutional forms should conform closely within specific policy areas. In policy areas where outside options are unattractive, institutions should be designed with rules that set a high bar for redistributive change, which reinforces the position of inception members. This is a testable prediction that will be considered in subsequent chapters. As I will show, the empirical evidence is generally consistent with a limited form of rational design, in which policymakers attempt to rationally anticipate policy area characteristics, but make frequent misjudgments. This will be most evident when we examine Intelsat and variation among development lending institutions.

Absence of Distributive Conflict

The formal model presented in this chapter assumes zero-sum bargaining: that is, within the context of ongoing cooperation, if one country secures a greater share of the gains from cooperation, it comes at another's expense. This is a plausible assumption in most cases. By their nature, variables such as voting shares, influence over the allocation of finite resources, headquarter locations, and appointments of nationals to leadership positions are zero sum. However, there are conditions under which zero-sum distributive conflict may be mitigated or absent. This is particularly likely in cases where member states have very similar preferences over policy issues, a condition Keohane describes as "harmony,"[52] either because of inherent similarities of interests or because questions addressed during a specific time period happen to generate consensus among members. Under these conditions, nominal imbalances may persist for the trivial reason that they are inconsequential.

---

[51] Moe 1989.   [52] Keohane 1984, 51.

Zero-sum competition will always exist to some degree: no two countries have identical preferences, and there will be inevitable uncertainty over preferences concerning unforeseen, future policy questions. In addition, even where preferences are convergent, countries often seek relative gains in voting shares or personnel representation for international status and prestige.

However, for the purposes of empirical analysis, it is important to establish the existence of distributive conflict among member states to avoid misinterpreting harmony as path dependence. I will do so by clearly delineating the stakes involved in distributing bargaining among members in the particular institutional context in question and presenting qualitative evidence to illustrate behavior consistent with distributive conflict. This evidence will include official and private statements indicative of distributive conflict – for example, descriptions of conflicts over policy objectives among member states; statements demanding change; threats related to distributive demands – and behavioral indicators – for example, the creation of working groups to manage distributive demands; issue linkage of other important issues to distributive outcomes; the proposal or creation of alternative institutions or agencies; reallocation of resources from the institution.

Bounded Rationality

Jupille, Mattli, and Snidal argue that bounded rationality may offer one solution to the conundrum of institutional change and persistence.[53] Although policymakers desire institutional solutions well suited to the problems they confront, they may be limited in their ability to choose optimally due to cognitive and informational limitations, such as the ability to acquire information and assess alternatives. Hence, according to these scholars, policymakers have a tendency to satisfice by settling on the first satisfactory solution they encounter, which in many cases results in attempts to deal with problems through existing institutional mechanisms. On the other hand, novel problems that demonstrate glaring problems with existing arrangements can trigger significant change.

This is an important insight, and bounded rationality is certainly an important feature of international relations and politics more generally. The empirical chapters of this book provide many illustrations of how policymakers made mistaken assumptions about various features of their institutional settings, particularly at the stage of initial design. The theory

[53] Jupille, Mattli, and Snidal 2013.

proposed in this book and the bounded rationality model proposed by Jupille, Mattli, and Snidal are complementary in important respects. The model proposed in this chapter is useful primarily for explaining variations in institutional change *across* policy areas, while the bounded rationality model is more suitable for explaining when and how institutional change occurs *within* policy areas, a point underscored by the fact that the primary focus of Jupille, Mattli, and Snidal's book is a single policy area, international commerce. In addition, the model proposed here focuses on redistributive institutional change, while Jupille, Mattli, and Snidal instead focus on how policymakers use, select, change, or create institutions to resolve policy problems.

These caveats notwithstanding, the predictions of the two models arguably diverge in one important respect. The bounded rationality model makes the case for a strong status quo bias in international institutions: policymakers will tend to satisfice by using existing institutions or selecting among them before considering change or creation. In comparison, the model proposed in this chapter suggests that institutional change and creation should be pervasive in competitive policy areas. An explanation for institutional persistence based on satisficing sits uncomfortably with one feature of contemporary international diplomacy: foreign policy officials and policy-oriented academics are constantly proposing and producing new institutional arrangements featuring alternative combinations of members, rules and issue areas, leading to a massive explosion in the number, scope, and diversity of international institutions.[54] If policymakers have a strong tendency to satisfice by sticking to familiar solutions, it is odd that so many, oftentimes seemingly redundant institutional arrangements are constantly emerging.[55] The empirical chapters will show that, in some policy areas, institutional change and creation occurs with a frequency that is arguably inconsistent with the premise that policymakers follow the sequences of "use, select, change, and create (USCC)."

In addition, Jupille, Mattli, and Snidal assume that policymakers satisfice by choosing among "USCC" in descending order until a satisfactory solution is discovered. In comparison, my model predicts that these outcomes are deeply interrelated: the propensity for "change" to occur

---

[54] See discussion in Chapter 10; also Shanks, Jacobson, and Kaplan 1996.

[55] Note also that bounded rationality does not necessarily imply status quo bias: in the parlance of bounded rationality models, the rapid proliferation of international institutions in the contemporary era is arguably more consistent with a garbage can model of decision-making, in which actors, solutions, and problems combine somewhat randomly to produce new arrangements (Cohen, March, and Olsen 1972).

is directly related to the feasibility of "select" and "create." If the bounded rationality model is correct, institutional change should generally occur when selection has been explored but ruled out as infeasible, but before creation has been pursued. Instead, my model suggests that change will occur directly in response to *discussions, threats, and implementations* of outside options, that is, the selection and creation of alternative institutions. If the satisficing model is correct, we should generally not observe thoughtful contemplation and strategizing over outcomes that lie toward the end of the sequence (change and creation) when earlier outcomes are chosen (use and selection): this would run counter to the assumption that search costs or some other factor limit the ability of policymakers to choose optimally among the options. Hence, evidence of bargaining among policymakers that illustrate careful consideration of outside options, threats of exit, and the outright pursuit of alternative arrangements, particularly when the status quo ultimately prevails, are more consistent with my theoretical approach compared to the satisficing model.

Domestic Politics

Variation in institutional change can also arise from domestic political factors. On various occasions, the US Congress has stymied or delayed international renegotiation outcomes for reasons orthogonal to my theory, such as divided government or ideological skepticism toward international institutions. One recent example is the 2010 Fourteenth General Review of IMF quotas, which was blocked until 2016 due to congressional inaction despite securing more than 80 percent of affirmative support from IMF membership.[56] Similarly, renegotiation efforts are often initiated by political leaders responding to domestic pressures to secure commensurate status or influence internationally, such as when Japan and more recently China became the second largest economies in the world.

While domestic politics can be an important source of institutional change, the key explanatory variables of this book – policy area characteristics and institutional rules – are not country-specific. In addition, these variables are relatively static and unlikely to be systematically correlated with variation in the domestic political conditions of any

---

[56] Nelson and Weiss 2015.

particular state. As such, any direct threat to causal inference from domestic political variables should be fairly minimal. Nonetheless, it is important not to misjudge variation in institutional change attributable to domestic political variables as variation due to the proposed explanatory variables. Accordingly, in the empirical chapters, I will carefully consider domestic political factors in order to confirm that they do not account for the observed empirical evidence.

Norms and the Role of Individuals

Norms are an important source of change in both domestic politics and international relations.[57] The proliferation of international institutions itself reflects important normative shifts in how countries organize their relations with one another. Policymakers pushing for redistribution in international institutions also frequently appeal to normative factors, such as notions of fairness, equity, and justice. It is possible for normative factors to facilitate distributive change in international institutions, if, for example, representatives of member states respond to normative appeals or change their perspectives on what constitutes appropriate representation. Similarly, it is impossible to deny the influence of individual leadership and other idiosyncratic factors in specific instances of institutional change.

Since norms can change in a variety of ways, and beliefs are inherently difficult to measure, it is challenging to develop a direct test of norms-based explanations against the theoretical predictions proposed in this book. Analogously, the role of individual policymakers, while surely important, is idiosyncratic and difficult to generalize across institutional settings. We can, however, make several observations. First, normative and individual explanations of institutional change and the rationalist account articulated here are not mutually exclusive. These alternative factors surely account for an important degree of institutional change in international relations. However, they do not preclude other sources of change.

Second, it is unlikely that norms or individual factors covary with the key independent variables proposed in this chapter. In the empirical section of this book, I examine a wide range of cross-institutional and over-time variation in policy area characteristics. In the case of Intelsat,

---

[57] Finnemore and Sikkink 1998; Wendt 1999.

where distribution becomes more fluid over time along with outside options, it might be plausible that the institution was also responding to evolving norms that called for greater openness and fairness in representation. However, over-time variation in the League of Nations/UN cuts in the opposite direction, with institutional change becoming less frequent and more resistant against calls for inclusivity over time. ICANN, an institution established many years after Intelsat, has successfully resisted widespread, and normatively convincing, calls for more equitable representation. The wide variety of forms and contexts of institutional change presented in the empirical chapters of this book should give us confidence that norms and individual influences are not confounding factors.

Appendix

I use subgame perfection and stationarity to derive the equilibrium conditions. I start with the subgame after 1 has initiated a challenge.[58] Let 1 and 2's optimal offers in equilibrium at any stage of the game be denoted respectively by α_1^* and α_2^*. Given stationarity, 1 (2) chooses an optimal offer in any subgame that makes 2 (1) indifferent between accepting 1 (2)'s offer and the greater of exiting or receiving the discounted payoff from making its optimal offer in the following stage. Hence, 1's optimal offer $\alpha_1^* = \pi - \max\{\delta_2\alpha_2^*, x_2\}$. Likewise, $\alpha_2^* = \pi - \max\{\delta_1\alpha_1^*, x_1\}$. Solving for these conditions yields the following equilibrium offers:

$$
\alpha_1^* = \begin{cases}
\mu_1\pi & \text{if } x_2 \leq \delta_2\mu_2\pi \text{ and } x_1 \leq \delta_1\mu_1\pi \\
\delta_2 x_1 + (1 - \delta_2)\pi & \text{if } x_2 \leq \delta_2(\pi - x_1) \text{ and } x_1 > \delta_1\mu_1\pi \\
\pi - x_2 & \text{if } x_2 > \delta_2\mu_2\pi \text{ and } x_1 \leq \delta_1(\pi - x_2) \\
\pi - x_2 & \text{if } x_2 > \delta_2(\pi - x_1) \text{ and } x_1 > \delta_1(\pi - x_2)
\end{cases}
$$

$$
\alpha_2^* = \begin{cases}
\mu_2\pi & \text{if } x_1 \leq \delta_1\mu_1\pi \text{ and } x_2 \leq \delta_2\mu_2\pi \\
\delta_1 x_2 + (1 - \delta_1)\pi & \text{if } x_1 \leq \delta_1(\pi - x_2) \text{ and } x_2 > \delta_2\mu_2\pi \\
\pi - x_1 & \text{if } x_1 > \delta_1\mu_1\pi \text{ and } x_2 \leq \delta_2(\pi - x_1) \\
\pi - x_1 & \text{if } x_1 > \delta_1(\pi - x_2) \text{ and } x_2 > \delta_2(\pi - x_1),
\end{cases}
$$

where each player i always make the optimal offer, always accepts offer x_j ($i \neq j$) iff $x_j^* \geq x_j$, and exits iff $x_i^* < x_i$ and $\delta_i x_i^* \leq x_i$. $\mu_i = (1 - \delta_j)/(1 - \delta_i\delta_j)$. Since player 2 moves first in the repeated subgame, 2's optimal offer is

---

[58] The equilibrium conditions are akin to those found in Binmore, Shaked, and Sutton 1989; Muthoo 1999.

accepted in equilibrium, assuming no exit. The first two conditions of Proposition 1 follow immediately from the equilibrium conditions.

The proof of Condition 3 of Proposition 1: As $g \to 0$, $x_1 + x_2 \to \pi_0$. If $c = 0$, $\pi_0 = \pi$. Hence, $x_1 + x_2 \to \pi$, $\pi - x_2 \to x_1$ and $\pi - x_1 \to x_2$. Since $\delta_i < 1$ for $i = (1, 2)$, $x_1 > \delta_1(\pi - x_2)$ and $x_2 > \delta_2(\pi - x_1)$. Therefore, in equilibrium $\alpha_2 \to x_2$ and $\alpha_1 \to x_1$. Hence, $\alpha_1/\alpha_2 \to x_1/x_2$.

By backward induction, 1 will challenge when the payoffs obtained in the repeated subgame are equivalent to or exceed the payoffs obtained from abiding by the status quo or existing, that is $\pi - \alpha_2{}^* \geq \max\{\alpha_{1SQ}, x_1\}$. In addition, for 2 to make an offer rather than pursue exit, $\alpha_2{}^* \geq x2$. Hence, a successful redistribution will occur in equilibrium when:

$$\max\{\alpha_{1SQ}, x_1\} \leq (\pi_0 - c)(1 - \mu_2) \text{ and } \pi_0 - c \geq x_2/\mu_2 \quad \text{if } x_1 \leq \delta_1\mu_1\pi \text{ and } x_2 \leq \delta_2\mu_2\pi$$
$$\max\{\alpha_{1SQ}, x_1\} \leq \delta_1(\pi_0 - c - x_2) \text{ and } \pi_0 - c \geq x_2 \quad \text{if } x_1 \leq \delta_1(\pi - x_2) \text{ and } x_2 > \delta_2\mu_2\pi$$
$$\alpha_{1SQ} \leq x1 \text{ and } \pi_0 - c \geq x_1 + x_2 \quad \text{if } x_1 > \delta_1\mu_1\pi \text{ and } x_2 \leq \delta_2(\pi - x_1)$$
$$\alpha_{1SQ} \leq x1 \text{ and } \pi_0 - c \geq x_1 + x_2 \quad \text{if } x_2 > \delta_2(\pi - x_1) \text{ and } x_1 > \delta_1(\pi - x_2)$$

Proof of Proposition 2: Note that a higher cost of challenge (c) makes a successful challenge in equilibrium less likely under all conditions. When c is prohibitively high, for example, $\pi_0 < c$, the only possible equilibria are maintenance of the status quo or exit. If $\alpha_{1SQ} \geq x_1$, 1 will accept the status quo. If $\alpha_{1SQ} < x_1$, 1 will exit. Hence, small outside option payoffs will tend to make maintenance of the status quo more likely in equilibrium, and high outside option payoffs will make exit more likely in equilibrium.

N-PLAYER GAME

Assume an *n* player game similar to the two player game described in this chapter. The players bargain over potential agreements, each contributing $x_i > 0$, $i \in \{1, 2, 3, \ldots, n\}$, where the total payoff from cooperation is $x_1 + x_2 + x_3 + \ldots + x_n + g = \pi_0$, $g > 0$. Also assume the existence of a status quo partition $\alpha_{SQ} = (\alpha_{1SQ}, \ldots \alpha_{nSQ})$ of π_0. By some procedure, a new partition $\alpha = (\alpha_1, \ldots \alpha_n)$ of $\pi = \pi_0 - c$, $c > 0$, will be offered.

In any extensive form of the game, assume each player has the opportunity to exercise its outside option before accepting α. If so, in any subgame perfect equilibrium resulting in redistribution, $\alpha_i \geq x_i$ and $\alpha_i \leq \pi - \sum x_j$, $i \neq j$, for all i.

Assume c=0. As $\sum x \to \pi_0$, i.e., $g \to 0$, for any subgame perfect equilibrium resulting in redistribution, $\alpha_i \to x_i$ for all i. In the extreme, as outside options become maximally attractive, the only partition that can be supported redistributes cooperative payoffs according to each player's outside option. Any exogenous shift in a player's outside option will result in a redistribution of cooperative payoffs. On the other hand, as $x_i \to o$ for all i, i.e., $g \to \pi_o$, then for any $q > o$, since $x_k \to o$ then at some point $x_k < q$ so theoretically a_k can equal q and still satisfy the constraint $a_k \geq x_k$. Hence, as outside options become maximally unattractive, bargaining procedures producing any new partition α can be theoretically supported. In the intermediate range, the feasible range for α, $x_i \leq \alpha_i \leq \pi_o - \sum x_{-i}$, expands as each x_i strictly decreases and contracts as each x_i strictly increases. Hence, a greater theoretical range of partitions can be supported as the attractiveness of outside options diminishes.

Now assume $c > o$, such that bargaining entails some cost. As $c \to \pi_o$, no challenges are likely to occur regardless of the status quo distribution of payoffs. However, the equilibrium outcome will vary according the attractiveness of outside options. As $\sum x \to \pi_o$, $\alpha_i \to x_i$. However, since $\pi < \pi_o$, $\alpha_i < x_i$ for at least one i. Hence, unless the status quo distribution perfectly reflects the distribution of outside options, only exit can be supported as a subgame perfect equilibrium. On the other hand, as $x_i \to o$ for all i and $c \to \pi_o$, only the status quo can be supported in equilibrium.

3

The International Monetary Fund and the World Bank

When studying institutions, one needs to be cognizant of simultaneous variation in a range of potential explanatory variables. To date, comparative study of international institutions has been hampered by the fact that institutions such as the International Monetary Fund (IMF), United Nations Security Council, European Union, and World Trade Organization vary not only in their functions, but also in terms of myriad other factors such as membership composition and formal rules. Formal rules in particular, as discussed in Chapter 2, are likely to have a direct effect on the likelihood of institutional change.

In this chapter, I will exploit a quasi-experiment offered by features of the Bretton Woods Institutions – the IMF and World Bank – in order to test my theoretical predictions regarding outside options. These two institutions operate in different policy areas, but they are characterized by identical de jure rules governing changes in voting shares and essentially identical membership.[1] This allows us to observe bargaining outcomes featuring the same set of actors operating under the same set of rules, but in institutional settings featuring distinct outside options.

From the perspective of causal inference, the setup resembles a crossover study, in which distinct treatments are alternatively assigned to the same set of subjects longitudinally. The fact that the subjects are states rather than individuals present advantages as well as disadvantages. The setup does not involve random assignment, but due to the universalistic and parallel nature of the two institutions, there is no concern about

---

[1] As I discuss below, the only exceptions are a handful of minor island states.

biased selection into one treatment or another: the subjects essentially include the universe of countries in the international system, particularly after the Cold War, when former communist bloc countries joined the Bretton Woods institutions. In addition, the distinct treatments are effectively applied simultaneously, mitigating concerns about bias arising from temporal factors. As with other quasi-experiments in the social sciences, important caveats remain, which will be discussed in the empirical section. However, the results clearly show that bargaining outcomes across the IMF and World Bank have diverged in a manner consistent with the theoretical predictions.

This chapter will proceed as follows. I will first consider the policy areas of the Bretton Woods institutions to derive specific predictions for the purposes of the empirical test. Compared to that of the IMF, the policy area of the World Bank is characterized by lower network effects and barriers to entry. The World Bank therefore faces greater competition and availability of outside options for member states. My theory predicts that the World Bank should exhibit comparatively less path dependence: the institution will more quickly and accurately reflect underlying shifts in economic power.

I will then provide quantitative evidence in support of the theory, focusing on the cross-national distribution of voting shares in the IMF and International Bank for Reconstruction and Development (IBRD) of the World Bank. As predicted by my theory, shares in the IMF, the less competitive institution, exhibit greater path dependence and autoregressive properties. The evidence indicates that World Bank voting shares are closely related to contemporaneous levels and changes in shares of world gross domestic product (GDP). In contrast, IMF voting shares are primarily related to share distributions in earlier time periods and exhibit little change in response to shifts in the distribution of world GDP and other economic variables.

I will continue the analysis of the Bretton Woods institutions in Chapter 4 by analyzing Japan's experience in the two institutions, expanding the discussion to informal influence over institutional outcomes, causal mechanisms, and broader implications.

THE IMF AND WORLD BANK: PREDICTIONS

Traditionally, it has been challenging to study international institutions comparatively due to simultaneous variation in a range of factors, such as policy areas, rules, and membership. Since these factors are all likely to influence bargaining outcomes, it is difficult to isolate the independent effect of a single variable of interest. I will address this problem by exploiting common de jure features of the Bretton Woods institutions – the IMF and the IBRD of the World Bank.[2] The Bretton Woods institutions facilitate cooperation in different policy areas, but they share common internal rules and membership. This effectively allows us to examine how two separate treatments – applied simultaneously to an identical set of countries operating under the same set of rules – potentially produce divergent outcomes.

The IMF and World Bank have virtually identical membership due to Article II, Section 1, Article B of the IBRD Articles of Agreement, which makes IMF membership a precondition for joining the World Bank. For this reason, it has been customary for states seeking membership to apply simultaneously to both of the Bretton Woods Institutions. Of the 187, fully overlapping current members of the IMF, 152 joined each institution on the same date. Due to slight variation in the timing of membership approval, thirty-five joined each institution within a matter of months. Only three countries – San Marino, the Seychelles, and St. Vincent and the Grenadines – joined the World Bank with a lag exceeding a year. These are tiny island states with negligible shares of voting power and therefore highly unlikely to have a meaningful stake in bargaining outcomes or bear on the empirical results.

The IMF and World Bank also have identical de jure rules for the distribution of voting power. Voting power is predominantly determined according to the share of subscriptions held by each member state.[3] In turn, subscription shares are to broadly reflect a country's standing in the world economy, measured through indicators such as GDP, balance of payments, reserves, and the variability of current receipts. In both institutions, redistribution can occur as part of a general increase in capitalization or on an ad hoc basis for individual countries. Both institutions require a supermajority of 85 percent to approve any change in subscription shares.[4]

However, the de facto process for redistributing shares involves a highly politicized bargaining process.[5] While specific formulas are used

[2] I will use IBRD and World Bank interchangeably in the subsequent text.
[3] There is also a very small fixed component distributed equally to all members of 250 voting shares to each member.
[4] The threshold was adjusted in the 1970s from 80 percent to 85 percent to maintain the veto of the United States as its voting share declined below 20 percent. See De Vries 1987, 524.
[5] Horsefield 1969; De Vries 1987; Rapkin, Elston, and Strand 1997; Boughton 2001; Blomberg and Broz 2007; Boughton 2012.

as loose guidelines for calculating subscription shares, the formulas themselves have been the subject of much wrangling.[6] In fact, the Bretton Woods formulas have been adjusted ex post facto to produce results consistent with politically determined bargaining outcomes. For example, in 1963–1964, IMF staff revised the Bretton Woods formula by developing fifteen alternatives and settling on a five-formula solution that produced a reasonable approximation to existing quota distributions. As De Vries notes, "The number of formulas for quota calculations indicated the difficulty of deriving a single formula that would produce reasonable quota calculations for all members, while account was still taken of the existing structure of Fund quotas and the desirability of proceeding slowly with shifts in that structure."[7] By the 1980s, the complexity of formula calculations led one official to lament, "It was said that there are one-hundred-twenty ways by which to calculate a country's quota."[8]

Officially, subscription shares in the IBRD are to be derivative of and parallel to those in the IMF. However, significant discrepancies have developed over time due to divergent interstate bargaining outcomes. This discrepancy will be the focus of the empirical section of this chapter. Before turning to the empirics, I will characterize the policy areas of the Bretton Woods institutions in order to derive predictions about institutional change across the two institutions.

Policy Area Effects for the IMF and World Bank

In this subsection, I will examine the primary policy areas of the World Bank and IMF. I will argue that the primary activities of the IMF are characterized by higher network effects and higher barriers to entry compared to those of the World Bank. Consequently, compared to the IMF, the World Bank faces much greater competition from bilateral and multilateral development agencies as well as private sector lenders. World Bank member states therefore have more credible outside options. This makes the World Bank more of a "realist" institution – skewed distributional outcomes cannot be sustained, and the institution quickly reflects changes in underlying economic power. In comparison, the IMF

---

[6] The quota formulas used by the IMF during the relevant time period for this chapter are available in International Monetary Fund, "Financial Organization and Operations of the IMF," Washington, D.C., 2001, 57.
[7] De Vries 1987, 516.   [8] Ogata 1989, 12.

is predicted to exhibit greater path dependence and resistance to distributive change.

Broadly speaking, the organizational policy area of the World Bank may be characterized as development lending and assistance. Analogously, the IMF's policy area in recent years may be characterized as the maintenance of global financial stability through the prevention and resolution of financial crises and balance of payments difficulties, particularly through the use of conditional lending – for the sake of brevity, I will use "balance of payments lending" in the subsequent text.[9] This is an oversimplification by any measure – prior to 1971, the IMF's mandate also included managing the Bretton Woods system of fixed exchange rates. For this reason, during the 1970s, the IMF's international role was contested and less clear than the period before and after. Hence, for the purposes of empirical examination, I will focus on the subsequent period during which the IMF's role has been clearer. In addition, the de facto roles of the two institutions sometimes overlap, leading to criticism about "mission creep."[10] However, the overlap is relatively small when considering the aggregate lending activities of each institution.[11] After describing the network effects and barriers to entry associated with each of these policy areas, I will generate empirical predictions and discuss several potential caveats.

---

[9] For an overview of the IMF's functions and history, see Vreeland 2007, particularly Chapter 1.

[10] Einhorn 2001; Stiglitz 2002.

[11] The IMF has provided concessional financing to the world's poorest countries through the Trust Fund since 1977 and formally since 1986 through the Structural and Enhanced Structural Adjustment Facility and the Poverty and Growth Reduction Facility (PRGF). This financing overlaps to some degree with development lending, but the proportion of outstanding credit from these facilities to total outstanding credit has not exceeded 14 percent except for a brief period in 2006–2008 (which is outside the time period analyzed in this chapter), when the IMF's other lending activities declined sharply due to unusual global macroeconomic stability (*IMF Annual Report*, Various Years, appendix II). The Bank has also occasionally provided supplementary financing, along with other bilateral and multilateral development agencies, toward major IMF bailout packages, but the IMF has acted as lead negotiator and exercised control over the terms of such lending (e.g., see Blustein 2003, 103–04). In terms of the Bank's routine activities, structural adjustment lending (now development policy lending), which has been provided since 1980, has some similarities to IMF lending, such as the use of conditionality to remedy structural problems. However, the primary focus of this lending is addressing the long-term developmental consequences of structural adjustment rather than remedying immediate crises or balance of payments difficulties (e.g., see World Bank, *World Bank Annual Report*, 1985, 53).

Network Effects

Balance of payments lending is characterized by higher network effects compared to development lending due to several factors: political sensitivity associated with conditionality and cross-national rescues, the benefits associated with information pooling, and credibility in the event of a crisis. These factors make it comparatively more difficult and costly for countries to provide balance of payments lending on a bilateral or regional basis independent of the IMF.

First, political cover provided by universality is more valuable in balance of payments lending. Balance of payments lending involves severe moral hazard and agency problems, which necessitate the frequent use of conditionality.[12] However, such intrusive conditions are inevitably associated with political controversy in the target state and difficult for countries to negotiate bilaterally. While conditions may be partially determined by parochial member state interests,[13] the IMF provides "cover" by virtue of its universality and technocratic expertise to reduce the impression of overt foreign intrusion in the recipient country's domestic affairs.[14] It is more difficult for regional institutions to provide such cover due to narrower, uneven membership and local political sensitivities. This is well-illustrated by the decision of East Asian states to tie the plurality of Chiang Mai Initiative lending to IMF conditionality – as I will discuss in Chapter 4, the prospect of China or Japan being implicated for imposing harsh conditions on regional neighbors such as Korea has been considered politically unacceptable. Analogously, Greek public perceptions toward Germany plummeted during the Euro Crisis, as Germany's dominant position in the Eurozone made it an obvious target for frustration over austerity measures.[15] Universal membership can help to diffuse such political sensitivities.

The political cover afforded by the IMF also enables countries to launder funds,[16] sidestepping domestic opposition to international

---

[12] Williamson 1983; Haggard 1985; Haggard and Kaufman 1992; Drazen 2002; Stone 2002; Gould 2003; Vreeland 2003; Dreher and Vaubel 2004; Stone 2004; Stone 2008.

[13] Kahler 1993; Thacker 1999; Oatley and Yackee 2004; Dreher and Jensen 2007; Stone 2008; Copelovitch 2010.

[14] This is the international analogue of the more common domestic variant, which holds that the IMF can provide political cover to push through unpopular domestic political reforms – for example, Remmer 1986; Vreeland 2003; Mukherjee and Singer 2010.

[15] For example, "European Unity on the Rocks," *Pew Research Center*, May 29, 2012.

[16] Abbott and Snidal 1998.

bailouts. Like rescues of domestic financial institutions, foreign bailouts are often criticized for using public funds to reward profligate behavior abroad. For example, the rescue package for Mexico in 1995 was opposed by 80 percent of the US public and came under heavy scrutiny from congressional Republicans.[17] The IMF not only allows countries to channel funds in a less overtly public manner, but the IMF's universality and perceived independence can also reassure skeptical publics in creditor states that bailouts will be accompanied by tough conditions. This appears to be a critical reason why German Chancellor Angela Merkel insisted on IMF involvement during the Euro Crisis. Facing a skeptical German public, Merkel argued forcefully against a Europe-only bailout plan on the grounds that IMF involvement was the only way to credibly impose austerity on profligate member states such as Greece and deter additional requests for aid.[18]

Comparatively speaking, political cover is less salient for development lending. Actual motives aside, development lending is often associated with generosity and responsible global citizenship – something donors prefer to publicize rather than conceal.[19] Monitoring and enforcement of development projects can be done diffusely on a project-specific basis, blunting headline impact and political salience. Only a subset of development lending benefits from political cover – for example, structural adjustment lending – and even there, the need is comparatively mitigated by the fact that negotiations can occur over long time horizons outside the politically charged atmosphere created by financial crises or balance of payments difficulties.

Second, there are greater network effects associated with information pooling for balance of payments lending. Because of globalization and interconnected capital markets, balance of payments crises frequently produce contagion – for example, the Asian Crisis of 1997–1998 affected seemingly unrelated countries such as Korea, Russia, and Brazil. As such, there are inherent and fundamental benefits associated with global surveillance and universal coverage, a point often highlighted by the IMF itself.[20]

---

[17] Morris and Passé-Smith 2001.

[18] For example, Walker, Marcus, Charles Forelle and Brian Blackstone, "On the Secret Committee to Save the Euro, a Dangerous Divide," *The Wall Street Journal*, September 24, 2010.

[19] For example, the UN has promoted the norm that developed countries should contribute 0.7 percent of GDP toward official development assistance. For a detailed description, see Botcheva and Martin 2001.

[20] For example, "In today's globalized economy, where the policies of one country typically affect many other countries, international cooperation is essential. The IMF, with its

Information sharing and combining of expertise might also incrementally benefit development lending – for example, some development projects have cross-border environmental consequences – but there is no comparable imperative for universality.

Third, the need for credibility makes balance of payments lending subject to greater network effects. International financial crises are a game of confidence. In responding to a balance of payments crisis, the perception of credibility by private sector actors can be as important as the amount of lending provided.[21] An economic hegemon with the will and capacity to support the system, if one exists, may exhibit such credibility.[22] In the absence of a hegemon, individual states will find it more difficult to restore confidence acting alone – hence an institution such as the IMF, which represents virtually all major creditor states in the international system.[23] Similar credibility issues do not arise in development lending, although multilateral pooling can mitigate risk and hence some modest network effects may be present.

Barriers to Entry

Barriers to entry are also likely to be higher in balance of payments lending compared to development lending. First, even prior to the issue of credibility, a balance of payments organization must have the capacity to mobilize a sizable pool of credit in the event of a major financial crisis. This will be difficult to achieve for incipient international institutions with limited membership, except in cases where members are well-endowed with reserve assets. Development lending usually does not require the rapid mobilization of such liquidity, and a small organization has the option to focus on small-scale projects.

Second, the IMF collects sensitive data from member countries such as available reserves. Countries are often reluctant to offer such data bilaterally or to economically proximate countries with potentially subversive motivations, placing limitations on the surveillance capabilities of alternative arrangements. For example, Japan had to reject a bilateral bailout of Thailand early in the Asian Crisis because Thai authorities

---

near-universal membership of 186 countries, facilitates this cooperation." (IMF, "International Monetary Fund Factsheet: Surveillance," August, 2006).

[21] For example, see Rubin 2004, 215.   [22] Kindleberger 1986.

[23] Kindleberger 2000, 211–38.

would only share crucial information regarding the status of their reserves to the IMF.[24]

Third, a balance of payments organization derives benefits from greater jurisdictional coverage over internationally active private financial institutions. This allows the institution to more effectively organize private sector "bail-ins" should they become necessary, as banks will be more willing to compromise if the institution can credibly guarantee that other banks will also hold steady.[25] Incipient organizations may find it difficult to establish broad jurisdictional coverage or develop relationships with a sufficiently wide range of private sector creditors.

Fourth, while both the IMF and World Bank have extensive professional bureaucracies that would be costly to reproduce, the costs may be somewhat higher to replicate an IMF. Because many governments participate to varying degrees in bilateral international development assistance, a domestic pool of bureaucratic expertise exists.[26] In contrast, bilateral involvement in international crisis lending tends to be more ad hoc and reliant on the IMF, limiting the available pool of outside specialists.[27]

Predictions and Discussion

Table 3.1 summarizes the preceding points and the implications for competition and outside options in each institution. The conditions underpinning balance of payments lending are associated with greater network effects and barriers to entry compared to development lending. The IMF is predicted to face less policy area competition and offer unattractive outside options for member states compared to the World Bank. Consequently, distributional outcomes in the World Bank will be less path dependent and more reflective of underlying economic capabilities.[28]

---

[24] Sakakibara 2001, 170.   [25] Gould 2003.

[26] This is, of course, a second-order effect of the other factors.

[27] This factor is more ambiguous than the others. For example, the size of IMF staff (2400) is smaller than that for the World Bank (10,000+), which could make it more costly if states wished to replicate the institutions in their entirety.

[28] The internal rules of each institution, which specify periodic redistribution according to predefined (if not meticulously followed) criteria, combined with a supermajority rule, are not obviously flexible or rigid. Empirically, there have been no instances of outright exit by important member states from either institution, and the financial resources of each institution have increased relatively consistently over time since inception. Hence, the costs of challenging existing share distributions in each institution appear not to have

TABLE 3.1 *The IMF and World Bank: Policy Areas and Path Dependence*

	Network Effects	Barriers to Entry	Outside Options	Distributive Outcomes
Balance of Payments Lending (IMF)	**Higher** – Political Cover – Laundering – Information Sharing (Contagion Risk) – Credibility Arising from Broad Membership	**Higher** – Sufficient Credit Availability in Crisis – Coverage over More Banks for Bail-ins – Access to Sensitive Information – Bureaucratic Expertise	Less Attractive	More Rigid
Development Aid (World Bank)	**Lower** – Pooling Funds – Pooling Information	**Lower** – Bureaucratic Expertise	More Attractive	More Flexible

Before moving to empirical analysis of redistributive outcomes, it should be noted that the predictions regarding the intervening variable – level of competition and hence outside options in the policy area – are consistent with the empirical evidence. In the field of development lending, myriad regional development agencies perform functions similar to the World Bank – among others, the Asian Development Bank, Inter-American Development Bank, Central American Bank for Regional Integration, African Development Bank, Islamic Development Bank, European Bank of Reconstruction and Development, Council of Europe Development Bank, Caribbean Development Bank, etc. On a yearly basis, the Asian Development Bank and Inter-American Development Bank each disburse about 40 percent of the lending of the World Bank.[29] A host of countries also provide bilateral development assistance through domestic aid agencies. In 2006, the largest bilateral donor, the United

been so high as to facilitate exit: according to the theory, this implies that World Bank share distributions will be determined according to outside options, and IMF share distributions according to relative patience, which is predicted to be less responsive to underlying shifts in power.

[29] Asian Development Bank, *ADB Annual Report* (various years); Inter-American Development Bank, *Annual Report* (various years); World Bank, *World Bank Annual Report* (various years).

States, provided roughly $27 billion in aid, comparable to the total provision of the World Bank loans of $24 billion.[30] Private financing is also a reasonable, though generally more costly, alternative for borrowers with access to capital markets. Countries dissatisfied with the World Bank's policies can turn to a wide range of credible alternatives.

There has been no comparable proliferation of bilateral or regional analogues to the IMF, and where they exist, they have been limited in scope or have relied heavily on IMF involvement. The Arab Monetary Fund has provided limited balance of payments lending to member states in the Arab League. However, total cumulative lending by the Arab Monetary Fund since inception only amounts to about $4 billion,[31] which is a tiny fraction of lending provided by the IMF. As will be discussed in Chapter 4, East Asian nations have developed a multilateral currency swap arrangement, but a plurality of lending is tied to IMF conditionality, and the funds have never been tapped. The IMF also played a central role in the Euro Crisis alongside European financial authorities.

Independent, bilateral provision of balance of payments lending was common in the period before World War II,[32] but has become comparatively rare after the establishment of the IMF: there are a few exceptions, but they tend to be small in scale. For example, Japan extended a $2.5 billion short-term loan to Malaysia during the Asian crisis.[33] China agreed to several bilateral currency swap arrangements after 2008, but these were symbolic measures in the absence of Yuan convertibility.[34] More significantly, US financial authorities entered into bilateral currency swap arrangements with several countries during the global economic crisis of 2008.[35] Tellingly, the "swap lines put the Fed in a politically uncomfortable position of having to choose which US allies were good enough credit risks," leading US financial authorities to seek a transfer of future decision-making over short-term foreign-exchange swaps operations to the IMF.[36]

---

[30] United States Agency for International Development, *U.S. Overseas Loans and Grants: Obligations and Loan Authorizations, July 1, 1945–September 30, 2007*; World Bank, *World Bank Annual Report 2008*, World Bank Lending by Theme and Sector.

[31] Arab Monetary Fund, 2003.   [32] Kindleberger 2000.

[33] Ministry of Finance (Japan), "The Road to the Revival of the Asian Economy and Financial System – Sustainable Growth in the 21st Century and Building of a Multi-layered Regional Cooperative Network," appendix 2 (7), June 20, 2000.

[34] For example, Chen, Bob, and Judy Chen, "China to Boost Yuan Swaps, Payments on Dollar Concern," *Bloomberg*, February 4, 2009.

[35] Kim, Jae-kyoung, "Korea, US Sign $30 Bil. Currency Swap Deal," *Korea Times*, October 30, 2008.

[36] Talley, Ian, "IMF Plan Sees Role for Fund in Crises." *The Wall Street Journal*, March 22, 2011.

For sure, the IMF does not monopolize all aspects of balance of payments lending. For small-scale balance of payments difficulties that do not require conditional lending, countries frequently turn to private markets. However, the credibility of these sources as outside options is limited by the potential for market disruptions as well as the possibility of more serious future difficulties that necessitate conditional lending from the IMF. There are some states, such as most advanced industrialized countries, that have largely ceased to use IMF resources.[37] Nonetheless, these states still have a strong interest in the determination of when and how conditional lending is provided, particularly in the presence of close economic, financial, or security ties.[38] As I discuss in Chapter 4, the difficulty of providing such lending without IMF involvement critically constrained Japan's response during the Asian Crisis.

The IMF also frequently relies on other sources of funding – public and private – during major international crisis episodes, such as the Mexican Crisis of 1994 and the Asian Crisis of 1997/1998, and hence does not monopolize the actual funding of rescue programs. In theory, such instances may provide opportunities for the contributors of ad hoc funds to exercise influence and push for redistributive gains within the institution as a quid pro quo for providing funds. The 1998 IMF quota redistribution favoring East Asia, although limited in magnitude, is consistent with such a possibility. However, both primary and secondary accounts indicate that both the World Bank and Japan, which contributed heavily to rescue packages in East Asia, found themselves largely shut out from the IMF's decision-making process.[39]

Empirically, any factors that potentially make the IMF more subject to redistributive forces will be associated with a bias against finding empirical results consistent with my hypotheses. For example, if states can secure greater leverage over the IMF by threatening to hold up funding during a large bailout operation, distributive outcomes in the IMF will be more fluid and more closely resemble those in the World Bank. Hence, the direction of bias is such that my empirical tests will understate, not overstate, the true difference in policy area effects between the two institutions.[40]

---

[37] Blomberg and Broz 2007

[38] Thacker 1999; Oatley and Yackee 2004; Dreher and Jensen 2007; Stone 2008; Copelovitch 2010

[39] For example, Blustein 2003, 159; Sakakibara 2000, discussion with various relevant officials.

[40] King, Keohane, and Verba 1994.

Measures of Policy Area Competition for the IMF and World Bank

For illustrative purposes, it is useful to consider some quantitative measures of the degree of competition in the policy areas of the IMF and World Bank. I use two pre-existing data sources to classify multilateral institutions according to policy area. The IMF has published a report identifying multilateral financing arrangements that were "established to avert financing instability and/or safeguard regional integration" or due to "dissatisfaction with Fund conditionality and concerns about Fund governance."[41] Tierney et al. have similarly compiled a database of multilateral development aid institutions including the World Bank.[42] Although these lists are not definitive, they contain a plausible and comparable set of institutions that facilitate cooperation in the areas of balance of payments and development lending.

According to this data, during the period 1978–2005, there were six international institutions engaged in the provision of balance of payments lending: the IMF, the Arab Monetary Fund, the Latin American Reserve Fund (Andean Reserve Fund), North American Framework Agreement, the Balance of Payments Assistance Facility of the European Union, and the Chiang Mai Initiative. In comparison, there were twenty-eight development institutions of various sizes engaged in the provision of development aid.

Large numbers of institutions do not necessarily indicate greater competition. Figure 3.1 depicts a measure of market concentration commonly used by antitrust regulators and economists to measure market competition – the Herfindahl–Hirschman Index – from 1978–2005 for balance of payments lending and development lending. The index is calculated according to the sum of the squares of the gross distribution shares of each institution within the respective policy areas.[43] Higher numbers indicate greater concentration, with the maximum value, 1, indicating monopoly, while values approaching 0 are associated with perfect competition. As the figure shows, in balance of payments lending, the Herfindahl–Hirschman Index generally hovers close to 1 and averages 0.88 during the entire time period. In comparison, the Index value is consistently lower for development lending, averaging 0.22. For reference, the US Department of Justice considers markets with values between 0.15 and 0.25 to reflect moderate concentration, and markets exceeding

[41] IMF 2013, 1.   [42] Tierney et al. 2011.
[43] Data is obtained from the annual reports of each agency as well as Henning 2002.

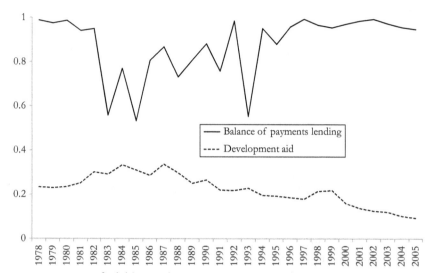

FIGURE 3.1 Herfindahl–Hirschman Concentration Indexes, Multilateral Disbursement of Balance of Payments Lending and Development Aid
Note: Classification of institutions in relevant policy areas are based on IMF (2013) and Tierney et al. (2011).

this level are classified as highly concentrated.[44] During this period, the IMF accounted for approximately 94.3 percent of disbursements in its policy area, compared to 31.1 percent for the World Bank. While the World Bank clearly faces considerable competition in pursuing its activities, the IMF's analogues either disburse funds very rarely (the European Balance of Payments Assistance Facility) or in much smaller magnitudes compared to the IMF.

Besides multilateral organizations, the IMF and World Bank also face potential competition from bilateral sources. Unfortunately, comprehensive data on bilateral balance of payments lending is not publicly available.[45] However, this data is available for one important bilateral source, the United States.[46] This data likely exaggerates overall bilateral provision

[44] "Herfindahl–Hirschman Index," US Department of Justice.
[45] Several governments, such as those of Japan and the United Kingdom, do not make this information publicly available as a matter of policy. I thank Daniel McDowell for confirming this point as well as pointing me to the US Exchange Stabilization Fund (ESF) data source.
[46] The US government has compiled and released data on its bilateral balance of payments lending activities, which have been principally conducted through the ESF and Federal Reserve's System Open Market Account. The Treasury only provides information on ESF funding. However, it notes that "Historically, U.S. intervention has been jointly financed

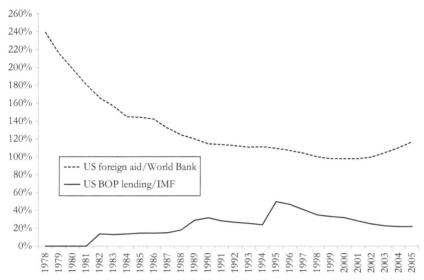

FIGURE 3.2 Cumulative Ratio of US Bilateral Disbursements vs. IMF and IBRD Disbursements by Policy Area

Note: High values indicate higher US bilateral disbursements compared to disbursements by the IMF or World Bank. US aid excludes military aid. US BOP lending includes commitments drawn upon and therefore likely overstates actual disbursements. Cumulative values are presented due to the lumpy pattern of distributions of US bilateral balance of payments lending.

of balance of payments lending for two reasons: first, the US Treasury only provides data on the size of commitments drawn upon, while the IMF data is funds actually disbursed; second, the United States has exercised an outsized global leadership role and financial preponderance,[47] making it a more likely source of balance of payments lending compared to lesser states. The cumulative proportions of US bilateral disbursement to the disbursements of each institution are presented in Figure 3.2. According to this data, between 1978 and 2005, cumulative US economic aid disbursements exceeded World Bank disbursements by 16 percent. In comparison, cumulative disbursements by the IMF were about 4.6 times greater than

by both the ESF and SOMA, and the financing has been equally shared between the two accounts." Hence, for the period in question, I double ESF commitments to obtain an estimate of total US bilateral balance of payments lending. (See "History, Exchange Stabilization Fund," US Department of the Treasury, www.treasury.gov/resource-center/international/ESF/Pages/history-index.aspx.)

[47] Simmons 2001.

US balance of payments figures, despite the latter being considerably overstated. This data is consistent with the theoretical premises that multilateral and bilateral provision of balance of payments lending is relatively less feasible compared to development aid.

Of course, direct measures of competition are subject to several important problems, whether applied to private markets or public policy areas. The most important of these is the issue of implicit competition: even in a market or policy area that appears to contain a small number of concentrated actors, competitive pressures may be intense due to the ease of potential entry. Antitrust regulators usually complement measures of explicit competition with attempts to ascertain market power by considering the implications of implicit competition on the behavior of firms and consumers by examining metrics such as price elasticities and profitability. The theory developed in this book generates the policy area analogue of these metrics: if the IMF faces greater implicit competition than implied by the direct measures of competition, an observable implication is that this should be reflected in redistributive dynamics, making the institution relatively malleable to institutional change. As I will show, the evidence is consistent with the IMF facing less explicit as well as implicit competition in comparison to the World Bank.

It is worth emphasizing that the IMF and World Bank are chosen for comparison because they offer *variation* in external policy area features, not necessarily because they lie at extremes. In this section, I have sought to establish that, for member states, outside options vis-à-vis the IMF are generally less attractive or more limited than those vis-à-vis the World Bank. This variation in the attractiveness of outside options leads to the prediction that the World Bank will be comparatively more prone to redistributive institutional change.

EMPIRICAL EXAMINATION: QUANTITATIVE ANALYSIS OF SUBSCRIPTION SHARES

Subscription shares in the IMF and World Bank are the predominant determinants of voting shares.[48] The shares are therefore a simple and reasonable way to quantify distributional change in each institution. In

---

[48] Voting shares are calculated by adding a small fixed component (250 shares) to subscriptions. Hence, running the analysis using voting shares produces nearly identical substantive results. The discussion in this section does not reflect reforms associated with the

this section, I will provide analysis based on two datasets. The first dataset was obtained directly from the IMF and includes all member states as of 2004, with information on subscriptions, economic variables used as inputs in the IMF formulas, and the IMF formula outputs.[49] This dataset is useful as we can be certain that the variables used in the analysis are identical to those used internally by the IMF. I added World Bank subscription shares for 2004 as well as subscription information from prior years from the relevant *Annual Reports*. I use this data to test the following hypothesis:

H1. The distribution of subscription (voting) shares in the IMF, compared to the World Bank, should be more greatly affected by the distribution of shares in previous time periods, i.e. the institution will be characterized by greater path dependence in distributional outcomes. World Bank shares should more readily reflect underlying economic power as measured by economic variables, primarily GDP.

In order to test this hypothesis, I first averaged the countries' shares across the two institutions in 2004 to rank all countries by combined average voting share. I then restricted the sample to the top forty countries. The combined average allows me to use the same set of countries for both institutions to make sure the results are not driven by the particular set of countries chosen. I restrict the number of countries to exclude countries whose positions are so small as to make bargaining over voting shares unlikely. As indicated earlier, subscriptions may be adjusted ex post to legitimize bargaining outcomes among large member states – smaller states often experience a shift in their relative shares as an externality. For the smallest members, proportional shares frequently shift due to extraneous factors – for example, in the Eighth General Review of IMF quotas, Maldives received an 11 percent increase in its shares relative to other members due to rounding of its shares to the next 0.1 millionth Special Drawing Right.[50] As a point of reference, the IMF granted ad hoc quota increases to China, Korea, Mexico and Turkey in 2006. In terms of rank in the dataset, these countries were respectively number 8, 22, 17, and 35. It therefore seems reasonable to include member states in this range as countries large enough to have an independent stake in their voting share.

Fourteenth General Quota Review, which are in the process of implementation at the time of writing and fall outside of the time period analyzed.

[49] Data was obtained from *International Monetary Fund: Quotas, Updated Calculations*, IMF Report Prepared for the Finance Department, 2006.

[50] Boughton 2001, 859.

Including all member states or using alternative cut-offs such as the top thirty or fifty states does not alter the substantive conclusions in the subsequent analysis.

Also included in the models are economic variables used by the IMF that indicate a country's position in the world economy: nominal GDP (average of 2002–2004), reserves (twelve month average for 2004), current receipts (average of 2000–2004), current payments (average of 2000–2004), and variability of current receipts (average of 1992–2004). Throughout, I keep the statistical models sparse, reflecting the fact that the empirical strategy holds constant the set of countries and time periods included for each institution. This effectively controls for country- or time- specific factors that have common effects across the institutions. It is still necessary to consider factors that might affect bargaining leverage asymmetrically between the two institutions, an issue I will return to in the robustness checks.

The dependent variable is the share of subscriptions in each institution in 2004. The key independent variable is share of subscriptions in 1984, that is, the dependent variable lagged by twenty years. I use the twenty year lag in light of the fact that the IMF's mandate was contested in the 1970s after the collapse of the Bretton Woods System – the period thereafter offers a more relevant test of my theoretical propositions. The results of the analysis are robust to the selection of alternative lag periods, such as fifteen years and twenty-five years. My predictions about path dependence imply that World Bank shares lagged by twenty years should have less predictive power over World Bank shares in 2004 than the same for IMF shares. All variables are log transformed.[51]

The OLS results are presented in Table 3.2. For reference, the first two specifications are run with only the economic control variables. It appears that GDP most reliably predicts subscription shares in each institution. The next two specifications include the dependent variable lagged by twenty years. The result is consistent with *H1*. For the IMF, shares from twenty years prior are a strong predictor of contemporary subscriptions: a one percentage point increase in 1984 shares is associated with a 0.81 percentage point increase in contemporary shares (0.73–0.89 with 95 percent confidence). After controlling for 1984 subscription shares, the key economic variable, GDP, has no relationship with contemporary IMF shares. In comparison, the twenty-year lagged dependent variable is more

---

[51] This is done to avoid potential bias caused by correlation between the variance of errors and the magnitude of predicted subscription shares.

TABLE 3.2 *Path Dependence in IMF and World Bank Subscription Shares (OLS)*

Indep/Dep Variables	IMF Subscription Shares (2004)	World Bank Subscription Shares (2004)	IMF Subscription Shares (2004)	World Bank Subscription Shares (2004)	IMF Subscription Shares (2004)
GDP	0.77*	0.99*	0.05	0.72*	0.05
	(0.13)	(0.12)	(0.04)	(0.15)	(0.04)
Reserves	-0.23*	-0.19*	0.03	-0.13*	0.00
	(0.08)	(0.07)	(0.01)	(0.04)	(0.02)
Current Receipts	0.44	0.08	0.32*	-0.08	0.22*
	(0.58)	(0.61)	(0.11)	(0.46)	(0.10)
Current Payments	-0.83	-0.80	-0.25*	-0.53	-0.35*
	(0.50)	(0.52)	(0.10)	(0.41)	(0.13)
Variability Of Receipts	0.55*	0.59*	0.07	0.43*	0.01
	(0.19)	(0.19)	(0.04)	(0.16)	(0.06)
Dependent Variable (1984)			0.81*	0.35*	0.79*
			(0.04)	(0.12)	(0.05)
IMF Formula					0.28
					(0.17)
Constant	-7.33*	-6.90*	-7.76*	-7.20*	-4.73
	(0.59)	(0.55)	(0.17)	(0.47)	(1.82)
n	40	40	40	40	40

Note: Numbers in parenthesis are Huber–White standard errors. All variables are logged. Star denotes a coefficient at least two standard errors removed from zero.

81

weakly associated with contemporary World Bank shares: a one percentage point increase in 1984 World Bank subscription shares is associated with a 0.35 percentage point increase in contemporary shares (0.11–0.60 with 95 percent confidence). More importantly, even after controlling for the lagged variable, GDP remains a strong predictor of World Bank subscriptions: a one percentage point increase in GDP is associated with a 0.72 percentage point increase in subscription share (0.41–1.03 with 95 percent confidence).

The last column of Table 3.2 repeats the analysis for the IMF including the IMF Quota Formulas as calculated by Fund staff. The results demonstrate that once historical subscriptions are controlled for, the IMF formulas have no predictive power over current subscriptions.[52] This result is consistent with the stylized fact that IMF quota formulas are used as loose guidelines at best.[53]

One alternative way to test H1 is to consider *changes* in subscriptions over time as a function of changes in GDP over time. If the World Bank more readily reflects underlying changes in economic power compared to the IMF, shifts in GDP should be more clearly associated with shifts in subscriptions. In this analysis, the dependent variable is the percentage change in subscriptions for each country from 1984 to 2004. The key independent variable of interest is the percentage change in GDP over the same time period. As controls, I include analogous percentage changes for reserves, current payments, and current receipts.[54] The results are presented in Table 3.3. Consistent with H1, ceteris paribus, there is no statistically significant relationship between changes in GDP and changes in IMF subscriptions between 1984 and 2004. On the other hand, changes in GDP are strongly associated with changes in World Bank subscriptions.

---

[52] Although not reported in the table, the results for World Bank subscription shares are the same – the IMF formulas are not significant predictors of contemporary subscription shares after controlling for the economic variables and the lagged dependent variable.

[53] As a robustness check, I also ran these regressions including the key independent variables from Blomberg and Broz 2007: θ (deviation in income share relative to the median), R (right wing government), and the interaction term $R*\theta$. These variables have the expected relationship with shares in both the IMF and World Bank prior to inclusion of the lagged dependent variables (negative for $R*\theta$, positive for θ). However, these variables are not significant predictors of shares after the lagged dependent variables are included, and the regression results produce substantively identical results to those reported in Table 3.2.

[54] Variability of current receipts is dropped from the analysis as there is too much missing data for 1984.

TABLE 3.3 *Percentage Changes in IMF and WB Subscriptions (OLS)*

Indep/Dep Variables	%Δ IMF Subscriptions (1984 to 2004)	%Δ World Bank Subscriptions (1984 to 2004)
%Δ GDP	−0.02	0.46*
	(0.02)	(0.09)
%Δ Reserves	0.00	−0.00
	(0.00)	(0.01)
%Δ Current Receipts	0.03	0.53
	(0.09)	(0.57)
%Δ Current Payments	0.07	−0.90
	(0.10)	(0.73)
Constant	1.02*	1.78*
	(0.08)	(0.30)
n	40	40

Note: Numbers in parenthesis are Huber–White standard errors. Variability of Current Receipts is dropped from the analysis due to missing data for 1984. Star denotes a coefficient at least two standard errors removed from zero.

Shifts in economic power have translated into greater voting power in the World Bank over time. In the IMF, on the other hand, the shadow the past has proven remarkably resilient. Consistent with my theory, despite identical de jure rules, subscription shares in the IMF have exhibited greater path dependence.

To provide an additional test of my theory, I examine a different data set, which contains time series information on the relevant variables from 1975–2014.[55] I use this data to test the following hypothesis:

H2. IMF subscription shares are more autoregressive compared to World Bank shares.

On a year-by-year basis, an institution that is relatively "sticky" should experience less change in the variable of interest and therefore greater correlation across time periods. The raw data is consistent with this hypothesis. I first consider the proportion of countries undergoing meaningful changes in voting shares on a year-by-year basis. To omit trivial

[55] Excluding the 1970s from this data does not alter the substantive conclusions that follow. The economic variables in this dataset are not necessarily the same ones used by Fund staff in original quota calculations, as they were collected independently. Part of this data was collected by Brock Blomberg and Lawrence Broz, whom I thank for making their data available.

variation caused by the entry of new members and the adjustment of the shares of other countries, changes are counted as "meaningful" when year-on-year share changes exceed 1 percent. According to this measure, 14.7 percent of country-year observations in the World Bank are associated with a meaningful change in voting shares, compared to only 5.5 percent of IMF country-years. At least one meaningful change in voting shares occurred in the World Bank during 27 out of 38 years analyzed (71.1 percent), compared to 12 out of 38 for the IMF (31.6 percent). The magnitude of changes is also larger in the World Bank, as measured by the percentage of total shares that shifted hands during a given year in each institution. On average, about 2.8 percent of World Bank shares shifted hands every year, compared to 0.7 percent for the IMF. The maximum percentage of shares to shift hands during a given year was also greater in the World Bank, at 10.7 percent, compared to 5.5 percent for the IMF.

For the statistical test, I restrict the sample to a set of large countries comparable to the previous analysis – countries that had subscriptions shares averaged across the IMF and World Bank in excess of 0.5 percent at any point in time.[56] All variables are log transformed as in the previous analyses. I estimate OLS models with panel-corrected standard errors. Due to data availability, I proxy the variability of current receipts with a more crude measure, one standard deviation of current receipts during the trailing three year period.[57]

The results are presented in Table 3.4 and are consistent with *H2*. The first column shows that, after controlling for subscription shares from the previous year, none of the economic variables are meaningfully associated with IMF subscription shares. A one percentage point increase in lagged IMF shares is associated with a 0.99 percentage point increase in IMF shares (0.98–1.00 with 95 percent confidence). In other words, there is remarkably little year-on-year variation in IMF shares, and any change that occurs is not explained by underlying economic variables. The second column presents comparable results for World Bank shares. Compared to IMF shares, World Bank shares exhibit meaningfully greater

---

[56] There were forty-six such countries. As in the previous analysis, the precise cutoff does not change the substantive conclusions that follow.

[57] The IMF quota formulas calculate variability of current receipts as one standard deviation from a centered five-year moving average from a recent 13-year period. Due to missing data, particularly for early years in the panel, it is impractical to calculate variability according to the official methodology. As Table 3.4 shows, the variability measure has little bearing on the substantive results.

TABLE 3.4 *IMF and WB Subscriptions (OLS with Panel-Corrected Standard Errors)*

Indep/Dep Variables	IMF Subscription Shares (1976–2014)	World Bank Subscription Shares (1976–2014)	IMF Subscription Shares (1976–2014)	World Bank Subscription Shares (1976–2014)
GDP	0.00	0.05*	0.00	0.05*
	(0.01)	(0.02)	(0.01)	(0.02)
Reserves	–0.00	–0.01	–0.00	–0.01
	(0.00)	(0.01)	(0.00)	(0.01)
Current Receipts	0.04	0.05	0.04	0.04
	(0.03)	(0.04)	(0.04)	(0.04)
Current Payments	–0.04	–0.05	–0.04	–0.04
	(0.03)	(0.04)	(0.05)	(0.04)
Variability Of Receipts	0.00	–0.00		
	(0.00)	(0.01)		
Dependent Variable (t-1)	0.99*	0.91*	0.98*	0.92*
	(0.01)	(0.02)	(0.01)	(0.02)
Constant	–0.08	–0.52*	–0.09	–0.48*
	(0.06)	(0.14)	(0.07)	(0.13)
n	1454	1454	1514	1514

Note: Numbers in parenthesis are panel-corrected standard errors. All variables are logged. Star denotes a coefficient at least two standard errors removed from zero. Due to data availability, variability of receipts is proxied using the standard deviation of current receipts over a trailing three-year period (this variable is dropped in the last two columns).

variability year-on-year. A one percentage point increase in lagged World Bank shares is associated with a 0.91 percentage point increase in World Bank shares (0.87–0.95 with 95 percent confidence). In addition, even after including lagged shares in the model, GDP is positively associated with contemporaneous World Bank shares. The last two columns of Table 3.4 omit Variability of Current Receipts from the models, as I used a proxy for this variable. As the columns show, the substantive results are unchanged.[58]

One contributing factor to the results in Table 3.4 is the prevalence of ad hoc subscription increases outside of general reviews in the World

[58] Again, I performed a robustness check by running these regressions including the key independent variables from Blomberg and Broz 2007. These variables are not significant predictors of subscriptions once the lagged dependent variables are controlled for, and the substantive results are virtually identical to what is reported in Table 3.4.

Bank. While institutional rules allow both institutions to grant ad hoc increases in subscriptions at any time subject to approval by a super-majority, the World Bank has concluded a far greater number of such increases in the time period analyzed. A review of minutes from the IMF/ World Bank Annual Meetings reveals that World Bank subscriptions have been increased frequently on an ad hoc basis during years where no general review of subscriptions was taking place. For example, in 1987 alone, nineteen countries were granted such ad hoc increases. On the other hand, the IMF provided ad hoc increases outside of general reviews on only four occasions during the entire time period analyzed.[59] Consistent with my theoretical predictions, ad hoc share redistributions in the IMF have been fewer in number and smaller in cumulative magnitude.

ALTERNATIVE EXPLANATIONS AND ROBUSTNESS CHECKS

I have argued that the IMF and World Bank provide conditions approximating a quasi-experiment that allow us to isolate the effect of outside options on institutional change. One general objection to the empirical strategy outlined in this chapter is that although the comparison of the IMF and World Bank allows us to control for some of the most salient alternative explanations for institutional change – variation in actors, rules, time periods, geographic location of headquarters, etc. – there may be some sources of variation aside from outside options that remain unaccounted for. This is a common limitation of quasi-experiments in the social sciences.[60] Analogously, we must guard against the possibility that some other difference between the IMF and World Bank aside from outside options accounts for the empirical findings. To address this concern, I will consider several remaining sources of potential variation in this section. I will also provide an additional test of the causal mechanism by examining subscription shares in the immediate post–World War II period, when the aftermath of the war limited the outside options for the

---

[59] China in 1980 (change in representation from Taiwan to PRC), Saudi Arabia in 1981 (to bolster fund liquidity and conclude borrowing arrangement), Cambodia in 1994 (resumption of fund relations), and China, Korea, Mexico, and Turkey in 2006 (to increase quotas for the most underrepresented members).

[60] For example, the seminal work by Posner 2004 on cultural cleavages in Malawi and Zambia takes advantage of cross-border ethnic divisions to demonstrate the salience of differences across borders, but the research design is less helpful for identifying which *specific* cross-border difference accounts for variations in the political salience of cleavages.

World Bank. Additional evidence in favor of the proposed causal mechanisms will be presented in Chapter 4.

One possible source of remaining variation across the IMF and World Bank is underlying power asymmetries in the respective policy areas. A neorealist may argue that underrepresented states, such as developing countries and East Asian states, exert greater influence over the World Bank because they have greater relative power in development lending, while overrepresented, primarily West European countries, have relatively greater power in balance of payments lending (note that the United States has not been formally overrepresented in the IMF and is generally not the primary opponent to redistribution).[61] However, this claim is difficult to square with the evidence. East Asian states such as Japan, China, and Korea, are among the top holders of foreign exchange reserves in the world, far exceeding the reserve holdings of West European countries. If international balance of payments lending were simply a matter of capacity, East Asian countries ought to be in a commanding position to "go it alone" through bilateral and regional mechanisms and exert significant pressure on the IMF. More broadly, the quantitative analysis includes variables such as GDP and international reserves, which should correlate closely with a country's unilateral capacity to discharge balance of payments lending. The evidence indicates that these factors are not strongly associated with bargaining outcomes in the IMF once prior share distributions are controlled for.

It is possible that some countries, such as the United States, the United Kingdom, France, and Germany, exhibit power in international finance not captured by the variables included in the models due to factors such as hegemony, status as international financial centers, or role in regional monetary arrangements. These factors may make the shares of these countries particularly resistant to change in the IMF. I therefore performed robustness checks by omitting these countries from the statistical analyses. Along similar lines, I reran the models including financial sector share of GDP as a control variable.[62] In both cases, the substantive conclusions were unchanged across the specifications. It is also plausible that strong geopolitical ties to influential countries such as these might provide an advantage in bargaining over representation. I therefore reran the models including a common measure of political affinity: proximity of voting

---

[61] The United States does hold a unilateral veto over important decisions and exercises informal influence over the IMF that is out of proportion with its formal voting shares, for example, see Stone 2011.

[62] Data from O'Mahony and Timmer 2009; Timmer and Vries 2009.

profile in the UN General Assembly to the United States, United Kingdom, France, or Germany.[63] The substantive results were again unchanged.

Although the institutional rules governing change in the IMF and World Bank are the same, IMF subscriptions have an additional function that could potentially lead to divergent bargaining outcomes. In addition to determining voting shares, a country's IMF quota is formally tied to its ability to draw on the institution's resources – for example, a country can draw on 25 percent of its quota without conditionality for the purposes of minor fluctuations in its balance of payments.[64] In theory, this factor may lead states to bargain more aggressively to resist a loss in IMF subscriptions, making it more difficult to reach a redistributive agreement.

There are several reasons why this alternative explanation is unlikely to account for the observed variation presented in this chapter. In both the IMF and the World Bank, it is extremely unusual for any country's absolute subscription level to decline. Share redistributions have almost always accompanied a general increase in capitalization or taken the form of selective ad hoc increases for member states.[65] Hence, an increase in one country's *relative* subscription share is generally achieved without consequence for another country's ability to draw on IMF resources. This is particularly true if the country receiving the increase is a creditor state that is unlikely to borrow from the IMF. Japan's experience, which will be discussed in greater detail in the following chapter, provides a strong counterpoint to this alternative explanation. Japan was unable to secure greater representation in the IMF in the 1980s despite being a highly unlikely candidate for an IMF loan: flexible exchange rate, large and persistent current account surpluses, and the largest stock of international reserves in the world. In addition, underrepresented countries such as Japan and China have frequently contributed to IMF special funds in a manner that does not affect their quota (one of the arguments made for greater voting rights stems from this "taxation without representation"). As such, concerns about potential drains on IMF resources could have been mitigated by simply tying increases in quota shares to additional non-quota contributions to fund resources.

As a related robustness check, I considered the possibility that the quantitative results are affected by the inclusion of likely IMF borrowers. Following along the logic above, the results may be biased if a subset of

---

[63] Gartzke 2010.   [64] Vreeland 2003, 26–27.
[65] For example, See Boughton 2001, 861.

states is perceived as particularly risky and therefore persistently prevented from obtaining greater subscriptions in the IMF, but not in the World Bank. I therefore reran the analyses, separately omitting developing countries, which have dominated IMF borrowing since the 1980s[66] and countries that participated in an IMF program at any point during the years analyzed.[67] In no case did the removal of these countries alter the substantive results reported in Tables 3.2–3.4.[68] Hence, the statistical findings are not driven by countries that are likely to require access to IMF resources.

Finally, I exploit over-time variation in the policy area of the World Bank to test an additional observable implication of the theory. Although the World Bank faces widespread competition in its activities in the current period, this was less true during its earliest years. Immediately after World War II, the ability of major economies aside from the United States to engage in development lending had been decimated, and large regional development banks, such as the Inter-American Development Bank (est. 1959) and Asian Development Bank (est. 1966), had yet to come into existence. Hence, the conditions of the immediate postwar period temporarily suppressed the general attractiveness of outside options for member states of the World Bank. If the causal mechanism proposed in this chapter is correct, World Bank share distributions during this period should have exhibited greater rigidity compared to the contemporary period. Table 3.5 replicates the analysis from Table 3.2 using subscription shares in 1950–1960. The results show that, in the 1950s, World Bank voting shares were indeed more rigid and closely resembled those of the IMF – that is, share distributions responded primarily to prior distributions rather than GDP. Over subsequent decades, World Bank share distributions became more flexible and responsive to GDP, while there was no comparable trend for IMF shares.

DISCUSSION

In this chapter, I took advantage of a quasi-experiment offered by the common rules and common membership of the Bretton Woods

---

[66] For example, Blomberg and Broz 2007. I restricted the sample to "advanced economies" as identified by the IMF.

[67] I thank James Vreeland for making the data on IMF participation available from Vreeland 2003 and Vreeland 2007.

[68] That is, the coefficients related to GDP and lagged shares continued to exhibit the expected hypothesized relationships and with statistical significance at the 95 percent level.

TABLE 3.5 *Path Dependence in IMF and World Bank Subscription Shares, 1950–1960 (OLS)*

Indep/Dep Variables	World Bank Subscription Shares (1960)	IMF Subscription Shares (1960)	World Bank Subscription Shares (1960)	IMF Subscription Shares (1960)
GDP	0.70*	0.66*	−0.03	−0.14
	(0.14)	(0.11)	(0.14)	(0.08)
Reserves	−0.21*	−0.22*	0.06	0.06
	(0.11)	(0.11)	(0.10)	(0.06)
Current Receipts	0.40	0.29	0.52*	0.21*
	(0.25)	(0.20)	(0.17)	(0.08)
Current Payments	0.31	0.28	−0.57*	−0.37*
	(0.31)	(0.28)	(0.22)	(0.11)
Dependent Variable (1950)			0.93*	1.06*
			(0.16)	(0.08)
Constant	−16.43*	−14.87*	−0.03	2.52
	(0.94)	(0.79)	(2.82)	(1.34)
n	52	52	37	37

Note: Numbers in parenthesis are Huber–White standard errors. All variables are logged. Star denotes a coefficient at least two standard errors removed from zero. Variability of receipts is omitted from this analysis due to availability of data.

institutions to isolate the effect of institutional competition on institutional change. The comparison illustrates how the same set of states operating under the same set of rules produced sharply divergent bargaining outcomes in the IMF and World Bank. The divergence is consistent with my theoretical predictions. The World Bank, which faces widespread competition from other development institutions, bilateral aid agencies, and private sources, has responded more flexibly to underlying shifts in economic power. In contrast, the IMF, which faces relatively limited or circumscribed competition, has resisted change, and share distributions show very little responsiveness to underlying shifts in power.

This chapter focused on formal voting shares to proxy for distributive outcomes in the Bretton Woods institutions. In Chapter 4, I will focus on the experience of Japan in each institution to offer additional qualitative evidence in support for the proposed causal mechanisms. In addition, I will examine more informal measures of influence – influence over lending outcomes and ideology – that extend beyond formal voting shares.

4

Japan in the International Monetary Fund and the World Bank

In Chapter 3, I examined formal voting shares as a proxy for bargaining outcomes in the Bretton Woods institutions. However, voting shares do not necessarily confer influence over outcomes. In many international organizations, states exercise informal influence out of proportion with rankings implied by formal voting shares.[1] In addition, the statistical analysis does not fully address the question of causal mechanisms: whether or not leverage attributable to outside options accounts for divergent outcomes between the International Monetary Fund (IMF) and World Bank.

To address these issues, in this chapter, I will examine Japan's attempts to secure greater representation in the Bretton Woods institutions. Japan's experience is illustrative for several reasons. First, Japan's rapid economic growth in the mid-to-late twentieth century opened up a large gap between its perceived economic status and its position in the Bretton Woods institutions. At the beginning of the 1980s, the magnitude of change needed to close this gap, in formal terms, was comparable across institutions and the widest among member states in absolute terms. It was also clear that Japan's informal influence lagged behind its newfound economic status. Hence, the Japanese case offers the strongest leverage with which to examine the proposed causal mechanisms.

Second, Japanese officials undertook a diplomatic campaign in the early 1980s to obtain greater representation and voice in the Bretton Woods institutions, and officials indicate that each institution was

---

[1] Stone 2011.

accorded equal priority. This makes it unlikely that any difference in outcomes is attributable to indifference or differential effort on the part of Japanese policymakers.

Third, by the early 1980s, Japan had become the second largest economy in the world, making it the most important dissatisfied state. Japan's status and influence over the Bretton Woods institutions was a major foreign policy issue, not only for Japan, but also for other states. In the United States, revisionist narratives of Japan's economic rise had led to considerable consternation and "Japan-bashing."[2] Although the countries remained diplomatic allies, economic relations were tense. In light of Japan's success, policymakers in many developing states had begun to consider Japan's state-led developmental model as a plausible strategy for their own economies. Japan's influence over the Bretton Woods institutions was therefore not just a matter of status or prestige, but also a contest between two major economic powers over alternative visions of how the institutions should manage crucial features of the global economy.

Finally, along with greater voting shares, Japanese policymakers also sought to increase their informal influence over decision-making in the Bretton Woods institutions. A particularly important goal of Japanese policymakers was securing greater recognition for the Japanese or Asian developmental model, which left greater scope for political intervention than the orthodox policy prescriptions of the IMF and World Bank. We can therefore consider Japan's success in light not only in terms of voting shares, but also in terms of informal factors such as influence over lending decisions and ideological recognition.

This chapter will proceed as follows. I will first describe Japan's diplomatic campaign for greater representation in the Bretton Woods institutions. Second, I will present qualitative evidence that Japan has achieved greater success in the World Bank rather than the IMF, and show that this is due in important measure to the credibility of Japan's outside options vis-à-vis the World Bank in comparison with the IMF. Third, I will consider Japan's informal influence over the IMF and World Bank, and show that outcomes are largely consistent with voting shares: Japan has been more successful in securing informal influence over policy outcomes at the Bank than it has at the IMF. I will close by discussing the substantive importance of path dependence in the IMF, focusing on the

[2] For example, Vogel 1979; Johnson 1982; Prestowitz 1988.

experience of Japan and other East Asian states and the imbalances stemming from the massive accumulation of international reserves by countries with limited influence over the institution.

JAPAN'S DIPLOMATIC CAMPAIGN FOR GREATER VOICE

Ever since the Meiji Restoration, the desire for international status and recognition has been an important motivator of Japanese foreign policy. After resounding defeat in World War II delegitimized colonialism and militarism as means to this end, Japanese national energies have focused on economic growth. The attainment of economic superpower status in the 1980s propelled diplomatic efforts to secure a commensurate place for Japan in major international institutions.

In the early 1980s, Japanese policymakers initiated a campaign for greater representation and voice in the Bretton Woods institutions. Japanese representatives made it clear that they felt the existing distribution of shares failed to reflect underlying economic reality.[3] In funding bills that authorized financing for international financial corporations, the Finance Committee of the Japanese Diet conspicuously attached conditions stipulating that the economic position of member countries should be reflected in the organizations' governance structures.[4] In particular, Japan pushed for unambiguous number two status in terms of voting shares – commensurate with the size of its economy – with an unofficial target set at around 8 percent of shares.[5] Simultaneously, Japan sought greater representation of its nationals as employees and greater ideological recognition for the merits of the "Asian Development Model."

Japanese officials pursued an aggressive bargaining strategy, threatening to withhold financial contributions to the institutions and deploy them elsewhere if its objectives were not met.[6] As its economy grew and generated large surpluses, Japan had made contributions to both institutions above and beyond amounts required by its quotas.[7] These included financing for the soft-loan windows of the World Bank

---

[3] For example, Statement by Haruo Mayekawa (Alternative Governor of the Fund and the Bank of Japan), *Summary Proceedings of the IMF-World Bank Annual Meetings*, 1981, 59; Statement by Michio Watanabe (Governor of the Fund and the Bank of Japan), *Summary Proceedings of the IMF-World Bank Annual Meetings*, 1982, 59.

[4] Ogata 1989, 10.   [5] Rapkin, Elston, and Strand 1997, 178.

[6] Personal interview, Ministry of Finance Officials, 2006. Also see discussion in Ibid., 177–78.

[7] Ibid., 178.

and capital-recycling plans and special funds for the IMF, which were considered irregular contributions and therefore did not count toward formal voting shares. Japan threatened to withhold these irregular contributions unless it received an increase in voting shares commensurate with its global standing.[8] Japanese officials emphasized that domestic political conditions made it imperative for Japan's voice in these institutions to be increased in order to maintain public support for expanded contributions.[9] Finance Minister Ryutaro Hashimoto issued a statement in 1989 that Japan would find it difficult to finance the IMF unless given "the proper ranking to reflect our economic power."[10]

Although voting shares were analyzed in great detail in Chapter 3, a simple comparison of Japan's shares in the IMF and World Bank makes it clear that Japan's objectives were met more rapidly and meaningfully in the World Bank. Figure 4.1 shows the ratio of Japan's shares of world gross domestic product (GDP)[11] and subscriptions compared to the United States. The ratio is used to omit exogenous changes in subscription shares caused by the entry of new member states, particularly at the end of the Cold War. After it initiated its diplomatic campaign for greater representation in the early 1980s, Japan's share in the World Bank increased considerably from a level comparable to its IMF share. By the late-1980s, Japan's shares in the Bank had increased to a level where Japanese officials considered their primary objective accomplished. In comparison, IMF shares consistently lagged behind: by 1989–1990, policy statements from Japanese officials clearly reflect dissatisfaction with Japan's position in the IMF but not in the World Bank.[12] As indicated earlier, one of Japan's major foreign policy goals was securing unambiguous number two status in each institution. The timing of Japan's attainment of unambiguous number two status is indicated by the gray dots. This goal was attained in 1985 for the International Bank for Reconstruction and Development (IBRD) but not until 1998 for the IMF, a lag of thirteen years.

A study of IMF quota and voting shares since the institution's inception concludes that "Germany and Japan look to be underrepresented: their

---

[8] Ogata 1989, 11; Rapkin, Elston, and Strand 1997, 178.   [9] Ogata 1989, 10.

[10] Rowen, Hobart, "Japanese Intensify Push for Higher IMF Ranking," *Washington Post*, September 26, 1989.

[11] Nominal GDP is used rather than purchasing power parity (PPP) as this is the input used by the IMF in its quota formulas.

[12] See Statements by Ryutaro Hashimoto, *Summary Proceedings of the Annual Meeting of the IMF and World Bank*, 1989 and 1990.

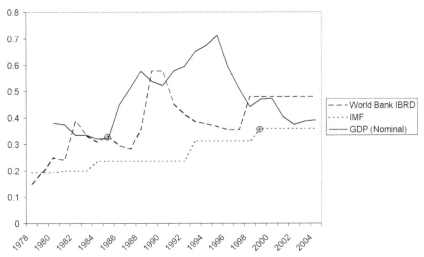

FIGURE 4.1: Relative Voting Shares of Japan and the United States in the World Bank and IMF

Note: Gray dot indicates attainment of unambiguous number two status by Japan. Relative shares are presented to eliminate variation in shares due to membership changes in each institution.

importance in the world economy is not fully reflected in their voting shares."[13] The same holds true for many of Japan's Asian neighbors, who were also absent at the initial negotiations creating the Bretton Woods institutions. For example, prior to the redistribution at the onset of the Asian Crisis, South Korea's share in the IMF stood directly below that of Libya, a pariah state. Relative to the IMF, member states' vote shares of the World Bank have more closely aligned with their positions in the world economy.

JAPANESE INFLUENCE IN THE WORLD BANK AND IMF

Japan's experience also illustrates the sharp difference in policy area features associated with development aid and balance of payments lending. Specifically, in development aid, Japan has formidable outside options, principally its bilateral development lending program, which is one of the world's largest,[14] and the ADB, which is a regional institution

---

[13] Rapkin, Elston, and Strand 1997, 184.

[14] For example, in the early 1990s, Japan's bilateral Official Development Assistance (ODA) disbursement averaged about $11 billion, while total IBRD lending averaged about $16 billion (*World Bank Annual Report* and *Japan ODA Annual Report*, various years).

dominated by Japan.[15] These options gave Japan leverage vis-à-vis the World Bank that was unavailable in the context of the IMF. In securing its objectives, Japan repeatedly threatened to withhold funding from other World Bank programs if its demands were not met. During the 1983–1984 negotiations, during which Japan secured unambiguous number two status in the World Bank, the primary bargaining strategy of Japanese financial authorities was to make International Development Association (IDA) contributions contingent on a boost in IBRD voting shares.[16] This threat to reallocate resources was highly credible in light of the country's own development lending capacity and alternative institutions.

Japan's leverage also brought it a measure of ideological influence in the World Bank. In the early 1990s, Japan pressured the World Bank to move away from its traditional neoclassical approach that emphasized economic liberalization and "shock therapy" for the new post–Soviet Republics. A formal statement of this criticism came in 1991 with the issuance of "Overseas Economic Cooperation Fund (OECF) Occasional Paper No. 1," which emphasized government-oriented growth measures and sharply criticized the World Bank orthodoxy. Around this time, Japan's economic success had led to revisionist accounts touting the merits of the Japanese and Asian models. Japan's criticism of the World Bank followed these lines. The significance of the OECF paper is demonstrated by the fact that it prompted a response, albeit a negative one, from then World Bank chief economist Lawrence Summers.

Japan took the further step of funding the "The East Asian Miracle" study,[17] which examined the rapid growth of Asian economies and conceded that state intervention can facilitate rapid, egalitarian growth under certain conditions. While the Miracle Report provided many caveats, including the probable inapplicability of the Asian model to countries lacking an efficient bureaucracy, convincing the World Bank to accept the partial validity of Japan's developmental principles was seen as a significant triumph.[18] These initiatives also had a subtle impact on subsequent Bank policies, as Wade notes:

---

[15] Yasumoto 1983; Lim and Vreeland 2013.
[16] Ogata 1989; Rapkin, Elston, and Strand 1997; also interviews with various current and former Japanese Ministry of Finance Officials.
[17] World Bank 1993.   [18] Awanohara 1998, 166–77.

the Bank's softening of its stand against directed credit, as of 1995, owes something to the wider Japanese pressure on the Bank. Compared to the 1980s, the Bank is now less likely to insist that directed credit and interest rate subsidies should always be avoided. It is more likely to insist simply that the onus must be on the proposer to explain the special circumstances justifying directed credit in a given case. The shift is small but not trivial, and gives the Bank more flexibility in responding to Japan's continued use of directed credit.[19]

Japanese Ministry of Finance officials in charge of relations with multilateral development lending agencies perceive Japan's contemporary voting shares and influence over World Bank lending policies as reasonably commensurate with Japan's economic standing, particularly in areas such as donor coordination and policies related to infrastructure and industrial development.[20]

In comparison, Japan's leverage vis-à-vis the IMF has been severely limited. This was particularly evident during the Asian Financial Crisis of 1997–1998. The crisis occurred in a region where Japanese financial authorities felt they had considerable expertise and where core Japanese economic interests were at stake. Japanese officials generally argued that the crisis was a short-term liquidity problem that did not require harsh conditionality or structural reform.[21] In line with the World Bank's *Miracle Report*, Japanese policymakers viewed East Asian economies as pursuing fundamentally sound policies that did not require fundamental revision. For example, then Vice Minister for International Affairs Eisuke Sakakibara recounts negotiations with the IMF over Indonesia as follows:

At the time, the main issue at stake was whether to construct a 'large package' dictating large-scale reform of the Indonesian economy and exceeding the $17.2 billion Thai package, or a 'small package' focusing on stabilization of the exchange rate... It is true that Suharto's regime was corrupt, and we also believed that the National Car Project should be eliminated – however, we were opposed to the IMF sticking its nose into these sorts of political or structural problems.[22]

Sakakibara and his deputy, Tatsuro Watanabe, engaged in a two-hour heated argument with the IMF mission chief, at one point threatening that "If you ignore the opinion of the Japanese government to this extent, we will have to consider our options."[23] However, despite this overt intervention and threats of unilateral action by the highest-level Japanese

---

[19] Wade 1996.
[20] Personal Interview, Japanese Ministry of Finance Officials, 2005; 2011.
[21] Sakakibara 2000; Amyx 2002; Lipscy 2003; Lee 2006; Grimes 2008.
[22] Sakakibara 2000, 196.   [23] Ibid., 196.

international financial authorities, IMF policy remained dismissive of Japan's position. As one IMF official noted, "Like the U.S. did it for Mexico, Japan seemed to think that it was fine for Japan to do the same role... At the same time, the IMF figured out that the IMF's attack on the so-called Asian model was a bit too harsh for Japan to endure, given its track record of selling the model to the rest of Asia."[24]

Japanese officials proposed a regional alternative to the IMF during the crisis – an Asian Monetary Fund – but this failed due to divided support within East Asia, particularly Chinese ambivalence, and active US opposition.[25] After the crisis, Japanese financial authorities took an active role in the creation of the Chiang-Mai Initiative (CMI), later upgraded to the Chiang-Mai Initiative Multilateralization (CMIM), a currency-swap network designed to provide balance of payments lending to Asian economies in crisis. Some Japanese officials view its continued development as a mechanism to apply pressure vis-à-vis the IMF to take East Asian interests into account – that is, an outside option.[26]

However, Japan's experience with the CMIM clearly illustrates the dilemmas associated with pursuing balance of payments lending outside of the IMF. Creditor states in the CMI, most prominently China and Japan, are hesitant to provide access to their reserves without any conditions whatsoever.[27] However, if the CMIM were to impose conditionality, it would be difficult for China or Japan to escape blame – in the CMIM, the two countries account for 64 percent of funds and voting shares.[28] The regional framework, because of its limited membership and skewed economic power, does not provide sufficient political cover for China and Japan to provide balance of payments lending in an effective and credible manner independent of IMF conditionality. For this reason, Japanese policymakers have sought to make CMI and CMIM financing contingent on IMF conditionality, and 80–90 percent of its bilateral currency swaps are tied to the presence of an IMF program.[29] Strikingly, despite considerable need from countries such as Korea and Singapore, the CMI disbursed no funds during the global turbulence associated with

---

[24] IMF Official as quoted in Lee 2006, 352.   [25] Lipscy 2003.

[26] Personal Interview, Japanese Ministry of Finance Official, 2006. A similar perspective is offered by Katada 2004 and Grimes 2011.

[27] Sakakibara 2001.

[28] ASEAN, "The Joint Media Statement of The 12th ASEAN+3 Finance Ministers' Meeting," Bali, Indonesia, May 3, 2009.

[29] Amyx 2005, 6; Shamim, Adam, "Asia Reserve Pool Should Reduce IMF Links, Asean's Surin Says," *Bloomberg*, May 3, 2009.

the 2008 US subprime crisis – the prospect of having to initiate an IMF program to access CMI funds was deemed politically unacceptable.[30] Hence, the utility of the CMIM as a credible outside option vis-à-vis the IMF remains marginal despite over a decade of development and participation by some of the largest holders of foreign exchange reserves in the world.

Japan's experience illustrates the significant asymmetry in the attractiveness of outside options vis-à-vis the IMF and World Bank. Despite its deep dissatisfaction with the IMF and formidable economic resources – Japan was the number two economy and number one holder of foreign reserves at the time – Japan has had little choice but to grudgingly rely on the IMF. In development lending, Japan has leveraged its credible outside options to achieve a satisfactory level of representation and influence in the World Bank.

INFORMAL INFLUENCE OVER WORLD BANK LENDING

Did Japan's gains in formal standing in the World Bank, along with a measure of ideological recognition, correspond to an increase in material influence over the lending policies of the institution? It is possible that Japan was "bought off" with higher voting rights and some acknowledgement of the merits of its development model without any substantive influence over Bank policymaking.

To assess Japan's informal influence over the Bank, I replicate and extend a statistical model used by Fleck and Kilby[31] to measure US influence over the institution. The panel dataset covers 110 countries that received lending from the World Bank during the period 1968–2002. The key dependent variable is a country's share of total World Bank lending during a given year. In order to measure US influence, Fleck and Kilby include variables that proxy for US interests and economic exposure. Share of total bilateral US aid is used as measure of revealed preference: the United States would presumably prefer the Bank also support countries that the United States already supports through its foreign aid program. Shares of total US exports and imports and commercial financial flows (inward and outward) are included as proxies for countries in which the United States has a strong economic interest. Fleck and Kilby find that these variables are strongly correlated with World Bank lending

---

[30] Grimes 2011.   [31] Fleck and Kilby 2006.

outcomes, implying that the United States exerts considerable influence over the institution's lending activities, though the nature of US interests appears to vary across presidential administrations.[32]

I obtained the data, successfully replicated the original results, and extended the dataset to include equivalent proxies for Japanese interests over the distribution of World Bank lending. For the purposes of comparison, I also collected equivalent information for three large European donors – France, Germany, and the United Kingdom – and averaged their shares to generate a proxy for European interests in Bank lending outcomes. Unlike the original study, we are not interested in which particular measure of economic activity motivates influence over Bank lending. Hence, I combine the economic indicators into a single measure of economic exposure. The combined measure represents the average share of total Japanese/European/American trade volumes (import + export) and commercial flows (inflows + outflows) to the country in question.

As with the original analysis, I estimate a feasible generalized least squares model with a first-order autoregressive (AR1) error structure.[33] I also retain control variables that are likely to have some impact on determining where Bank lending flows: population, population^2, annualized population growth rate, per capita GDP, per capita GDP^2, annualized per capita GDP growth rate, and region dummies. For consistency, I also include a combined measure of world economic exposure, which represents the average share of world trade volumes and commercial flows.

In order to test how Japan's influence over Bank lending has varied over time, I separate the dataset into two periods based on the year Japan successfully attained unambiguous #2 status in the Bank in terms of voting shares: 1985. This year also conveniently divides the data into seventeen year segments with roughly the same number of observations. Hence, the data is split into two time periods: 1968–1985 and 1985–2002. Alternative splits of the data using any year during the 1980s do not alter the substantive results. If Japan meaningfully increased its influence over policymaking at the World Bank as its economy grew, we should observe a greater association between proxies for Japanese interests over Bank lending and outcomes during the second period. If, on the other hand, Japan was bought off using formal voting rights without a material increase in influence over policy outcomes, this should be reflected in a weak association between the variables across both time periods.

---

[32] Ibid., 230–37.   [33] Additional details are available in Ibid.

The substantive results of interest are presented in Table 4.1. For the sake of presentation, I only include coefficients and standard errors for the key variables of interest. The first two columns show the results from the full model. As the results show, neither Japanese foreign aid allocations nor economic exposure was strongly related to World Bank lending allocations during the period 1968–1985. In contrast, during the period 1985–2002, both Japanese foreign aid allocations and economic exposure are positively associated with World Bank lending, suggesting that Japanese interests were being reflected in Bank policymaking. Consistent with existing research, US economic exposure is positively and meaningfully associated with World Bank lending across time periods, suggesting that US influence in the Bank has been considerable over the years. The results for Europe are more ambiguous, but they are consistent with the premise that European countries have exercised a measure of influence over Bank lending during both time periods. Interestingly, Bank lending appears to have become more responsive to economic exposure for all three of Japan, the United States, and European countries over time.

TABLE 4.1 *Influence over World Bank Lending (Cross-Sectional Time-Series Feasible Generalized Least Squares Allowing for Common AR1 Across Panels)*

Indep/Dep Variables	World Bank Lending (Pre-1985)	World Bank Lending (Post-1985)	World Bank Lending (Pre-1985)	World Bank Lending (Post-1985)
Japanese Foreign Aid	0.006 (0.014)	0.081* (0.011)		
Japan Econ. Exposure	0.016 (0.013)	0.069* (0.012)	0.016 (0.014)	0.074* (0.012)
US Foreign Aid	0.039* (0.018)	−0.035* (0.016)		
US Econ. Exposure	0.016* (0.007)	0.047* (0.010)	0.016* (0.008)	0.041* (0.011)
Europe Foreign Aid	0.023* (0.010)	−0.006 (0.008)		
Europe Econ. Exposure	0.011 (0.007)	0.040* (0.008)	0.010 (0.007)	0.042* (0.009)
n	1267	1234	1267	1234

Note: Numbers in parenthesis are standard errors. Star denotes a coefficient at least two standard errors removed from zero. Variables included in the model but omitted from the table for the sake of presentation: population, population^2, annualized population growth rate, per capita GDP, per capita GDP^2, annualized per capita GDP growth rate, and region dummies.

For both the United States and Europe, the association between bilateral foreign aid allocation and Bank lending has weakened during the more recent time period.

Since bilateral foreign aid programs are highly likely to be influenced by bilateral economic interests, there may be some concern that including both aid and economic exposure in the model could bias the coefficient on exposure: there is a danger that we would be controlling for a variable that is the effect of a key variable of interest. In addition, it is possible that countries allocate bilateral foreign aid strategically, treating bilateral aid and influence over Bank lending as substitutes. Hence, in the third and fourth columns of Table 4.1, I rerun the analysis omitting foreign aid from the models. The results closely mirror those from the first two columns.

This analysis shows that World Bank lending became more responsive to indicators of Japanese interest at roughly the same time Japan secured greater voting rights and ideological recognition within the institution. This is consistent with the subjective assessment of Japanese policymakers regarding their position in the Bank: Ministry of Finance officials indicate that they are satisfied overall with the degree of influence their country exercises within the institution. In particular, Japanese officials note that the Bank accords significant recognition to their development priorities, which in recent years have emphasized investment in infrastructure projects that facilitate rapid industrialization, particularly in East Asia and sub-Saharan Africa.[34] As this section illustrates, Japan's successful renegotiation of the status quo in the Bank was not simply a matter of status: the country has secured a measure of influence over Bank lending that it did not previously exercise.

INFORMAL INFLUENCE OVER IMF LENDING

In this section, I use data on IMF lending to examine Japanese informal influence over outcomes in the institution. As I will show, in contrast to the World Bank, there is very little evidence that Japanese policymakers have been able to influence the substance of IMF policy regardless of the time period in question. As with the Bank, informal influence over policy

---

[34] Personal interview, Ministry of Finance (Japan) Official responsible for handling relations with multilateral development institutions, 2005, Tokyo Japan, and follow up interviews, 2011.

outcomes in the IMF closely mirrors the patterns observed in formal voting rights and qualitative case study evidence.

In order to assess informal influence over the IMF, I replicate and extend data originally used by Barro and Lee,[35] which analyzes IMF lending (Standby Agreements and Extended Loan Facilities) from 1975–2000. The data contains information on 130 countries in five year increments. There are three dependent variables of interest – the size of IMF loans as a share of the receiving country's GDP averaged over each five year period, the fraction of months during each five-year period that a country operated under an IMF loan program,[36] and a dichotomous variable indicating an approval of any new IMF programs during the five year period. Standard economic controls for determinants of IMF lending are included in all statistical models, measured at the beginning of each five year period. These are international reserves as a proportion of imports, per capita GDP, logged absolute GDP, the lagged GDP growth rate,[37] and a dummy variable indicating membership in the Organisation for Economic Co-operation and Development (OECD). As noted by Barro and Lee, other economic variables such as magnitude of current account deficits and inflation are not meaningful predictors of IMF lending once lagged GDP growth and international reserves are included. The squares of per capita and absolute GDP are included to account for the possibility of a nonlinear relationship between those variables and IMF lending. The models also include dummy variables for each five year period.

I also include as controls several variables that have been identified in previous studies as indicators of potential political influence by the recipient of IMF lending. First, a country's quota/voting shares may provide a measure of formal leverage to secure lending. Second, a country may be able to exert informal pressure if its nationals comprise a large percentage of IMF employees. Hence, I control for the share of recipient state nationals among IMF professional staff.

The key independent variables of interest for this study are indicators of creditor state ties with the potential recipient of IMF lending. I include such variables for the United States, Japan, and averages for three major

---

[35] Barro and Lee 2005.

[36] For example, if a country had an IMF program for the entire period, this variable would be 1. If it had a program for 57 out of 60 months, the variable would be 57/60 = 0.95, etc.

[37] That is, for the previous five year period.

European states – France, Germany, and the United Kingdom.[38] I collected data on three sets of economic indicators. First, data on total foreign claims on individual countries by creditor state banks was obtained from the Bank for International Settlements Consolidated Banking Statistics. This proxies for the level of financial sector exposure to the recipient state. Second, I include a measure for intensity of trade between each creditor and potential recipient of IMF lending. This is measured as the value of bilateral trade divided by the countries' GDP.[39] Third, I include a measure of foreign direct investment stocks by country as another indicator of potential non-financial private sector exposure.[40] For all explanatory variables, values from the first year of the five year period are used to avoid endogeneity problems, and values are logged to avoid undue influence of outliers.[41]

Following previous studies, I also include affinity scores based on United Nations General Assembly voting with the United States, Japan, and European states. This variable ranges from one to zero based on the fraction of General Assembly votes for which the relevant creditor state and the potential recipient voted identically during each five year period. High scores can be interpreted as a sign of diplomatic affinity and may therefore proxy for private benefits attainable from supporting a friendly state using IMF resources.

Many existing studies of IMF lending have focused on one or two specific proxies for political influence over the institution, and this has led to somewhat inconsistent results. IMF lending appears to be influenced by a recipient's diplomatic ties to the United States as expressed by proximity of voting profile in the United Nations General Assembly,[42] intensity of trade with the United States,[43] and bank lending from United States financial institutions.[44] However, these studies have generally analyzed these variables piecemeal and have often produced contradictory results.

---

[38] I combine the variables for the European states as they are not the main focus of the study. Including the countries separately does not have any meaningful impact on the substantive results concerning the United States and Japan.

[39] Running the statistical analyses instead with absolute levels of bilateral trade does not alter the substantive conclusions.

[40] This data was obtained from the OECD. As there were a considerable number of missing cells in this data, I used multiple imputation (King et al. 2001) to avoid potential bias.

[41] For the Bank for International Settlements (BIS) bank lending data, years prior to 1983 are unavailable. Hence, I use the value for 1983 for the 1980–1985 periods. Dropping this period from the analysis does not alter the substantive conclusions.

[42] Thacker 1999.   [43] Barro and Lee 2005.

[44] Oatley and Yackee 2004; Broz and Hawes 2006.

For example, while some find that find that General Assembly voting is a useful predictor of IMF lending,[45] others find no evidence of this.[46] Some scholars have found that a high level of exports from the United States is negatively related to IMF lending,[47] while others find the opposite.[48] Variables found to be significant predictors of IMF lending, such as employment of home country nationals among IMF economists, in some studies,[49] are omitted from most others.

Policy officials who deal directly with international financial crises and IMF lending generally note that political decision-making over such issues are based on broad assessments of potential macroeconomic consequences rather than a specific indicator or the interests of a single, narrow group, such as commercial financial institutions.[50] Accordingly, I construct an index variable that proxies for economic exposure by combining bank lending, trade, and foreign direct investment (FDI) between each creditor state and potential IMF borrower. The variable is constructed by normalizing the log of each variable to vary between zero and one based on empirical minimum and maximum values and taking a simple average. Alternative specifications of this variable, such as a simple average, produce similar substantive results. I also ran an alternative specification by using factor analysis to obtain the largest principal component from a principal components model that is a linear combination of the economic variables. Using this variable produces coefficients in the same direction as the reported results but with larger standard errors. Using a more conventional measure, bank lending, by itself, also produces substantively similar results.

Since this data is only available for the period after which Japan initiated its diplomatic campaign for influence in the Bretton Woods Institutions, I focus on the period 1985–2000. As the previous subsection demonstrated, during these years, there is evidence that suggests Japan exerted considerable informal influence over the World Bank's lending profile. In contrast, my expectation is that Japan's influence over IMF lending should be limited.

In Tables 4.2, 4.3, and 4.4, I run several model specifications to account for features of the data that may bias the empirical results. The size of IMF lending and participation in IMF programs are continuous variables. I therefore begin with a simple OLS specification with robust standard errors. I also run a random effects specification to account for

---

[45] Thacker 1999; Oatley and Yackee 2004.   [46] Broz and Hawes 2006.
[47] Thacker 1999; Bird and Rowlands 2001.   [48] Barro and Lee 2005.   [49] Ibid.
[50] Personal conversations with officials at the US Treasury, Japanese Ministry of Finance, and IMF. Also see the accounts in Rubin 2004 and Greenspan 2007.

TABLE 4.2 *Determinants of IMF Loan Size, 1980–2000*

	OLS	Random Effects	Tobit	Tobit RE
US	0.0184*	0.0843*	0.0471*	0.0462*
Economic Ties	(0.0063)	(0.0059)	(0.0114)	(0.0119)
Europe	0.0091	0.0108	0.0322*	0.0353*
Economic Ties	(0.0054)	(0.0071)	(0.0136)	(0.0144)
Japan	−0.0092*	−0.0097	−0.0226*	−0.0228*
Economic Ties	(0.0040)	(0.0058)	(0.0107)	(0.0113)
US	−0.0014	−0.0012	−0.0036	−0.0031
UN Affinity	(0.0017)	(0.0029)	(0.0062)	(0.0063)
Europe	0.0023	0.0021	0.0109	0.0097
UN Affinity	(0.0028)	(0.0049)	(0.0098)	(0.0099)
Japan	0.0009	0.0009	0.0127	0.0128
UN Affinity	(0.0019)	(0.0031)	(0.0077)	(0.0078)
Quota Share	0.0048*	0.0045*	0.0089*	0.0084*
	(0.0020)	(0.0015)	(0.0028)	(0.0030)
IMF Staff	0.0007	0.0005	0.0020	0.0018
Share	(0.0005)	(0.0007)	(0.0011)	(0.0012)
Per Capita	−0.0271*	−0.0269	−0.0612*	−0.0596*
GDP Growth	(0.0123)	(0.0150)	(0.0293)	(0.0296)
Real GDP	−0.0005	−0.0005	0.0008	0.0007
Per Capita	(0.0003)	(0.0004)	(0.0011)	(0.0012)
Real GDP	0.0000	0.0000	−0.0002*	−0.0002*
Per Capita^2	(0.0000)	(0.0000)	(0.0001)	(0.0001)
Log Real GDP	−0.0031	−0.0032	−0.0003	−0.0003
	(0.0028)	(0.0030)	(0.0056)	(0.0060)
Log Real GDP^2	−0.0000	−0.0000	−0.0003	−0.0003
	(0.0001)	(0.0002)	(0.0003)	(0.0003)
Reserves	−0.0003*	−0.0003	−0.0010*	−0.0010*
	(0.0002)	(0.0002)	(0.0004)	(0.0004)
OECD	−0.0037*	−0.0037	−0.0160	−0.0160
	(0.0017)	(0.0033)	(0.0085)	(0.0088)
n	435	435	435	435

Note: Control variables included in the models and not shown in the table: panel dummies. Standard errors in parentheses. Star denotes a coefficient at least two standard errors removed from zero.

the possibility that unexplained factors may lead the IMF to favor specific countries across time periods.[51] As the dependent variables are bounded,

---

[51] I used Hausman tests to confirm the consistency of this modeling choice against fixed effects specifications.

TABLE 4.3 *Determinants of IMF Program Participation, 1985–2000*

	OLS	Random Effects	Tobit	Tobit RE
US	0.531 *	0.498 *	1.072 *	0.944*
Economic Ties	(0.127)	(0.156)	(0.303)	(0.337)
Europe	0.495*	0.552*	1.163*	1.247*
Economic Ties	(0.168)	(0.181)	(0.369)	(0.400)
Japan	−0.404*	−0.377*	−0.652*	−0.595
Economic Ties	(0.135)	(0.159)	(0.286)	(0.335)
n	435	435	435	435

Note: Control variables included in the models and not shown in the table: per capita GDP growth rate, real GDP per capita and its square, log real GDP and its square, international reserves per months of imports, US–UN Affinity, Europe–UN Affinity, Japan–UN Affinity, OECD dummy, and panel dummies. Standard errors in parentheses. Star denotes a coefficient at least two standard errors removed from zero.

TABLE 4.4 *Determinants of IMF Program Approval, 1985–2000*

	Probit	Probit RE
US	2.275 *	2.165 *
Economic Ties	(0.909)	(1.053)
Europe	2.247*	2.550*
Economic Ties	(1.127)	(1.300)
Japan	−1.535	−1.449
Economic Ties	(0.833)	(1.000)
n	435	435

Note: Control variables included in the models and not shown in the table: per capita GDP growth rate, real GDP per capita and its square, log real GDP and its square, international reserves per months of imports, US–UN Affinity, Europe–UN Affinity, Japan–UN Affinity, OECD dummy, and panel dummies. Standard errors in parentheses. Star denotes a coefficient at least two standard errors removed from zero.

I also use Tobit and random effects Tobit specifications[52] to avoid potential bias from censoring.[53] For the dichotomous approval variable, I use

[52] Tobin 1958; Amemiya 1984.

[53] For example, IMF lending is bounded by zero at the lower limit. Hence, the Tobit specification is:

$$L_{it}^* = \alpha + \beta X_{it} + \delta^* time_t + u_{it}, L_{it} = \max[0, L_{it}^*],$$

whereas program participation is bounded between zero and one, hence the specification is:

$$P_{it}^* = \alpha + \beta X_{it} + \delta^* time_t + u_{it}, P_{it} = \min[1, \max(0, P_{it}^*)],$$

where L_{it} and P_{it} are the relevant dependent variables, the vector X_{it} denotes country specific independent variables as shown in the regression tables and footnotes, and u_{it} is a

probit and random effects probit.[54] The substantive results are generally consistent across all specifications.

Tables 4.2, 4.3, and 4.4 suggest that Japanese informal influence over IMF policies was weak even after 1985. While economic ties with the United States and European countries are generally positively and meaningfully associated with both IMF program participation and program approval, economic ties with Japan are either unassociated or negatively associated with both outcomes. The substantive effects are quite large. Holding other variables constant, a country with strong economic ties to the United States – such as Brazil or Mexico in 1995–2000 – is expected to receive an IMF loan about 4 percent of GDP greater than a country with minimal ties to the United States. In comparison, a country with strong economic ties to Japan – for example, Thailand in 1995–2000 – is expected to receive an IMF loan about 2 percent of GDP smaller than a country with minimal ties to Japan. Similarly, controlling for all other factors, a country with strong economic ties to the United States analogous to the previous example is predicted to receive loan approval 53 percent more often and participate in IMF programs on average about 75 percent more of the time than a country with minimal ties, while a country with strong economic ties to Japan is predicted to receive loan approval 26 percent less often[55] and participate about 48 percent less of the time than a country with minimal ties.

SUBSTANTIVE EFFECTS OF IMF PATH DEPENDENCE ON POLICY OUTCOMES

In this section, I will consider how distributive path dependence in the IMF can have broader consequences that go beyond the parochial interests of creditor states vis-à-vis specific crises. Most East Asian countries occupy a position in the IMF analogous to that of Japan: due to rapid economic development over the past several decades, representation in and influence over IMF policymaking has not kept up with these countries' economic

---

random error term. "$time_t$" denotes period dummies to control for common external factors such as world macroeconomic conditions.

[54] That is:

$$A_{it}^* = \alpha + \beta X_{it} + \delta^* time_t + u_{it}, \ A_{it} = 1 \text{ if } A_{it}^* > 0 \text{ and } A_{it} = 0 \text{ if } A_{it}^* \le 0.$$

Variable definitions are analogous to the previous footnote.

[55] This effect is not statistically distinguishable from zero. All other reported substantive results are statistically different from zero with 95 percent confidence.

weight in the international system. This lack of influence contributes to several important political and economic distortions in the world economy.

Formal underrepresentation in the IMF has been a major, lingering diplomatic concern of East Asian states. Quotas have been heavily tilted towards the US and developed Europe, and attempts at reform have generally produced only modest adjustments. Prior to reforms associated with the Fourteenth General Quota Review, which came into force in 2016, ASEAN+3 accounted for about 22 percent of world GDP in nominal terms and 27 percent in terms of PPP, but the region's share of IMF voting rights was only 13 percent, compared to 17 percent for the United States and 30 percent for the European Union (EU). ASEAN+3 also lags in informal measures of influence, such as representation of nationals among staff; ASEAN+3 has only a 7 percent share of IMF economists, compared to 24 percent for the United States and 30 percent for the EU. The IMF managing directorship has gone to a European national by convention, and the location of the institution's headquarters in Washington, D.C. gives US economic policymakers easy and immediate access to the institution. For all of these reasons, government officials in East Asia have held that the IMF does not appropriately reflect their preferences and economic standing in the world economy.

These concerns came to a head during the 1997–1998 Asian Financial Crisis, when many regional policymakers felt that the IMF systematically ignored their views and imposed inappropriate policy measures preferred by the United States and European states. Delays in IMF disbursement prompted nations with ailing economies to question the ability of the Fund to deal with international economic emergencies swiftly and effectively.[56] Washington's reluctance to participate in the Thai rescue package of 1997 – in contrast to the 1994 bailout of Mexico – particularly angered policymakers in Southeast Asia.

Their perceived lack of influence in the IMF is an important factor that has compelled East Asian countries to secure alternative forms of economic insurance for potential future crises. One such avenue has been the creation of regional swap agreements – the Chiang Mai Initiative and Chiang Mai Initiative Multilateralization – but these mechanisms remain largely dysfunctional and have not been utilized. The other main responses have been self-insurance through reserve accumulation and

---

[56] Speech by John Lipsky, First Deputy Managing Director of the International Monetary Fund, at the 2009 Federal Reserve Bank of San Francisco Conference, Santa Barbara, California.

bargaining for greater say in the IMF. Former South Korean President Lee Myung Bak stated that, "The main reason for the sharp increase of currency reserves is that the IMF and the World Bank have failed to set up effective systems for the prevention of a crisis."[57] A Japanese Ministry of Finance official concurred, noting that "Now, each country wants to have its own insurance policy and not rely on the IMF," even though reserves represent a costly and "inefficient" form of insurance.[58] John Lipsky, former first Deputy Managing Director of the IMF, conceded as much, noting that, "If a broader set of countries could rely on trusted counterparties or a multinational agency like the IMF in a crisis, we wouldn't have a world where countries are holding 20 or 30 or 40 percent of their GDP in reserves."[59]

China was not as severely affected by the Asian Crisis, and it enacted exchange rate reform prior to the crisis in 1994, pegging its unified currency to the US dollar. However, the Asian Crisis provided an additional impetus for reserve accumulation after 1997–1998. In light of the crisis, Chinese financial officials viewed IMF intervention in China as inconceivable and pursued reserve accumulation and capital controls to buttress the economy against the possibility of a future crisis.[60] Deputy Governor of the People's Bank of China, Gang Yi, remarked that "Our abundant foreign exchange reserves could protect the banking industry from the impacts of financial crisis."[61] Simultaneously, China started advocating aggressively for greater voice in the IMF, as Prime Minister Wen Jiaobao noted, "We believe it is imperative that we should first undertake reform in international financial institutions, including the IMF. And through reform, we should increase the voting share, the representation, and the say of developing countries."[62]

[57] "IMF and World Bank Should Carry Out Reforms," *Yeonhap News*, September 25, 2009.
[58] "Why is Asia Building a Cache of Dollars?; Asean+3 will Breathe New Life into 'Dead' Asian Monetary Fund Proposal When They Meet on the Sidelines of the ADB's Annual Meeting in May," *The Business Time Singapore*, March 10, 2005.
[59] Speech by John Lipsky, First Deputy Managing Director of the International Monetary Fund, at the 2009 Federal Reserve Bank of San Francisco Conference, Santa Barbara, California.
[60] Personal Interview, Chinese NDRC Official, June 2010.
[61] Gang Yi, Director, State Administration of Foreign Exchange; Deputy Governor, People's Bank of China, Remarks made at the Press Conference for the Third Session of the 11th National People's Congress, March 13, 2010.
[62] Premier Wen Jiabao's Interview with the Financial Times. www.fmprc.gov.cn/eng/zxxx/t535971.htm

It is informative to compare the Asian Crisis to the Mexican Crisis of 1994. At the initial stages, these two crises were comparable in their potential consequences for the world financial system. Aggregate global bank exposure to Mexico and Thailand was about the same, at $50–60 billion.[63] However, the distribution of economic exposure, both financial and non-financial, varied considerably. The United States was heavily exposed to Mexico and other Latin American countries where contagion was most likely – Mexico alone represented about 25 percent of US lending to developing countries on the eve of the crisis. In contrast, Japan was heavily exposed to Thailand and other East Asian states on the eve of the Asian Crisis, with Thailand accounting for about 25 percent of lending to developing countries.

In concert with the US Treasury, the IMF responded quickly to the 1994 Mexican financial crisis. Less than a month into the December 1994 currency crisis in Mexico – during which the Peso was allowed to float following a steep devaluation – the IMF assembled a $30 billion emergency loan package on top of the $20 billion financial support package of loans and credits promised by the United States.[64] This swift response was partially to prevent the crisis from spreading to or unleashing a wave of migrants into the United States, the largest shareholder in the IMF, which also exercises outsized informal influence. The Mexican bailout was also generally perceived as less onerous than those applied to East Asian countries.[65]

Biased application of policy prescriptions by the IMF is an issue of concern not only for developing countries vulnerable to balance of payments crises. There are also potential consequences for macroeconomic performance in closely-integrated developed economies. US banks were heavily exposed on the eve of the 1994 Mexico Crisis. The IMF rescue measures left US financial institutions largely unscathed, in direct contrast to Japanese financial firms, which were the most exposed to East Asia during the 1997–1998 crisis. As Figure 4.2 demonstrates, Japanese financial institutions increased loan loss provisions dramatically in 1997–1998, while no such trend is observed for US institutions during the Mexican Crisis. Japan was suffering through its own financial

---

[63] Data from the Bank for International Settlements.

[64] "Use of the Exchange Stabilization Fund to Provide Loans and Credits to Mexico," from Memorandum to Edward S. Knight, General Counsel, Treasury Department (Accessed from the Department of Justice website; www.justice.gov/olc/esf2.htm)

[65] For example, according to data compiled by Copelovitch 2010, the Mexican package contained 6 total conditions, compared to 9 for Thailand, 10 for South Korea, 17.5 for Indonesia.

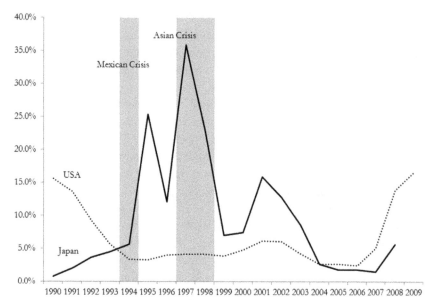

FIGURE 4.2: Financial Institutions: Loan Loss Provisions/Capital
Note: Japanese financial institutions incurred major losses from the 1997–1998 Asian
Financial Crisis. Despite a comparable level of financial exposure, US financial institutions
were not significantly affected by the 1994 Mexican Crisis. Source: OECD

difficulties at the time, so the increase in provisions cannot be attributed
to the crisis alone. However, other indicators make it clear that the crisis
had a serious adverse impact on Japanese financial institutions. Moody's
downgraded all major Japanese financial institutions in 1997–1998,
explicitly citing exposure to the Asian Crisis. There were no downgrades
of US institutions in 1994 citing the Mexican episode. In addition, esti-
mates by the OECD suggest the Asian Crisis shaved 0.8–1.3 percent off of
Japanese GDP growth. The crisis therefore also affected Japanese financial institutions through their domestic loan book. One potential consequence of this policy inconsistency is that the IMF may give US and
European financial institutions an unwarranted advantage by lowering –
and therefore distorting – the risk of loss from their international lending
activities.

The Asian Financial Crisis clearly revealed to East Asian leaders that the
IMF did not adequately reflect Asian interests. As Table 4.5 shows, in
China, South Korea, and ASEAN countries, the volume of reserves (measured as the 10 year average of reserves in imports) surged by 80 percent,
216 percent, and 42 percent, respectively, following the 1997 regional

TABLE 4.5 *Ten Year Average of Reserves (Months of Imports) before and after Asian and Mexican Crises*

	Before Crisis 1987–1996	After Crisis 1998–2007	% Change
China	6.28	11.28	80%
South Korea	2.22	7.02	216%
ASEAN Average	2.97	4.21	42%
Taiwan	14.62	13.78	−5%
	1984–1993	1995–2004	% Change
Mexico	2.65	2.57	−3%

Note: Whereas East Asian states that are IMF members dramatically increased their reserve holdings after the Asian Crisis, Taiwan's reserves remained stable at high levels, and Mexico did not increase its reserves after the 1994 crisis. Taiwan is not an IMF member and is therefore not subject to moral hazard. Mexico's economic and geographic proximity to the United States means generous treatment by the IMF is likely.
Data Source: International Financial Statistics, IMF; Statistical Database of the Central Bank of the Republic of China (Taiwan).

meltdown.[66] In contrast, the Mexican Crisis of 1994 did not lead to a change in Mexico's level of international reserves, which actually fell by 3 percent in the years after its crisis. Despite its crisis and involvement with the IMF, Mexico has not pursued aggressive self-insurance. In addition, Mexico was the first country to express interest in the IMF's Flexible Credit Line (FCL) during the 2008 financial crisis and was provided $47 billion dollars in April 2009, less than a month after its initial application. The attitude of Asian countries toward the Fund again stood in a stark contrast to that of Mexico. While many Asian countries had access to the FCL, a short-term loan lacking the stringent requirements typical of longer-term IMF loans, both the South Korean and Indonesian governments explicitly ruled out any type of IMF aid.[67] When the Wall Street Journal reported that South Korea was one of the countries set to receive the FCL, the South Korean government vehemently rejected any potential association with the IMF, arguing that Korea does not need external support with its economy soundly backed by sizeable foreign reserves.[68]

One common alternative explanation for reserve accumulation in East Asia is that it is a byproduct of export-oriented policies. The underlying

---

[66] IMF, International Financial Statistics.
[67] WSJ 'Korea, Singapore reject IMF funding for emerging countries,' *FNN News*, March 23, 2009.
[68] "MB government, do you intend to receive IMF funding?" *Pressian*, December 15, 2008.

logic is that Asian central banks purchase foreign exchange to keep their currencies weak and thus promote exports. However, East Asian countries have been pursuing export-oriented industrialization for decades, long before the Asian Financial Crisis. This explanation cannot account for the sharp acceleration in reserve accumulation subsequent to the crisis. Another counterpoint to the export-based explanation for Asian reserve accumulation is the behavior of Taiwan. Taiwan is essentially the only major economy that has not been an IMF member since it was replaced by the People's Republic of China in 1980. US government officials of the American Institute in Taiwan, the de facto embassy, confirm that there are no arrangements, formal or informal, for a rescue of Taiwan in the event of a financial crisis. For this reason, Taiwan offers a unique opportunity to examine the counterfactual case of a major economy without any prospect of being subject to IMF moral hazard. Importantly, Taiwan is not distinguished from other East Asian countries in terms of its export-orientation – its export-oriented developmental policies are often compared to other Asian "Tigers" such as South Korea and Singapore.

Taiwan has traditionally adopted an extremely conservative policy of self-insurance. Despite its relatively small size, Taiwan's international reserves are the fourth largest in the world, only exceeded by China, Japan, and Russia.[69] Taiwan has also adopted a cautious stance toward financial liberalization and capital inflows, and it has no sovereign wealth fund, choosing to invest its reserves primarily in US Treasuries and gold. This behavior is driven by the realization that no international organization will come to Taiwan's rescue in the event of a crisis.[70]

Taiwan's policies after the Asian Financial Crisis provide further support for the notion that the IMF's policies were at least partially responsible for a significant portion of reserve accumulation in the region since 1997–1998. While other major East Asian countries sharply increased their foreign reserve holdings after the 1997–1998 crisis, Taiwan's reserves were more stable in comparison – reserves measured in months of imports averaged 14.6 during the ten years before 1998 and 13.8 in the ten years thereafter. Although many observers have described the reserve accumulation of states such as China and Korea to be "excessive," they generally remained below or comparable to levels maintained by Taiwan,

---

[69] "Taiwan's Foreign Reserves 4th Largest in World," *The China Post*, April 6, 2011.

[70] This description of Taiwan's policies and motivations is based on discussions with Taiwanese officials in the Ministry of Economic Affairs and Foreign Affairs, as well as US representatives as the American Institute in Taiwan, the de facto US Embassy.

as shown in Table 4.5. In effect, East Asian states have been converging toward self-insurance at levels consistent with minimizing the prospect IMF involvement.

Statistical Analysis

Do political imbalances in the IMF contribute to broader imbalances in the global economy? To investigate this question further, I revisit the statistical models used in the prior section to investigate Japanese informal influence over IMF lending. However, in this case, I consider two alternative dependent variables: international reserves and the incidence of currency crises. As discussed earlier, Japan, along with major East Asian states, are underrepresented in the IMF, while the United States and major European countries exercise relatively greater formal and informal influence. This means IMF policymaking may be administered in a biased manner cross-nationally. Countries with dense economic ties to the United States and European states are likely to be subject to moral hazard: underpreparing for crises on the assumption that generous rescues from the IMF will be forthcoming. In comparison, countries with strong ties only to Japan may feel compelled to pursue self-insurance out of fear that IMF lending will not be forthcoming or that any involvement will be accompanied by excessively stringent terms.

I first consider reserves. The dependent variable is international reserves, expressed in months of imports. The tobit model includes the control variables used in the earlier analysis: per capita GDP and its square, GDP and its square, the lagged GDP growth rate, the rate of inflation, exports, imports and a dummy variable indicating membership in the OECD. In addition, I control for a dichotomous indicator for currency peg and a measure of currency undervaluation.[71] These are included to account for the possibility that high reserves are a side effect of export-oriented policies. The substantive results are shown in Figure 4.3. Holding all other variables to their mean values, I plot the predicted levels of reserves and 95 percent confidence intervals as a function of the economic exposure of the United States, European Countries, and Japan.[72] As the figure shows, while high European and

---

[71] Sources are: Rodrik 2008; Shambaugh 2004.
[72] Economic exposure is defined the same way it was used for the analysis of IMF lending conducted earlier: an index variable that proxies for economic exposure by combining bank lending, trade, and FDI between each creditor state and potential IMF borrower.

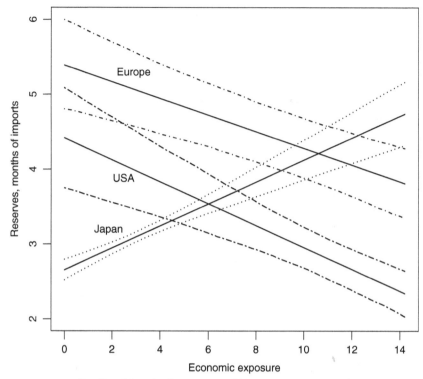

FIGURE 4.3: Predicted Level of Reserve Holdings as a Function of Economic Exposure from Selected Countries

Note: This figure plots the predicted level of reserves simulated from the tobit model described in the text. The vertical axis is the predicted level of reserves, in months of imports. The horizontal axis is the degree of economic exposure (a combined measure of bank exposure, trade, and FDI) from the countries depicted. The figure illustrates that countries that have large economic exposure from the United States and Europe tend to hold much less reserves than countries with low exposure, while the opposite is true for Japanese economic exposure.

American economic exposure is associated with lower reserve holdings, higher economic exposure from Japan is associated with greater reserve holdings. This is consistent with a moral hazard story: the expectation of a generous bailout from the IMF rises along with economic exposure from the United States and European countries, leading countries to underinsure by holding a lower level of reserves. In contrast, higher exposure from Japan is associated with *greater* holdings of reserves. This

The variable is constructed by normalizing the log of each variable to vary between zero and one based on empirical minimum and maximum values and taking a simple average.

is a more conventional response to elevated foreign economic inflows, which could leave countries vulnerable in the event of a sudden reversal. It is clear, however, that high Japanese economic exposure is not associated with any signs of moral hazard among counterpart countries.

Next, I consider the incidence of currency crises. The variable is dichotomous with one indicating any occurrence of a currency crisis during the relevant five year period, and zero otherwise.[73] I use a probit specification as the dependent variable is dichotomous.[74] The control variables are the same ones used in the previous model. The substantive results are depicted in Figure 4.4. Economic exposure from the United States and European countries is associated with an increase in the likelihood of currency crisis, though the association is very weak for European countries. On the other hand, high economic exposure from Japan is associated with a decline in the likelihood of currency crises. Countries in which US and European economic interests are exposed not only tend to under-insure by holding lower levels of reserves, but also experience more frequent crises. There is no corresponding association between Japanese economic exposure and the occurrence of currency crises.

To make sure the results are not completely contingent on the East Asian dynamics described in the preceding subsection, I included region dummies and omitted the 1995–2000 period, which corresponded with the incidence of the Asian Financial Crisis. I also reran the models with random effects to account for unobserved heterogeneity among individual countries. To account for oil producers, who tend to hold a high level of reserves for unrelated reasons, I also included a dummy variable for oil exporters. None of these alternative specifications changed the substantive findings.

DISCUSSION

In this chapter, I focused attention on the experience of Japan in the Bretton Woods institutions. As a country on the losing side of World War II, Japan was not involved in designing these institutions. As the

---

[73] I use the coding for currency crisis incidence from Hutchinson 2001.

[74] That is, $C_{it}^* = \alpha + \beta X_{it} + \delta^* time_t + u_{it}$, $C_{it} = 1$ if $C_{it}^* > 0$ and $C_{it} = 0$ if $C_{it}^* \leq 0$.
where C is a dichotomous variable indicating the occurrence of a currency crisis, the vector X_{it} denotes country specific independent variables as shown in the regression tables and footnotes, and u_{it} is a random error term. "$time_t$" denotes period dummies to control for common external factors such as world macroeconomic conditions.

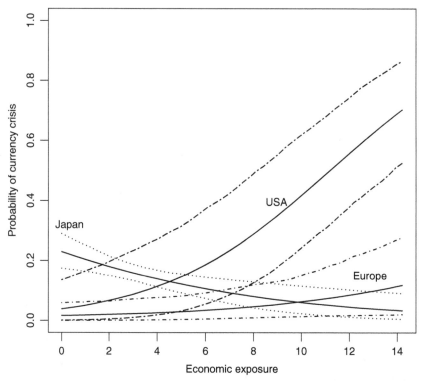

FIGURE 4.4: Predicted Probability of Currency Crisis as a Function of Economic Exposure from Selected Countries

Note: This figure plots the predicted probability of a currency crisis simulated from the probit model described in the text. The vertical axis is the predicted probability of a currency crisis during a five year period. The horizontal axis is the degree of economic exposure (a combined measure of bank exposure, trade, and FDI) from the countries depicted. The figure illustrates that countries that have large economic exposure from the United States (and to a lesser degree Europe) are more likely to experience a currency crisis, while the opposite is true for Japanese economic exposure.

Japanese economy grew rapidly in the late twentieth century, a large gap opened up between the country's initial position in the Bretton Woods institutions and its weight in the world economy. The evidence in this chapter demonstrates that the World Bank adjusted swiftly in order to accommodate Japan's newfound status. The IMF did not.

Japan's experience lends support to the causal mechanisms proposed in Chapter 2. Japanese financial authorities bargained aggressively, threatening to withhold financial contributions from the World Bank and IMF if its objectives were not met. In the policy area of the World Bank, Japan's outside options – its bilateral aid program and the ADB – made its threats of exit credible. In contrast, Japanese policymakers have struggled to create an alternative to the IMF, primarily due to concerns that bilateral or regional alternatives would not provide sufficient cover for the purposes of imposing conditionality. The absence of a credible outside option limited the ability of Japanese policymakers to threaten exit from the IMF.

Japan secured greater influence over the World Bank not only through the acquisition of formal voting rights, but also by gaining greater recognition for its developmental principles. Statistical tests indicate that Japan's informal influence over World Bank lending rose concurrently with formal voting rights and ideological recognition. Within a few years of initiating a political campaign for greater voice, Japanese policymakers were satisfied with their position within the World Bank.

Japanese policymakers have faced far greater headwinds in the IMF. Voting share increases have consistently lagged behind those at the Bank. Japan's lack of influence was underscored during the 1997–1998 Asian Financial Crisis, in which Japanese financial officials were powerless as the IMF ignored their pleas for conditions more attuned to regional realities and Japanese interests. Statistical analysis indicates that Japan exercised little influence over IMF policymaking even as its influence over the Bank increased sharply.

This chapter also illustrates the substantive importance of institutional path dependence. I showed that the rigidity of the IMF has been a major political issue for East Asian states with real economic consequences. I also presented suggestive evidence that institutional rigidity in the IMF may be a contributing factor to one of the most significant economic distortions of contemporary international economic relations: Bretton Woods II, or the combination of international reserve accumulation by East Asian states and US current account deficits. The outsized influence of the United States and European countries in the IMF may be contributing to asymmetrical moral hazard, in which some countries – such as Mexico – follow irresponsible macroeconomic policies on the assumption of favorable treatment from the IMF, while others – such as major East Asian states – pursue aggressive self-insurance to reduce the likelihood of IMF involvement. Biased influence over IMF lending may also put financial institutions outside the United States and Europe at an unfair competitive disadvantage.

5

Policy Area Discipline

Development Institutions and Regional Integration Projects

One important implication of my theory is the concept of *policy area discipline*, an analogue to market discipline in the private sector. Institutions that facilitate cooperation in competitive policy areas face strong pressures to distribute representation and influence appropriately according to the underlying capabilities of members. Institutions can adapt to policy area pressures through direct renegotiation or by reforming internal rules and structures to incorporate greater flexibility. According to my theory, institutions that fail to respond to policy area pressures should be marginalized as members shift to alternative policy vehicles. Consequently, competitive policy areas should be characterized by the "survival of the fittest," where fittest is defined as flexible institutional rules that are capable of rapidly accommodating underlying shifts in power.

The operation of policy area discipline need not be immediate: much as uncompetitive firms often linger on for many years,[1] institutions inappropriately designed for their policy areas may be able to survive for some time. It is not uncommon for states to remain in an institution until a crucial policy disagreement demonstrates the incompatibility of their own interests and an organization's decision-making structures: for example, although League of Nations rules always underrepresented powerful

---

[1] For example, although General Motors was widely seen as uncompetitive in the automotive sector since the 1980s due to high legacy labor costs, the firm did not formally declare bankruptcy until 2009. Similarly, many "zombie" Japanese firms have managed to stay in business for several decades despite de facto insolvency (Caballero, Hoshi, and Kashyap 2008).

states, Japan only left when confronted with an adverse decision over the disposition of Manchuria. To avoid disruption and international censure, states may choose to quietly and gradually reduce participation rather than walking out dramatically. However, even if the process of decline is gradual and informal, we should be able to observe signs of conflict and marginalization. These may include episodes of irreconcilable internal conflict, erosion of membership, and the reduction of resources under the institution's control.

In this chapter, I will examine policy area discipline in development institutions and regional integration projects. As explained in Chapter 3, the provision of development aid is a policy area in which a variety of cooperative forms are possible and actively pursued: multilateral, regional, bilateral, and private. This reflects relatively low network effects and barriers to entry: there is no compelling rationale for universality in development aid, and small donors can focus on small-scale projects. In turn, widespread competition makes it difficult for development institutions to sustain unbalanced representation while remaining relevant: dissatisfied states have plenty of alternative venues through which to distribute or receive aid.

It is useful to clarify how the empirical approach in this chapter differs from that in Chapters 3 and 4. Chapters 3 and 4 isolated the impact of policy areas on redistributive change by comparing the International Monetary Fund (IMF) and World Bank, which operate in different policy areas but according to the same internal rules governing redistribution. This chapter instead holds policy area constant (e.g., development aid), while examining variation in internal rules among institutions.

In Chapters 3 and 4, we saw that formal voting power and influence over outcomes in the World Bank have closely mirrored underlying shifts in gross domestic product (GDP). This was possible in part because, like the IMF, the World Bank is characterized by relatively flexible internal rules: voting power is weighted and can therefore be flexibly adjusted; there are frequent, formal, and predetermined opportunities to initiate renegotiation; and unanimity is not required for approving redistributive change. For sure, even more flexible rules could be implemented, for example by eliminating the supermajority rule for reform or mechanically tying voting shares to underlying economic variables such as GDP. Nonetheless, as I will show, among development institutions, the World Bank's rules for redistribution are relatively flexible and capable of accommodating underlying shifts in relative power.

My theory predicts that, among development aid institutions, those with flexible structures like the World Bank should benefit from policy area discipline at the expense of less flexible institutions. Within competitive policy areas like development aid, my theory predicts that:

1. institutions with flexible internal rules (i.e., challenges are less costly) will see frequent renegotiation in line with underlying capabilities;
2. institutions with rigid internal rules will see exit as underrepresented members become frustrated and seek alternative policy avenues where they can exert greater influence.

Hence, over time, cooperation within a competitive policy area should shift from inflexible to flexible institutions.

The evidence presented in this chapter supports these predictions. Using an original data set of aid disbursements by multilateral development institutions, I show that there has been a dramatic shift of resources in favor of institutions utilizing flexible internal rules over the past four decades. Institutions that operate according to one-country-one-vote principles, which are particularly rigid as they do not allow any weighting of voting power, have oftentimes seen their disbursements decline in real terms despite considerable growth in overall global aid. Meanwhile, disbursements from weighted-voting institutions have increased dramatically. I will also present several qualitative case studies to support the validity of my proposed causal mechanisms. The experience of the International Fund for Agricultural Development (IFAD) is particularly informative: the institution saw widespread disengagement and declining disbursements under rigid internal rules, but participation and disbursements increased sharply after the adoption of a weighted voting scheme.

The last section of this chapter considers policy area discipline in one additional policy area: regional integration projects. Regional integration projects are by definition bounded, and the economics of integration argue against ever greater expansion of membership.[2] Hence, there are limited network effects and no tendency toward universality. Alternative configurations of members are always conceivable, as is rejecting the restraints on sovereignty imposed by an integration project entirely in

---

[2] For example, optimum currency areas are limited by factors such as correlation of economic shocks and labor mobility, which are in turn influenced by geography, economic specialization, common language and culture, etc. (Mundell 1961; Bayoumi and Eichengreen 1994).

favor of unilateralism. However, barriers to entry may intensify as integration deepens. For example, while a free trade area does not foreclose the possibility of pursuing similar agreements with other sets of states, exclusive arrangements such as a common legal system or common currency are much more costly to reverse, reducing the attractiveness of exit.[3] Hence, policy area discipline should also be most observable among regional integration projects during early phases before exclusive arrangements are implemented. I will present evidence that is consistent with this proposition based on the formal rules and track record of all regional integration projects initiated during the post–World War II period.

POLICY AREA DISCIPLINE IN DEVELOPMENT INSTITUTIONS

As discussed in earlier chapters, development institutions are generally characterized by weak network effects and barriers to entry, making outside options highly credible. As I demonstrated in Chapters 3 and 4, competition in the provision of development aid is fierce, and the World Bank has been more responsive to demands for distributive change compared to the IMF. Consistent with rational design principles,[4] the internal rules of development institutions generally reflect this reality: compared to other policy areas, development institutions are more likely to be characterized by weighted voting rules that can be adjusted flexibly in response to underlying shifts in power.[5] However, not all development institutions came into existence with rules that conform to the realities of their policy areas. In this section, I will exploit this fact to examine the effect of policy area discipline on competitive international institutions.

Weighted Voting vs. One-Country-One-Vote Institutions

There are many ways in which institutional voting rules can fail to correctly reflect underlying realities. However, the most straightforward indicator for rigidity is a voting scheme that makes no allowance for

---

[3] For example, Eichengreen 2010 argues that the Euro would be extremely costly to exit, as any credible signs of exit would trigger large scale bank runs as depositors seek to move their funds out of the domestic banking system, and efforts to prevent this would create a large macroeconomic shock.

[4] Koremenos, Lipson, and Snidal 2001.

[5] Blake and Payton 2009. Also research presentation by Erica Gould on decision making rules in intergovernmental organizations (IGOs) at the Summer Research College Workshop, Stanford University, July 29, 2013.

flexibility. The one-country-one-vote rule is one such scheme. By construct, the one-country-one-vote rule does not allow for differentiation
according to underlying factors such as geopolitical or economic power.
The rise and fall of member states cannot be reflected in voting power,
unlike weighted voting systems that have more scope for accommodation.
As established in Chapter 3, the provision of development aid is a policy
area in which competition is widespread and outside options are attractive. Hence, institutions adopting one-country-one-vote rules should tend
to experience exit as large countries dissatisfied with their influence over
institutional policies reallocate their resources elsewhere.

Although a large number of development institutions in existence
today have adopted weighted voting schemes, there are also a good
number that use one-country-one vote principles (Figure 5.1).[6] In the
early years after World War II, one-country-one-vote organizations out-
numbered weighted voting organizations, and only with the proliferation
of regional development organizations in the 1960s and 1970s did this
trend reverse. One-country-one-vote rules are adopted for a range of
reasons. Small membership appears to be associated with such rules
due to the relative ease of achieving consensus: for example, the North
American Development Fund, which is a cooperative venture between the
United States and Mexico, and the Nordic Development Fund, which
includes only five members. However, such organizations are also generally small distributors of aid. More interesting are universalistic aid
organizations that have nonetheless adopted one-country-one-vote rules,
such as the United Nations Development Programme (UNDP) and United
Nations Population Fund (UNFPA). As United Nations (UN) specialized
agencies established relatively early on (1966 and 1969 respectively),
these organizations tended to conform to the broader UN principle that
each member country would receive equal say in organizational decision-
making. These two organizations directly adapted the decision-making
rules of the Economic and Social Council of the UN, which follows one-
country-one-vote. Hence, the design of decision rules in development
organizations do not strictly conform to rational design principles: international norms and available precedents guided early decisions on rule
making. This provides useful variation with which to examine the interaction of institutional rules and policy area competition.

---

[6] Organizations that do not specify a voting rule but operate on consensus or unanimity
principles are classified as one-country-one-vote.

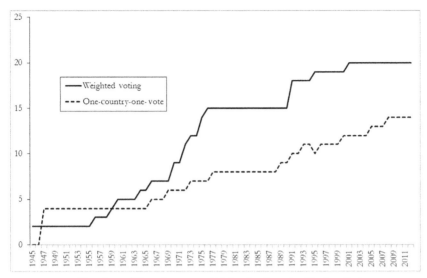

FIGURE 5.1 Number of Development Aid Institutions by Voting Rule
(1945–2012)
Source: Annual reports and websites of development aid organizations. The universe of aid
organizations is adapted from Aid Data 2.0.[7]

Figure 5.2 plots the ratio of total aid disbursed by aid organizations
with weighted voting rules and those with one-country-one-vote rules
since 1969.[8] Data on disbursements was collected directly from the
annual reports of each institution. Disbursements that circumvent

---

[7] Tierney et al. 2011.
[8] The data covers the following organizations: Weighted Voting Organizations: African
Development Bank, African Development Fund, Arab Bank for Economic Development in
Africa, Arab Fund for Economic & Social Development, Asian Development Bank, Asian
Development Fund, Caribbean Development Bank, European Bank for Reconstruction
and Development, European Union (EU) Institutions, Inter-American Development Bank,
International Fund for Agricultural Development (after 1995), Islamic Development Bank,
Organization of the Petroleum Exporting Countries (OPEC) Fund for International
Development, World Bank (International Bank for Reconstruction and Development
[IBRD], International Development Association [IDA], International Finance Corporation
[IFC]). One-Country-One-Vote Organizations: Congo Basin Forest Fund, Global Alliance
for Vaccines & Immunization, Global Fund to Fight Aids Tuberculosis and Malaria, Joint
United Nations Programme on HIV/AIDS, Nordic Development Fund, North American
Development Bank, United Nations Children's Fund, United Nations Democracy Fund,
United Nations Development Programme, United Nations Economic and Social Commis-
sion for Asia and the Pacific, United Nations Economic and Social Commission for
Western Asia, United Nations Economic Commission for Europe, United Nations Popula-
tion Fund (UNFPA).

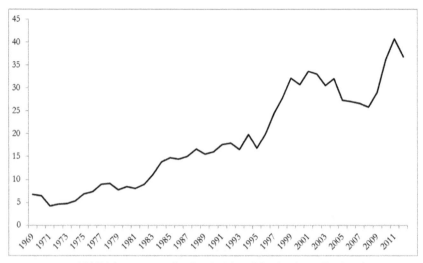

FIGURE 5.2 Aid Disbursements by International Institutions: Ratio of Institutions with Weighted Voting Rules/Those with One-Country-One-Vote Rules
Source: Annual Reports of Various Development Organizations; See footnote 8 for list of organizations covered.

institutional decision-making procedures, such as co-financing arrangements and earmarked funds, are omitted from the analysis and will be discussed later. As the figure shows, in the early 1970s, weighted-voting organizations, such as the World Bank and Asian Development Bank, tended to disburse about five times the amount of funds disbursed by one-country-one-vote organizations such as UNDP and the Nordic Development Fund (NDF). The ratio climbed steadily to about forty times by 2012. In part, this reflects the proliferation of weighted-voting organizations that disburse large quantities of aid, such as regional development banks, as well as absolute increases in the amounts that these organizations disburse.

Since gross disbursement figures may be biased by the composition of aid – for example, the measure makes no distinction between grant aid and development lending – I also calculated a similar ratio using Organisation for Economic Co-operation and Development (OECD) data on Official Development Assistance (ODA) commitments, which attempts to net out the grant element from the various modalities of aid.[9]

---

[9] OECD, "Creditor Reporting System (CRS) Aid Activities Database." www.oecd.org/dac/stats/crsguide.htm

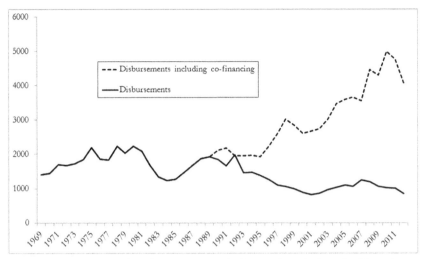

FIGURE 5.3 UNDP Aid Disbursements Including and Excluding Co-Financing (Millions of 2012 US$)
Source: *UNDP Annual Report*, various years.

Although this data is not available for most institutions going back many years, in 2011, aid commitments by weighted voting organizations was about ten times greater at $49.1 billion compared to $4.8 billion for one-country-one-vote organizations. According to this dataset, the International Development Association (IDA) – the World Bank's concessional arm that uses a weighted voting rule – alone distributed about 3.5 times the ODA of all one-country-one-vote organizations combined.

Another important factor boosting the relative share of weighted-voting development institutions is the stagnation of aid disbursement by one-country-one-vote organizations. UNDP is illustrative. Figure 5.3 plots the real disbursement of aid by UNDP since 1969 in millions of 2012 US dollars. As the figure shows, core aid disbursements by UNDP stagnated and then declined in real terms beginning in the early 1990s. UNDP depends almost entirely on contributions by member states to support its activities. However, large donor states, such as the United States and Japan, have numerous other avenues through which to distribute foreign aid – bilateral aid programs, regional development institutions, and other universalistic institutions that give them greater voting power. This has led to "stagnant or declining" commitments to

UNDP's resources.[10] In 1996, the United States unilaterally slashed its funding to UNDP by 55 percent, seriously impacting the institution's operations.[11] Competition with the World Bank has proved particularly challenging, as Klingebiel notes:

Most of [UNDP's] problems are ... due to the UN member states themselves ... The erosion of the funding role is a vivid example, as is the governments' inability in the various political supervisory bodies of the UN system to ensure that effective coordination is possible ... Important manifestations of disintegration are also associated with UNDP's growing competition with the World Bank for [technical cooperation] resources.[12]

In 1970, UNDP distributed about 1.5 times the aid level of IDA, the World Bank's concessional arm. By 2010, the relationship had reversed in dramatic fashion: IDA was distributing 10.5 times the aid level of UNDP.

To compensate for the shortfall in funding, UNDP has increasingly relied on "co-financing" or "non-core" arrangements, in which UNDP employees act as agents responsible for the implementation of projects proposed and designed by donor and recipient governments. In return for administering the projects, UNDP receives a small fee (such as 3 percent of project delivery costs).[13] For example, the central government of Brazil has hired UNDP employees to implement what are essentially national fiscal projects under the rubric of co-financing in order to take advantage of the privileges and immunities the UNDP enjoys from local taxation and regulations.[14] These arrangements have been important in keeping UNDP involved in developing countries, but they are a far cry from traditional aid projects proposed, designed, and implemented by the organization. As Klingebiel notes, "One of the main problems is that UNDP and its Executive Board have very little influence on the use of [non-core] resources."[15] These concerns were aired by the UNDP itself, which in an internal report on the topic points out that:

It is thus feared that UNDP may be used for purely administrative functions (i.e., a simple crown agent or fiduciary role), as a hedge against currency fluctuations, or as a convenient device to bypass national tax legislation or generally applicable limitations on public service staffing and salaries.[16]

---

[10] Galvani and Morse 2004, 312.   [11] Klingebiel 1999, 119.   [12] Ibid., 296.
[13] Galvani and Morse 2004, 314.   [14] Ibid., 316.   [15] Klingebiel 1999, 123.
[16] North et al. 1996, chapter 1.

The increasingly predominant share of co-financing arrangements in UNDP's budget has also transformed the agency's relationship with developing countries:

In order to cope with this new role, UNDP Brazil has upgraded its administrative capacity and taken on a more 'aid business' orientation which recognises that its [developing country] clients can move their funds elsewhere if their demands are not satisfied[17]

In effect, UNDP is increasingly abandoning the field of development aid and evolving into a fee-based consultancy and subcontractor for developing countries.

Similar problems have arisen across UN specialized agencies that utilize one-country-one-vote procedures. Non-core funding has risen from 19 percent of UNICEF disbursements in 1970 to 68 percent in 2012; and from 0 percent of UN Food Program disbursements in 1996 to 55 percent in 2012. This has prompted calls for greater contributions from donor countries to core resources, but the issue of representation has proved a major sticking point. A UN report on the topic concludes that limited steps in the direction of greater representation on behalf of donors, though politically difficult, may be necessary to stem the tide of declining resources:

One key issue is how to handle burden-sharing among different donors. The international financial institutions have traditionally dealt with burden sharing by linking voting rights and representation on their boards with each donor's share of capital ... burden-sharing as addressed in financial institutions would require major adjustments before application to United Nations agencies, funds or programs. Although it is unlikely that the pilot introduction of negotiated replenishments ... would significantly modify burden-sharing among donors and bring about substantial change in the short-term, it may serve to start a discussion process between the United Nations entities and Member States that could lead to significant funding results in the long-term.[18]

In the next subsection, I will examine one UN specialized agency that reformed its decision-making rules in the direction of greater flexibility, and illustrate how this mitigated distributive conflict and reversed what appeared to be an inexorable decline in resources.

---

[17] Galvani and Morse 2004, 317.
[18] Funding for United Nations Development Cooperation: Challenges and Options 2005.

International Fund for Agricultural Development

International Fund for Agricultural Development (IFAD) is a development aid institution that specializes in food security issues. Similar aid is provided by other bilateral and multilateral aid agencies such as the US International Food Assistance Program and the World Bank. Hence, there are plenty of attractive outside options available for member states. However, unlike the World Bank, the internal rules governing the voting structure of IFAD were rigid at inception. Article 6, Section 3 of the governing document of IFAD dictated a static allocation of votes in which each of the OECD, the Organization of the Petroleum Exporting Countries (OPEC), and developing countries maintained one third of the institution's voting power.[19] A change to the voting rules required a four-fifths majority of votes, effectively necessitating consensus among the three voting blocs. Hence, IFAD was an institution characterized by attractive outside options but rigid internal rules governing redistribution. IFAD is a useful case study because these inflexible voting rules were eventually modified in the direction of greater flexibility, allowing us to examine the effect of the rule change on the decisions of countries to maintain participation in the organization.

IFAD is one of the specialized agencies of the UN, established in 1977 during the aftermath of the 1974 World Food Conference. That Conference had been organized to brainstorm an effective response to the food crises of the early 1970s that primarily affected the Sahelian countries of Africa. IFAD was created to "finance agricultural development projects primarily for food production in the developing countries," and to address food insecurity and famine in developing countries.[20] The purpose of IFAD was to provide long-term loans at low interest to poor, developing countries in order to enable farmers to improve their production methods with new plows or seeds or other methods.[21] However,

---

[19] Article 6, Section 3, stipulated that "The total number of votes in the Governing Council shall be 1800, distributed equally among Categories I, II and III. The votes of each Category shall be distributed among its members in accordance with the formula set out for that Category in Schedule II, which forms an integral part of this Agreement." According to Schedule II of the Agreement (prior to amendment), within each category, the 600 votes were divided among individual Members as per the 3 voting blocs mentioned earlier in the paper.

[20] "Who We Are," International Fund for Agricultural Development, www.ifad.org/govern ance/index.htm

[21] Dionne, E.J., U.N. Farm Agency Settles a Dispute, *New York Times*, March 2, 1985.

IFAD was dogged by controversy and major disagreements over the distribution of voting rights among its member states from the mid 1980s to 1995.

IFAD started out in 1977 with a system of equal voting rights coupled with unequal financial contributions for three blocs of countries: OECD, OPEC, and the rest of the world. Each bloc was allocated one-third of the total votes. However, only the OECD and OPEC blocs contributed financing to the organization, with OECD contributing 58 percent and OPEC the remaining 42 percent. The rest of the membership consisted of developing countries that did not contribute funding.[22] The allocation of voting rights within each bloc was left to bloc members, and the OECD and OPEC blocs chose weighted voting, while the developing country bloc chose a one-country-one-vote structure.

IFAD's voting scheme was controversial from the outset. The United States expressed its opposition early on, preferring a "less rigid, more informal coordinating structure" for development aid, and arguing that any incremental agricultural aid for developing countries should be channeled through existing aid institutions and programs.[23] However, the United States relented after OPEC promised to contribute a large share of the funding for IFAD in the spirit of utilizing surplus oil revenues for international development purposes.

An intense, distributive conflict arose in the early 1980s following a decision by the OPEC bloc to unilaterally cut its share of financial contributions to IFAD. OPEC reasoned that its financial capacity had diminished sharply due to the ongoing collapse in oil prices, and several of its members – Iran, Iraq, and Libya – had ceased participation for geopolitical reasons. The United States, supported by other OECD countries, demanded that OPEC members contribute a proportion of financial contributions in line with their voting shares.[24] The United States threatened to withdraw from IFAD if its demands were not met.[25] This threat was highly credible in light of the country's recent

[22] www.ifad.org/gbdocs/repl/7/iii/e/REPL-VII-3-R-6.pdf, IFAD Consultation on the Seventh Replenishment of IFAD's Resources-Third Session: Voting Rights of Member States and Membership of the Executive Board, Report No. REPL.VII//3/R.6, June 15 2005, 1.

[23] Talbot 1980, 263.

[24] John Madeley, "Wrangle over Contributions Threatens UN Farm Aid Fund," *The Globe and Mail*, October 19, 1984.

[25] Victoria Brittain, "Third World Review: US Squeezer/International Fund for Agricultural Development," *The Guardian*, November 2, 1984.

withdrawal from the International Labour Organization (ILO), International Atomic Energy Agency (IAEA) and United Nations Educational, Scientific and Cultural Organization (UNESCO).[26]

In 1985, IFAD President Idris Jazairy of Algeria proposed a compromise, in which the contributions of OECD and OPEC would be adjusted slightly to 60 percent and 40 percent respectively, with no change to voting shares.[27] While other OECD members were willing to accept this compromise, the United States held out, arguing that "the new ratio constituted an unacceptable erosion of the OECD–OPEC partnership on which IFAD was originally established."[28] US diplomats were concerned about accepting even a minor adjustment in contribution shares without a concurrent reform of voting shares. In 1986, the 60–40 compromise was finally accepted, but OECD states sharply curtailed their funding for IFAD, reducing the resources available to the institution to $500 million, a 45 percent decline compared to previous levels.[29] OECD countries continued to demand a greater share of voting rights as a condition for additional contributions to the institution.

During the fourth replenishment negotiations in 1989, IFAD resources were cut back again as controversies over voting shares and contributions continued.[30] During these negotiations, OECD countries proposed an overhaul of the institution's voting structure in light of the sharply diminished capacity of OPEC to contribute to IFAD's finances. Seeing that the main source of contributions to IFAD's operations would be jeopardized if no action was taken, other IFAD member countries eventually conceded to amend Article 6, Section 3 of the original 1977 Agreement establishing IFAD, which governed the institution's voting structure. On February 1994, the Governing Council of IFAD proposed that governance reforms should follow several principles:

(i)   There should be a link between individual contributions and voting rights so as to provide an incentive to all Member Countries to increase their contributions to IFAD's resources;

---

[26] Imber 1989.
[27] Don A. Schanche, "Last-Minute Compromise May Rescue U.N. Farm-Help Agency," *Los Angeles Times*, March 2, 1985.
[28] North-South Monitor 1985.
[29] Dionne, E.J., "U.N. Farm Agency Settles a Dispute," *New York Times*, March 2, 1985.
[30] "Donors to U.N. Farm Body Reach Deal on Cutback," *The Global and Mail*, June 13, 1989.

(ii) The total votes should be divided into two parts: membership votes, which would be distributed equally among Members, irrespective of the level of their contributions; and contribution votes, which would be distributed in accordance with cumulative payment of contributions.[31]

These proposals were adopted by the IFAD Governing Council in January 1995. This led to a sharp increase in the voting share of OECD countries from 33.3 percent to about 50 percent, a level roughly commensurate to the OECD share of world GDP. Financial contributions to the institution increased considerably as a result of the rule change, a point underscored in IFAD's *Annual Report*:

The Fund's formal governance structure of three Categories with fixed membership was eliminated and Member States can now choose to align themselves in informal constituencies of flexible composition. This has important implications for future replenishments of the Fund by eliminating the whole question of "burden-sharing" among Categories of Membership, previously a hindering element in replenishment negotiations.[32]

Prior to 1995, replenishments occurred at a pace of one every six years. Subsequently, the pace accelerated to one every 2.5 years. During the decade of 1985–1995, when the voting controversy was at its peak, there was only one replenishment of IFAD resources, totaling $550 million. This compares to four replenishments totaling about $2 billion during the subsequent decade.

Figure 5.4 compares the disbursement of funds by IFAD and the average of major one-country-one-vote UN Agencies (UNDP, UNICEF, and UNFP), with figures normalized to one in 1995. As with Figure 5.2, co-financing is excluded from the figure to focus on funds directly under the institutions' control. As Figure 5.4 illustrates, IFAD disbursements declined sharply after controversies over voting shares and contributions came to the fore in the early and mid-1980s. However, after voting reform in 1995, IFAD distributions have more than doubled while distributions from institutions that maintained one-country-one-vote rules have stagnated.

In effect, the 1995 rule change shifted IFAD from an institution with rigid rules in a competitive policy area to one with flexible rules. Under

---

[31] www.ifad.org/gbdocs/repl/7/iii/e/REPL-VII-3-R-6.pdf, IFAD Consultation on the Seventh Replenishment of IFAD's Resources-Third Session: Voting Rights of Member States and Membership of the Executive Board, Report No. REPL.VII//3/R.6, June 15, 2005, 3.
[32] *IFAD Annual Report*, 1997, 120.

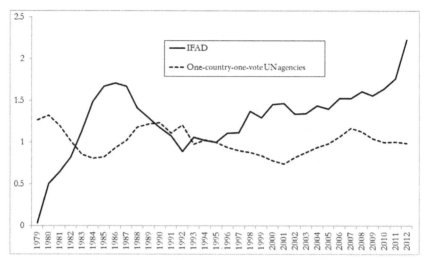

FIGURE 5.4 Disbursements by IFAD and One-Country-One-Vote UN Agencies, Normalized to =1 in 1995 (1979–2012)
Source: Annual Reports for IFAD, UNDP, UNICEF, and UNFP, various years.

the rigid voting rules established in 1977, dissatisfied OECD states chose exit by withholding and redirecting resources away from the institution. After the rule change made representation more malleable, voting shares converged toward levels commensurate with underlying economic capabilities, and cooperation through the institution flourished.

The findings in this section illustrate the operation of *policy area discipline*. As predicted, policy area competition tends to favor institutions that respond flexibly to underlying shifts in capabilities and power. I have demonstrated three mechanisms through which this occurs:

1. the transfer of resources away from rigid institutions in favor of existing, flexible institutions;
2. the creation of new institutions that use flexible rules, such as the proliferation of regional development banks;
3. the reform of rigid institutions into flexible institutions.

Judging from the track record in development aid, the first two mechanisms appear to be more common than the third. Aside from IFAD, it is difficult to identify development institutions that overhauled decision rules in the direction of greater flexibility. Generally, developing countries, which predominate in one-country-one-vote arrangements, have been unwilling to give up power even as their outsized influence undermines the institutions they control. This may reflect other considerations, such as norms favoring equality in the context of the UN, or the use of positions in international institutions as a form of patronage, which can be sustained as long as some income is generated, be it from development or other activities.

REGIONAL INTEGRATION PROJECTS

Regional integration projects, which seek to foster political and economic integration of nation states, have become an increasingly important form of international cooperation in recent years, although early efforts can be traced back to the Kalmar Union of the fourteenth century. Myriad explanations for regional integration projects have been proposed – the entrepreneurial initiative of policymakers, the economic incentives of private actors, and the rational calculation of political leaders – largely inspired by the experience of the European Union (EU).[33] Rather than revisiting these well-established debates, I will focus more narrowly on the question of whether empirical patterns among regional integration projects are also consistent with the operation of policy area discipline.

A priori, there are reasons to expect policy area discipline to affect regional integration projects, at least during early phases of cooperation. By definition, regional integration projects are bounded. There is no impetus for universality or the inclusion of ever more states. Furthermore, because the notion of a region is often contested and could be defined according to many different criteria – such as geography, heritage, religion, culture, or language – numerous unique combinations of countries could plausibly form the basis for a regional integration project. The inclusion of a country in one integration project does not preclude participation in another. Although regional integration may bring significant benefits – for example, the removal of barriers to economic flows, pooling of resources for common defense, and greater diplomatic recognition – there are also important costs, such as the sacrifice of control over tariffs, monetary policy, regulatory policy, and legal administration, as well as the prospect of being forced to make sacrifices on behalf of other

---

[33] See, for example, Haas 1968; Moravcsik 1998; Mattli 1999. For a general overview of scholarship on the European Union, see Pollack 2005.

members. The optimal scope of integration projects is generally limited by economic factors such as the synchronicity of macroeconomic shocks and labor mobility as well as underlying characteristics such as geography, level of development, economic specialization, language, and culture.[34] Hence, regional integration projects should face explicit or implicit competition from a wide range of alternatives. Outside options vis-à-vis regional integration projects should be generally attractive, making it difficult for such arrangements to sustain unbalanced distributive arrangements among members.

These propositions are unlikely to hold under all circumstances. First, unbalanced arrangements are obviously sustainable if integration is involuntary – for example, the forceful reintegration of the South by the United States in 1861–1865 or Chechnya by Russia after 1994. Since the premise of my theory is that states can freely enter or exit from cooperative arrangements, I will focus on *voluntary* integration projects,[35] while acknowledging that the theoretical predictions will have less relevance for coercive episodes of political integration.

Second, integration projects may be able to sustain greater rigidities by incorporating exclusive institutions. An integration project is effectively a bundle of institutions. These are most commonly focused on the elimination of barriers to the free movement of goods, services, capital, and people, for which outside options are generally credible: opening one's borders to one counterpart does not preclude doing so vis-à-vis another counterpart. However, as cooperation deepens, integration projects may also incorporate institutions that are characterized by high barriers to entry by virtue of exclusivity and high costs of reversal. A quintessential example is a currency union. Because it is impractical and tedious for a country to maintain multiple currencies, joining a currency union implies abstention from competing currency arrangements. Furthermore, a common currency is difficult to abandon without triggering financial and macroeconomic instability.[36] Consequently, threatening to exit a regional integration project may become less credible once a currency union is implemented.

In this section, I will therefore focus on non-coercive, early-stage regional integration projects to examine the operation of policy area discipline. Among these integration projects, my theory predicts that

---

[34] For example, Mundell 1961; Bayoumi and Eichengreen 1994.
[35] This is the same class of integration projects examined by Mattli 1999.
[36] Eichengreen 2010.

institutions with flexible distributive rules should achieve greater success than those with rigid rules. I will close with a discussion of the EU and how the establishment of the Euro may have fundamentally altered the bargaining context within the institution.

Competition among Regional Integration Projects

Table 5.1 presents one illustration of competition among regional integration projects. The table lists regional integration projects with at least three members formally reported to the General Agreement on Tariffs and Trade (GATT) or World Trade Organization (WTO), separated by region.[37] The list includes many integration projects with clearly overlapping membership. For example, in the Asia Pacific, both Laos and the Philippines are members of the Association of Southeast Asian Nations (ASEAN), ASEAN Free Trade Area (AFTA), and the Asia Pacific Trade Agreement (APTA); Brunei and Singapore are members of both AFTA and the Trans-Pacific Strategic Economic Partnership (TPSEP); New Zealand is a member of AFTA, TPSEP, the ASEAN–Australia–New Zealand Free Trade Agreement (AANZFTA), and the South Pacific Regional Trade and Economic Cooperation Agreement (SPARTECA). The list probably understates competition, since it does not include institutions and groupings that could plausibly serve as platforms for regional integration but were not formally reported to the GATT/WTO: in East Asia, institutions such as Asia-Pacific Economic Cooperation (APEC), ASEAN +3, ASEAN Regional Forum, and the East Asia Summit.

There are several practical problems that arise when attempting to code the success and failure of integration projects. First, many integration projects are recent developments, meaning their ultimate viability remains an open question. Figure 5.5 plots integration projects over time by date of creation.[38] According to this data, a majority of integration

---

[37] World Trade Organization, Regional Trade Agreements Information System, http://rtais .wto.org/UI/PublicMaintainRTAHome.aspx.; regional coding is my own. In order to code regional integration projects, I include "economic integration projects," "customs unions," and "partial scope agreements:" These three categories each contain at least several institutions that aimed to foster political or economic integration that went beyond the simple removal of trade barriers. I exclude clearly extra-regional agreements, such as the Tripartite Agreement (Egpyt, India, Yugoslavia), and treaties between existing multilateral organizations and bilateral third parties or non-sovereign territories.

[38] Data source is the same: the WTO Regional Trade Agreements Information System. See previous discussion for which agreements are included.

TABLE 5.1 *Regional Integration Projects by Region*

Region	Institution Name
Africa	
	African Common Market
	Common Market for Eastern and Southern Africa (COMESA)
	East African Community (EAC)
	Economic and Monetary Community of Central Africa (CEMAC)
	Economic Community of West African States (ECOWAS)
	Equatorial Customs Union - Cameroon Association
	Southern African Customs Union (SACU)
	Southern African Development Community (SADC)
	West African Economic and Monetary Union (WAEMU)
Americas	
	Andean Community
	Caribbean Community and Common Market (CARICOM)
	Central American Common Market (CACM)
	Central American Free Trade Area (CAFTA)
	Colombia - Northern Triangle (El Salvador, Guatemala, Honduras)
	Dominican Republic - Central America
	Dominican Republic - Central America - United States Free Trade Agreement (CAFTA-DR)
	Latin American Free Trade Area (LAFTA)
	Latin American Integration Association (LAIA)
	North American Free Trade Agreement (NAFTA)
	Southern Common Market (MERCOSUR)
Asia/Pacific	
	ASEAN - Australia - New Zealand (AANZFTA)
	ASEAN Free Trade Area (AFTA)
	Asia Pacific Trade Agreement (APTA)
	Melanesian Spearhead Group (MSG)
	Pacific Island Countries Trade Agreement (PICTA)
	South Pacific Regional Trade and Economic Cooperation Agreement (SPARTECA)
	Trans-Pacific Strategic Economic Partnership (TPSEP)
Europe	
	Central European Free Trade Agreement (CEFTA)
	Common Economic Zone (CEZ)
	European Community (EC) Treaty
	European Economic Area (EEA)

Region	Institution Name
	European Free Trade Association (EFTA)
	Central European Free Trade Agreement (CEFTA)
Former USSR / Central Asia	
	Commonwealth of Independent States (CIS)
	Economic Cooperation Organization (ECO)
	Eurasian Economic Community (EAEC)
	Russian Federation - Belarus - Kazakhstan
	Treaty on a Free Trade Area between members of the Commonwealth of Independent States (CIS)
Middle East / North Africa	
	Gulf Cooperation Council (GCC)
	Pan-Arab Free Trade Area (PAFTA)
	Arab Common Market
South Asia	
	South Asian Free Trade Agreement (SAFTA)
	South Asian Preferential Trade Arrangement (SAPTA)

Note: Coding is based on WTO Regional Trade Agreements Information System. List only includes regionally based economic integration agreements, customs unions, and partial scope agreements with membership exceeding three countries.

projects have track records no longer than two decades. This is likely not enough time to determine the ultimate success or failure of these projects.

Second, compared to development aid institutions, where activity can be simply and plausibly quantified by annual disbursements, regional integration projects are more multifaceted, seeking a diverse range of objectives such as removal of trade barriers, the unfettered movement of people, fiscal union, monetary union, a unified legal system, avoidance of mutual conflict, and common defense against a third party.[39] A large budget does not necessarily imply a successful integration project. Improvements in indirect measures, such as intraregional trade shares, may not necessarily be attributable to the presence of an institution: for example, intraregional trade in North and Southeast Asia has increased dramatically in recent years despite the absence

---

[39] For an early discussion, see Nye 1968.

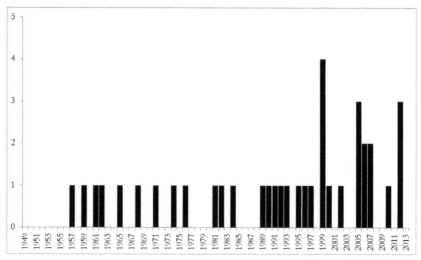

FIGURE 5.5 Number of New Multilateral Economic Integration Agreements and Customs Unions, 1949–2013
Source: World Trade Organization Regional Trade Agreements Information System

of a common institution facilitating integration. Comprehensive efforts to evaluate proxies for integration have generally shown that the EU stands out compared to other integration projects, particularly when political dimensions are considered.[40] This is consistent with conventional wisdom, but these measures are less useful for comparing variation among lesser projects: any ranking would be determined by arbitrary decisions concerning which indicators to include and what weights to assign to them.

Third, there is limited variation in formal voting rules adopted among regional integration projects. Table 5.2 lists multilateral economic integration agreements and customs unions reported to the GATT/WTO along with voting rules, date of entry into force, and current status.[41] I only list organizations established during the twentieth century, as organizations established subsequently have a clearly limited track record. As the table shows, until the Eurasian Economic Community (EAEC) was established in 1999, the European Community (EC, now the EU) was the only regional integration project that adopted a weighted voting scheme for at least some aspect of its formal decision-making

---

[40] Lombaerde 2006; Capannelli, Lee, and Petri 2009.
[41] See previous discussion for agreements that are included.

TABLE 5.2 *Integration Projects by Voting Rule, Date of Entry into Force and Status*

Institution Name	Voting Rule	Established	Inactive as of 2013
European Community Treaty	Weighted	1957	
European Free Trade Association (EFTA)	Equal	1959	
Central American Common Market (CACM)	Equal	1961	
African Common Market	Consensus	1962	X
Arab Common Market	Equal	1965	X
Caribbean Community and Common Market (CARICOM)	Equal	1974	
Asia Pacific Trade Agreement (APTA)	Equal	1976	
South Pacific Regional Trade and Economic Cooperation Agreement (SPARTECA)	Consensus	1981	
Latin American Integration Association (LAIA)	Equal	1982	
Gulf Cooperation Council (GCC)	Equal	1984	X
Andean Community	Equal	1990	
Southern Common Market (MERCOSUR)	Equal	1991	
Economic Cooperation Organization (ECO)	Equal	1992	
North American Free Trade Agreement (NAFTA)	Consensus	1993	
Common Market for Eastern and Southern Africa (COMESA)	Equal	1995	
European Economic Area (EEA)	Consensus	1996	
South Asian Preferential Trade Arrangement (SAPTA)	Consensus	1997	
Eurasian Economic Community (EAEC)	Weighted	1999	
Economic and Monetary Community of Central Africa (CEMAC)	Equal	1999	
Melanesian Spearhead Group (MSG)	Consensus	1999	
West African Economic and Monetary Union (WAEMU)	Equal	1999	

Note: List includes multilateral economic integration agreements, customs unions, and partial scope agreements reported to the GATT/WTO. Extra-regional agreements, such as the Tripartite Agreement between Egypt, India, and Yugoslavia, are excluded. Voting rule is classified as "weighted" if the founding document of the institution includes any kind of provision for weighted voting, "equal" if each country received one vote under formal voting procedures, and "consensus" if decision require unanimity or no voting procedures are explicated.

procedures. Other organizations either stipulated decision-making by consensus or majority vote based on one-country-one-vote principles. Compared to development institutions, there is strikingly limited variation in voting rules across integration projects.

These practical limitations make it difficult to assess the operation of policy area discipline among integration projects. However, Table 5.2 illustrates several empirical patterns consistent with policy area discipline. The only organizations that fell into inactivity were those that adopted inflexible rules early on: that is, organizations with rigid decision-rules for which we have a reasonably long timeframe for observation. The rigid organizations that did survive have not fared well. The Central American Common Market (CACM) was suspended after the 1969 war between two of its members (Honduras and El Salvador) and only reinitiated activity in the early 1990s. The Caribbean Community and Common Market (CARICOM) has survived, but it is widely recognized as a minimalist project that prioritizes autonomy over integration.[42] Similarly, APTA has primarily served as a framework for modest reductions in trade barriers with minimal institution building.[43]

The EU, the only organization to have adopted weighted voting procedures at an early date, is also generally considered sui generis in terms of successful contemporary integration projects.[44] The clearest competition between a weighted voting institution and a one-country-one-vote institution on the list is between the EU and the European Free Trade Association (EFTA). EFTA was established shortly after the EC, the predecessor to the EU, drawing on countries in Western Europe that were plausible members of the EC. EFTA founding members sought to create an institution that would bring the benefits of trade liberalization without the deep, political integration envisaged by the EC.[45] At inception, EFTA had seven members, one more than the EC, and represented slightly more than half the population and economic size of the EC. However, EFTA has gradually declined over time as members left to join the EU, and the institution now only retains four members representing 3 percent of the population and 7 percent of the GDP of the EU.

---

[42] Nicholls et al. 2000; Bravo 2005, 148; "Caribbean Integration: Centrifugal Force," *The Economist*, February 6, 2012.

[43] Mukherji 2005.   [44] For example, see discussions in Caporaso et al. 1997; Mattli 1999

[45] Bjarnason 2010, chapter 2–2.

Of course, the relative failure of EFTA can also be attributed to factors aside from formal rules, such as lack of geographic contiguity and enthusiasm among its members for more ambitious integration. There is clearly insufficient variation in voting rules and outcomes to make strong inferences about policy area discipline among regional integration projects. Nonetheless, the general pattern we observe is consistent with the operation of policy area discipline: the only unambiguously successful regional integration project in the postwar period is also the only one that adopted flexible internal rules at an early date.

In the remainder of this section, I will focus on the EU in order to evaluate the validity of my proposed causal mechanisms. The EU has thus far proved durable, and it is widely regarded as the epitome of a flourishing regional integration effort. As such, my theory predicts that the EU should be characterized by relatively flexible distributive outcomes.

The representativeness of EU institutions is a contested issue among scholars and policymakers, and unlike the paired comparison of the Bretton Woods institutions, there is no "alternative EU" characterized by unattractive outside options against which to draw comparisons. Nonetheless, there is one useful measure through which to evaluate my theoretical predictions: the voting shares of new members compared to existing members on the Council of the European Union. I will show that, unlike path dependent institutions, such as the IMF and UN Security Council, voting shares in the EU Council have traditionally exhibited no bias against new entrants.

I will also present qualitative evidence consistent with the premise that, despite deep integration, outside options vis-à-vis the EU have remained plausible and attractive: states have often succeeded in securing concessions in the EU by threatening various forms of exit, and states that have chosen to abstain have nonetheless managed to secure many of the benefits of formal membership. I will close by discussing the European Monetary Union – an exclusive institution with high potential costs of reversal – which has reduced the attractiveness of exit for members and arguably transformed the bargaining context of the EU in the direction of greater rigidity.

The European Union

The origins of European Union (EU) can be traced to the European Coal and Steel Community, which was established in 1951 among Belgium, France, West Germany, Italy, the Netherlands, and Luxembourg as a mechanism to facilitate economic cooperation between France and Germany to prevent a recurrence of conflict. Cooperation was subsequently deepened with the establishment of the European Economic Community (EEC), a customs union, in 1957, and the Maastricht Treaty in 1993, which among other things created a single currency and formally established the EU. For presentational convenience, I will refer to the EU and its predecessor institutions as the "EU" in subsequent text. The EU is widely considered a model for regional integration, and despite considerable distributive disagreements, the institution has expanded and deepened over time.[46]

Much has been written about distributive conflict in the EU, and there is considerable controversy about whether or not EU institutions properly reflect underlying distributions of power among states. Focusing on the distribution of votes in the Council of Ministers (or the Council of the EU), widely recognized as the most important decision-making authority in the institution, Aksoy and Rodden have argued that small countries have been overrepresented, resulting in a favorable distribution of transfer payments within the union.[47] On the other hand, Stone points out that the formal underrepresentation of large states, particularly Germany, was remedied in the EU's early years thanks to informal control, which allowed large states to block legislation that infringed upon their interests: Germany's de facto veto over currency union is a prime example.[48] According to Stone, it was only when these informal mechanisms eroded that large states demanded a greater share of formal voting power.[49]

Yet another set of scholars argue that the distribution of voting weights in the Council have historically mapped up remarkably well with the square root rule, which has the attractive property of equalizing the *indirect* representation of citizens within countries in the union under certain conditions.[50] Intuitively, since country representatives may be elected into office with the support of a small majority of their citizens, giving representatives voting power proportionate to population size can inflate the voting power of the majority view within large states. Assuming independence of opinion among citizens, the square root rule maximizes the indirect influence of citizens on decision-making in the union, while a more direct rule that makes voting power proportionate

---

[46] For an excellent analysis of bargaining associated with EU expansion, see Schneider 2009.

[47] Rodden 2002; Aksoy and Rodden 2009.   [48] Stone 2011, 104–29.   [49] Ibid., 110.

[50] Felsenthal and Machover 1997, 39; Penrose 1946; Felsenthal and Machover 1998.

to population size is appropriate if there is high correlation of opinion within countries.[51]

Since the substantive question of whether or not the formal and informal structure of the EU properly distributes underlying power is highly contested among experts, I will focus instead on an alternative indicator of distributive rigidity: the relative representation of new members versus current members. As shown in other chapters, path dependent institutions tend to produce distributive outcomes favoring inception or current members at the expense of new entrants. Voting shares in the IMF have tilted consistently toward inception members compared to the Axis Powers of World War II, which were not present during the initial bargaining process. The P5, the only permanent members and veto holders in the UN Security Council, were the major power victors of World War II. As I will show in Chapter 6, during the early years of the International Telecommunications Satellite Organization (Intelsat), when the institution monopolized its policy area, the United States guaranteed itself a 50 percent+ voting share by limiting the total voting power of new entrants to no more than 17 percent. The governance structure of the Internet Corporation for Assigned Names and Numbers (ICANN) drastically overrepresents the influence of the United States, the founder, at the expense of all other countries.

If it is true that: 1. the EU has faced significant competition due to its status as a regional integration project, and hence current and potential members possess attractive outside options; and 2. the EU has thrived and not thus far been split apart by intractable distributive imbalances; we should be able to observe the effect of policy area discipline by comparing the status of new members against current members of the institution. More specifically, institutional competition should restrain the ability of current members of the EU to maintain representational bias against new members.

To test this proposition, I examine voting power in the Council of Ministers, which is generally considered the most important decision-making body in the EU. Following others, I use the Shapley-Shubik score to express voting power in the Council to account for voting weights as well as the specific majority requirements that have been utilized over time.[52] Figures 5.6–5.9 plot the relationship between shares of square root of population and voting power according to the Shapley-Shubik

---

[51] Kirsch 2013.
[52] The use of other voting power indices generally produces similar findings. See Felsenthal and Machover 1997; Rodden 2002; Antonakakis, Badinger, and Reuter 2014.

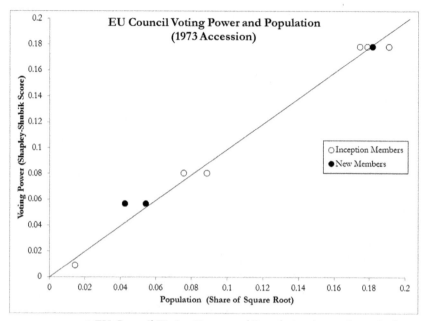

FIGURE 5.6 EU Council Voting Power and Population (1973 Accession)

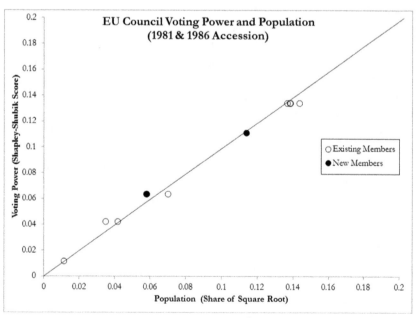

FIGURE 5.7 EU Council Voting Power and Population (1981 & 1986 Accession)

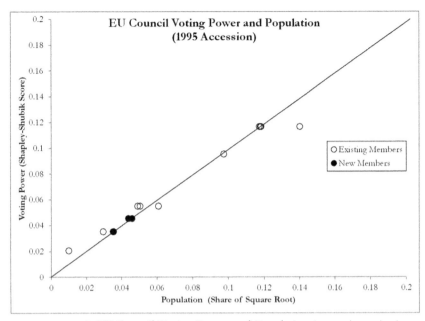

FIGURE 5.8 EU Council Voting Power and Population (1995 Accession)

FIGURE 5.8 EU Council Voting Power and Population (1995 Accession)

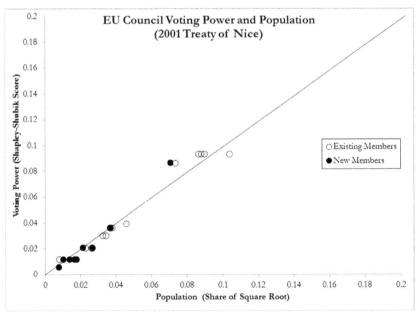

FIGURE 5.9 EU Council Voting Power and Population (2001 Treaty of Nice)
Source: Antonakakis et al. (2014), Eurostat

TABLE 5.3 *Overrepresentation of Prior Members in the Council of Ministers after Accession Episodes*

	1973 Accession	1981 & 1986 Accession	1995 Accession	2001 Treaty of Nice	2007 Treaty of Lisbon
Average Difference, SS Voting Power – √Population	−1.5%	−0.9%	−0.1%	−0.1%	2.7%
Average Difference, Voting Share – Population	1.5%	−5.5%	−6.7%	−9.7%	0%

Note: Positive numbers are indicative of overrepresentation of existing members, while negative numbers indicate overrepresentation of new entrants. Numbers are calculated after new voting rules come into effect. Calculations for the Treaty of Lisbon are as of 2014 when the new voting rules were implemented and include Croatia, which joined the EU in 2013.

Score in the Council of Ministers for EU member states during all accession episodes from 1973 through the 2001 Treaty of Nice. As discussed previously, the distribution of voting power during this period corresponds very closely to the square root principle, as indicated by the clustering of countries around the 45 degree line. More importantly for present purposes, the figures show that there has been no bias against new members in terms of the allocation of voting power on the Council: new members frequently lie above the line.

Table 5.3 depicts bias in voting power in the Council of Ministers according to two measures calculated for existing members of the EU during specific accession episodes. The first measure is the average difference of Shapley-Shubik voting power and the share of square root of population size, as discussed earlier. The second is the average difference of unadjusted voting share and share of total population. Positive values indicate that existing members, on average, were overrepresented compared to new members, while negative values indicate that new members were overrepresented. The table shows that bias in the allocation of voting power between existing and new members has been minimal, and has tended to tilt against existing members according to the more naïve measure of voting share against population size, reflecting the relatively small size of new entrants in the EU.

For both measures, it is clear that distributive outcomes have not been systematically biased against new entrants.

A possible exception to this pattern is the voting rules adopted by the Treaty of Lisbon in 2007 and implemented in 2014. The new voting rules reallocate voting power in the Council by making votes directly proportional to population size for the first time. Rather than renegotiating voting weights periodically, the new rules simply make affirmative votes contingent on the support of 55 percent of member countries representing 65 percent of the Union's population. As a practical matter, this allocation rule favors large countries such as Germany and France.[53] This was a highly contentious issue, as it represented a departure from the Union's previous de facto norm of roughly adhering to the square root principle: Poland in particular pushed hard for the formal adoption of the square root rule.[54] Stone argues that large states were no longer willing to concede formal voting power to smaller states as they lost their informal influence over the operation of the EU.[55] The last column of Table 5.3 also shows that the new voting rules represent a departure from the traditional pattern: new members were somewhat disadvantaged according to the square root rule, though they were treated fairly according to population weighting.

Outside Options and Threats of Exit in the EU

There is considerable qualitative evidence suggesting that exit remained a viable and credible option for much of the existence of the EU and its predecessor institutions. This may have changed in recent years, at least for a subset of member states, with deepening integration and particularly the adoption of a common currency.

Over the years, many institutions have been proposed and implemented alongside the EU that could plausibly serve as the basis for alternative integration projects. Among others, these include the European Defense Community, The North Atlantic Treaty Organization (NATO), the Nordic Council, the OECD, the Organization for Cooperation and Security in Europe, the Union for the Mediterranean, and the Western European Union. Particularly notable is EFTA, which evolved in

[53] Koczy 2012.
[54] James G. Neuger, "Merkel Sees Snags over EU Treaty as Poland Holds Firm," *Bloomberg*, July 18, 2007.
[55] Stone 2011, 104–29.

parallel with the EU, attracting the membership of countries that desired closer economic integration without the supranational political structures of the EU. Although seven countries have left EFTA in favor of the EU, Switzerland, Norway, Iceland, and Liechtenstein have chosen to remain in EFTA despite heightened economic interdependence with the rest of the region. These countries have enjoyed many of the benefits of EU membership through bilateral or multilateral agreements, such as the European Economic Area (EEA) and Schengen Treaty, which abolished immigration and passport controls among signatories. The EU has exerted some pressure to encourage more formalized cooperation: for example, in 2012, the European Council notified Switzerland that future cooperation would need to occur on an institutionalized basis rather than the country's preferred, bilateral mechanisms.[56] However, the Swiss public has repeatedly voted down measures for formal integration, including the EEA, and prospects for joining the EU are not promising.

There have been several efforts to quantify the costs and benefits of EU membership. A report by the Swiss government, published in 2006, concluded that EU membership would involve a net cost about six times higher than the government's status quo bilateral approach, primarily due to the high share of budgetary contributions that Switzerland would be required to chip in as a relatively wealthy member of the Union.[57] Another study, focusing on the United Kingdom, concluded that EU membership entailed significant costs and risks with few clear economic benefits.[58] An analysis focusing on Iceland in 2010 estimated that the government would incur a net cost of about 0.25 percent GDP by joining the EU, but this would be outweighed by macroeconomic benefits stemming from economic and monetary union to the tune of about 6 percent of GDP.[59] However, the purported benefits of integration, particularly monetary union, have been called in question in recent years as the Euro Crisis demonstrated the negative consequences of abandoning independent monetary policy and currency devaluation as adjustment mechanisms.[60] Although quantifying the value of EU membership is by nature an inexact science, these studies suggest that it is not obvious that the

---

[56] Council of the European Union. "Council Conclusions on EU relations with EFTA countries," August 1, 2013.

[57] Swiss Federal Council 2006.　　[58] Minford, Mahambare, and Nowell 2005.

[59] Bjarnason 2010, 245.

[60] For example, Charles Forelle, "In European Crisis, Iceland Emerges as an Island of Recovery," *The Wall Street Journal*, May 21, 2012.

benefits of the EU significantly outweigh the costs, particularly where reasonably comparable alternative arrangements are available.

In essence, although full disengagement from the EU – including loss of access to the common economic market – would surely be costly, this has not been the realistic second-best option for member states and potential members. EFTA countries illustrate that many of the benefits of EU membership can be obtained without formal accession. This has placed significant limits on the degree to which the EU can maintain imbalanced structures of representation among its members.

Aside from countries that have abstained from joining the EU, the relatively modest costs of exit from the institution are illustrated by the decision of Greenland to formally leave in 1985. Greenland had voted against membership in the EEC in 1972, but as a territory of Denmark, it was forced to join in 1973. In 1979, home rule was established for the territory. On a per capita basis, Greenlanders received a large share of EEC subsidies,[61] but they found restrictions on fisheries imposed by the institution unacceptable.[62] In a referendum in 1983, by a 52–48 percent margin, Greenlanders voted to secede from the union. However, EEC members, eager to secure continuing access to fishing in adjacent waters, agreed to continue aid in an amount roughly equal to what would have been provided had Greenland remained a formal member.[63] In effect, Greenland was able to secure an economic outcome comparable to continuing membership in the EU without being bound by the political obligations union membership would have entailed. An EU member that exits from the institution in the future will likely be able to negotiate analogous arrangements: in light of the give and take and mutually beneficial nature of much of the cooperation that takes place under the EU, it is not credible to threaten a departing state with severe punishment.

Historical distributive conflicts within the EU also illustrate how threats of exit have been effective in constraining the institution from adopting policy measures that would run counter to the interests of member states. In 1965, Charles de Gaulle, President of France, boycotted the EEC over the decision to introduce qualified majority voting in the Council, which would have deprived individual countries of veto power, even considering issues that affected core national interests. De Gaulle's boycott paralyzed the EEC and led to a unanimity norm in the Council

---

[61] "Greenland Pulls out of the European Community," *The Evening Independent*, February 2, 1985.
[62] House of Commons Deliberation (United Kingdom) 1984.   [63] Leonard 2006.

during the subsequent fifteen years.[64] The United Kingdom repeatedly secured concessions from the union by threatening to exit or withhold funding. A prime example is Margaret Thatcher's threat to withhold contributions to the Common Agricultural Policy and shut down the EEC budget unless the country received a sizable rebate on account of its small agricultural sector, a concession that was granted by other members.[65]

In recent years, policy area discipline may have weakened vis-à-vis the EU due to the adoption of exclusive institutions. As discussed in the theory chapter, exclusive institutions are those for which simultaneous membership in multiple institutions is impossible or impractical. Exclusivity is a barrier to entry: ceteris paribus, it is more costly to pursue alternative institutions or policy instruments if doing so is impossible without giving up cooperation through an existing institution.

In the context of the EU, there are several potential sources of exclusivity, such as legal integration and harmonization of standards, which may be difficult to pursue simultaneously vis-à-vis multiple, disparate institutions. However, the most potent illustration of exclusivity is the single European currency, the Euro. An agreement for a common currency was included in the Treaty on European Union, more commonly known as the Maastricht Treaty, which came into force in 1993. The European Central Bank was established in 1998, and the Euro was introduced to international financial markets in 1999, with physical circulation following in 2002. As of 2015, 19 out of 28 EU members have adopted the Euro.

The Eurozone is characterized by high exclusivity for several reasons. First, there are practical reasons why countries prefer not to maintain multiple currencies within their national borders, most obviously the transaction costs associated with handling and maintaining multiple currencies for everyday transactions. Second, there are legal barriers to pursuing outside options vis-à-vis the common currency. The Maastricht Treaty legally obligates members of the EU who adopt the Euro to maintain a "single" currency, monetary policy, and exchange rate policy, effectively prohibiting multiple exchange rate agreements.[66] In addition, unlike exit from the EU itself, which is governed by Article 50 of the

---

[64] Dedman 2010, 103.

[65] For example, "Thatcher May Stop U.K. Payments to the Common Market," *Ottawa Citizen*, March 22, 1984; "After the Haggling, a Little Cordiale in the Entente," *The Sydney Morning Herald*, January 7, 1984.

[66] Article 3a, 2.

Lisbon Treaty, the EU treaties do not include any formal provisions for exit from the single currency.[67] Third, exit from a common currency involves highly uncertain and potentially severe economic costs. If the departing state cannot credibly maintain a fixed exchange rate during and after the transition period, exit is likely to trigger bank runs and financial instability, which Eichengreen has described as the "mother of all financial crises."[68]

The exclusivity of the Eurozone – member countries cannot simultaneously adopt a competing policy arrangement or join an alternative institution – acts as a barrier to entry that diminishes the attractiveness of outside options for members. In turn, the adoption of the Euro may have reduced the bargaining leverage countries can obtain from explicit or implicit threats of exit from the EU, weakening the operation of policy area discipline.

There is some evidence that suggests that the EU has indeed faced less policy area discipline in recent years. Bargaining during the Euro Crisis, particularly the harsh treatment of Greece despite threats of "Grexit," suggests that monetary union has eroded the credibility of exit threats as a bargaining strategy.[69] As discussed earlier, formal voting weights in the Council of Ministers historically exhibited remarkably little bias against new entrants through the rules adopted in the 2001 Treaty of Nice, but more recent voting rules established under the Treaty of Lisbon arguably break this trend.

DISCUSSION

International institutions do not exist in a vacuum. Institutions that facilitate cooperation in policy areas subject to intense competition face strong pressures to adopt structures of representation and influence that properly reflect underlying distributions of power. I call this *policy area discipline*. This chapter sought to demonstrate the operation of policy area discipline in two sets of institutions: development institutions and regional integration projects.

Development institutions that employ inflexible representational structures – in this chapter, I focused on one-country-one-vote rules – have faded as resources are reallocated to institutions that adjust more flexibly to underlying shifts in economic power. Inflexible organizations, such as

---

[67] Phoebus 2009.   [68] Eichengreen 2010.
[69] For example, "Bitter Cup," *The Economist*, July 7, 2015.

UNDP, have survived by increasingly shifting into different policy areas, such as acting as middlemen in the implementation of domestic fiscal policy. I also examined an institution that altered institutional rules in response to competitive pressures – IFAD – and showed how this enabled the institution to move from stagnation to growth.

Regional integration projects are similarly characterized by attractive outside options during early phases of cooperation, making effective cooperation difficult without flexible rules that are able to accommodate the conflicting demands of member states. As I demonstrated, the EU was unique among post–World War II regional integration projects for adopting flexible, relatively balanced internal rules early on, and this has contributed to its unparalleled success. An interesting question is how bargaining patterns within the EU will change moving forward as monetary union, along with other forms of exclusive cooperation, increasingly diminish the credibility of exit threats among members. It is possible that the EU will be characterized by greater path dependence moving forward, particularly among members of the Eurozone.

One interesting question about policy area discipline is why survival of the fittest ought to be necessary in the first place. According to proponents of rational design, states craft international institutions with considerable foresight, optimizing various features of institutions to achieve effective cooperation. Among development aid institutions and regional integration projects, the prevalence of one-country-one-vote decision rules is puzzling in this light. Why would countries create institutions with provisions that make them uncompetitive and prone to failure?

As I argued in the theory chapter, rational design may fail for a variety of reasons: for example, uncertainty or misperceptions about the salient features of a policy area, normative pressures to adopt inefficient rules, or intentional inefficient design by a subset of states that prefer an ineffectual institution. Relatively speaking, the logic of rationalist renegotiation is straightforward and less prone to misjudgement: it only requires that states understand the narrow context of redistributive bargaining and act in their own best interests. Aid institutions associated with the UN have often adopted one-country-one-vote rules to conform to the principle of sovereign equality embedded in the UN Charter. The prevalence of this norm appears to be weakening over time as it becomes increasingly clear that rigid rules are incompatible with effective cooperation in a policy area characterized by widespread competition. Among regional integration projects, one-country-one-vote rules have also predominated, with the notable exception of the EU. However, in recent years, this norm appears to be shifting, with diverse organizations such as the Eurasian Economic Community, Economic Community of West African States, and Mercosur experimenting with weighted voting rules, either explicitly or through the creation of elected parliaments. If my theory is correct, flexible distributive arrangements of this sort will mitigate formal or informal exit and contribute to the long-term viability of these institutions.

6

International Telecommunications Satellite Organization

The International Telecommunications Satellite Organization, or Intelsat,[1] established in 1964, was an intergovernmental organization that specialized in satellite telecommunications. Intelsat achieved considerable success, facilitating the creation of the first commercial global satellite communications system. Intelsat was also responsible for the first globally broadcast television program, featuring the Apollo 11 moon landing in 1969, which simultaneously reached 500 million viewers across the globe.[2] However, Intelsat is also an unusual example of a major, essentially universal-membership international organization that ceased to function on an intergovernmental basis. Intelsat was privatized in 2001 and now trades on the New York Stock Exchange with the ticker symbol "I."

The evolution of Intelsat is a useful case study for several reasons. First, like the Bretton Woods Institutions, Intelsat offers variation in policy area characteristics that can be exploited to examine how outside options influence institutional change. In the case of Intelsat, the salient variation is *over time* rather than across institutions. Satellite telecommunications requires the development and maintenance of a global satellite network and associated infrastructure. When Intelsat was created in the 1960s, the technology and capacity for launching communications satellites was largely monopolized by the United States within the Western Bloc.

---

[1] Intelsat and INTELSAT were both used frequently in source documents since the organization's inception, and I will use Intelsat throughout this book for expositional convenience, except when quoting source documents that use INTELSAT. Technically, INTELSAT was the formal designation for the intergovernmental organization that existed until 2001, and Intelsat is the formal designation for the private firm that has existed thereafter.

[2] Taylor 2009.

Consequently, member states of Intelsat had extremely limited outside options vis-à-vis the organization. Over time, technological diffusion eroded barriers to entry in the field of satellite communications, gradually increasing the attractiveness of outside options for member states. By the 1990s, technology evolved to the point where Intelsat faced competition not only from public organizations, but also from communications firms in the private sector. If the theory is correct, this increasing competition and attractiveness of outside options should correspond to an evolution of Intelsat from path dependence to flexible redistribution or exit.

Second, the early diffusion of satellite communications technology offers an opportunity to test the validity of outside options as a causal mechanism. Barriers to entry vis-à-vis Intelsat did not erode at the same rate for all member states. During the renegotiation of Intelsat's founding documents in 1969–1973, several, but not all, countries aside from the United States acquired credible outside options by developing their own communications satellites or launch capabilities. I will show that states with these credible outside options enjoyed asymmetrical gains in the bargaining process, an outcome that is consistent with the theoretical premises.

Third, a large volume of internal communications of the US government regarding Intelsat was declassified in 2010. These documents offer a firsthand look at how US policymakers and negotiators thought about Intelsat and approached the interstate bargaining process. The internal communications offer another validation of the proposed causal mechanisms. US policymakers were deeply concerned about potential competition vis-à-vis Intelsat and carefully evaluated the credibility of outside options as they formulated their bargaining strategies. The countries cited by US negotiators in private communications as potentially capable of exercising exit were also those that gained the most in the voting share redistribution that occurred in 1973.

This chapter will proceed largely chronologically, discussing Intelsat's formation, the major renegotiation that took place in 1969–1973, and privatization. Throughout, I will incorporate internal communications of US negotiators that illustrate how assessments of competition in Intelsat's policy area evolved over time. I will also present data on Intelsat voting shares to illustrate the evolution of the institution from rigidity to flexibility.

THE FORMATION OF INTELSAT

In the early 1960s, US policymakers began to contemplate the creation of a global communications satellite system. Although US policy sought to develop global satellite communications in a manner consistent with commercial interests, political concerns were front and center. President John F. Kennedy made clear that global coverage should be pursued even in cases "where individual portions of the coverage are not profitable."[3] This reflected a consensus among US congressional representatives and administration officials that the proposed satellite system would be a natural monopoly,[4] and therefore rolling out the system rapidly under US influence and control would bring significant advantages. These policy objectives were written into law in the Communications Satellite Act of 1962, which stated that, "The Congress declares that it is the policy of the United States to establish, in conjunction and in cooperation with other countries, as expeditiously as practicable a commercial communications satellite system, as part of an improved global communications network, which will be responsive to public needs and national objectives, which will serve the communication needs of the United States and other countries, and which will contribute to world peace and understanding."[5] The Act created the Communications Satellite Corporation (COMSAT), which was organized as a private corporation in name but designed to operate as an instrument of US foreign policy: COMSAT had a board appointed by the President and its policies were subject to review by the Department of State.[6]

Initial US policy favored the unilateral establishment of a global communications network with COMSAT as the primary operator. Other states would be allowed to "plug into" the US system and receive access. President Kennedy wrote to Congress in 1961 indicating that the role of COMSAT would be the "assurance of global coverage; co-operation with other countries; expeditious development of an operational system; the provision of service to economically less developed countries as well as industrialised countries"[7]

The Stakes in International Satellite Telecommunications

What were the stakes in the policy area of international satellite telecommunications? A US-dominated system was considered an important foreign policy objective by US policymakers for several reasons. First, radio and video communications were seen as crucial mediums for conveying information to and influencing illiterate populations, particularly in

---

[3] *US Department of State Bulletin*, August 4, 1961, 273.   [4] Katkin 2005, 9.
[5] Communications Satellite Act 1962.   [6] Levy 1975, 659.   [7] Wilson 1971, 75.

developing countries. Second, within the context of Cold War competition, establishing a satellite communications network ahead of the Soviet Union would bring "political and prestige advantages" and preempt an expansion of Soviet propaganda output. Third, real time contact with policymakers in foreign countries would avoid frustration arising from delayed communication and misperceptions of US diplomatic neglect. Fourth, effective and rapid communication with underdeveloped countries was seen as crucial as these countries held "the numerical balance of power in international organizations" such as the United Nations.[8]

US plans to move ahead with a global communications system on a largely unilateral basis met with concern from counterparts in developed economies, primarily Western European countries and Japan. These countries were deeply concerned that a US-dominated telecommunications system would undermine their ability to control the flow and content of information within their traditional spheres of influence. Control over Intelsat was contested because, as Levy notes, states desire "... to structure the flows of communication so that they parallel politically desired patterns of international transactions, ideological groups, and influence."[9] Prior to the advent of satellites, telecommunication networks conformed to established colonial and regional relationships, enabling metropole states to monitor, impede, and manipulate information flows to suit their preferences. As US President Johnson emphasized as he made the case for Intelsat, "A telephone call from Rangoon to Djakarta must still go through Tokyo. A call from Dakar, Senegal, to Lagos, Nigeria, is routed through Paris and London. Such an archaic system of international communications is no longer necessary."[10] Hence, the prospect of a US-dominated satellite telecommunications system stoked fears among countries such as the United Kingdom, France, and Japan that they would lose access to valuable information and an important lever of influence over countries considered core to their national interests.

Early Bargaining: US Technological Monopoly and Domination

Informal exchanges concerning COMSAT and satellite communications policy were held with various countries through 1962 and 1963. The first official intergovernmental discussion on global satellite communications

---

[8] Welsh, E.C. (National Aeronautics and Space Council). "Memorandum for Honorable Leonard H. Marks Jr." Declassified Government Communication, January 10, 1966.
[9] Levy 1975, 656.   [10] As quoted in Ibid., 657.

systems took place in October 1962, in Washington, D.C., and involved representatives from the United States, Canada, and United Kingdom. Several other states were consulted on a semi-official basis, including other European states, South American states, and Japan.

Opposition to US plans solidified in 1963, when Western European states formed the European Conference on Satellite Telecommunications (CETS). Although European countries did not yet have the technical capacity to compete with the US system, they attempted to exert leverage by threatening to opt out of global satellite communications altogether. As Wilson notes, "There are two people involved in a telephone conversation; there are two ends to a telephone wire; you don't have to answer when the bell rings."[11] This threat was not entirely credible, as it would deprive European states of access to a new and likely crucial means of international communication. However, the United States was willing to concede some ground in order to expedite the development of the satellite system, which was an important objective for US policymakers concerned about the potential for a competing Soviet system: "[CETS] paradoxically had the effect of accomplishing one US objective: that of moving ahead with dispatch. The CETS resolved most of the differences among European countries before European representatives appeared at the conference table, thereby reducing the number of parties involved in the negotiations."[12]

The United States ultimately accepted a European proposal for an international consortium that included broad international participation. However, as Krasner notes, the bargaining reflected "a distribution of power in which the United States controlled vital technology but other states still regulated access to their national systems."[13] For example, European negotiators attempted to include a clause that would weaken the US monopoly by explicitly allowing for competing systems, but the United States refused and at this point, "the Europeans held no bargaining power."[14] Official negotiations for the international consortium commenced in February 1964, involving the participation of countries accounting for 80 percent of transnational communication traffic at the time: the United States, Western European countries, Australia, and Japan.[15] The United States also invited participation of the USSR and held bilateral talks with Soviet representatives. However, the USSR dropped out of the negotiations when it became clear that its voting share

[11] Wilson 1971, 77.   [12] Ibid., 78.   [13] Krasner 1991, 358.   [14] Hills 2007, 71.
[15] Wilson 1971, 78.

would be miniscule in the proposed organization due to the fact that the USSR only accounted for about 1–2 percent of international communication traffic.[16] Developing countries were largely excluded from initial negotiations.[17]

In June 1964, nineteen signatories signed the Interim Agreement establishing the Interim Communications Satellite Committee (ICSC), the precursor to Intelsat. The governing body consisted of representatives of nationally designated communications entities, such as COMSAT. Voting shares were weighted on the basis of initial forecasts of satellite telecommunications traffic, and the formula heavily favored the United States, which dominated traffic at the time. In addition, voting shares were effectively frozen at these initial levels that tilted the scales in favor of the United States. Although voting shares were adjusted as new members joined the organization, the adjustments were made through a pro-rata reduction of all existing members' shares, thus maintaining status quo voting share distributions.[18] By design, US voting shares could not fall below 50 percent. The dominance of the United States was checked only by a rule that mandated that all votes require passage with 12.5 percent of votes in addition to the votes of the member with the largest share.[19] The United States further entrenched its dominance over the organization by installing COMSAT as the agent responsible for "management in the design, development, construction, establishment, operation, and maintenance of the space segment."[20] In effect, Intelsat was created as an international organization formally and informally dominated by the United States.

Despite US domination, major European states and Japan derived important benefits from Intelsat. These states enjoyed access to US technologies and technical data through contract work on production of hardware for Intelsat satellites and ground infrastructure. Technological transfer was a major early priority of non-US participants, who strongly objected to efforts by COMSAT to conduct research and development (R&D) in house and sought access to joint ventures wherever feasible. As one European aerospace executive pointed out, "This is one of the few vehicles by which we can today participate in this growing and vitally important field. Both the technology and the feeling of being on the ground floor are important to us."[21]

---

[16] Trooboff 1968, 76.   [17] Krasner 1991, 358.   [18] Trooboff 1968, 51.
[19] Krasner 1991, 358.   [20] Levy 1975, 660.   [21] Ibid., 662.

THE SINGLE SYSTEM CONCEPT AND EARLY US
CONCERNS ABOUT COMPETITION

In the next two sections, I will examine internal US communications that
shed light on how policymakers viewed Intelsat as it was established and
evolved during the 1960s and early 1970s.[22] From an early stage, US
policymakers sought to establish Intelsat as the principal provider of
satellite communication services as a means of entrenching US interests
over the system. A 1966 White House memorandum describes the US
government approach as follows:

> *Single System Concept: The concept of a single global system, which
> has been a key element in U.S. Government policy in this field, has
> enormous political appeal. Although the concept cannot be defined
> with precision, at a minimum it would seem to require that INTEL-
> SAT be looked to in the first instance to provide satellite capability in
> response to identified communications needs of all sorts, special uses
> such as educational television, as well as common carrier inter-
> continental communications. If, after thorough analysis, INTELSAT
> is found unable to provide such capability, whether for technical,
> economic or national interest reasons, alternative solutions should
> then be considered.[23]*

US policymakers actively sought to entrench Intelsat by rolling out the
satellite network quickly and tying countries into the system through
investments in ancillary facilities such as ground stations. In effect, the
goal of US policy was to establish Intelsat as a monopoly institution
within the policy area of satellite telecommunications:

*Another potent factor in favor of assisting the establishment of ground stations is
the need to preclude the Soviet Union from establishing a separate system competing with our single system concept, and also, to counter the Soviet Union's
political efforts in the United Nations and elsewhere to disrupt INTELSAT. The
political efforts expended to broaden the consortium from the initial eleven
signatories in August 1964 to the present 48 were not only accomplished for the
basic policy reasons set out in the 1962 Act, but also to preclude the Soviets (or
French or others) from moving into this field. The rapid and successful*

---

[22] Most of the records cited here are available in the Library of Congress, Clay Thomas
Whitehead papers, 1927–2012, MSS85763.

[23] Agency for International Development, "Memorandum for: White House Working
Group on Communications Satellite Ground Stations." Declassified Government Communication, 1-10-1966.

establishment of a space segment and earth stations widely distributed geographically should certainly tend to wed the consortium members to the single system concept – and thwart efforts by others to set up competing systems.[24]

The White House formulated policy based on a detailed assessment of the potential for other actors to undermine Intelsat by offering competitive systems. A 1966 memo from a White House working group on communications satellites is illustrative:

Thus, the full global communications network sponsored by the United States and envisaged by the Communications Satellite Act of 1962 will be in operation according to plan by 1968. Meanwhile, there may be opportunities for other countries to challenge the American leadership in the creation of a single global communication system.

– *The Soviet Union has already orbited two communications satellites and is reported to be exploring the possibility of setting up their own rival system emphasizing communications links with Europe, Asia and Africa.*
– *European countries may also be a source of opposition. There has been a certain reluctance among Europeans to support fully American dominance in international communications. This attitude is based on (a) a desire to protect present European investments in cable and radio facilities whose obsolescence they fear will be hastened by the communications satellite network and (b) on political prestige reasons, tied to resentment of American domination of the space-communications field.*
– *Japan has announced plans to orbit its own communications satellite next year (Comsat cannot verify).The Japanese are known to be discussing construction of earth stations with Latin American governments.*

The memo concludes that:

The most practical way to head off these pressures is to get the global system into full worldwide operation as quickly as possible ....Completion of such a program ... will not only confirm the global character of the system, but also integrate these countries more firmly to a truly single global system, in which the U.S. is the dominant figure.[25]

In effect, the goal was to establish Intelsat as a monopolistic institution and assure US domination of Intelsat. This was viewed as an achievable objective because Intelsat members had limited outside options in satellite

---

[24] Jordan, William J. (Deputy Assistant Secretary for Public Affairs). "Memorandum to The Honorable Leonard H. Marks, Director, U.S. Information Agency." Declassified Government Communication. January 12, 1966.
[25] White House Working Group on Communications Satellite Service for Less-Developed Countries. "Information Supporting Working Group Recommendations." Declassified National Security Action Memorandum, January 17, 1966.

telecommunications. The United States held a large lead in relevant technologies and was the only country among Intelsat members at the time with the infrastructure capable of launching satellites into orbit. Other major Intelsat members could derive some leverage over the United States by threatening to delay or limit the roll out of Intelsat's network, but this threat was not highly credible, as the primary beneficiary of an undermined Intelsat would have been a common adversary: the Soviet Union.

US internal communications also repeatedly describe the demands of other participants, particularly European countries, for technological transfers, for example:

Minister Lefevre (of France) stressed the importance to Europe of total access to detailed technical data to the level of production know-how across the full spectrum of tasks ... including all detailed technical data developed by the US in performing development tasks not undertaken by Europe.[26]

The United States sought to establish Intelsat as a monopoly dominated by the United States by rapidly rolling out the satellite network and locking other countries into the system. The participation of other developed countries was secured at the cost of access to US proprietary technologies, which would eventually allow them to develop their own communications satellite capabilities. However, US policymakers calculated that despite this technological diffusion, the network effects arising from early establishment of the Intelsat system would mean that future satellite launches by other countries would closely tie into a US-dominated system rather than serving to undermine it.

EVOLVING US ASSESSMENTS OF COMPETITION IN INTELSAT'S POLICY AREA

By the late 1960s, US internal assessments of outside options vis-à-vis Intelsat had begun to shift considerably. A 1969 memorandum outlines the development of potential threats to Intelsat as follows:

Certain countries of the world are restive under the alleged domination of the United States [of Intelsat] which comes about by reason of our technical progress and capabilities in space. In addition, there is an incentive to try and retain or re-establish the communication domination which the major colonial countries had over other countries in the colonial era.

---

[26] "Department of State Telegram Summarizing Discussion with Minister Lefevre and Other Representatives of the European Space Conference (ESC)," October 9, 1970.

French activity: There have been press reports of French plans to promote a European-African regional system in order to strengthen her traditional political and economic influence in her former African colonies; There have been reports of possible French interests in placing the management of the International Satellite Consortium under the UN; France alone among the INTELSAT members has indicated the desire to restrict INTELSAT service to international commercial communications, excluding aeronautical and other services which might be provided by satellite.

German activity: There have been reports of German–French discussions toward creating a European Regional Satellite System employing a portion of the German Olympia program.

Japanese activity: Japan, whose technological capability in telecommunications is great and growing, gives some evidence of a latent desire to establish a regional system which would include the Japanese islands, the Far East, and probably South East Asia.

Canadian activity: Canada is studying the desirability of setting up its own domestic satellite system.

Russian activity: USSR has established its own system using non-synchronous satellites. It has the technical capability to do much more and has expressed dissatisfaction with INTELSAT because of the alleged domination by the U.S.[27]

This enhanced competitive activity was seen as a "substantial threat to the future" of Intelsat,[28] but by this time US policymakers had begun to soften their view that a US-dominated Intelsat would be able to maintain monopolistic control over global satellite telecommunications. This reflected a fundamental feature of the policy area of Intelsat, which was not fully recognized in the early 1960s before the system was in place. Once technological diffusion eroded barriers to entry, enabling the development and launch of communications satellites by Intelsat members other than the United States, there was essentially no impediment to the development of competitive communication systems. The underlying technology of satellite telecommunications was not subject to a high degree of network effects as US policymakers had initially predicted. Among states with the technological capability to set up their own systems, outside options had become attractive and highly credible.

---

[27] O'Connell, J.D. (Director of Telecommunications Management Executive Office of the President). "Initiation of the Pilot Program for Domestic Communications Satellite System in the United States." Declassified Government Memorandum, April 4, 1969.

[28] O'Connell, J.D. (Director of Telecommunications Management Executive Office of the President). "Letter to the Honorable Anthony M. Solomon, Assistant Secretary of State for Economic Affairs, Department of State." Declassified Government Communication, August 23, 1968.

US policymakers had initially assumed the global satellite system would be subject to strong network effects, and therefore unattractive outside options, once the system became operational. This was not an unreasonable assumption: the system required considerable initial investments and standard-setting to ensure compatibility among satellites, ground transmitters, and ground receivers. However, although the universal system offered some cost advantages arising from scale economies, switching costs proved to be minimal for several reasons. First, although it was costly to establish the infrastructure necessary to engage in satellite telecommunications, the ground infrastructure was not specific to the global network and could be easily reoriented to accommodate alternative systems. Second, once established, common standards could be utilized in alternative systems and therefore did not serve as an impediment to exit. Third, regional networks could offer meaningful differentiation by offering locally relevant broadcast programming and lower prices. As the Intelsat network became operational, US policymakers increasingly realized that exit from the network would not be as costly as initially predicted:

> ... some [INTLESAT members] might be persuaded by the Soviet Union or others to abandon INTELSAT, because their investment and commitment are not that great. Even if [their investment] were substantial and earth stations were in existence in those countries, there would be no insuperable problem in reorienting the earth station antenna toward a different space segment.[29]

Several internal memos contain direct evidence that the credibility of outside options was consciously evaluated by US policymakers, and concessions calibrated, to address the potential threat of exit. In a 1971 memorandum evaluating whether or not the United States should renegotiate a memorandum of understanding concerning aeronautical satellites with Europe, one of three reasons cited as an argument against reopening negotiations is "Attempts to renegotiate may cause the Europeans to threaten a unilateral program in the Atlantic with no cooperation."[30] Assessments of this threat varied across agencies, with opinions split between the Department of Transportation and Federal Aviation

---

[29] O'Connell, J.D. (Director of Telecommunications Management Executive Office of the President). "Letter to the Honorable Anthony M. Solomon, Assistant Secretary of State for Economic Affairs, Department of State." Declassified Government Communication, August 23, 1968.

[30] Whitehead, Clay T. (White House Office of Telecommunications Policy) "Memorandum for the President: Aeronautical Communication Satellite Service." Declassified White House Communication, December 13, 1971.

Administration on the one hand and the Department of State on the other. A recommendation to accept the agreement without renegotiation argued that:

[Renegotiation] would lead to an independent European/Canadian action in the Atlantic (since they have the technology, the funds, and the assurance of a U.S. launch) which would put the U.S. Government and industry at a clear disadvantage with respect to an operational system and create vested interests effectively precluding a broad based approach to oceanic mobile communications in the future ...[31]

A recommendation to renegotiate the agreement contended that the threat of unilateral action was less credible:

[Renegotiating] will avoid short-term unhappiness on the part of the French, Germans, and British. State contends that any delay or renegotiations would cause Europe to build their own system for the Atlantic; however, ESRO [European Space Research Organization] is a faltering organization, and we doubt they have the resources or resolve to do so.[32]

In 1968, the directors of the Franco-German Symphonie communications program had requested that NASA provide facilities to launch and service its satellites. The United States had made it clear that it would only do so with an understanding that the satellites were "experimental" in nature and in compliance with Intelsat rules, which barred the creation of regional systems. The Symphonie directors understood this to mean that the United States would not launch European communications satellites for operational purposes, and there was very little that they could do given the absence of an independent Franco-German launch capability.[33]

However, US internal documents indicate that threats of exit, particularly by European countries, had come to be taken very seriously by US policymakers by the early 1970s. A 1971 Department of States telegram notes that, in a private meeting:

German officials were surprised and shocked by what they universally described as the 'hard line' taken by the US ... They expressed fear that it will be impossible for Europe to participate in the post–Apollo program and dismay that Europe will

---

[31] Whitehead, Clay T. (White House Office of Telecommunications Policy) "Memordandum for the President: Aeronautical Communication Satellite Service." Declassified White House Communication, December 13, 1971.

[32] Whitehead, Clay T. "Memorandum for Brigadier General Haig, The White House." Declassified White House Communication, November 29, 1971.

[33] Sebesta 1997.

find it necessary to develop an independent launcher capacity which would be wasteful and also a divisive element in US-European cooperation.[34]

German officials argued that the exercise of this outside option would allow European nations to independently launch their own communications satellites regardless of US preferences, and therefore the United States ought to offer them a mutually preferable solution that produced a similar outcome:

Randermann and Von Kyaw made the following points. If Europe is forced to develop the Europa III launcher, Europe will be in a position to launch a European communications satellite with or without US assistance or INTELSAT approval. Consequently the US might as well guarantee launching services [by NASA] now.[35]

This credible outside option convinced US policymakers to offer NASA launching services for European satellites, including satellites involved in the creation of regional systems, that is, those that could pose direct competition to Intelsat's communication network. The point is summarized in a White House memorandum, which concludes that the United States must meet the European demand for free access to launch facilities on the grounds that:

In view ... of the significant investment which the Europeans may have made to participate "substantially" in the development of the system, and particularly if they have set aside the further development of their own launch capability (EUROPA-III) in order to participate substantially, we could not reasonably sustain a specific US override on their use of the system to launch communication systems separate from INTELSAT so long as they meet the requirements of the INTELSAT Agreement at the time ... we should withdraw the US-imposed limitation as to their use of the space transportation system for launching communications satellite systems separate from INTELSAT.[36]

This policy was formalized in 1972 according to a declaration by President Nixon that the United States would provide launch assistance not only to satellites deemed appropriate by Intelsat, but also in cases where the counterpart country "considers in good faith" its Intelsat obligations.

---

[34] "German Reactions to Post–Apollo Meeting," Department of State Telegram, February 1971.

[35] Ibid.

[36] "Second Discussion with Representatives of the Euorpean Space Confernce Concerning Euroepan Participation in the post–Apollo Program." White House Internal Memo, February 8, 1971, 30.

This was designed to signal flexibility of the United States vis-à-vis launch requests, even in cases where they could not secure support from Intelsat.[37]

In sum, outside options functioned just as predicted by the theory. Although US policymakers clearly preferred not to facilitate satellite systems that posed direct competition to Intelsat, they were forced to offer NASA facilities to launch competing European satellites because not doing so would have resulted in European exit and an essentially identical outcome, only with an independent European launch infrastructure. The credible outside option (independent launch capability) resulted in a dramatic narrowing of the ability of the United States to sustain an institutional arrangement that heavily favored its own interests at the expense of other participants.

RENEGOTIATION OF INTELSAT

By 1969, the interim agreements that had governed Intelsat's satellite network came under increasing strain. The interim agreements, despite their international character, had given COMSAT de facto control over Intelsat's operations: Intelsat was housed within COMSAT's headquarters, and because COMSAT was a US domestic company, the organization fell under the regulatory scrutiny of the Federal Communications Commission (FCC). FCC directives at times overturned internationally negotiated terms in the interim agreements, causing considerable consternation among Intelsat members.[38] The Foreign Office of Britain complained that "The general feeling in Europe particularly ... is that the American COMSAT Corporation ... is abusing its dominant position and denying the cooperative international character of ICSS."[39] COMSAT lobbied aggressively to have the interim agreements extended or incorporated with minimal change into a new international agreement. However, US negotiators quickly realized that this would be an unattainable outcome.

By the late 1960s, through transfers and development of indigenous technologies, several Intelsat members were beginning to acquire the ability to place their own satellites into orbit. These states were no longer willing to accept US dominance of the international satellite telecommunications network. In addition, Intelsat membership had grown rapidly,

---

[37] Sebesta 1997, 153.   [38] Hills 2007, 72.   [39] Ibid., 72.

raising questions about the adequacy of existing governance structures.[40] Hence, negotiations for definitive arrangements took place, culminating in a formal agreement that entered into force in February 1973.

These negotiations took place under circumstances that fundamentally differed from the early 1960s, when the initial agreement was hammered out.[41] The United States no longer possessed a clear monopoly over the technologies pertaining to satellite launches, and several members, primarily major European countries and Japan, had obtained – or were on the verge of obtaining – credible outside options. The renegotiated agreement clearly reflected this shift.

Several countries demanded that the administrative role of COMSAT be downgraded. This resulted in a compromise, in which a Director General would take on management functions that had previously been fulfilled by COMSAT after a five-year transition period. The organization was split into a Board of Governors, Meeting of Signatories, and Assembly of Parties. The Assembly, although relatively limited in its authority, was designed to consider issues of relevance in telecommunications from the perspective of sovereign states, and it operated on one-country-one-vote principles, which represented a departure from the US vision of an organization represented by telecommunication entities.

A particularly crucial concession by US policymakers was in the area of regional systems that would potentially pose direct competition to Intelsat. Major developed countries aside from the United States were concerned that Intelsat would occupy a "central and monopolistic position in satellite communications,"[42] precisely the role that was envisioned by US policymakers for the organization. They therefore sought to relax the restrictions Intelsat placed on the development of regional systems. Developing countries generally supported the US position, fearing that fragmentation of the telecommunications system would leave them uncovered or dependent on former colonial masters.

In 1968, European countries used the threat of creating their own separate system to force the US acceptance of a proposal that "groups of countries in a closely integrated land mass like Europe should have corresponding rights which a single large country like the U.S.A might have to provide a satellite for domestic traffic."[43] The United States viewed this as a limited concession that would still bar the threat of regional systems that would proceed independently of Intelsat, but it

---

[40] Levy 1975, 667.   [41] Nixon 1970.   [42] Levy 1975, 671.   [43] Hills 2007, 73.

was becoming increasingly clear that US leverage was eroding. The United States sought to persuade Intelsat members to commit "that they shall not establish or join in the establishment of, or use, any space segment to meet international public telecommunications service requirements,"[44] with breaches punishable with expulsion from the organization. This draft was resisted fiercely by developed country delegates, particularly the French, and it was ultimately replaced by a far less stringent requirement that "the establishment or use of such [regional] facilities shall not prejudice the establishment of the direct communications link through the INTELSAT space segment among all the participants."[45] Although the Board of Governors could make nonbinding recommendations regarding proposed regional systems, regional systems could not be vetoed without a resolution in the Assembly of Parties, which operated on a one-country-one-vote basis and therefore minimized US influence. As a practical matter, Intelsat was not given any means to enforce sanctions even if a regional system was deemed inappropriate.[46]

The renegotiated Intelsat, which formally commenced operations in 1973, thus reflected a much greater compromise between the original US vision and the interests of other, particularly developed, countries. The concept of a unified global telecommunications network dominated by the United States was not to be: exit from the network proved far less costly than US policymakers had initially envisioned, and this gave countries credible outside options as the terms of the organization were renegotiated. The United States sought to discourage competition artificially by including strong rules that would bar the creation of regional systems, but this was resisted successfully by countries that by at this point possessed the capability to create such competing arrangements.

INTELSAT VOTING SHARES

Voting shares in Intelsat initially reflected the objective of US policymakers to create a monopoly organization in which their country would be the dominant actor. Voting shares nominally derived from investment shares, which in turn were based on projected shares of telecommunications traffic. However, the de facto allocation was based on a formula that assured the United States a "perpetual veto."[47] More specifically, voting shares were primarily allocated according to international traffic,

---

[44] Levy 1975, 6/1.   [45] Ibid., 671.   [46] Katkin 2005, 9.   [47] Hills 2007, 71.

but domestic traffic over two thousand kilometers was also taken into account. This was specifically designed to inflate the US share by including the territories of Guam and Puerto Rico in the calculations. In addition, new signatories to Intelsat were restricted to a 17 percent total share, assuring that the US position would not fall below 50.5 percent, a guaranteed veto.[48] Finally, adjustments to voting shares resulting from new entrants were to be accommodated by proportionately reducing the shares of existing members, which froze into place initial allocations that heavily advantaged the United States over other initial members.

During the negotiations for the definitive arrangements, COMSAT pushed hard to retain the interim agreements, which guaranteed its status as administrator and a US veto over the institution's decisions.[49] However, US policymakers had by this point abandoned the earlier objective of creating a monopolistic organization dominated by US interests:

It appears to us that the concern about the voting power, although expressed in general terms, is directed primarily at what appears to be the disproportionate share of voting power the U.S. would have under a use formula which ties investment and voting together. We recognize that there is merit in these concerns, whatever theoretical justification there may be for a direct relationship between use, investment and voting. It follows, then, that an international organization now composed of 68 members, and hopefully encompassing all nations of the world in the future, should not be controlled by any single country.[50]

The multilateral negotiations over the determination of the future voting shares of Intelsat generated a wide range of proposals. Among the most significant issues debated were: 1. whether voting shares should be based on international or domestic telecommunications traffic. The inclusion of domestic traffic would tend to inflate the voting shares of large countries, particularly those with distant territories separated by the sea: archipelago states such as Japan and the United Kingdom, as well as countries in possession of overseas colonies and territories; 2. whether additional criteria should be incorporated, such as investment in base stations. These additional factors, should they be incorporated, would generally shift voting shares in the direction of developing countries, which were relatively less intensive users of the telecommunications network; 3. whether there should be an absolute cap on the voting shares of any single country. The cap was widely understood to apply only to the United States, which

[48] Ibid., 71.   [49] Ibid., 74.
[50] O'Malley, J.J. "Significant Issues in the INTELSAT Conference," 1969. Declassified White House Memorandum.

went into the negotiations with a voting share in excess of 50 percent; and 4. whether or not differentiated pricing could be used by Intelsat's operators. COMSAT saw price discrimination as a potential tool to forestall competition from regional systems: in areas where regional systems were threatened, prices could be cut preemptively. However, price differentiation also had implications for voting rights. Since traffic would be measured by total utilization charges during the prior six month period,[51] price reductions, if not fully offset by increased utilization, would reduce the voting rights of targeted countries. This mechanism would give COMSAT considerable leverage to not only undercut regional systems on price, but also to reduce the political clout of recalcitrant countries.

The bargaining dynamics reflected asymmetrical outside options available to Intelsat members at the time of the negotiations. Developed economies, particularly major European states and Japan, had acquired considerable technical knowhow through participation in the interim arrangements and could credibly threaten to leave the global network should the outcome not reflect their interests. Other countries had comparatively limited outside options. Developed economies lacking independent satellite technology and launch capabilities could not credibly threaten exit. Developing countries were among the strongest supporters of Intelsat's global architecture. This reflected fears that competing systems would raise their costs of communication: competing systems would deprive Intelsat's satellites of traffic over which to spread out fixed costs, and duplicate antennas would need to be constructed to communicate with multiple systems.[52] Developing economies not strongly aligned with the West attempted to exert some leverage over the negotiations by threatening to defect to the Soviet Intersputnik system, which, although still nascent and possessing far less capacity than Intelsat, would be established as a competing international organization in November 1971.[53]

The negotiation outcome ultimately reflected this asymmetrical alignment of outside options. Intelsat's new voting rules were based on international as well as domestic traffic, which inflated the shares of the major developed countries with credible outside options. Simultaneously, a hard

[51] Agreement Relating to the International Telecommunications Satellite Organization, 1973, Article 6.
[52] U.S. Delegation to the INTELSAT Conference. 1969. "Memorandum for Governor Stanton: Emerging Patterns on the Basic Issues before the Conference." 26.
[53] Hills 2007, 73.

cap of 40 percent was placed on voting shares, diminishing US influence in the organization and assuring that the United States would not enjoy the benefits of counting domestic traffic in the calculations. Uniform pricing was instituted, removing the possibility that Intelsat could undercut regional systems on price or through reduction in voting power. Calculation methods that would increase the weight of developing countries, such as counting investments in base stations, were rejected.

Figure 6.1 provides a more intuitive presentation of the negotiated outcome over voting shares. The figure plots, for Intelsat inception members, cumulative communication satellites placed into orbit during the period 1964–1978[54] against voting share changes during the same period.[55] 1964 is the year Intelsat was established, and 1978 is the first year Intelsat published an *Annual Report*, which presents comprehensive voting share distributions under the definitive arrangements. It should be noted that the figure includes communications satellites placed into orbit for several years after the definite arrangements were negotiated. As a practical matter, the United Kingdom was the only non-US Intelsat member to place a satellite into orbit prior to the conclusion of the definitive arrangements. However, the planning and construction of satellites takes time, and it is clear from the negotiation records that policymakers took into account not only current satellites in orbit but also technological capabilities and the prospect of launches in the near future. The number of launches through 1978 should therefore serve as a reasonable, if crude, proxy for credible outside options during the bargaining process. Launches undertaken as part of a consortium are included as fractional based on the number of countries participating. The figure illustrates how countries that had developed the technological skills to manufacture communications satellites during this time period tended to benefit the most from Intelsat's new voting scheme.

Similarly, countries that demonstrated an independent launch capability before or during the negotiations concerning the definitive arrangements[56] benefited the most under the new voting scheme. Besides possessing the capacity to develop communications satellites, these countries could sidestep NASA and put their satellites in orbit unilaterally.

[54] The data is from McDowell 2013.
[55] Voting share data was obtained from the *Intelsat Annual Report* for 1978, and US Department of State 1964.
[56] France (1965), Japan (1970), and the United Kingdom (1971). The next country to perform an independent launch for the first time was India in 1980. The European Space Agency performed its first launch in 1979.

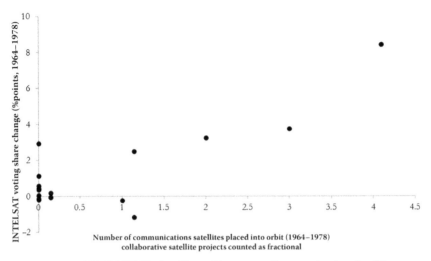

FIGURE 6.1 INTELSAT Voting Share Change vs. Communication Satellites Placed into Orbit (1964–1978)
Source: McDowell (2013); Intelsat Annual Report (1978); US Department of State (1964)

Among inception members and excluding the United States, countries with independent launch capabilities increased their voting shares on average by 5.1 percentage points between 1964 and 1978, compared to 0.4 percentage points for countries without launch capabilities.

Table 6.1 presents a simple regression to consider the possibility that these associations are attributable to other variables. In the first two columns, the dependent variable is Intelsat voting shares in 1978. Following the methodology used to analyze path dependence in IMF and World Bank voting shares in Chapter 3, I include voting shares from ten years prior (1968) along with several explanatory variables of interest. It is possible that the development of communications satellites and launch capabilities are simply proxying for large, powerful countries. I therefore include the log of nominal GDP for the year of the dependent variable.[57] Another possibility is that technical sophistication in the field of aerospace is associated with economic development, which may inflate utilization of satellite telecommunications traffic due relatively higher penetration of telephones. To account for this possibility, I include

---

[57] Source: World Bank World Development Indicators.

TABLE 6.1 *Outside Options and Intelsat Voting Shares (OLS)*

Indep/Dep Variables	Intelsat Voting Shares (1978)	Intelsat Voting Shares (1978)	Intelsat Voting Shares (1988)	Intelsat Voting Shares (1998)
Intelsat Voting	0.67*	0.85*	0.41	0.43
Shares (1968)	(0.29)	(0.25)	(0.25)	(0.26)
Satellites Placed	1.06*		1.68*	0.35
in Orbit	(0.45)		(0.49)	(0.51)
(1968–1978)				
Independent		2.63*		
Launch		(1.07)		
Ln GDP	0.10	0.09	0.12	0.32*
	(0.10)	(0.10)	(0.11)	(0.13)
Telephone	−0.02	−0.01	−0.01	−0.01
Penetration	(0.01)	(0.01)	(0.01)	(0.01)
Major Language	−0.13	−0.23	0.09	−0.28
	(0.31)	(0.27)	(0.23)	(0.21)
Constant	−1.57	−1.34	−2.37	−7.09
	(2.24)	(2.30)	(2.53)	(3.09)
n	52	52	60	60

Note: Numbers in parenthesis are Huber–White standard errors. Star denotes a coefficient at least two standard errors removed from zero.

fixed-telephone subscriptions per 100 inhabitants.[58] Finally, I include a dummy variable for countries in which the primary language spoken is English, French, or Spanish, on the grounds that this may facilitate international telecommunications traffic with foreign nationals who share a common language.[59] As the first two columns of Table 6.1 show, the positive association between satellites placed into orbit and launches on the one hand and voting shares on the other remains after controlling for these variables.

The third and fourth columns of Table 6.1 rerun the first specification for Intelsat voting shares in 1988 and 1998 respectively.[60] As the columns show, although the association between voting shares and satellites placed into orbit in 1968–1978 remains positive and statistically

[58] Source: International Telecommunications Union World Telecommunication/ICT Indicators.

[59] Source: Central Intelligence Agency World Fact Book.

[60] The specifications in the table use satellites placed in orbit, but launches produce the same substantive result.

significant in 1988, by 1998 the association weakens considerably. This reflects factors such as decolonization, the proliferation of regional systems, and the advancement of alternative telecommunications technologies, which all served to dilute the link between the voting rule established in 1973 and the characteristics of the countries that stood to benefit at the time. For example, although Japan, as an archipelago state, benefited from the inclusion of domestic traffic in voting share calculations early on, by the 1980s and 1990s most domestic traffic was being routed through undersea cables. Hence, the bargaining leverage attributable to early launches was helpful in securing a favorable distributive outcome initially, but the advantage did not persist indefinitely.

Developing countries secured no significant concessions on voting rights in the Board of Governors, the executive organ of Intelsat. However, the creation of the Assembly, administered according to one-country-one-vote rules, gave them the ability to shape the overall direction of the organization and vote on any proposed changes to the operating agreement. The Assembly's voting rule was a response to Intersputnik, which, although only able to utilize a fraction of the capacity of Intelsat, sought to attract developing countries and operated under a one-country-one-vote rule.[61]

Figure 6.2 plots the US share of communications satellite launches among Intelsat members alongside the US voting share in Intelsat.[62] As the figure shows, during the early years, when the US dominated communication satellite launches, voting shares in Intelsat were highly stable by design, changing only in response to new members and guaranteeing a 50 percent+ share to the United States. As the US monopoly on launches began to erode, the institution's voting shares also became more flexible. The US share fell to 40 percent with the implementation of the definitive arrangements in 1973, and rapidly declined thereafter as Intelsat grew and more member countries began to actively utilize satellite telecommunications. From the mid-1970s through the privatization of the organization in 2001, share distributions adjusted completely flexibly, mechanically reflecting utilization of the space segment by member states. This adjustment mechanism was more flexible than weighted voting rules used in most economic institutions such as the IMF and World Bank, in which adjustments of weights usually occurs through negotiation.

---

[61] Buck 1998, 160.
[62] Intelsat did not keep consistent records of voting shares in the early years. To fill in missing data, some of the early data is calculated from the organization's voting rules that prevailed at the time. Several missing years prior to 1978 are imputed from available data.

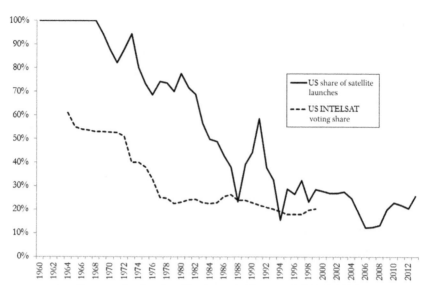

FIGURE 6.2 Communication Satellite Launch Share and INTELSAT Voting
Share of United States

Source: McDowell (2013); *Intelsat Annual Report*, Various Years; US Department of State
(1964); Various declassified US government documents

THE PROLIFERATION OF COMPETITION AND PRIVATIZATION

Competition against Intelsat proliferated dramatically over the course of
the 1980s and 1990s. Technological diffusion gradually made it possible
for a larger set of actors to develop communication satellites and place
them into orbit. By the 1990s, over twenty countries were capable of
placing satellites into orbit, either unilaterally or through the European
Space Agency. Although the costs of individual launches remained high,
technological developments, particularly increases in the power transmission capabilities of satellites, led to dramatic reductions in setup costs.[63]
In addition, undersea fiber optic cables and cellular telephony became
capable of replicating many of the functions of communications satellites
at competitive cost.

The proliferation of competition turned many of the debates of the
1960s on their head. The global satellite telecommunications

---

[63] Whalen 2010 points out that the cost of a typical earth station declined from about $45
million in the 1960s to $30,000 or less by the 1990s due to improvements in the
transmission power of communications satellites.

infrastructure became less central as a means to obtain and disseminate information, and winning the hearts and minds of developing countries receded in importance along with decolonization and the end of the Cold War. Major developed countries, particularly the United States, began to see private sector provision of satellite telecommunications services as preferable to the global architecture embodied in Intelsat.[64] Although the voting rules of the Board of Governors of Intelsat had been made highly flexible during the negotiations over the definitive arrangements, the Assembly, a one-country-one-vote organ, had been given partial authority over fundamental changes to the organization. This set up a confrontation between major developed countries, which sought to reform and ultimately privatize Intelsat, and developing countries, which sought to block changes in order to enjoy the benefits of access at a reasonable price guaranteed by a global network.[65] As predicted by the theory, ease of exit allowed developed countries to largely sidestep developing country opposition to change.

In 1979, Intelsat formally approved Western Europe's European Telecommunications Satellite Organization (EUTELSAT), a separate, regional system that would pose direct competition to Intelsat's services. Regional systems quickly proliferated, with Palapa (Southeast Asia) and the Arab Satellite Communications Organization (Middle East) following in quick succession.[66] This clear breakdown of Intelsat's global monopoly in turn strengthened the hand of private communications providers in the United States, which saw an opportunity to challenge COMSAT's dominance of the US-based satellite communications market. The Pan American Satellite Corporation (PanAmSat), which was established in 1984, launched a particularly aggressive lobbying effort, taking out colorful full page advertisements in the *Wall Street Journal* featuring a cartoon dog mascot urinating on politicians and declaring "The triumph of truth and technology over bull**** and bureaucracy."[67] In a major about face, in November 1984, US President Ronald Reagan formally determined that "separate international communications satellite systems [were] required in the national interest."[68] He directed the FCC to examine the establishment

---

[64] Hahn and Kroszner 1990.   [65] Ayish 1992.   [66] Katkin 2005, 10.

[67] John R. Quan, "Beaming Up Business (Corporate Profile of PanAmSat." *New York Stock Exchange Magazine,* 2005.

[68] Katkin 2005, 10.

of private US satellite systems that would compete directly with Intelsat's services.

Despite having advocated for the creation of competing regional systems, non-US Intelsat members strongly objected to the creation of a US-based competitor to Intelsat. All 109 member states aside from the United States supported a resolution opposing the FCC's proposal to license a separate system as risking Intelsat's "prosperity and political harmony."[69] European countries were concerned that a new US-based competitor capable of providing trans-Atlantic services would undermine EUTELSAT. Developing countries expressed concerns that competition would fail to extend into their markets, leading to higher prices as Intelsat was forced to compensate for lost revenues in the US market. Nonetheless, the FCC went ahead with its decision to authorize separate systems. In 1988, PanAmSat began posing private competition to Intelsat in the lucrative US and trans-Atlantic markets.

Intelsat's position was also being eroded by technological change outside the satellite communications field. In the late-1980s, large telecommunications firms such as American Telephone & Telegraph (AT&T) began laying submarine cables across the Atlantic and Pacific, allowing telecommunications traffic to bypass the satellite systems entirely. By the mid-1990s, communications traffic via transoceanic fiber optic cables exceeded those via satellite. Undersea cables were not subject to delays associated with satellite relays and also offered a cost advantage.[70]

Rapid increase in competition from public as well as private sources altered the landscape for Intelsat dramatically. As a universal-membership international organization, Intelsat's decision-making structure was slow and laborious, making it difficult to compete with more nimble private competitors. Major Intelsat members, particularly developed countries including the United States, ironically began to view Intelsat's modest constraints on separate systems as an impediment to their unilateral plans for private development of satellite telecommunications. On the other hand, developing countries had come to see Intelsat as a beneficial arrangement, primarily due to restrictions on price discrimination across market segments. In order to compete with public and private providers in developed markets, Intelsat was being forced to lower prices, and these price declines were directly applied to developing

[69] Ibid., 10.   [70] Ibid., 11.

countries, where prices would have otherwise been far higher. Because the Assembly of Intelsat operated on one-country-one-vote principles, and the organ needed to approve major changes to the organization, this created a conflict between developing countries, which sought to protect the status quo, and developed countries that sought change.

The numerical strength of developing countries in the Assembly gave them formal authority to veto significant changes to the governing structure of Intelsat. However, the attractive outside options that characterized Intelsat's policy area by this point meant that resistance would only fuel a shift of telecommunications traffic from Intelsat's system to competing systems. This gave reform-minded developed countries decisive leverage. In 1990, the United States, United Kingdom, and Australia successfully pushed for an amendment of Intelsat's constitution that formalized the acceptance of private regional systems that posed direct competition to the organization.[71] The United States and United Kingdom also began to advocate for the privatization of Intelsat. In 1997, the US House of Representatives passed H.R. 1872, an act "to amend the Communications Satellite Act of 1962 to promote competition and privatization in satellite communications." This law was passed without consultation with Intelsat, as Diane Hinson, the Vice President and General Counsel for Intelsat, pointed out, noting that Intelsat signatories felt "a little baffled ... at how the United States Congress purports to pass legislation that governs them."[72] However, developing countries ultimately came around to the view that a privatized Intelsat with modest protections for their interests was the best bargain they could secure. Refusing to alter the status quo would eliminate implicit subsidies for developing countries in any case, as exit by developed economies would cause Intelsat to rapidly lose traffic in its most lucrative markets. In 1999, the Intelsat Assembly formally adopted a resolution moving the organization toward privatization.[73]

US President Clinton signed the ORBIT (Open Market Organization for the Betterment of International Telecommunications) Act into law in March 2000, setting forth conditions that a privatized Intelsat would need to meet in order to continue business in the US market. In a November 2000 meeting of the Intelsat Assembly, a privatization plan was approved with unanimous consent of all 144 government members. All assets, liabilities, and operations of the organization were transferred

[71] Hills 1994, 184.   [72] McCormick 2008, 62.
[73] INTELSAT Assembly of Parties Decision, 1999, AP 24-24-3E Final.

to Intelsat Ltd., a private holding company based in Bermuda. Intelsat Limited Liability Company (LLC), a Delaware-incorporated subsidiary, was granted possession of satellites and licenses, and the main service subsidiary remained in Washington, D.C.[74]

Developing countries advocated for and secured the creation of a new organization, which maintained the name, "International Telecommunications Satellite Organization," but had a new acronym, ITSO. The organization's purpose was to "ensure, through the Public Services Agreement, that [Intelsat] provides, on a commercial basis, international public telecommunications services, in order to ensure performance of the Core Principles, [which are] (i) maintain global connectivity and global coverage; (ii) serve its lifeline connectivity customers; and (iii) provide non-discriminatory access to the Company's system."[75] This was enforced through a contractual public services agreement with Intelsat, which provided for a transition period during which Intelsat was obligated to provide services to countries that were at risk of being cut off from the global network under private incentives. These agreements were designed to expire after twelve years, at which point the future of ITSO would be open for additional discussion.[76]

DISCUSSION

As predicted by the theory, Intelsat became more flexible and responsive to distributive shifts as barriers to competition eroded and outside options for member states became more attractive. During the initial phase, US policymakers sought to create a monopolistic organization that they could dominate. Without credible outside options, other member states had no choice but to largely accept US prerogatives. As the US monopoly on communications satellite technology and launch capabilities eroded, exit became a plausible option for several states, primarily the United Kingdom, France, and Japan, and these states negotiated a more flexible arrangement that reflected their interests. Intelsat's voting rules in the Board of Governors evolved from near-total rigidity – freezing initial share allocations and guaranteeing the United States a 50 percent + share – to mechanical flexibility – rising and falling in direct proportion

---

[74] Privatization of Intelsat 2001; Thussu 2001.
[75] "Agreement Relating to the International Telecommunications Satellite Organization (as amended on 17 November 2000)," Article III.
[76] Katkin 2005.

to utilization of the satellite telecommunications network. Although Intelsat's voting rules became highly flexible in regards to operational issues, important rigidities remained, particularly with respect to decisions requiring consent of the Assembly, which operated on one-country-one-vote principles. As competition intensified further in the 1980s and 1990s, particularly from private sector sources, these rigidities became a source of discontent for several developed countries. These countries exercised exit by flouting Intelsat's prohibition on competing systems and ultimately succeeded in forcing dramatic change, transforming the institution into a private corporation.

Intelsat also illustrates the limitations of rational design in the formation of international organizations. US policymakers clearly miscalculated the degree of network effects that would be present in Intelsat's policy area, investing heavily in a rapid rollout that was designed to preempt alternative systems from being established first. Once the satellite system was operative, it became clear that network effects were limited, and outside options were attractive for states with requisite technical capabilities. Intelsat was designed as a monopoly institution that would perpetuate US dominance in a policy area that eventually proved highly competitive. By the 1990s, the United States was leading an effort to dismantle the global architecture it had itself championed three decades earlier. Similarly, states that had secured credible outside options early, such as Britain, France, and Japan, negotiated for a voting rule that generated clear advantages for themselves early on, but these advantages did not persist. Intelsat's structure was a reflection of bounded rational design: confronted by a new policy area with uncertain characteristics, policymakers made mistakes and bargained for short-term gains that proved transient.

The evolution of Intelsat also illustrates the discipline imposed on international institutions by policy area competition. The initial mismatch between Intelsat's rigid structure and the increasingly competitive nature of its policy area was quickly resolved as credible threats of exit foreclosed the possibility that unbalanced representation among member states could be sustained. Similarly, in the 1980s and 1990s, developing countries had the formal authority to block privatization, but widespread competition meant that maintenance of the status quo would lead to exit by dissatisfied developed states and render the organization unsustainable. Recognizing this, developing countries conceded to privatization.

7

Internet Corporation for Assigned Names and Numbers

Chapter 6 examined Intelsat, an institution proposed by US policymakers with the intent to establish a monopoly organization dominated by US interests. This goal was undercut by features of Intelsat's policy area: satellite telecommunications was not subject to strong network effects due to modest switching costs, and technological diffusion eroded barriers to entry over time. Intelsat faced competition from regional satellite systems as well as alternative communication technologies, eroding the ability of the United States to maintain its dominance over the institution.

In this chapter, I will present a case study of an institution that bears many similarities to Intelsat: the Internet Corporation for Assigned Names and Numbers (ICANN). ICANN was established to manage a new policy area that emerged along with the development of the internet, much as Intelsat sought to manage the nascent satellite telecommunications system. As was the case with Intelsat, the United States played a central role in creating and designing ICANN, and the initial development of the institution followed a similar blueprint: the United States sought to minimize foreign influence, install US-based private actors in central administrative roles, and place the organization under the regulatory authority of domestic US agencies. However, compared to Intelsat, ICANN governs a policy area with powerful network effects. This enabled the United States to sustain dominance over the institution to a much greater degree. Despite the rapid international proliferation of the internet and repeated calls by other, powerful countries to transfer ICANN's governance functions to an explicitly intergovernmental framework, the United States has been largely able to dictate the terms of reform.

THE POLICY AREA OF ICANN

The internet operates based on a unique set of identifiers – the domain name system (DNS), internet protocol (IP) addresses and autonomous system (AS) numbers, and protocol port and parameter numbers. Until 1998, the regulation of such identifiers was under the direct purview of the Department of Defense of the United States. This authority was transferred in 1998 to ICANN, a nonprofit organization based in California. Bargaining over the creation of ICANN primarily took place between US government authorities and private sector actors with little involvement of other states.[1] As internet use globalized and expanded to include a wide range of functions traditionally regulated by sovereign states, other nations developed an interest in internet governance. The institution therefore closely reflects the theoretical assumptions proposed in Chapter 2: essentially unilateral institutional design, followed by international renegotiation efforts by states that had no role in establishing the institution.

The Issues at Stake

What are the stakes in ICANN's policy area? Distributive conflict over ICANN has been intense due to the ubiquitous nature of the internet and its rising importance for purposes such as intelligence, cyber warfare, and control of domestic information flows.[2] Interest in ICANN governance runs the gamut from symbolic questions to more "high politics" concerns such as whether the current regulatory regime might give the US military an upper hand in cyber warfare or other non-conventional uses of the internet.

Symbolism has been an important source of contestation over ICANN. A major early source of frustration stemmed from ICANN's decision to only accept domain names based on the English alphabet, which prompted accusations of linguistic imperialism from China and other developing countries.[3] ICANN's authority over the DNS has also been used for explicitly political purposes. Afghanistan's country domain ".af" was registered by expatriate Afghanis rather than the Taliban-controlled

---

[1] Franda 2001, 55.

[2] For example, Swaine 2013; David Kravets, "NSA Leaks Prompt Rethinking of U.S. Control over the Internet's Infrastructure," *Wired*, October 14, 2013.

[3] "English Dominance Sparks 'Digital Divide,'" *The Toronto Star*, January 12, 2004.

Afghan government in the 1990s,[4] and the Palestinian authority was granted ".ps" in 2000 before receiving recognition as a sovereign state.[5] Similarly, Taiwan was granted ".tw" without any consultation with China, an outcome unthinkable in a traditional intergovernmental organization.[6] One former ICANN board member noted that, "We've got a California corporation, working under the Department of Commerce, deciding who's a country. Where does statehood begin?"[7]

However, symbolism is not the only issue at stake in the contestation over ICANN: control over domain names can produce both economic and geopolitical advantages. The United States has used its asymmetrical influence over ICANN to unilaterally seize global domain names that allegedly violated federal copyright and trademark laws, replacing the websites with a US IP address that informs visitors of the seizure.[8] A major security issue concerning ICANN is the possibility that US authorities could unilaterally disrupt internet traffic to entire countries by manipulating or deleting identifying information from servers under US jurisdiction.[9] In addition, ICANN remains under the jurisdiction of the US court system, including the Foreign Intelligence Surveillance Court, which means the organization is obligated to provide information upon request to US intelligence agencies such as the National Security Agency.[10] Autocratic governments that seek to maintain a tight grip over domestic information flows, such as China, have been particularly vocal in expressing dissatisfaction and seeking greater authority over ICANN's policy area.

Policy Area Characteristics

The policy area of ICANN epitomizes network effects.[11] If France used one set of identifiers that overlapped with identifiers used in Germany,

---

[4] "Countries, Companies Debate U.N. Control over Internet," *Associated Press Worldstream*, March 27, 2004.

[5] "Will U.N. have Role in Internet Name Game?; Some Countries Think the U.S. Has too much Influence," *Associated Press*, March 28, 2004.

[6] Cukier 2005.

[7] "Will U.N. Have Role in Internet Name Game?; Some Countries Think the U.S. Has too much Influence," *Associated Press*, March 28, 2004.

[8] David Kravets, "NSA Leaks Prompt Rethinking of U.S. Control over the Internet's Infrastructure," *Wired*, October 14, 2013.

[9] "Countries, Companies Debate U.N. Control over Internet," *Associated Press Worldstream*, March 27, 2004.

[10] David Kravets, "NSA Leaks Prompt Rethinking of U.S. Control over the Internet's Infrastructure," *Wired*, October 14, 2013.

[11] David 1985.

network users would not be able to locate each other globally. Once a standard for identification is established, it is extremely costly to unilaterally deviate to an alternative naming standard. There are strong incentives for all actors to coordinate on one system of assigning unique identifiers to avoid chaos. Although alternatives to the DNS controlled by ICANN have been proposed by various organizations, none have taken off due to this fundamental issue.[12] The policy area is therefore characterized by extremely unattractive outside options for states wishing to renegotiate a more globalized regulatory regime for the internet.

In addition, costs of renegotiating ICANN can be considered high. There is no formal mechanism for a dissatisfied state to bring a proposal to the table to increase its decision-making authority over ICANN. While the US Department of Commerce has played a central role in overseeing and regulating ICANN, other states have no formal jurisdiction over the institution. Hence, bringing a challenge to the ICANN regime requires costly consensus-building outside the institution and challenging the United States through diplomatic channels. In addition, the policy area is highly technical and dominated by private actors, making it challenging for governments to formulate actionable reform proposals.

The US government has consistently taken the position that internet governance should be coordinated by ICANN under the initiative of the private sector with minimal government interference. The United States has vehemently resisted transferring authority to international organizations such as the United Nations (UN) or International Telecommunications Union (ITU), which operate under one-country-one-vote principles and would therefore severely reduce US influence over internet governance.[13] Many policymakers in the US view authority over the internet as a reasonable return on investment given the technical and financial resources invested during the early stages of development.[14]

As I will show, the combination of highly unattractive outside options and high costs of challenging the status quo have allowed the United States to dominate ICANN and dictate the course of reform for over three decades despite repeated attempts by other countries to alter the status quo. This does not mean a shift to international governance is impossible.

[12] "Open Root: The Grandfather of the Internet Takes on ICANN," *TechWeekEurope*, October 29, 2012.
[13] "UN Summit to Focus on Internet," *Technews*, December 5, 2003.
[14] "U.N. Internet Confab Takes on ICANN, or Does It Really?" *Telecom Policy Report*, November 6, 2006.

However, it does mean that the United States has wide latitude in choosing if, when, and how to allow institutional change, a luxury it does not possess in policy areas subject to intense competition.

THE EMERGENCE OF ICANN

The concept of host names to organize internet communication can be traced to 1972, when Peggy Karp, an early pioneer of internet standards, produced the first hosts.txt file, which was the precursor of the modern root file. Control over the file shifted over time, first being transferred to the Stanford Research Institute Network Information Center (SRI-NIC), and then to the Defense Data Network (DDN-NIC), and finally the Defense Information Systems Agency (DISA-NIC). These organizations also served as domain name registrars for generic top-level domain names. Beginning in 1977, a graduate student at the University of California, Los Angeles, Jon Postel, became responsible for handling the assignment of IP numbers to specific domain names. These functions were then transferred to the Internet Assigned Numbers Authority (IANA), which remained under Postel's management and Defense Department support.[15]

In the mid-1980s, IANA established the DNS, which formalized the assignment of domain names to numerical IP addresses. Decisions about the overall architecture of the internet were handled informally through consultation among several interested parties, primarily the IANA and the Internet Engineering Task Force (IETF), which was charged with the management of IPs.[16] As the internet grew, the US government recognized that a more formal managerial organization would be needed. In 1991, the National Science Foundation (NSF) took over responsibility for coordinating and maintaining the internet. In 1993, the NSF signed an agreement with Network Solutions to manage domain name assignments for top-level domains such as ".com," and ".org."[17] By 1997, the importance of the internet and the value of domain names became more clearly recognized, and other firms began to lobby for authority to act as registrars alongside Network Solutions.[18]

Up until this point, the internet had evolved largely as a project regulated and guided by the US government, despite the participation of international experts and users since early stages. With the explosive,

[15] Froomkin 2000, 51–53.   [16] Crawford 2004, 412.   [17] Ibid., 412.
[18] Froomkin 2000, 61.

international growth of internet use in the 1990s, along with the growing recognition of the commercial and geopolitical implications of the medium, the US government monopoly over the root file became increasingly controversial. Governments began to criticize US unilateral control over an important feature of what was rapidly becoming a global network. Controversies also arose over how to reconcile international commercial trademarks with similar or identical domain names.

A proposal to transfer management of the DNS to a more international framework emerged in 1997, largely without US government participation. The Internet Society (ISOC), a group of researchers involved in the development of the internet, formed an International Ad Hoc Committee (IAHC) to discuss management of the DNS. The IAHC invited participation from a broad range of interested international parties, such as the International Trademark Association (ITA), World Intellectual Property Organization (WIPO), and the ITU. The IAHC put together the Generic Top Level Domain Name Memorandum of Understanding (gTLD-MoU), which proposed that the governance of the internet should be assigned to an agency within the ITU. The gTLD-MoU was signed in a formal ceremony overseen by the ITU in Geneva. The US government refused to accept the gTLD-MoU and sharply criticized the ITU for failing to secure authorization from its member states. US antipathy toward the ITU stemmed from a history of contestation in the organization over issues such as global data networking standards and the perception that US interests were not adequately represented under the one-country-one-vote rule of the organization.[19]

In July of 1997, US President Clinton directed the Secretary of Commerce to privatize the DNS in order to deflect international criticism of US domination. The US government, along with US commercial firms such as AOL, IBM, and MCI, were concerned that internationalization of internet governance would be unruly and inefficient. Primary among these concerns was that the assertion of territorial jurisdiction would curtail the growth of electronic commerce.[20] The Department of Commerce formed an interagency group, led by Ira Magaziner, tasked with the privatization and regulation of the DNS. Magaziner's group issued a White Paper that established basic principles for a new internet infrastructure: "stability, competition, private bottom-up coordination, and representation."[21] The White Paper rejected the approach outlined in the gTLD-MoU,

[19] Drezner 2004, 494.   [20] Mueller, Mathiason, and Klein 2007, 238.
[21] Froomkin 2000, 67.

calling for a private entity to take control over the DNS: "overall policy guidance and control of the TLDs and the Internet root server system should be vested in a single organization that is representative of Internet users around the globe."[22] The White Paper made it clear that the private sector would take the lead in managing the DNS, and the US government role would be to "empower" rather than actively participate. Similarly, international participation by private actors was encouraged, but not foreign government involvement.[23]

In November 1998, the recommendations of the White Paper were largely implemented in an agreement between the Department of Commerce and IANA. This resulted in the creation of ICANN, a non-profit corporate entity headquartered in California that would be responsible for management of the DNS. ICANN controlled top-level domain names, giving it a central role in the management of the internet.

To give some voice to foreign governments and international organizations over the organization, a Governmental Advisory Committee (GAC) was formed within ICANN, with participation open to all nations. However, ICANN bylaws severely limit the authority of the GAC over the organization. The GAC has no formal decision-making authority: it was initially prohibited from seating a representative on the ICANN Board of Directors, and subsequently granted one, non-voting liaison. Although the bylaws state that the GAC should be consulted concerning issues that affect "various laws and international agreements or ... public policy issues,"[24] and mutually acceptable solutions should be sought, the ICANN Board can ultimately ignore any GAC suggestions, only being required to "state in its final decision the reasons why the Governmental Advisory Committee advice was not followed."[25] In addition, the GAC is a universal membership organization with a consensus decision-making structure, limiting the scope for actions that directly challenge the interests of any specific member, including the United States. In effect, the GAC serves as a forum for governments to exchange information with ICANN, but it has no formal influence over policy outcomes.[26]

---

[22] Department of Commerce National Telecommunications Information Agency 1998.
[23] Ibid.
[24] Internet Corporation for Assigned Names and Numbers 2014, ARTICLE XI, section 2.
[25] Ibid., ARTICLE XI, section 2.   [26] Mueller, Mathiason, and Klein 2007, 239.

THE RENEGOTIATION OF ICANN

Despite its legal status as a nonprofit organization with non-government representatives from across the globe, ICANN has been subject to the direct jurisdiction of the US government.[27] Aside from the United States, government input is restricted to providing advice through the largely toothless GAC.[28] In practice, ICANN has largely operated under the leadership of private sector actors under the loose oversight of US government agencies such as the Department of Commerce.

This asymmetrical position of the United States in ICANN has led to repeated calls for internationalization of governance over the internet. Other developed states, such as members of the European Union, have expressed frustration with the US-dominated system and called for a greater regulatory role by international organizations. However, the greatest source of dissatisfaction is among governments of developing, particularly autocratic states, which perceive the free flow of information over the internet as a potential threat to regime stability. Former UN Secretary General Kofi Annan noted:

> developing countries find it difficult to follow all these processes and feel left out of Internet governance structures. The United States deserves our thanks for having developed the Internet and made it available to the world. For historical reasons, the United States has the ultimate authority over some of the Internet's core resources. It is an authority that many say should be shared with the international community.[29]

Dissatisfied states, particularly developing countries that prefer greater state regulation over internet activity, have argued in favor of moving authority away from ICANN toward international organizations such as the UN and the ITU.[30] The one-country-one-vote rule in most UN organizations such as the ITU tends to favor developing countries, which lag in technology and economic development but can often outvote developed countries on account of their numerical advantage.

Efforts to internationalize ICANN have been ongoing since the establishment of the organization. In 2001, the UN General Assembly voted to authorize the World Summit on the Information Society (WSIS), a forum

---

[27] Thierer and Crews 2003, x.   [28] Feld 2003, 346–58.

[29] Annan, Kofi, "The U.N. Isn't a Threat to the Net," *The New York Times*, November 5, 2005.

[30] "External Forces Chip Away at Internet's Overseer," *The International Herald Tribune*, March 8, 2004.

to discuss the digital divide between developed and developing societies. One major agenda item for WSIS was to evaluate the role of ICANN in internet governance and consider a shift of the organization toward a more international direction. The first WSIS summits were held in Geneva in 2003 and Tunisia in 2005.[31]

The 2003 WSIS discussed various alternatives to ICANN's role in internet governance. Brazil, China, South Africa, and other developing countries condemned the structure of ICANN and argued in favor of a revised arrangement.[32] Many delegates questioned the dominant role the US government played in regulating ICANN and expressed concerns that the United States would seek to unilaterally manipulate internet governance in favor of its narrow interests. David Gross, the State Department's coordinator for international communications and information policy, made it clear that the United States had no intention of compromising ICANN's role in internet governance, and asserted that "We think that ICANN has in place opportunities for input from governments."[33] In effect, the United States expressed a clear preference in favor of the status quo.

Several alternatives to the status quo were discussed at the 2003 WSIS. One option was to elevate the role of the GAC within ICANN from a pure advisory body to an organ with policymaking authority. GAC membership was open to all national governments as well as international organizations such as the EU and ITU. However, it was perceived that developing countries would hold limited influence in an upgraded GAC due to their lack of technical expertise and financial resources.[34] This made the GAC option an attractive one for developed countries aside from the United States.

Another option was to shift DNS authority from ICANN to the ITU. The ITU is generally viewed as an institution favorable to developing country interests due to its one-country-one-vote rule and its stated mission of supporting economic development through the expansion of telecommunications services. Since developing countries were already well-established in the governance structures of the ITU, this option was seen as more attractive than an upgraded GAC. However, developed countries, even aside from the United States, had significant reservations about shifting regulatory authority over the internet to the ITU. This

---

[31] Mueller, Mathiason, and Klein 2007, 240.   [32] Ibid., 240.
[33] "US Ready for Battle at Information Summit," *AFP*, December 3, 2003.
[34] Klein 2004, 408–9.

stemmed from the perception that the ITU tended to support entrenched national telecommunications monopolies, particularly in developing countries, at the expense of competitive service providers based in developed economies.[35]

The summit bogged down as the United States opposed modifications to the status quo and other participants could not converge on a coherent alternative plan. The summit created a Working Group on Internet Governance (WGIG), composed of forty representatives from business, government and civil society. In turn, the WGIG published a report recommending the creation of a multi-stakeholder forum to discuss internet governance issues. The substantive recommendations of the WGIG sidestepped the thorny issue of governance, recommending merely that government should focus on "public policy" while civil society groups and the private sector should manage "day to day operation" and "technical management" of the internet.[36]

The second WSIS was held in Tunisia in November 2005. The summit largely followed the script of the previous meeting, with developing countries lined up against the US-dominated status quo. Brazil, Cuba, South Africa, and Syria expressed deep disapproval of the existing arrangement centered around ICANN. The representative from Zimbabwe declared that internet governance represented a "form of neocolonialism."[37] Brazil, China, Iran, and Saudi Arabia argued aggressively in favor of greater international oversight over ICANN. China proposed the establishment of a new international organization to manage the internet.

The EU, spearheaded by the French delegation, proposed the creation of an international forum that would determine ICANN policies. This was couched as a proposal to "mov[e] from unilateralism to multilateralism in Internet governance."[38] Martin Selmayr, spokesman for the EU Directorate on Information Society and Media, explained that "We believe in freedom of speech and the freedom of the Internet ... We're not asking for enhancing government's role" in the operation of the internet.[39] Rather, "the E.U. is proposing moving from unilateralism to multilateralism in Internet governance. Public policy principles ... issued in the future should be discussed internationally."[40]

---

[35] Ibid., 409.   [36] Mueller, Mathiason, and Klein 2007, 241.   [37] Cukier 2005, 7.
[38] Jonathan Krim, "U.S. May Face World at Internet Governance Summit," *The Washington Post*, October 13, 2005.
[39] Ibid.   [40] Ibid.

The United States stood firm in its opposition to any modification of the status quo and conceded no ground. The United States had announced earlier in 2005 that it would maintain the Department of Commerce's oversight role over ICANN, citing the need to maintain security of the internet. At the WSIS, Gross made it clear that the United States would not accept any new entity exercising an oversight role over ICANN, stating that, "We are firm in our position ... This is not a negotiation."[41]

The 2005 WSIS concluded by proposing the development of "globally-applicable principles on public policy issues associated with coordination and management of critical Internet resources" and the creation of another multi-stakeholder forum, the Internet Governance Forum (IGF), which would continue discussing issues of internet governance.[42]

US policymakers did agree to the replacement of the memorandum of understanding between ICANN and the Department of Commerce with a Joint Project Agreement (JPA). The JPA stated that ICANN need not formally report to the Department of Commerce, but that it must have regular "consultations" with the US agency.[43] The JPA was a modest step, but it was seen as "a step into the right direction, of reduced governmental involvement in the day-to-day operation of the management of the internet resources."[44] Following the 2005 WSIS, ICANN also undertook some efforts to emphasize its international character and responsiveness to international concerns. In 2006 and 2007, regional offices were established in Europe and Asia respectively. Joint working groups and task forces were set up between ICANN and the GAC in a bid to improve communication and mutual understanding.

In 2009, the US Department of Commerce replaced the JPA with an Affirmation of Commitments with ICANN that shifted oversight over the organization from the US government to a series of review panels composed of independent experts, representatives of the ICANN board, and the Department of Commerce.[45] ICANN chief Rod Beckstrom noted that the shift in US policy was prompted by concern that US dominance was leading some countries to consider alternatives to the internet despite the costs of developing parallel networks: "It's rumoured that there are multiple experiments going on with countries forking the internet, various

---

[41] Ibid.   [42] Mueller, Mathiason, and Klein 2007, 241–42.
[43] Bauer, Benedek, and Kettemann 2008, 24.   [44] Ibid., 24.
[45] Grant Gross, "New ICANN Agreement Runs into Criticism," *Reuters* October 1, 2009.

countries have discussed this ... This is a very significant shift because it takes the wind out of our opponents."[46]

However, ICANN's survival continued to depend on the willingness of the Department of Commerce to grant authority to administer the DNS. As the Department of Commerce described, "Critical to the DNS is the continued performance of the Internet Assigned Numbers Authority (IANA) functions ... The Internet Corporation for Assigned Names and Numbers (ICANN) currently performs the IANA functions, on behalf of the US Government, through a contract with the National Telecommunications and Information Administration (NTIA)."[47] In 2011, the Department of Commerce briefly refused to extend ICANN's contract over concerns that the organization was approving too many top-level domain names.[48] No other country possessed comparable leverage over ICANN.

The Affirmation of Commitments retained the US government's asymmetrical position of influence over ICANN. Rather than enhancing the oversight role of foreign governments, the agreement primarily increased the role of private and non-governmental stakeholders and granted ICANN greater autonomy from regulation.[49] This was largely consistent with US policy objectives, which sought to minimize foreign government oversight over ICANN while maintaining the open architecture of the internet.

In 2014, the Obama administration proposed to relinquish the Department of Commerce's direct authority over ICANN in the wake of Edward Snowden's revelations about US cyber espionage activities. However, the proposal focused on ceding authority to private and non-governmental stakeholders and explicitly noted that, "we will not accept a proposal that replaces NTIA's role with a government-led or an inter-governmental solution."[50] Even this modest step was blocked by Congress, which defunded the transition and forced the Commerce Department to

---

[46] Bobbie Johnson, "US Relinquishes Control of the Internet," *The Guardian*, September 30, 2009.

[47] National Telecommunications & Information Administration of the Department of Commerce, "IANA Functions Contract," www.ntia.doc.gov/page/iana-functions-pur chase-order.

[48] Eric Engleman, "Commerce Department Keeps Icann as Web's Address Manager," *Bloomberg*, June 3, 2012.

[49] Grant Gross, "New ICANN Agreement Runs into Criticism," *Reuters* October 1, 2009.

[50] Lawrence E. Strickling, "Promoting Internet Growth and Innovation through Multistakeholder Internet Governance," US Department of Commerce, March 19, 2014.

maintain its authority over ICANN.[51] ICANN remains under the jurisdiction of the US court system, including the Foreign Intelligence Surveillance Court, which means the organization is obligated to provide
information upon request to the National Security Agency.[52] In essence,
the US government has been able to approach the evolution of ICANN as
if it were a purely domestic political issue, and foreign government
demands have been met with minimal, largely cosmetic concessions.

CHINESE EFFORTS TO CREATE AN ALTERNATIVE INTERNET

As I argued earlier, an important reason why dissatisfied states have been
unsuccessful in their efforts to renegotiate ICANN's US-dominated structure is their lack of credible outside options, which in turn stems from the
powerful network effects that characterize the institution's policy area. To
demonstrate this point, it is useful to examine China's attempts to develop
an alternative internet architecture that competes with ICANN. China is
now a major geopolitical and economic power second only to the United
States, and it has not shied away from creating institutions – such as the
Asian Infrastructure Investment Bank and New Development Bank – to
compete with what it perceives as US-dominated incumbent institutions.
In addition, the Chinese regime is famously obsessed with controlling
information flows into and within its borders and possesses well-
developed censorship and cybersecurity capabilities.[53] Hence, of all countries in the international system, China would appear to have the
strongest combination of motivation and capability to develop an outside
option vis-à-vis ICANN. However, Chinese efforts in this direction, along
with those of all other countries, have been uniformly unsuccessful.

Along with concerns about US dominance articulated earlier in this
chapter, China's initial objections to ICANN centered on the organization's decision to treat Taiwan no differently from other sovereign states:
Taiwan was given the top-level domain name ".tw" and welcomed as a
participant in the GAC alongside other countries. This led China to cease
sending official representatives to ICANN in 2001.[54] China returned to
ICANN's GAC in 2009 when cross-Strait relations improved with the

[51] "Remarks by Lawrence E. Strickling Assistant Secretary of Commerce for Communications and Information," State of the Net Conference, Washington, D.C., January
27, 2015.
[52] David Kravets, "NSA Leaks Prompt Rethinking of U.S. Control over the Internet's
Infrastructure," *Wired*, October 14, 2013.
[53] Among many others, see King, Pan, and Roberts 2013.   [54] Deibert et al. 2012, 182.

election of Ma Ying-jeou, and Taiwan was formally re-designated "Chinese Taipei" in line with other international organizations.

Concurrently, Chinese policymakers sought to develop a "Chinese" internet that would be based on the Chinese language and directly subject to government control. In 1998, the Chinese government launched the China Public Multimedia Network (widely known as the "169 network" from the dial-up access number used to connect to it), which operated on the Chinese language and limited access to the global internet.[55] In addition, in 2001, Chinese authorities proposed the C-Net Strategic Alliance, which was touted as "a completely new, second-generation proprietary communications and data network that is intended to replace the global internet."[56] Furthermore, in 2006, the *People's Daily*, the official newspaper of the Chinese Communist Party, created international alarm when it reported that Chinese authorities would create their own top-level domains in the Chinese language independent of ICANN.[57] The report was quickly denied by ICANN and Chinese government officials, who clarified that the Chinese-language domains would operate under the exiting ".cn" domain, which is part of the DNS managed by ICANN.[58] However, the article was widely interpreted as a signal of discontent by the Chinese government over its powerlessness in ICANN and inability to secure reform through international efforts.

Despite clear dissatisfaction and repeated pronouncements that it would create its own, alternative internet, China has remained firmly within the status quo internet architecture overseen by ICANN. Proposals for a "Chinese" internet were largely cosmetic in nature: for example, the illusion of original Chinese top-level domain names was created by using browser plug-ins to suppress the ".cn" extension, which is within the DNS overseen by ICANN.[59] In 2009, ICANN undercut a major source of Chinese frustration when it started approving internationalized country code top-level domains, that is, top level domains expressed in non-English languages.[60] These official Chinese-language top-level domain names were quickly snapped up by users in China as well as the Chinese government itself.[61]

---

[55] Franda 2002, 198–99.   [56] Ibid., 202.

[57] "China Adds Top-level Domain," *People's Daily Online*, February 28, 2006.

[58] "Inaccurate Report Sparks Fears China May Split Net," *PC World*, IDG News Service, March 2, 2006.

[59] "ICANN Disputes China Domain Report," *IDG News Service*, March 1, 2006.

[60] Deibert et al. 2012, 184.

[61] E.g., "Chinese Government Buys 20,000 New IDN Domain Names," *Domain Name Wire*, March 19, 2014.

China's experience underscores the powerful network effects that characterize ICANN's policy area. As Franda accurately notes:

Chinese business and government leaders have a huge potential stake in selling Chinese products to the rest of the world over the Internet, but the degree of success they can aspire to in this regard will be highly dependent on the ability of Chinese producers and sellers to communicate in cyberspace in a relatively free and open manner with potential customers, suppliers, and business partners in the rest of the world ... the likelihood is that a Chinese intranet that is walled off and shielded from the rest of the world's Internet regime would create serious impediments to a flourishing e-commerce.[62]

Exiting the ICANN regime may have been credible for the relatively insular China of the 1970s or North Korea. However, the information flows necessitated by economic globalization and multinational production chains make it highly impractical for a country to opt out of the existing DNS. In effect, Chinese leaders cannot credibly threaten to exit the ICANN regime without risking considerable economic, and by implication, political costs. This has given the United States and ICANN considerable latitude to resist Chinese demands for greater authority and control over the internet architecture.

DISCUSSION

Given the unattractive outside options in the policy area of internet domain name assignment, it is unsurprising that the United States has been largely able to maintain its dominant position over ICANN despite repeated international challenges. ICANN remains a non-profit organization with limited international oversight, as intended by US policymakers from the outset. The United States has made modest, cosmetic concessions in response to global concerns about US domination and to preempt consideration of alternative networks. However, since threats of exit are not highly credible, the United States has faced little incentive to cede significant authority over ICANN to other countries. In addition, the absence of direct internal mechanisms to challenge US domination, stemming from the exclusion of foreign governments in the initial phase of ICANN, made it cumbersome for foreign governments to challenge the US position. The result, as predicted by the theory, has been path

---

[62] Franda 2002, 203.

dependence, in which a highly skewed status quo has been sustained despite the explosive growth of global internet use.

For sure, it is possible that future developments will undermine the ability of the United States to secure its policy preferences over ICANN. Innovation is unpredictable, and new technologies may make it more attractive to contemplate regional or national alternatives to the internet. The rise of social networks and proprietary mobile applications platforms, which allow users to sidestep the traditional internet, may make it more credible for countries to threaten exit from the ICANN regime. Alternatively, concerns over US domination, particularly in areas that touch on national security, such as surveillance and cyber security, could escalate to a level where some countries view exit as the lesser evil despite high costs. Nonetheless, the experience of ICANN clearly demonstrates that highly skewed arrangements governing international cooperation can be sustained in policy areas characterized by high network effects and barriers to entry.

8

The League of Nations and the
United Nations Security Council

Since the early twentieth century, the League of Nations and United Nations (UN) Security Council have been the subject of recurrent distributive conflict among member states. The governance of the League was contested constantly throughout its existence. Similarly, UN Security Council reform has been a perennial topic of debate, with the P5, the permanent members of the council (China, France, Russia, the United Kingdom, and the United States), lined up against rising and aspiring states in pursuit of greater recognition.

The League of Nations and UN have occupied central positions in the architecture of global institutions since the early twentieth century. The League was established in 1919 during the Paris Peace Conference that ended the First World War. The conflict widely became known as the "war to end all wars,"[1] and the postwar settlement drew heavily on US President Woodrow Wilson's ideals, which centered on principles such as open diplomacy, national self-determination, and the establishment of peace through international cooperation.[2] Paramount among the functions of the League was the notion of collective security, which committed League members to "enforcement by common action of international obligations."[3] The League is widely regarded as a failure, and it was ultimately abandoned in favor of the UN, which was established in 1945 at the tail end of World War II, attempting to remedy the perceived failures of the League.

---

[1] Wells 1914.   [2] Housden 2012.
[3] *The Covenant of the League of Nations*, 1924, Article 8.

Much existing work has examined the political failures of the League,[4] and an equally voluminous literature examines the contemporary role of the UN in the international system.[5] However, less attention has been devoted to the contrasting pattern of bargaining and institutional change between the League and the UN. As I will show, member states have continuously sought greater status, representation, and authority in both institutions. However, the nature of contestation differs markedly. Disagreements over the rules and structures of the League frequently escalated into brinksmanship, with dissatisfied members threatening to abandon the institution entirely unless their demands were met. Although the dramatic departures of Japan, Germany, and Italy from the League are infamous, they were preceded by equally impassioned threats of exit by more obscure members such as Brazil, Costa Rica, and Poland. Comparable threats and actions have been exceedingly rare vis-à-vis the UN Security Council. Brinkmanship led to frequent renegotiation in the Council of the League of Nations, which was reformed at the rate of once every 3.2 years, compared to just one reform during the UN Security Council's nearly seventy years of existence. What accounts for this variation in the patterns and outcomes of distributive conflict?

I will argue that several factors explain the relative stasis of the UN Security Council compared to the League. For the broader objectives of this book, paramount among these is variation in outside options and institutional rules across the two institutions. Both the League and the UN Security Council sought to become sources of collective international legitimacy, either by directly securing the peace through collective action or by legitimating the international uses of force. By its nature, collective legitimization draws upon strength in numbers. As Inis Claude Jr., who coined the term collective legitimization, observed, "[statesmen] ... are keenly conscious for the need for approval by as large and impressive a body of other states as may be possible, for multilateral endorsement of their positions."[6] Because the value of collective legitimization is increasing in the number of states participating, it is effectively subject to network effects. Collective legitimacy and universality are mutually self-reinforcing: greater membership strengthens an institution's ability to claim that it represents the views of the broad international community, and in turn, the ability to confer legitimacy limits incentives for members to exit. However, there are limits to the tendency for collective legitimacy

---

[4] Goodrich 1947; Scott 1974; Claude Jr. 1984; Housden 2012.
[5] For an overview, see Weiss et al. 2013.   [6] Claude Jr. 1966, 370.

to suppress competition: by its nature, collective legitimization will not always be forthcoming, and hence states have incentives to create or seek second-best options, and barriers to entry are relatively low due to the fact that existing multilateral institutions set up for other purposes can be utilized for legitimization. Nonetheless, the UN has been far more successful in achieving universality than the League, and has hence established itself as the first-best option for collective legitimization. Consequently, exit from the UN is far less attractive than exit from the League, limiting the attractiveness of outside options for states seeking reform.

There are several reasons why the League failed to attain universality. The League aspired to become a collective security mechanism, displacing traditional security arrangements such as alliances, spheres of influence, and the balance of power. However, this put the institution in direct competition with alternative security mechanisms that oftentimes possessed greater military capabilities and flexibility. These served as credible outside options vis-à-vis the League.[7] In addition, the League was beset with several internal imbalances that displeased its member states. For powerful members, the most problematic were the co-equal status of the Council and the League, which underrepresented the voting power of powerful states, and the interested-party principle, which led to a loss of say over issues most fundamental to a country's geostrategic interests. Underdeveloped states, which were structurally overrepresented, also had reasons to be dissatisfied with their terms of participation in the League, as the financial burdens of participation – membership dues and the costs of sending delegations to Geneva – loomed large. Consequently, the League never attained anything close to universality of membership, and major geopolitical powers were consistently absent from its ranks: this limited the organization's ability to play an effective legitimization or informational role. As predicted by the theory, the combination of attractive outside options and rules that failed to reflect underlying interests and power relationships led to frequent abstention and outright exit by dissatisfied states, particularly the most powerful states of the era.

---

[7] For example, a crucial reason for US abstention from the League was views among Republican congressional representatives that the Monroe Doctrine, which sought to limit foreign intervention in affairs of the American continent, was a superior mechanism for guaranteeing US security interests than the League, which could facilitate European meddling in the Americas and divert US armed forces abroad. See, for example, Henry Cabot Lodge, "Senate Speech Opposing the League of Nations," February 28, 1919.

The UN Security Council remedied the underrepresentation of great powers through several reforms, namely the elimination of the veto for all but the permanent five members of the Council (P5), elevation of the status of the Council vis-à-vis the Assembly, and abandonment of the interested party rule. In addition, departure was discouraged by explicitly omitting exit clauses from the UN Charter. Formally underrepresented developing countries were enticed by tying membership to foreign aid from related UN agencies – rather than incurring a financial burden, these countries now stood to benefit from participation in UN activities. This alignment of institutional rules with the underlying objectives and power relationships of members dramatically reduced the incentives for members to exit from the UN.

Along with internal rules that better reflected underlying geopolitical realities, the UN Security Council has leveraged the near-universality of UN membership to establish itself as the first-best option for the legitimization of international uses of force, particularly since the end of the Cold War.[8] This has further diminished the attractiveness of exit for members. As a consequence, compared to the League, the UN Security Council has been prone to exhibit greater path dependence in distributive outcomes. As I will show, this factor is critical in explaining the ongoing membership of an important group of dissatisfied states: large, powerful states excluded from the P5, such as Japan, India, Germany, and Brazil.

The League and the UN Security Council are useful cases from an empirical standpoint for several reasons. First, the preeminence of these institutions means that they have been subject to frequent redistributive challenges entailing the investment of considerable diplomatic and financial resources. Policymakers clearly care about the terms of representation in these institutions, and the stakes are high, in terms of both international prestige and the ability to influence the provision of international legitimization. Second, the two institutions offer numerous examples of countries threatening to exercise their outside options, and in several instances, countries carried through on their threats. This gives us an opportunity to carefully examine the relationship between exit and institutional change across a large number of instances involving a diverse set of countries. Third, because the UN succeeded the League with no overlap, we can examine over-time variation in key variables of interest and how they affected the course of institutional change.

---

[8] E.g., see discussion in Voeten 2008.

However, simultaneous variation is a limitation of the empirical analysis in this chapter: many things changed as the League gave way to the UN – among other things, membership composition, the global balance of power, international norms, and the advent of nuclear weapons. Compared to preceding chapters, the comparison of the League and the UN Security Council provides less direct leverage to empirically isolate the impact of my key explanatory variables on institutional change. I will therefore focus on evaluating the proposed causal mechanisms through an analysis of bargaining patterns and outcomes throughout the history of each institution. In addition, the plausibility of several alternative explanations will be considered at the end of the chapter.

The remainder of this chapter will proceed as follows. I will first characterize the policy areas of the League and the UN Security Council. Second, I will present three case studies of threatened use of outside options in the League: Costa Rica, the first country that departed from the League; Brazil and Spain, two countries that threatened exit over distributive conflict in the Council; and Japan, which walked out of the League after failing to secure a de facto veto over the disposition of Manchuria. The cases illustrate the attractiveness of outside options in the League and the limitations of the internal rules that made it difficult to respond to the demands of dissatisfied states. I will then consider how the planners of the UN sought to remedy these shortcomings, and examine three cases where threats of outside options were used in distributive conflicts over the Security Council: the Soviet boycott, the "Uniting for Peace" resolution, and Indonesia's formal departure from the UN. An analysis of UN Security Council reform efforts and a brief discussion will follow.

POLICY AREAS OF THE LEAGUE AND UN SECURITY COUNCIL

In this chapter, I will focus attention on the principal executive organs of the League and the UN. In the League, executive authority was shared in parallel between the Assembly and the Council. The League Charter contained identical language in regards to each organ's core responsibilities: "[The Assembly / The Council] may deal at its meetings with any matter within the sphere of action of the League or affecting the peace of the world."[9] The Council was not to be considered "as an upper

---

[9] *The Covenant of the League of Nations*, 1924, Article 3 and Article 4.

chamber" or "as invested with the executive" power.[10] In practice, each organ formally agreed to give deference on issues that first came to the attention of the other.[11] The Council generally took up matters of pressing importance that required immediate action, as the Assembly only convened annually, while the Council met about four to six times a year. On the other hand, when both organs were meeting concurrently, the Assembly was considered the higher authority, and the Council could transfer difficult questions to the Assembly as it did on many crucial decisions such as the Manchurian question in 1933, which led to Japan's exit from the League.[12] For convenience, I will refer to the Assembly and the Council of the League as simply "the League" in the subsequent text.

In the UN, the principal executive organ is the Security Council, as indicated in Article 24 of the UN Charter: "In order to ensure prompt and effective action by the United Nations, its Members confer on the Security Council primary responsibility for the maintenance of international peace and security, and agree that in carrying out its duties under this responsibility the Security Council acts on their behalf."[13] Unlike the League, the General Assembly (GA) is explicitly given an advisory role on geopolitical issues, with provisions to "make recommendations" and "call the attention" of the Security Council to "questions relating to the maintenance of international peace and security."[14] Furthermore, unsolicited recommendations from the Assembly are forbidden once the Security Council is actively considering a dispute or situation.[15] As discussed below, the GA's role was elevated temporarily in the 1950s, but it has since largely receded back into irrelevance.

The policy areas of the League and UN Security Council are somewhat tricky to delineate compared to the economic and technical institutions examined earlier in this book. This reflects several complicating factors. First, these are institutions at least partially founded on aspiration, and the stated goals of the institutions do not necessarily reflect their de facto roles in international relations. Second, to an important degree, the institutions were designed to be transformative, reshaping the fundamental nature of their policy areas. This differs from institutions set up to

---

[10] Myers 1935, 37–40.   [11] Spencer 1930, 6-7.   [12] Burkman 2008, 171–172.
[13] *Charter of the United Nations*, Article 24, Section 1.
[14] *Charter of the United Nations*, Article 10–17.
[15] "While the Security Council is exercising in respect of any dispute or situation the functions assigned to it in the present Charter, the General Assembly shall not make any recommendation with regard to that dispute or situation unless the Security Council so requests." *Charter of the United Nations*, Article 12.

facilitate cooperation over policy issues with exogenously given characteristics. Third, legitimacy, which is inherently subjective and challenging
to measure, plays an important role in understanding the policy areas of
the League and UN Security Council.[16] In this section, I will rely on
existing scholarly work to characterize the de facto policy areas and the
role of legitimacy in each institution.

Collective Security

The League of Nations differs from many other international organizations, in that it was not created to manage a particular set of policy
problems, but rather to fundamentally transform the nature of a policy
area. The League was founded on the principle and language of *collective
security*. As defined by Inis Claude Jr.:

> Collective security was the name given by the planners of a new world order after
> World War I to the system for maintenance of international peace that they
> intended as a replacement for the system commonly known as the balance of
> power. The new system as they envisaged it involved the establishment and
> operation of a complex scheme of national commitments and international mech-
> anisms designed to prevent or suppress aggression by any state against any other
> state, by presenting to potential aggressors the credible threat and to potential
> victims of aggression the reliable promise of effective collective measures, ranging
> from diplomatic boycott through economic pressure to military sanctions, to
> enforce the peace.[17]

In effect, the aspiration of the League was to transform a highly competitive policy area, in which international peace and security had been (not
very successfully) maintained by competing alliances and the balance of
power, into one dominated by a single international institution. The
League was in effect the first major attempt by statesmen to create an
international institution that would artificially monopolize its policy area.

In the ideal form, a collective security institution faces essentially no
competition. Collective security was proposed as an organizing principle
of international relations based on the threat of retaliation by "an overwhelming collection of restraining power assembled by the mass of
states," in contrast to the competitive dynamics of the balance of power
system.[18] As such, "a collective security system demands substantial
universality of membership."[19] By definition, a collective security

---

[16] Hurd 2008. [17] Claude Jr. 1984, 247. [18] Ibid., 247. [19] Ibid., 256.

organization contemplates no meaningful competition, except to the limited extent that an occasional miscreant engages in aggression.

However, as a practical matter, neither the League nor the UN Security Council has ever functioned as a collective security organization in this ideal form. Neither institution has been able to muster overwhelming deterrent force, the kind of which would be necessary to forestall armed aggression by the great powers, and both institutions have existed alongside myriad traditional security arrangements such as alliances, doctrines, informal guarantees, and threats of unilateral military action.

A key practical shortcoming for the collective security ideal was the reluctance of member states to make a priori commitments of their military forces for the purpose of deterring and punishing aggression. The League founders aspired in the abstract to design an institution that could function as a collective security mechanism, and the League acted on several occasions in a limited manner consistent with this mandate, for example by imposing economic sanctions in response to the Italian invasion of Abyssinia in 1935. However, with non-universal membership and without the commitment of military forces by its powerful members, League sanctions proved largely ineffectual.[20]

In effect, the League aspired to monopolize a policy area that is by its nature highly competitive. For the purposes of guaranteeing national security and sovereignty, large, powerful states do not have strong incentives to pursue universality: a small number of allies, or even unilateral action, can be more attractive, particularly when obtaining consensus among a large number of countries is cumbersome or costly. Analogously, weaker states can seek security by aligning themselves with the more powerful or by maintaining neutrality. The League lacked a mechanism to forestall such competition, akin to predatory pricing in the private sector.

The UN Security Council fundamentally suffers from analogous problems as a collective security organization. With limited, partial exceptions enabled by special circumstances, such as the Korean War and the Persian Gulf War, the UN Security Council has not come close to the collective security ideal articulated by early proponents of the League. On the other hand, the Security Council has been somewhat more successful in establishing itself in two related policy areas: limited enforcement of the peace through peacekeeping missions, and the legitimization of international uses of force.

[20] Housden 2012, 106.

Peacekeeping

The UN Security Council has authorized sixty-eight peacekeeping operations since 1948, with a sharp increase in activity since the end of the Cold War.[21] Peacekeeping operations are best characterized as a public good: although all states stand to benefit from the maintenance of peace and order, each individual state has incentives to free ride on the efforts of others.[22] As such, the policy area characteristics of peacekeeping operations are analogous to collective action. There is an imperative for universality in an aspirational sense, in order to ensure equitable contributions and discourage free riding. However, individual states do not face strong incentives to remain within a universalistic framework: the optimal outcome is to uniquely abstain from an otherwise effective institution that delivers global public goods. For these reasons, peacekeeping operations are unlikely to limit the attractiveness of outside options for member states.

Legitimization of International Uses of Force

More interesting is the UN Security Council's role as a source of international legitimization. As Inis Claude Jr. defined it:

> While statesmen have their own ways of justifying their foreign policies to themselves and their peoples, independently of external judgments, they are well aware that such unilateral determinations will not suffice. They are keenly conscious of the need for approval by as large and impressive a body of other states as may be possible, for multilateral endorsement of their positions – in short, for collective legitimization.[23]

Since the end of the World War II, the Security Council has facilitated cooperation by acting as a source of collective legitimization.[24] This role has become particularly salient with the end of policy paralysis associated with the Cold War, although US intervention during the Korean War can be interpreted in a similar light.[25] In effect, the UN Security Council serves as a mechanism to signal strong international consensus for or against the actions of a state or set of states, either by serving as a focal point or by providing reliable information about the preferences of the international

---

[21] As of November 2013. "Peacekeeping Factsheet," United Nations, www.un.org/en/peace keeping/resources/statistics/factsheet.shtml
[22] E.g., see Bennett, Lepgold, and Unger 1994.　　[23] Claude Jr. 1966, 370.
[24] Claude Jr. 1984, 270.　　[25] Dunbabi 2014, 177.

community.[26] This role draws on the Security Council's position as an organization representing the universe of states, but sidesteps its major shortcoming: the lack of commitment from members to carry out the Council's wishes. Collective legitimization clearly benefits from universality. Universality increases the ability of an institution to claim that its decisions represent the views and norms of the international community as a whole, and it also helps convey information about the state of international opinion that may be useful in generating domestic support for action.[27]

Collective legitimization and universality are mutually self-reinforcing. Universality enhances an institution's ability to legitimate, and in turn, the opportunity to utilize collective legitimization provides strong incentives to remain in an institution. In effect, collective legitimization is subject to network effects: the value of legitimization to a given state is directly dependent on the number of other states participating. However, for several reasons, these network effects do not constrain outside options to the same degree as an institution such as the Internet Corporation for Assigned Names and Numbers (ICANN). First, by its nature, collective legitimization is only forthcoming if the collective can reach a common judgment. When disagreements cannot be resolved among the universe of states, leaders seeking collective legitimization may turn to second-best solutions, that is, smaller groupings of like-minded states. In effect, the UN Security Council is akin to a global internet that frequently shuts down and becomes unavailable: although limited alternatives such as regional or country-specific networks may be less preferable ceteris paribus, they are better than nothing if the most attractive network is down. Second, collective legitimization depends primarily on numbers, is not exclusive, and does not require sophisticated technical or financial capabilities. Hence, barriers to entry can be considered relatively low. As a practical matter, the United States has often repurposed existing institutions set up for different goals, such as the North Atlantic Treaty Organization (NATO) and the Arab League, as second-best sources of collective legitimization.

Compared to the UN, the League consistently suffered from limited membership, which constrained its appeal as a potential source of legitimacy or information. For example, when Japan left the League in 1933, the institution lacked representation from, among others, the United

---

[26] Hurd 2002; Voeten 2005; Thompson 2006.   [27] Thompson 2006.

States, the Union of Soviet Socialist Republics (USSR), Brazil, and Argentina. Combined with problematic institutional rules that I discuss below, this made exit an attractive option for many members, and exit further reduced the utility of the institution.

The UN Security Council does not possess a monopoly over international legitimization. I will discuss potential competition from the General Assembly later in the chapter. The Unites States has also sought to leverage support from other organizations as second-best options, most prominently NATO, to legitimate action in conflicts such as the Kosovo intervention of 1998–1999.[28] However, ceteris paribus, a country seeking legitimization would surely prefer UN Security Council authorization to the support of a limited-membership organization such as NATO or the Arab League, which in turn would be preferred to unilateral action.[29] The status of the Security Council as the most-preferred option for legitimization places limits on the attractiveness of exit for member states. The nature of future international crises is uncertain, as is the likelihood that Security Council approval will be forthcoming for a particular contingency. As such, countries choosing to leave the Security Council entirely sacrifice expected utility in several respects: 1. Giving up the opportunity to utilize the first-best option for legitimization in future conflicts; 2. Losing the ability to shape and influence future decisions over international legitimization; and 3. Facing the risk that antagonistic countries will use the Security Council to legitimate hostile actions.

As I will discuss in the case studies, the architects of the UN Security Council have also succeeded in erecting modest barriers against potential competition. The UN Charter contains no formal provisions for exit, an intentional omission by planners seeking to prevent states from using the threat of exit to obtain leverage over the organization as so many had done vis-à-vis the League. In addition, as the UN system has grown and incorporated an expanding number of institutions, the credibility of exit threats have diminished, particularly for developing countries that depend on UN institutions for financial support: as the Indonesian case will illustrate, attempting to influence the Security Council by exercising exit can jeopardize aid flows from related UN agencies. In combination, these factors have mitigated the attractiveness of exit vis-à-vis the UN Security Council compared to the League.

---

[28] Voeten 2001.   [29] This is consistent with the preference ordering in Ibid.

DISTRIBUTIVE CONFLICT IN THE LEAGUE

I will begin with an examination of distributive conflict in the League. As the preceding discussion illustrates, the League was established under the principle that it would serve as an artificial monopoly concerning matters of international peace and security. However, the institution had no mechanism to forestall competition, and states faced few disincentives when pursuing more traditional arrangements to guarantee their security, such as alliances and unilateral action. The League faced particularly severe competition from traditional security arrangements in regions outside of Europe, where League intervention was either precluded by the Covenant or geopolitical realities.

This ease of exit was compounded by important distributive imbalances and inflexibilities in the League's governance structure. As I will illustrate below, distributive outcomes were not completely inflexible in the League: the Council was reformed on several occasions to accommodate the demands of disgruntled states. However, given the relatively weak position of the Council within the institution, these reforms did not sufficiently remedy imbalances in the League's structure. In particular, the League underrepresented the interests of the great powers by adopting a strict one-country-one-vote unanimity rule and placing the Assembly on de jure co-equal status alongside the Council. Furthermore, the League abided by the "interested party rule," whereby countries with a direct stake in an ongoing dispute or conflict lost their voting rights on the matter completely. In effect, the League was an institution with relatively rigid institutional rules that were also heavily tilted against the most powerful states of the era.

The combination of attractive outside options and rigid, unbalanced representation led to the outcome predicted by the theory: frequent exit. This is illustrated in Table 8.1, which lists episodes of exit from the League and United Nations. On average, about one country left the League per year during the life of the organization. In comparison, only Indonesia has voluntarily withdrawn from the United Nations since the organization's inception in 1945, and it rejoined within a year of exit. Exit from the League was especially prevalent among major powers of the era – aside from Japan, Germany, and Italy, the United States abstained from participation and the USSR only joined for five years before being expelled – and countries outside of Europe, especially Latin American countries.

TABLE 8.1   *Episodes of Voluntary Exit from the League of Nations and United Nations*[30]

Year	Countries
	League of Nations
1925	Costa Rica
1926	Brazil, Spain (withdrawal rescinded)
1933	Japan, Germany
1935	Paraguay
1936	Guatemala, Honduras, Nicaragua
1937	Italy, Salvador
1938	Chile, Venezuela
1939	Hungary, Peru, Spain
1940	Romania
1942	Haiti
	United Nations
1965	Indonesia

Costa Rica

Although the most infamous instances of countries storming out of the League involve the Axis Powers in the 1930s, the first country to formally exit was actually Costa Rica. Costa Rica had several reasons to be dissatisfied about the League. First, although Costa Rica, along with other Latin American countries, had seen the League as a potential counterweight to the United States in the Americas, US non-membership had rendered this idea moot.[31] In addition, the United States had pressed for the inclusion of Article 21 in the League Covenant, which stated that "Nothing in this Covenant shall be deemed to affect the validity of international engagements, such as treaties of arbitration or regional understandings like the Monroe doctrine, for securing the maintenance of peace."[32] Since the Monroe Doctrine considered any external intervention in North or South America an act of aggression, Article 21 arguably made the League irrelevant for the Americas.

The Costa Rican government also viewed the financial costs of participation in the League as excessively burdensome. For a small, poor country in the era of steamships, sending a formal delegation to the Assembly

---

[30] Source: van Ginneken 2006, 217–218; Involuntary exit, such as annexations and expulsion, are omitted.

[31] Leonard 2011, 97.   [32] The Covenant of the League of Nations, 1921, Article 21.

annual meetings was a nontrivial affair. Even Japan, which was a major power at the time, had urged Assembly meetings to be held biennially or triennially to mitigate the costs of sending high-ranking government personnel on months-long trips to Geneva.[33] In addition, Costa Rica felt that League dues, though already reduced, remained excessively burdensome for underdeveloped, small countries.[34]

The impotence of the League in the Americas was underscored during Costa Rica's brief border conflict with Panama in 1922. Although both belligerents were members of the League and communicated by telegram with the Council and Secretariat during the conflict, the League held back and allowed the United States to intervene diplomatically to settle the dispute.[35] The Costa Rican delegation to the League was further incensed when, in 1924, the Assembly passed a resolution allowing the Secretary General "to make representation," or official complaints, to Latin American countries in regards to their dues in arrears.[36] In December of 1924, the Costa Rican delegation sent a letter to the Secretary General announcing its intention to withdraw from the League. The letter included a check for $18,677 covering back dues for the years 1921–1924.[37]

The League attempted to persuade Costa Rica to return, but the League's irrelevance in the Americas and the financial burden of participation proved to be a continuing sticking point. The League had adopted an ambiguous position regarding the applicability of the Monroe Doctrine to its activities in the Americas. In 1928, as a condition of returning to the League's ranks, Costa Rica demanded that the institution clarify its interpretation of the Monroe Doctrine.[38] In reply, the League indicated that the Monroe Doctrine was outside of its scope and "that such a regional understanding was not within the power of the League to modify or expand."[39] Within League circles, this interpretation was understood as not necessarily precluding Latin American countries from taking up their disputes with the League.[40] However, the answer was unsatisfactory for Costa Rica, and the country never returned to the League's ranks.

---

[33] Burkman 2008, 116.   [34] Burns 1935, 44.   [35] Levermore 1922, 41–43.

[36] Burns 1935, 44.

[37] *Reading Eagle*, "Costa Rica, Sore at Critics, Quits League," January 22, 1925.

[38] "Costa Rica Asks League's View of Monroe Doctrine: Interpretation Requested before It Decides on Membership Question," *The Christian Science Monitor*, August 15, 1928.

[39] "Monroe Doctrine Is Beyond League," *The Miami News*, September 9, 1928.

[40] "League of Nations Refuses to Rule on the Monroe Doctrine," *Associated Press*, September 2, 1928.

Costa Rica's exit from the League underscores the failure of the League to preclude outside options despite its mandate as a collective security mechanism. Although the League's authority in theory extended to all corners of the world, the institution was largely powerless in the Americas. The Monroe Doctrine, backed by the threat of US force, was the preeminent security mechanism for the region, and the doctrine precluded intervention by the League. Costa Rica sought to make its membership in the League more valuable by making the institution a plausible counterweight to US influence and by minimizing its financial contributions. When these conditions were not met, the country exited the League.

As a small state in an institution organized according to principles of unanimity, Costa Rica was structurally overrepresented in the League. However, the country's primary concern and source of dissatisfaction was the financial burden of participation. The proximate cause of exit was $5,000 in annual dues (about $70,000 in 2013 US dollars), compounded by the costs of sending annual delegations to Geneva. Prior to the advent of economic foreign aid, the League had no effective means with which to address this source of discontent. Hence, the structure of the League managed to simultaneously alienate its powerful members, who were underrepresented in terms of voting rights, and its weakest, who were primarily concerned about budgetary inequities.

Contestation over the League Council

When the League of Nations was established in 1920, there were four permanent members in the Council: France, Italy, Japan, and the United Kingdom. Three minor Allies of World War I – Belgium, Brazil, and Greece – received nonpermanent seats, along with Spain. The Second Assembly adopted a resolution concerning the procedures for electing nonpermanent members: nonpermanent members would be elected for a period of three years, with a third of them renewed each year. Retiring members would not be eligible for reelection until after three years.[41] The number of nonpermanent seats would be expanded to six. Several states objected to this arrangement. Foremost among them were Brazil and Spain. Brazil saw itself as a plausible candidate for a permanent seat as the largest League member from the Americas. Spain still fashioned itself a great

[41] Howard-Ellis 1928,139–140.

power despite losing most of its colonial possessions over the course of the nineteenth century.

The signing of the Locarno Treaties with Germany in November 1925 set up a major clash over the Council's composition. During the treaty negotiations, Germany promised to join the League in exchange for a permanent seat on the Council: Germany sought international recognition for its resurrection as a major power alongside Britain, Italy, Japan, and France. While many League members supported German membership, some states – namely Spain, Brazil, and Poland – objected on the grounds that they also deserved permanent status.

Spain felt entitled to a permanent seat as a former great power and a neutral nation. Spain also claimed to offer "cultural and moral leadership of the Latin American nations."[42] Spain warned early on that if it were not given a permanent seat, it would oppose Germany's entry and consider withdrawing from the League. Brazil argued that it was larger in area than the United States[43] and the greatest American power that remained in the League. Brazilian representatives reasoned that the American continent must be represented with a permanent seat on the Council, and made it clear that they would veto Germany's entry if their demands were not met. Poland argued that it could more effectively settle its disputes with Germany if given a permanent seat on the Council.

For its part, Germany declared it would oppose any changes to Council membership prior to its entry. Germany asserted that its agreement with the Locarno powers was predicated on the composition of the Council being unchanged from the status quo in November 1925. If the Council was altered in a way that would "diminish the importance and political effectiveness of her position and emphasize the 'Allied' element in that body,"[44] Germany would abstain from membership.

In March of 1926, the Assembly convened in an attempt to reconcile these contradictory objectives. The United Kingdom proposed a plan that would grant Spain a permanent seat in the Council while excluding Poland and Brazil. No additional changes in the Council would be made prior to German entry.[45] Predictably, Brazil and Poland raised vocal objections. The Brazilian delegation in particular refused to accept any plan that granted Germany a permanent seat without also giving Brazil equal status. From the Brazilian perspective, any plan that gave an additional seat to a European country was unacceptable without a new

---

[42] Ibid., 143.   [43] Note that this was true prior to the statehood of Alaska in 1959.
[44] Howard-Ellis 1928, 144.   [45] Scott 1974, 138.

permanent seat representing the Americas. The delegates had two choices: they could put the question to a vote and see it vetoed by Brazil, or they could adjourn and postpone the decision. Unable to come to a compromise, the Assembly adjourned. The League's failure to reach a workable compromise damaged its reputation, and the episode was seen as a fiasco.[46]

Before adjourning, the Assembly created a special committee to deal with the question of Council membership. The permanent and nonpermanent members of Council – France, the United Kingdom, Italy, Japan, Belgium, Brazil, Czechoslovakia, Spain, Sweden, and Uruguay – along with Germany, Argentina, Poland, and China, were appointed to the committee. Lord Robert Cecil of the United Kingdom dominated the committee's proceedings and proposed a draft plan. The committee proposal would expand the Council by four seats to fourteen: one new permanent seat would go to Germany, and three new seats would be nonpermanent. Elections would occur every three years, during which three out of nine nonpermanent members would retire. Crucially, a retiring state could become eligible again with two-thirds supermajority support in the Assembly.[47] The plan essentially foresaw the creation of "semi-permanent" seats, contingent on states being able to secure an Assembly supermajority. The three new semi-permanent seats were intended for Brazil, Spain, and Poland. Although Poland was willing to accept the compromise, Spain and Brazil remained dissatisfied. Spain resisted making its Council membership contingent on Assembly support, and Brazil would accept nothing short of outright permanent membership.

The committee adjourned, and efforts continued to convince Brazil and Spain to accept the compromise proposal. These efforts ultimately proved fruitless. At the June 1926 meeting of the Council, Spain announced it would exit from the League because it was unwilling to accept nonpermanent status in the Council. However, Spain agreed to ratify the compromise proposal prior to its departure.[48] Despite diplomatic pressure, Brazil also opted to withdraw from the League. The Brazilian delegation announced that, "It must be recognized how odious becomes the exclusion of America from representation by one of its States, in the permanent framework of the Council, in view of the fact that the privilege of such a representation is accorded to the other continents."[49]

---

[46] Ibid., 141.   [47] Howard-Ellis 1928, 145.   [48] Scott 1974, 151.
[49] Edwards 1929, 144.

Spain eventually rescinded its decision and returned to the League in 1928, while Brazil never returned.

This brief overview of contestation over the League Council illustrates the pervasive use of outside options as bargaining leverage. The threats were not entirely ineffectual: the dissatisfied states – Brazil, Poland, and Spain – though ultimately denied permanent membership on the Council, secured a compromise solution in which they would acquire semi-permanent status. However, this compromise solution was considered unacceptable by Brazil and Spain, which deemed that exit from the institution was preferable to semi-permanent status. This pattern of contestation contrasts sharply with more recent tussles over the UN Security Council, which will be discussed later in this chapter.

The Exit of Japan

On September 18, 1931, a bomb explosion triggered fighting between Chinese troops and Japanese guards on the South Manchurian Railway.[50] The Japanese Kwantung Army occupied the nearby city of Mukden the next morning and expanded the fighting into a large portion of South Manchuria. On September 21, 1931, China brought Japanese military actions to the League's attention, invoking Article 11 of the Covenant.[51] The next day, the Council discussed the Sino–Japanese dispute and urged "the Chinese and Japanese Governments to refrain from any action which might aggravate the situation"[52] and noted that the Council would work "in consultation with the Chinese and Japanese representatives, to find adequate means of enabling the two countries to withdraw troops immediately."[53] Japanese delegates asserted that their country had no designs for territorial conquest: the Japanese army was simply guarding the South Manchurian Railway to protect Japanese interests and citizens.[54]

---

[50] Burkman 2008, 166.

[51] Article 11 stated that. "Any war or threat of war, whether immediately affecting any of the Members of the League or not, is hereby declared a matter of concern to the whole League, and the League shall take any action that may be deemed wise and effectual to safeguard the peace of nations. In case any such emergency should arise the Secretary General shall on the request of any Member of the League forthwith summon a meeting of the Council. It is also declared to be the friendly right of each Member of the League to bring to the attention of the Assembly or of the Council any circumstance whatever affecting international relations which threatens to disturb international peace or the good understanding between nations upon which peace depends."

[52] Burkman 2008, 167.   [53] Ibid., 167.   [54] Ibid., 167.

The Council continued consultations as Japanese military actions expanded. In early 1932, Japanese forces entered Qiqihar and proceeded to invade Jinzhou and Northern Manchuria, occupying about 200,000 square miles of Chinese territory. After riots took place in Shanghai, Japanese warships were dispatched to the city and made onerous demands. The escalating conflict in Shanghai caused Japan to rapidly lose the sympathies of Western states, which had henceforth been somewhat ambivalent about Japanese prerogatives in Manchuria.[55]

As the conflict escalated, Japan pushed aggressively to promote a legal interpretation of the League Covenant that would minimize League interference over its actions in East Asia. Japanese delegates were essentially arguing in favor of a great power veto over core national interests. Yosuke Matsuoka, the head of the Japanese delegation to the League, made it clear that his country considered the Manchurian question a fundamental issue of national security and that compromise was impossible:

"It is true that international peace can be secured only upon the basis of mutual concessions. There are, however, with every nation, certain questions so vital to its existence that no concession or compromise is possible. The Manchurian problem is one of them. It constitutes such a problem to the nation of Japan. It is regarded by our people as a question of life and death."[56]

Matsuoka also asserted that no great power would accept international meddling over an area considered so vital to its national interests:

Again, the Draft Report makes an attempt to establish a measure of international control over Manchuria, where there has been and is no such control ... What justification is there for such an attempt on the part of the League of Nations? I cannot see. Would the American people agree to such control over the Panama Canal Zone? Would the British people permit it over Egypt? ... In this connection, let me state clearly once and for all that the Japanese people will, for reasons too patent for me to feel it necessary to explain, oppose any such attempt in Manchuria.[57]

Japan also emphasized its unique position as the preeminent regional power in East Asia, which meant League action against Japan would be

---

[55] Burton 1975, 296.

[56] Yosuke Matsuoka, "Address Delivered by Yosuke Matsuoka, Chief Japanese Delegate, at the Seventeenth Plenary Meeting of the Special Assembly of the League of Nations," February 24, 1933.

[57] Yosuke Matsuoka, "Address Delivered by Yosuke Matsuoka, Chief Japanese Delegate, at the Seventeenth Plenary Meeting of the Special Assembly of the League of Nations," February 24, 1933.

ineffectual: unilateral Japanese action was a credible outside option. Along these lines, Japanese delegates asserted that the Japan-Manchukuo relationship fell under Article 21, which exempted regional understandings akin to the Monroe Doctrine from the Covenant.[58]

Finally, Japanese diplomats explicitly threatened to exit from the League in the event that its demands were not met. On December 8, 1932, Matsuoka made an announcement to the media that they should prepare their cameras "in case I am historically obliged to withdraw from the Assembly."[59] On February 1, 1933, a spokesman of Japanese Foreign Minister Uchida said, "We are not hopeful that the league will accept our terms ... If they are refused, publication of a report by the league council as provided for in the covenant is inevitable. The nature of that report will determine whether Japan shall withdraw from the league."[60] On February 13, 1933, the Japanese government made its threat of exit explicit, delivering a decree to Geneva in the name of the Emperor. The decree made it clear that Japan would find the recognition of Chinese sovereignty over Manchuria unacceptable and stated that, "With deep regret, Japan will withdraw from the League of Nations if necessary."[61]

The League had neither the desire nor the flexibility to accommodate Japanese demands. Rather than carving out an exception for great powers, the League abided by its founding principles by adopting a legalistic approach, relying on expert interpretation of international law to determine the merits of the dispute. Particularly contentious was the question of which Articles of the Covenant should apply to the Sino–Japanese dispute. The Chinese government had invoked Article 10 and 15 of the League Covenant.[62] Japan instead pushed to resolve the matter under Article 11. The Japanese delegation argued that Article 15 did not

---

[58] Burkman 2008, 173.   [59] Lu 2002, 94.

[60] "Japan Drafts Terms on Which It Will Stay in League of Nations; Withdrawal Probable," *Associated Press*, February 1, 1933.

[61] "Japanese Emperor Authorizes His Nation to Leave League," *International News Service*, February 13, 1933.

[62] Article 10: "The Members of the League undertake to respect and preserve as against external aggression the territorial integrity and existing political independence of all Members of the League. In case of any such aggression or in case of any threat or danger of such aggression the Council shall advise upon the means by which this obligation shall be fulfilled."; Article 15, Paragraph 1: "If there should arise between Members of the League any dispute likely to lead to a rupture, which is not submitted to arbitration or judicial settlement in accordance with Article 13, the Members of the League agree that they will submit the matter to the Council. Any party to the dispute may effect such submission by giving notice of the existence of the dispute to the Secretary General, who will make all necessary arrangements for a full investigation and consideration thereof."

apply in this case because it was for the "final means of redress between members of the League,"[63] and asked that the Council continue to examine the situation under Article 11. Crucially, if Article 10 and 15 were invoked, the interested party rule would apply, depriving Japan of its veto over the dispute under the League's unanimity rules.[64] Council president Paul-Boncour initially took the position that proceedings could continue under Article 11, while not foreclosing the applicability of other provisions of the Covenant.

Japan also argued that China was not technically "entitled to the protection of the League Covenant," pointing to the Covenant's Preamble, which stated "the high contracting parties agree to the Covenant in order to promote co-operation and to achieve peace and security by the maintenance of justice and a scrupulous respect for all treaty obligations in the dealings of organized peoples with one another."[65] The Japanese government did not consider China to be an "organized people" due to the anarchic conditions that prevailed in that country.

China also invoked paragraph 9 of Article 15,[66] asking that the Sino–Japanese dispute be referred to the Assembly, whose members overall were seen as more sympathetic to the Chinese position. In light of Japan's continued protests regarding the applicability of Article 15, the Council adopted a strictly legalistic approach, assembling a Committee of Jurists to determine the validity of China's request.[67] The Committee ultimately validated China's request to refer the dispute to the Assembly.

In March 1932, the Assembly convened to consider the Sino–Japanese dispute. Delegates adopted a resolution confirming non-recognition of territories obtained through force and agreed to continue consultations.[68] In September, the Lytton Commission, which was formed to investigate Japanese actions in China, presented its final report, condemning

---

[63] Burton 1975, 297.

[64] Article 15, Paragraph 6: "If a report by the Council is unanimously agreed to by the members thereof other than the Representatives of one or more of the parties to the dispute, the Members of the League agree that they will not go to war with any party to the dispute which complies with the recommendations of the report."

[65] Burton 1975, 299.

[66] Article 15, Paragraph 9: "The Council may in any case under this Article refer the dispute to the Assembly. The dispute shall be so referred at the request of either party to the dispute, provided that such request be made within fourteen days after the submission of the dispute to the Council."

[67] Burton 1975, 295–298.

[68] League of Nations Photo Archive, last modified October 2002, www.indiana.edu/~league/1932.htm.

Japanese actions in harsh terms. The report declared that Japan had violated Chinese sovereignty and Japanese military operations "cannot be regarded as measures of legitimate self-defense,"[69] and further concluded that Manchukuo was not established by an independence movement but rather "was only made possible by the presence of Japanese troops."[70] In December, the Assembly created the Committee of Nineteen, a mediation committee tasked with submitting final recommendations concerning the dispute.

When the Assembly convened in February 1933, Japan's position had weakened considerably due to reports that Japanese troops were advancing into Manchuria to occupy the province of Jehol. The Assembly gathered to consider the Committee of Nineteen's recommendations that Japan withdraw troops from Manchuria and "restore the country to Chinese sovereignty."[71] After the Assembly's General Commission adopted the committee report, the Assembly proceeded to a vote. The vote was 42 to 1, with only Japan dissenting. Assembly President Hymans declared that the resolution to accept the Committee of Nineteen's report was adopted unanimously, as Japan's vote was omitted on account of the interested party rule. The Japanese delegation stormed out of the building. The head of the delegation, Yosuke Matsuoka, told the United Press "that means the withdrawal of our delegation from the league ... We can no longer co-operate on this question."[72]

The Japanese foreign ministry submitted a formal statement of withdrawal to the League on March 27, 1933. The statement noted that:

Because of the profound differences of opinion existing between Japan and the majority of the League in their interpretation of the Covenant and other treaties, the Japanese government have been led to realize the existence of an irreconcilable divergence of views, dividing Japan and the League on policies of peace, and especially as regard the fundamental principles to be followed in the establishment of a durable peace in the Far East.[73]

The emphasis on differing interpretations of the Covenant refers to Japan's repeated assertions that the Manchurian incident be handled in a manner that would allow Japan to veto unfavorable resolutions related to the Manchurian issue. In effect, Japan had been attempting to transform the informal norms of the League in the direction of a great power

[69] Burkman 2008, 170. [70] Ibid., 170.
[71] Stewart Brown, "Japan Stuns World, Withdraws from League," *United Press International*, February 24, 1933.
[72] Burkman 2008, 172. [73] Ibid., 175.

veto, or at minimum, special consideration for its position in East Asia akin to the deference given to the Monroe Doctrine in Article 21. These assertions were rejected, largely because the League was founded on legalistic ideals that sought to reject the prerogatives of power politics. The Covenant made no exceptions for great powers, and it was a legal stretch to apply Article 21, which was designed to address preexisting regional arrangements, to unilateral action by Japan in East Asia. In condemning Japan, the League had followed its own internal rules meticulously, repeatedly subjecting the Manchurian case to intensive legal scrutiny. In effect, even though Japan had enjoyed significant formal advantages in the League, including a permanent seat on the Council, these advantages were insufficient to protect what Japan viewed as core national prerogatives. Japan's military strength, combined with the League's limited means, particularly in East Asia, meant that formal exit was a highly attractive option for Japan.[74]

TRANSITIONING FROM THE LEAGUE TO THE UN

The planners of the UN sought to incorporate lessons from what they perceived as the errors of League governance.[75] Somewhat ironically, foremost among these was elevating the decision-making authority of powerful states. The Allied Powers sought to remedy the internal rules of the League that had effectively underrepresented powerful states and encouraged abstention or exit. In effect, the Allied Powers of World War II – the United States, USSR, and United Kingdom – secured for themselves what Japan had failed to obtain in 1933.

Voting rules were modified to eliminate unanimity requirements. Article 18 of the UN Charter established that only a two-thirds majority vote is needed for GA resolutions. Decisions in the Security Council required a two-thirds majority along with support from all permanent members. The exclusive veto power granted to permanent members dramatically strengthened their sway over Council decisions.

Unlike the League, where unanimity was required to make amendments to the Covenant, Article 108 of the Charter allowed for

---

[74] Japanese diplomats also calculated that the League would be less likely to impose economic sanctions if Japan was no longer a member (NHK (Nihon Hosou Kyokai) 2011). However, economic sanctions were applied anyway in 1938, prompting Japan to cease residual cooperation with League organs (Ministry of Foreign Affairs (Japan) 2011, chapter 4–3).

[75] Claude Jr. 1984, 60–61.

amendments with two-thirds majorities of UN members, along with support from all permanent members of the Security Council.[76] It should be noted, however, that as a practical matter, it is not clear that the UN's rules for institutional change are more flexible than those of the League. The UN now has 193 member states, meaning a two-thirds majority requires the support of 129 states, a much larger number than the League's peak membership of fifty-eight.

The Charter also elevated the role of the Security Council vis-à-vis the GA. In the League, the Council and the Assembly had the same competence, and little effort was made to differentiate their responsibilities. As indicated earlier, the Covenant included the same description for the responsibilities of each organ with respect to issues affecting the peace of the world. In contrast, the Charter makes it clear that the Security Council was specifically in charge of the maintenance of peace and security. A party to a dispute could no longer have its case transferred to the GA, as had been the case in the League.

One of the more contentious issues leading up to the establishment of the UN was how to handle the interested party rule, which was the proximate factor that led to Japan's exit from the League. The Soviet Union expressed a strong preference in the negotiations that the interested party rule be discarded, so that the veto power of the P5 would be absolute. The United States and Britain ultimately came around to this view, removing the requirement for abstention regarding issues related to the all-important Chapter VII of the Charter, which deals with "Action with Respect to Threats of Peace, Breaches of the Peace, and Acts of Aggression."[77]

Formally, the interested party rule survived in a limited form, relating to matters concerning peaceful adjustment. Article 27, paragraph 3 of the UN charter declares that "in decisions under Chapter VI, and under paragraph 3 of Article 52, a party to a dispute shall abstain from voting."[78] Chapter VI of the Charter deals with the Pacific Settlement of Disputes, while Article 52 deals with the Pacific Settlement of Local Disputes.

In the UN's initial years, member states generally adhered to the letter of Article 27 (3). However, confusion arose regarding the interpretation of the provision. Security Council members could deem a matter to be a

---

[76] Goodrich 1947, 9–11.   [77] Claude Jr. 1984, 144–145
[78] CHAPTER V: THE SECURITY COUNCIL, Charter of the United Nations, accessed August 2, 2013, www.un.org/en/documents/charter/chapter5.shtml.

"situation" rather than a "dispute," thus rendering Article 27 and the interested party rule inapplicable. Often, it was difficult to identify whether a member state was a "party" to a dispute because many states may not be directly involved in the matter but nonetheless take an interest in the outcome.[79] Several efforts were made in the 1940s to clarify these issues as it was a time "when members [of the Security Council] were especially concerned about the precedents being established."[80] Ultimately, no consensus could be reached on the distinction between a "dispute" and a "situation," and states were left largely to their own devices.[81]

From 1946 to 1951, there were eight documented cases in which the applicability of Article 27(3) was debated.[82] Occasionally, members abstained without formally raising the issue of invoking Article 27, and some members explicitly referred to the inapplicability of Article 27 (3) to the case at hand. In several cases, states clearly violated the letter of Article 27(3): for example, on October 25, 1948, France, USSR, United Kingdom, and the United States participated in voting on the Berlin question despite their clear stake in the dispute. From the 1950s on, the requirement to abstain on account of being an interested party in peaceful disputes was largely abandoned in practice, leading to the de facto evisceration of the interested party principle.

The cumulative effect of these changes – elimination of unanimity rule, granting of veto power only to the P5, elevation of the Security Council and gutting of the interested party principle – was to dramatically enhance the sway of the most powerful countries in the decision-making structure of the UN. One conventional, crude way to quantify the voting power of a member in a political arrangement is the Shapely-Shubik Power Index.[83] The score quantifies the de facto power of players in a voting game by calculating the proportion of vote sequences in which the player is pivotal. Although the index has important shortcomings, such as failing to account for coalitions or strategic voting, it provides a reasonable first approximation for the formal voting power of members in political institutions. For present purposes, other indices produce substantively similar results.[84] Figure 8.1 depicts Shapley-Shubik indices for the permanent members of the Councils of the League and UN. Also included are two proxies for the geopolitical power of the permanent members: share of military

---

[79] Higgins 1970, 2.   [80] Blum 1993, 196.   [81] Ibid., 198.   [82] Ibid., 204.
[83] Shapley and Shubik 1954.
[84] E.g., see Penrose 1946; Banzhaf 1965; Deegan and Packel 1978; Johnson 1978.

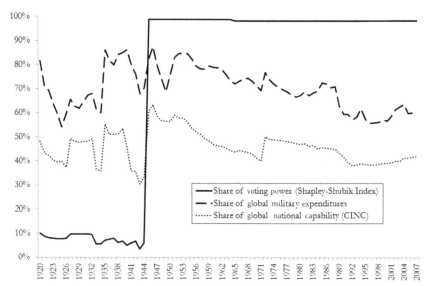

FIGURE 8.1 Shares of Voting Power and Geopolitical Power, Permanent
Members of the League & UN Councils, 1920–2007
Source: van Ginneken (2006) and Singer, Bremer, and Stuckey (1972)

expenditures and share of Composite Index of National Capability (CINC)
values among members of the institution.[85] The League data is based on
the Assembly, reflecting its status as the highest organ in the institution, and
the UN data is based on the Security Council.

Figure 8.1 shows that the relative military power of permanent members
has been relatively stable over time for both institutions: military expenditures have roughly ranged from about 60–80 percent, while CINC has
ranged between about 40–60 percent. These numbers were more volatile
for the League, which saw frequent exit and entry, but the exit of major
powers such as Germany and Japan were offset by the entry of others,
primarily the USSR. In contrast, changes in the UN Security Council are
more gradual, reflecting exogenous shifts in the composition of international
power, with the exception of the substitution of China for Taiwan in 1971.

In contrast to the relatively stable pattern of relative military power,
there is a remarkable difference in voting power across the institutions. In
the League, the voting power of permanent members was extremely low,

---

[85] Singer, Bremer, and Stuckey 1972.

generally not exceeding 10 percent. This is a consequence of the one-country-one-vote principal, unanimity rule, and the large number of countries present in the Assembly. In effect, League rules gave powerful states the same voting power as the weakest. On the other hand, voting power of the P5 in the UN has never fallen below 98 percent, reflecting the fact that the selective veto virtually assures that one of the P5 will be pivotal across possible voting sequences.[86]

For sure, voting power based on the Shapley-Shubik index overstates the differences between the two institutions. Formal voting power indices neglect informal sources of influence and coalition-building dynamics.[87] Council membership in the League certainly had some value, such as informal control over the agenda and priority over the Assembly when the latter was not in session. The index also understates the informal value of a nonpermanent seat on the UN Security Council, which provides access to information and influence over agenda setting.

On the other hand, Figure 8.1 *understates* the differences between the institutions in one crucial respect, because it does not account for variation in the salience of particular issues at stake. On average, great powers are more likely than smaller powers to have a stake in a major international dispute due to their power projection capabilities and global interests. In the League, the interested party principle meant that voting power effectively went to zero concerning issues that touched upon a country's core national interests. For the P5 of the UN Security Council, the opposite is true: veto power effectively gives countries unilateral authority to reject resolutions that threaten their core national interests. In sum, although voting power indices should be interpreted with some caution, it is abundantly clear that the UN dramatically boosted the formal authority of the permanent Council members compared to the League.

Having established a structure that tilted the scales in their favor, the P5 also sought to diminish the credibility of outside options as a bargaining device in the United Nations. UN planners felt the "possibility of withdrawal would give recalcitrant members the opportunity of securing concessions from the Organization by threatening to leave it."[88] Hence, procedures for withdrawal were omitted entirely from the Charter in order to reduce the leverage states could obtain through threats of exit.

The voting rules of the UN Security Council heavily favor P5 members. At first glance, this suggests that weaker states, which were originally

---

[86] Oneal, Russett, and Berbaum 2003.   [87] E.g., Voeten 2008; Stone 2011.
[88] Kelsen 1948, 29.

overrepresented in the League, would be deeply dissatisfied. This problem was remedied through the creation of specialized UN agencies that provided economic and technical assistance to developing countries. The aid available from these institutions effectively reversed the burdens of membership that had led underdeveloped League members, such as Costa Rica, to pursue exit. In addition, ambiguities concerning formal withdrawal from the UN have allowed status quo powers in the UN to threaten recalcitrant states with the severance of all benefits associated with UN membership, including assistance from agencies like the United Nations Development Programme (UNDP) and the Bretton Woods institutions.

Finally, the UN Security Council has also diminished the attractiveness of outside options by establishing itself as the primary source for collective legitimization in international relations.[89] The universality of the UN has been self-reinforcing, making the UN relevant in every part of the globe and enhancing its legitimacy as an organization that speaks on behalf of the international community as a whole. This contrasts with the League, which suffered from the nonparticipation of major powers, which in turn diminished the organization's relevance and ultimately undercut its legitimacy and prestige.[90] This success of the UN in achieving and maintaining near-universality has enabled the Security Council to become the first-best option for international legitimization, suppressing the attractiveness of outside options and reducing the bargaining leverage of states seeking to press redistributive claims.

DISTRIBUTIVE CONFLICT OVER THE UN SECURITY COUNCIL

There have been two notable cases where states utilized the threat of exit in order to press a distributive claim vis-à-vis the UN Security Council: The Soviet Union in 1950, and Indonesia in 1965. In both cases, the threat of exit was ineffectual and the states in question quickly reversed course.

The Soviet Boycott

The establishment of the People's Republic of China (PRC) in 1949 triggered debate over which state – the Republic of China,[91] now exiled to Taiwan, or the People's Republic, in control of the mainland – would be

---

[89] Hurd 2002; Voeten 2005; Thompson 2006.   [90] Tomuschat 1995, 79.
[91] For presentational purposes, I will refer to the Republic of China as "Taiwan" in the subsequent text.

represented in the UN. On January 10, 1950, Jacob Malik of the USSR declared, "the representative of Kuomintang . . . represents neither China nor the Chinese people."[92] He thus offered a draft resolution that would replace the Taiwanese delegation with representatives from the PRC. Malik's proposal came with an explicit threat of exit from the Council: "The delegate of the U.S.S.R will not participate in the work of the Security Council as long as the representative of the Kuomintang is not excluded from that body."[93] Malik was referring to Tsiang Tingfu, the President of the Security Council and a national of Taiwan. On January 13, 1950, the Soviet proposal to expel Taiwan was rejected with three in favor, six against, and two abstentions. As he had warned, Malik walked out of the Security Council, and representatives of the USSR and its satellite states refused to participate in further deliberations. The USSR concurrently established the World Peace Council, an international organization whose focus on global issues such as world peace, disarmament, and anti-imperialism "seemed designed to compete with the United Nations."[94]

The Soviet boycott backfired spectacularly in June 1950, when the United States succeeded in passing a series of resolutions condemning the North Korean invasion of South Korea, culminating in Resolution 84, which determined that the invasion constituted a breach of the peace and recommended that UN members furnish forces to repel the attack. Had the USSR remained on the Council, it could have exercised its veto to forestall the resolutions. Instead, the boycott allowed the United States to conduct its military operations as the leader of a multinational force operating under the legitimacy of the UN flag. The USSR realized its mistake and promptly reassumed its position in the Security Council, ready to exercise its veto aggressively.[95]

There were several factors that led the USSR to return to the Security Council, whereas many of the great powers of the League had simply walked away. A crucial motivation for the Soviet return was the legitimation function of the Security Council demonstrated during the Korean War. UN involvement in the Korean War fell far short of the collective security ideal, with the United States exerting full operational command and contributing the lion's share of forces. However, the Truman administration placed high priority on placing US forces under the UN banner to enhance the legitimacy of military intervention.[96] As Dunbabin notes,

[92] Briggs 1952, 199.   [93] Ibid., 199.   [94] Bosco 2009, 54.   [95] Pak 2000, 108–109.
[96] Bosco 2009, 57.

"UN support did much to legitimate, at home and abroad, a war in which the command, and all the crucial decisions, were taken by Americans."[97] Unlike the League, which had limited coverage in major regions of the world, the UN was truly global in scope largely due to the capability and willingness of the two superpowers to project power. In the context of the Cold War, the Soviet boycott made clear that exiting the UN would bring few benefits while ceding to one's adversary the legitimacy of UN-sanctioned interventions. Crucially, the combination of the P5 veto and abandonment of the interested party rule meant that P5 members had the ability to block any Security Council resolution at will. P5 members could deny the benefit of legitimacy to adversaries, but only if they remained within the institution. In combination, these factors have made exit highly unattractive for P5 members.

Indonesia's Exit from the UN

When Malaysia was created through the federation of Malaya and British crown colonies in Southeast Asia in September of 1964, Indonesia under Sukarno refused to recognize its existence and pursued a "policy of aggression,"[98] supporting guerilla forces to undermine the newly formed state. When Malaysia sought to join the Security Council as a nonpermanent member, Sukarno warned that Indonesia would withdraw from the UN should Malaysia be seated. These threats were ignored, and Malaysia was admitted as a member of the Council. As promised, in a letter dated January 20, 1965, the Deputy Prime Minister and Minister of Foreign Affairs of Indonesia informed the Secretary General of his country's withdrawal:

in the circumstances which have been created by colonial powers in the United Nations so blatantly against our anti-colonial struggle and indeed against the lofty principles and purposes of the United Nations Charter [the Government] felt that no alternative had been left for Indonesia but withdrawal from the United Nations.[99]

On February 26, 1965, the Secretary General replied to Indonesia's letter. The letter stated, "The position of your Government recorded therein has given rise to a situation in regard to which no express provision is made in the Charter."[100] This reflected the fact that there are no formal provisions for exit in the UN Charter. The Secretary General did

---

[97] Dunbabi 2014, 177.   [98] Schwelb 1967, 638.   [99] Livingstone 1965, 666.
[100] Ibid., 666.

not explicitly validate Indonesia's withdrawal and instead stated that Indonesia's intentions "have been noted." Neither the Security Council nor GA placed the issue on the agenda. Nonetheless, Indonesia's withdrawal was acknowledged in practice when the country's successors were elected onto committees of the Economic and Social Council.

Sukarno proposed the creation of an alternative organization to the UN, which was variously described as the New Emerging Forces Organization (NEFO) or Conference of Newly Emerging Forces (CONEFO).[101] Sukarno had fallen out with the International Olympic Committee earlier in 1962 over the politicization of the Asian Games Hosted in Jakarta. In response, Indonesia hosted the Games of New Emerging Forces (GANEFO) in 1963, intended to pose direct competition to the Olympic Games. Both efforts were actively supported by the PRC, which remained unrepresented on the UN and a nonparticipant in the Olympics due to its conflict with Taiwan.[102] Indonesia's exit caused considerable consternation at the UN, which was already reeling from internal discord over financial issues.[103] Internal assessments by US policymakers surmised that Indonesia was "pressing ahead full speed with plans to set up a rival to the United Nations known as the CONEFO," and worried that Sukarno would use Chinese technology to develop a nuclear bomb in order to attract Afro-Asian nations to the initiative.[104] However, unlike GANEFO, which was held twice and included the participation of over 4,000 athletes, CONEFO was never formally established.

On September 19, 1966, a little over a year after exiting, the Ambassador of Indonesia to the United States sent a telegram to the Secretary General informing him that the Indonesia government "has decided to resume full co-operation with the UN and to resume participation in its activities starting with the Twenty-First Session of the General Assembly."[105] The Foreign Minister of Indonesia also consulted with the Secretary General and the President of the GA. On September 29, the President of the GA informed the Assembly of Indonesia's desired to return, stating:

It would therefore appear that the Government of Indonesia considers that its recent absence from the Organization was based not upon a withdrawal from the

[101] "Sukarno May Try to Form New Nation Organization," *Associated Press*, January 4, 1965.
[102] "Sukarno Insists on Quitting U.N.," *Associated Press*, January 7, 1965.
[103] Blum 1967, 523.
[104] The George Washington University National Security Archive 1965, 274.
[105] Livingstone 1965, 668.

United Nations but upon a cessation of co-operation. The action so far taken by the United Nations on this matter would not appear to preclude this view.[106]

He then announced that given there are no objections, Indonesia would resume full participation in the activities of the United Nations. Seeing as no one objected, the representatives of Indonesia took their seats in the General Assembly, and the Foreign Minister of Indonesia thanked the President, Secretariat, and the Secretary General for "making our reparticipation in the United Nations a smooth and happy one."[107]

The proximate cause for Indonesia's rapid return to the UN was a shift in Indonesian domestic politics. Sukarno had faded from political power in Indonesia after Suharto's successful coup d'état in 1965. Indonesia's return to the UN was pursued over Sukarno's objections, despite the fact that he was still nominally president of the country. However, exit from the UN had also proven to be a disastrous course for Indonesia. Sukarno had expected widespread support for his stand against the UN and its "neocolonial" tendencies, but the move was roundly condemned by developing countries as well as the Soviet Union, resulting in diplomatic isolation. Only China, which itself had been excluded from the organization, supported Sukarno's move.[108] It became immediately clear that CONEFO would not succeed in attracting members away from the UN.[109] Only a few months after removing his country from the UN, Sukarno had privately signaled to US diplomats that he might be willing to formally recognize Malaysia if given a "pill sweetener" to "erase the humiliation and permit him a victory for international consumption."[110] In addition, Indonesia's exit from the UN had severed its access to multilateral foreign aid from UN agencies estimated to be around $50 million, exacerbating economic conditions and undermining Sukarno's hold on power.[111] A major motivation for Indonesia's return was the need to access foreign aid in light of the economic turmoil surrounding the twilight of Sukarno's rule.[112]

Indonesia's exit from the UN was nominally about the sovereign status of Malaysia. However, the backdrop for Sukarno's action was the

---

[106] Ibid., 669.   [107] Ibid., 669.   [108] Taylor 1965, 209.   [109] Ibid., 211.
[110] "Paper for Consideration at the National Security Council Meeting," May 9, 1964; as quoted in The George Washington University National Security Archive 1964, 104.
[111] "Sukarno Insists on Quitting U.N.," *Associated Press*, January 7, 1965.
[112] "Indonesia May Seek U.N. Seat Back," *Associated Press*, April 4, 1966.

nonparticipation of the PRC in the UN and Chinese attempts to under-mine the legitimacy of the organization by encouraging potential alterna-tives. This is evident from the parallel effort vis-à-vis the Olympics: China contributed the largest share of athletes to GANEFO and won the lion's share of medals in both games. Premier of China, Zhou Enlai, had encouraged Indonesia, declaring that:

The UN has committed too many mistakes ... In these circumstances, another UN, a revolutionary one, may well be set up so that rival dramas may be staged in competition with that body which calls itself the UN but which is under the manipulation of United States imperialism and therefore can only make mischief and do nothing good.[113]

Despite being the world's most populous nation and a major military power, China was unable to gain any sort of traction in proposing alternatives to the UN, and the country repeatedly sought to replace the Taiwanese delegation in the organization. This clearly illustrates the degree to which the UN succeeded in reducing the attractiveness of outside options compared to the League, which saw widespread volun-tary abstention and exit. If China had remained outside the UN indefin-itely, it seems plausible that more serious challenges along these lines could have emerged as the country developed economically and emerged as a preeminent economic and military power. The replacement of the Republic of China by the People's Republic in 1971 forestalled this possibility.

UNITING FOR PEACE AND THE 1963 SECURITY COUNCIL REFORM

As the preceding section demonstrated, threats of formal exit have been largely ineffectual vis-à-vis the UN Security Council due to institutional reforms and the achievement of near-universality, which made outright exit unattractive for most members. However, informal exit – remaining a formal member while shifting diplomatic attention elsewhere – is not precluded by these changes. In addition, because barriers to entry are relatively low for collective legitimization, it is possible for states to utilize existing institutions with sufficiently large membership as plausible alter-natives. The aggressive use of veto power by the Soviet Union after the Korean War effectively paralyzed the Security Council, rendering the

---

[113] Kent 2007, 45; See also Taylor 1965, 210.

institution irrelevant for the resolution of important international disputes. In this context, the United States pursued a form of informal exit by seeking to elevate the role of the General Assembly (GA) as a plausible alternative for collective legitimization.

In 1950, the UN General Assembly passed the "Uniting for Peace" Resolution 377(V), which asserted that the GA could circumvent the Security Council if the use of the veto led to paralysis. Specifically, the resolution stated that:

if the Security Council, because of lack of unanimity of the permanent members, fails to exercise its primary responsibility for the maintenance of international peace and security in any case where there appears to be a threat to the peace, breach of the peace, or act of aggression, the General Assembly shall consider the matter immediately with a view to making appropriate recommendations to Members for collective measures, including in the case of a breach of the peace or act of aggression the use of armed force when necessary, to maintain or restore international peace and security.[114]

The resolution arose in direct response to the Soviet Union's repeated exercise of its veto upon ending its boycott of the Security Council. US Secretary of State Dean Acheson condemned the Soviet abuse of the veto, asserting that, "We have been confronted with many and complex problems, but the main obstacle to peace ... has been created by the policies of the Soviet Union."[115] Concern about abuse of veto authority was also widespread among other members. Ambassador Belaunde of Peru echoed Acheson by stating that the "the veto has gone far beyond the purpose for which it was devised ... the veto was not a right but an obligation ... to seek unanimity."[116] During the early stages of the Cold War, the United States enjoyed strong majority support in the GA, and its decisions were not subject to a P5 veto. Hence, US policymakers sought to elevate the GA, calculating that the organ would serve as a reliable source of legitimation for US initiatives unencumbered by the Soviet veto.

The Uniting for Peace Resolution was clearly based on a "dubious reading of the charter,"[117] which foresaw no such role for the GA. However, the GA represented a plausible alternative source of international legitimization because it had an equal, if not stronger, claim to being representative of the universe of states. The United States, though not directly invoking Resolution 377(V), followed the procedures set

---

[114] UN General Assembly Resolution 377(V).   [115] Cronin and Hurd 2008, 179.
[116] Ibid., 179.   [117] Bosco 2009.

forth in the resolution to condemn Chinese participation in the Korean War in 1951.[118] In 1956, the United States secured condemnation in the GA against the French and British intervention in the Suez Crisis and the Soviet intervention in Hungary, both crises involving P5 members in which Security Council action was vetoed. These were followed by emergency GA sessions in 1958 and 1960 respectively to deal with crises in Lebanon and the Congo.[119]

Hence, by the early 1960s, the GA had emerged as a credible outside option with respect to international legitimization. This was an important reason for the only successful reform of the Security Council, which took place in 1963. Decolonization in the 1950s and 1960s, along with a US-Soviet agreement in 1955 not to block any future applications for UN membership, sharply increased the ranks of newly independent developing states in the GA.[120] This dramatically altered the composition of the institution, which had been previously dominated by Latin American and Commonwealth states sympathetic to the West. By 1963, African and Asian countries constituted a majority of membership and hence voting power in the GA.[121] In addition, developing countries founded the non-aligned movement in 1961, establishing a dominant voting bloc independent of both the US and USSR.

These factors created a unique opportunity for developing countries to exercise leverage over the UN Security Council. The GA, which had been emphasized and elevated by the US as an alternative to the paralyzed Security Council, had now come under the de facto control of unaligned developing countries. Developing countries used this leverage to effectively steamroll the P5 members, which were reluctant to expand the Security Council and dilute their own influence. The United States, United Kingdom, and France adopted a moderate stance toward Security Council expansion, supporting a limited expansion of two nonpermanent seats. This was in part to attract the sympathies of developing countries by drawing a sharp contrast with the USSR, which insisted that no reform could be possible without the inclusion of the PRC in the UN.[122]

Using their overwhelming numerical majority in the GA, developing countries pushed through Resolution 1991A, which added four nonpermanent members to the Council and allocated them according to region. The vote was 97 to 11. The USSR and France voted against the resolution, and the United States and United Kingdom abstained. Despite outright

---

[118] Cronin and Hurd 2008, 183.   [119] Binder 2006.   [120] Bourantonis 2004, 12.
[121] Ibid., 12.   [122] Bourantonis 2005, 20.

opposition from P5 members, who possessed the formal ability to veto the resolution, 1991A was ultimately ratified because the P5 feared alienating the dominant voting bloc in the GA, which had come to be seen as an influential institution. This concern was most paramount for the Republic of China, which feared that the GA would deprive it of its credentials as the sole representative of China. However, the USSR also ultimately reversed its stance and became the first P5 member to ratify 1991A out of concern that the country would be placed in "complete isolation in the UN with severe repercussions for its policies in the world organization."[123]

The 1963 reform of the Security Council reflected the circumstances of a unique period, when the GA had been promoted as a credible competitor to the Security Council. The GA acted as a source of international legitimization during several crises of the 1950s, when the Security Council had failed to act. This gave the GA a degree of legitimacy that it has not since enjoyed, and the dysfunction of the Security Council gave credence to arguments in favor of reform. However, by the end of the 1950s, the GA was transforming from an organ that reliably supported the West to an unruly body dominated by developing countries. A US National Security memo suggested that a return of authority to the Security Council would be advisable: "It is in the long-range interest of this country, as well as the USSR, that important matters such as peacekeeping go through the Security Council channel due to the present nature and composition of the General Assembly."[124] These sentiments were shared among the other P5 members, which came to an agreement to restore the primacy of the Security Council due to the increasing size and unpredictability of the GA. The credibility of the GA as a potential alternative source of international legitimization receded as its views came to be dominated by developing countries, which possessed limited power projection capabilities, and the P5 reverted to prioritizing the Security Council. These factors have limited the potential for the GA to serve as a credible outside option subsequent to the 1960s.

UN SECURITY COUNCIL REFORM PROPOSALS BY THE G4

In recent years, several countries have sought inclusion as permanent members of the UN Security Council on account of their international

---

[123] Bourantonis 2004, 24.   [124] Bosco 2009, 102.

stature. These are non-P5 major powers, such as Brazil, Germany, India, and Japan (the G4). On first inspection, it would appear that the G4 face strong incentives to bargain aggressively by threatening exit, much like the dissatisfied members of the League: these countries do not enjoy the favorable formal status of the P5, and Germany and Japan are developed countries that do not depend on foreign aid from UN agencies. The G4 have repeatedly pressed for UN Security Council reform in order to secure permanent seats for themselves, much as Brazil and Spain did vis-à-vis the League. However, despite repeated rejection of these demands, these countries have not threatened or pursued exit from the UN.

Although the collective legitimization function of the UN Security Council was largely paralyzed after the Korean War due to aggressive use of the veto by the USSR and the United States, the end of the Cold War opened up new opportunities for cooperation. This was most starkly demonstrated by Resolution 678 in 1991, which authorized the use of "all necessary means" to expel Iraqi forces from Kuwait during the Persian Gulf War. This was followed by resolutions authorizing the use of force in Somalia (1992), Haiti (1994), Rwanda (1994), Albania (1997), and East Timor (1999).[125]

Voeten points out that the United States has enhanced its bargaining leverage over the Security Council by threatening unilateral or more limited multilateral uses of force, an outside option.[126] However, no other state possesses anything approaching the global power projection capabilities of the US military or the second-order legitimacy that might be derived from the US multilateral alliance network. In fact, the G4 have generally attached high priority to the UN in their foreign policies and invested heavily in the legitimacy of the UN system through both financial and manpower contributions. G4 policymakers do occasionally refer to the possibility that the Security Council will be superseded by other institutions without reform. For example, in a speech to the GA, Ambassador Thomas Matussek of Germany stated, "One thing is clear – If the Security Council does not reform itself, there is a risk that other bodies will attempt to take its place. Such a rivalry would be detrimental to us all."[127]

However, in practice, there are few attractive multilateral alternatives to the Security Council for the G4. In recent years, Japan has proposed the

---

[125] Malone 2004, 136.   [126] Voeten 2001.
[127] Permanent Mission of Germany to the United Nations, "Statement by the Permanent Representative of Germany, H.E. Ambassador Thomas Matussek, before the 64th General Assembly of the United Nations," September 28, 2009.

"Quadrilateral Initiative," whose membership also includes Australia, India, and the United States, as well as the "Arc of Freedom and Prosperity," which encompasses democratic states on the outer rim of the Eurasian continent.[128] These initiatives may be seen as attempts to create a new source of international legitimization based on principles of democratic cooperation.[129] However, such initiatives are in nascent stages at best and hardly constitute a credible alternative to the Security Council. Germany is a member of several multilateral organizations such as the European Union (EU) and NATO, but using these as credible outside options to press for change in the Security Council is virtually impossible, since P5 members are important participants in both organizations. India and Brazil are also members of various regional and international groupings such as the Nonaligned Movement, which may confer a degree of legitimacy in limited contexts to their foreign policy proposals. However, these organizations are in most cases too narrow to serve as focal points[130] or sources of reliable information about the views of the broader international community,[131] key sources of the Security Council's legitimacy in authorizing force.

Hence, the outside options vis-à-vis the UN Security Council have been generally unattractive for the states interested in revising the status quo. For P5 members, outside options are arguably more heterogenous: the United States has a stronger network of alliances to claim legitimacy for military intervention outside the UN Security Council than China or Russia. However, as a privileged P5 member, the United States is not interested in threatening to exercise its outside option for the purpose of institutional change.

Although less onerous in theory than the unanimity rule of the League, Security Council reform still requires a high degree of consensus among UN members. Unanimity in the League required affirmative votes by fifty-eight states at most. In comparison, UN Security Council reform requires two thirds of UN membership, which now equates to the affirmative vote of 129 states, along with the unanimous support of the P5. While the UN Charter sets out a specific procedure for reform, there is no provision for periodic review or guidelines stipulating what type of states should merit inclusion on the Council. Hence, mounting a successful reform effort requires consensus-building to gather support from a plurality of GA

---

[128] Among other sources, see Aso, Taro, "Arc of Freedom and Prosperity: Japan's Expanding Diplomatic Horizons," Speech by Mr. Taro Aso, Minister for Foreign Affairs on the Occasion of the Japan Institute of International Affairs Seminar.
[129] Also see Ikenberry and Slaughter 2006.   [130] Voeten 2005.   [131] Thompson 2006.

members, a task that is often accomplished through costly checkbook diplomacy.[132] In addition, dissatisfied states must expend considerable resources justifying their status as deserving members given the ambiguous criteria for inclusion. Japan's candidacy was widely criticized for its historically limited manpower contributions to UN Peacekeeping Operations, an issue the Japanese government has sought to address through expanded participation in such efforts beginning in the 1990s.

In addition to the factors already mentioned, discussions over Security Council reform take place while the institution remains fully operative, and reform failure equates to maintenance of the status quo. While dissatisfied states must maintain costly lobbying efforts to keep reform initiatives alive, status quo states often face minimal costs as they can ultimately rely on their veto authority. Hence, status quo states can be thought of as being far more patient than dissatisfied states when it comes to efforts to redistribute authority over the UN Security Council. Dissatisfied states have weak bargaining leverage both in terms of relative patience and outside options. This means maintenance of the status quo is the most likely bargaining outcome.

Consistent with the predictions of the theoretical claims laid out in Chapter 2, UN Security Council reform has proven difficult despite repeated efforts. The only successful reform that has occurred to date is the 1963 expansion, which added four nonpermanent seats. No expansion of permanent seats has ever succeeded. Table 8.2 compares successful reforms of the Council of the League of Nations and the UN Security Council. Figure 8.2 provides a visual representation of similar information, depicting the number of nonpermanent and permanent members in the Councils of each institution. As the table shows, despite unanimity rules, brinksmanship forced the League Council to be reformed repeatedly throughout its history (either through efforts to accommodate a threatening member or adjustments necessitated by the exit of a permanent member) at the rate of one reform every 3.2 years. In comparison, reforms of the Security Council have occurred at the rate of one every sixty-seven years. Even if we include China's replacement of Taiwan as a reform of the Council,[133] the frequency would only be one every 33.5 years. This was not due to the absence of reform proposals. As Table 8.3

---

[132] For example, "Japans Opens Checkbook in Bid for Permanent Security Council Seat," *The Yomiuri Shinbun*, April 6, 2005.

[133] This was technically not a change in the composition of the membership of the Council, as the matter was considered one of credentials and settled by majority vote in the General Assembly with no countries able to exercise a veto.

TABLE 8.2 *Episodes of Successful Council Reform*[134]

Year	Details/Comments
	The Council of the League of Nations (1920–1939, 19 years)
1922	Nonpermanent seats expanded from four to six
1926	Germany admitted as permanent member, nonpermanent seats increased from six to nine, period of office for nonpermanent seats changed from one to three years
1933	Nonpermanent seats increased from nine to ten
1934	USSR admitted as a permanent member
1936	Nonpermanent seats increased from ten to eleven
1939	USSR expelled from the Council
	UN Security Council (1946–2013, sixty-seven years)
1963	Nonpermanent seats expanded from six to ten

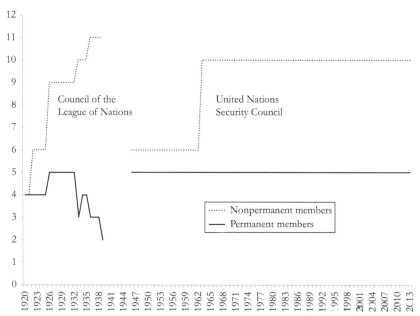

FIGURE 8.2: The Number of Nonpermanent and Permanent Members on the Councils of the League of Nations and United Nations (1920–2013).
Source: van Ginneken (2006)

shows, the UN Security Council has been subject to repeated proposals for reform since inception to date. In addition, as depicted earlier in Table 8.1, the absence of reform in the UN Security Council has not led

[134] Source: League of Nations Photo Archive 2002 and van Ginneken 2006.

TABLE 8.3 *Major Proposals Relating to Reform of the UN Security Council*

Year	Details/Comments
1956	Spanish and Latin American proposal to add two nonpermanent seats.
1963	A proposal to expand the UN Security Council's size to 15 was adopted. This is the only successful attempt to change the composition of the UN Security Council to date.
1979	Proposal to increase nonpermanent members from 10 to 14
1980	Proposal to add 6 nonpermanent members, proposed by a group of African, Asian, and Latin states
1991	Some talk of expanding the size of the permanent membership with the collapse of the Soviet Union. It was thought that USSR's seat would become vacant, but it was replaced by Russia.
1993	Launch of the Open-Ended Working Group on the Question of Equitable Representation on and Increase in the Membership of the Security Council and Other Matters Related to the Security Council
1995	Quick-fix Plan (adding Japan & Germany with veto)
1997	Razali Plan (adding 5P without veto /4NP)
2005	High-level Panel Report "For Larger Freedom" (Model A and Model B) -The G4 Resolution (adding 6P "without" veto/ 4NP) -The AU Resolution (adding 6P with veto /5NP) - The UfC Resolution (adding 10NP)
2008	Intergovernmental negotiations in the informal sessions under the General Assembly

to exit from the institution: there was far more widespread exit from the League despite accommodative changes in Council membership.

Hopes for some type of UN Security Council reform were raised from 2000 to 2004, when US Ambassador Richard Holbrooke expressed US openness to limited reform.[135] This was followed by proposals by the High-level Panel on Threats, Challenges and Change and the UN Millennium Project, culminating in a report by UN Secretary General Kofi Annan outlining two possible plans for Security Council reform.[136] However, the reform initiative stalled as Chinese protests against Japanese membership on the Security Council captured international attention[137] and US enthusiasm for reform waned.[138]

Despite repeated attempts and high-profile diplomatic efforts by some of the most influential states in the international system since the end of the

---

[135] Satoh 2001. [136] Anan 2005. [137] Weiss 2013.
[138] Personal Interviews, Ministry of Foreign Affairs Official, 2005; Ministry of Foreign Affairs Official, 2007; former Ministry of Foreign Affairs Official, 2008.

Cold War, UN Security Council reform efforts remain stalled. Negotiators point to the difficulty of achieving support from the heterogeneous group of developing states needed to secure a two-thirds majority in the GA as well as the veto-wielding P5.[139] Notably, despite these high-profile failures at securing Security Council Reform, G4 states remain committed to the UN system, and there has been virtually no talk of exit or cutting back on contributions to peacekeeping efforts or other aspects of UN operations.

Reform of the Security Council is not impossible. However, if reform materializes, it will likely be due to factors exogenous to my theory, such as normative persuasion or issue linkage. The bargaining leverage of dissatisfied states vis-à-vis status quo states is strikingly weak, and this will likely remain true unless an alternative, credible source of international legitimization, such as a Concert of Democracies, emerges.

DISCUSSION

The evolution of the League of Nations and United Nations provide evidence consistent with the theoretical predictions outlined in Chatper 2. The League of Nations was an attempt to create a collective security institution, an artificial monopoly in the policy area of international peace and security, which had traditionally been dominated by balance of power dynamics, formal and informal alliances, and unilateral action. The monopoly never materialized, and exit from the League was relatively attractive throughout its existence. The League's internal rules were fairly rigid, with one-country-one-vote rules that could not be adjusted according to power, and provisions requiring unanimous support for changes to the Covenant. Furthermore, the League was designed in a way that substantially underrepresented the interests of the most powerful member states while also imposing an unacceptable financial burden on smaller states. The one point of modest flexibility that the League could use to accommodate dissatisfied states – membership in the Council – was both controversial and insufficiently attractive given the institution's rules, such as co-equal status with the Assembly and the interested party principle. As predicted by the theory, the combination of attractive outside options and relatively rigid rules led to widespread exit despite diplomatic efforts to accommodate dissatisfied states. Abstention and exit further eroded the ability of the League to play an effective international legitimization role.

---

[139] Personal Interview, Japanese Ministry of Foreign Affairs Official, 2007.

The UN was created with an eye toward remedying many of the shortcomings of the League. Foremost among these was strengthening the position of the strongest powers in the governing structure of the institution through introduction of the selective veto, elevation of the status of the Council, and elimination of the interested party rule. Internal rules governing change remain inflexible: although unanimity was dropped in favor of a two-thirds majority rule, increase in membership means an affirmative vote from more than twice as many countries is needed for reform compared to the League. Planners of the UN sought to reduce the bargaining leverage obtainable from outside options by omitting provisions for exit from the Charter and attempting to tie membership with foreign aid from related UN agencies.

However, the competitive dynamics within the UN Security Council's policy area is also crucial. The Security Council has successfully established itself as the primary source for collective legitimization for the international use of force. Since the Council's ability to legitimate draws from its ability to claim representation of the broad, international community, the institution offers something of value to member states that is not easily obtainable from alternative unilateral, bilateral, or limited multilateral sources. This universality has been self-reinforcing: the institution is more legitimate because it is universal, which discourages exit and maintains universality. These factors make the Security Council an institution with relatively unattractive outside options and rigid rules that tilt the scales in favor of P5 members. As predicted by the theory, this has resulted in path dependence, and outright exit has been far less common in comparison to the League.

The analysis in this chapter has relied primarily on case studies in order to assess the causal mechanisms proposed by my theory. The observed bargaining behavior among states, as well as bargaining outcomes, are consistent with the theory. However, it is important to consider whether some unexamined variable might be responsible for the general observed variation in outcomes between the League and the UN Security Council. I will close this chapter by considering several plausible alternative explanations.

First, while the League operated under multipolarity, the UN has existed entirely under bipolarity and then unipolarity. Could it be that greater stability of the international system under bipolarity and unipolarity[140] has been conducive to less turbulence in the management of the primary

---

[140] Waltz 1979.

executive organ intended to address matters of international peace and security? This seems unlikely. Deliberations in the UN Security Council during and after the Cold War over conflicts such as Korea, Cuba, and Iraq, have been no less heated than comparable debates in the League. The post–World War II period has also seen major power shifts and realignments – the decline of France and the United Kingdom, the rise of China and Japan, the Sino–Soviet split, the end of the Cold War – that could have precipitated more serious contestation over the Security Council. Turbulence in the League was instigated by countries such as Brazil and Spain, which were hardly great powers, as well as minor states such as Costa Rica and Guatemala. Finally, this explanation would appear to provide limited leverage over the behavior of countries that were not deeply involved in the Cold War, such as nonaligned states.

Second, could it be that exit has become less attractive not due to policy area effects, but due to evolving international norms? It is plausible that international norms have evolved over the course of the twentieth century, strengthening the legitimacy of international institutions while reducing the legitimacy of exit. It is undeniable that the indelible image of Japanese delegates storming out of the League in 1933 makes exit from the UN a dicey proposition for contemporary dissatisfied states. Nonetheless, there is considerable evidence against the proposition that a norm against exit has developed. This is underscored by the frequent use of exit by prominent states as a means of leverage in contemporary international organizations aside from the UN Security Council. For example, the United States, United Kingdom, and Singapore ceased participation in the United Nations Educational, Scientific and Cultural Organization (UNESCO) in the 1980s over ideological conflicts,[141] and the United States, Canada, and Australia withdrew from the United Nations Industrial Development Organization (UNIDO) in the 1990s.[142] As a practical matter, norms in favor of institutions and against formal exit could be circumvented by maintaining nominal membership while investing resources in competing institutions, a strategy that G4 states have not pursued. It also seems implausible that the League would function effectively on the strengths of international norms alone if transported to the present era – the interested party principle alone would have presented tremendous problems for the United States and other major powers.

---

[141] Imber 1989.
[142] Patrick Goodenough, "U.S. May Rejoin a U.N. Agency It Once Dismissed As Ineffective," *CBS News*, 12-2-2009.

Third, to some degree, the Security Council's resilience and imperviousness to change surely reflects an element of luck. Much of the shift in the balance of international power since the end of World War II has occurred among the P5, avoiding gross disparities between representation and underlying power. This is apparent from Figure 8.1: despite the rise of countries such as Germany, Japan, and India, the P5 still control a commanding share of global military capabilities. As the Soviet Union waned, the United States and China have risen to take its place. Although the UN Security Council is clearly more prone to path dependence than the League, a major shift, such as a large movement in the global balance of power against the P5, would likely necessitate adjustments. However, based on current patterns of economic growth, such a shift is unlikely to occur for the foreseeable future.

Fourth, a notable exception to the distributive rigidity of the UN Security Council was the replacement of the representatives of the Republic of China (Taiwan) with those of the PRC (mainland China) in 1971. As I will discuss in Chapter 9, China–Taiwan competition offers an important "placebo" test for the theoretical propositions offered in this book. Because China and Taiwan engaged in zero sum competition in which the membership of one country precluded membership of the other, the impact of outside options on institutional change was suppressed: one cannot obtain bargaining leverage by threatening to exit if the topic of discussion is whether or not you will be allowed to stay. As I will illustrate in Chapter 9, the outcomes of China-Taiwan competition exhibit a distinctive empirical pattern consistent with my theoretical premises: there is no relationship between institutional change and the attractiveness of outside options across policy areas.

Finally, it is worth considering if domestic political factors were responsible for variation in bargaining patterns between the League and the UN Security Council. One conventional, widely accepted explanation for the failure of the League of Nations is the abstention of the United States, and the proximate cause for this was congressional opposition by isolationist Republicans.[143] It is undeniable that US domestic political conditions shifted dramatically between 1920 and 1945. However, it is also worth considering the counterfactual, i.e. how US domestic political opposition would have unfolded had the League incorporated internal rules akin to the UN. Notably, many Republicans in the Senate had been

---

[143] For example, Scott 1974; van Ginneken 2006; Housden 2012

willing to support a ratification of the League Treaty containing Henry Cabot Lodge's so-called "14 Reservations."[144] These reservations essentially sought to give the US unilateral freedom to reject League obligations and resist League intervention over issues central to its national interests. The League failed in the Senate because Republicans would not support ratification without Lodge's reservations, and many Democrats, including Wilson, would not accept ratification with reservations.[145] We cannot repeat history, and perhaps Republican opposition was insincere.[146] However, it is worth noting that one simple change that was later incorporated in the UN – abandonment of the interested-party principle – would have effectively addressed all major Republican criticisms by giving the United States an unambiguous, unilateral veto over the League's operations. It is at least conceivable that this would have shifted the handful of votes that were ultimately necessary to secure League ratification in the Senate.

Another plausible domestic political explanation is regime type. For example, Japan's approach to each institution was likely shaped in part by the fact that its government was autocratic in the 1930s and democratic in the post–World War II period. However, regime type is not a plausible explanation for much of the evidence described in this chapter. The first member to exit from the League, Costa Rica, was a democracy, and the most powerful democracy of the era, the United States, abstained from membership. In terms of absolute numbers, there have been more autocratic members of the UN than the League, but formal exit has been essentially non-existent. For sure, other country-specific factors, such as leadership, partisanship, and ideology, are surely relevant if one seeks to explain bargaining strategies and outcomes pertaining to a single state. However, these are unlikely to serve as satisfactory explanations for the systematic variations across many countries described in this chapter.

---

[144] Lodge 1919.

[145] The vote in favor of ratification with the 14 reservations was 39–55, with strong opposition from Democrats, and the vote in favor of unconditional ratification was 34–53, with strong opposition from Republicans. The final vote on a measure including a separate set of resolutions fell short of the required two-thirds majority, 49–35, due to opposition from Democrats who were not willing to accept the reservations.

[146] For example, see discussion of Lodge's intentions in Widenor 1980, 332–333.

9

China–Taiwan Competition over
International Organizations

Since 1949, when Mao Zedong proclaimed the People's Republic of China (PRC) and established de facto control over the Chinese mainland, the PRC and the Republic of China (ROC), which controlled Taiwan, have engaged in fierce competition over representation in major international organizations.[1] In the subsequent discussion, I will refer to the government of the PRC as "China" and the government of ROC as "Taiwan" for ease of exposition unless a distinction needs to be drawn when referring to the geographic territories denoted by those terms.

During the early stages of the Cold War, Taiwan maintained a strong advantage in this competition stemming from its status quo representation in major organizations, support from Western allies, and Chinese international isolation. China exacerbated its isolation by withdrawing from several major organizations, such as the Universal Postal Union and World Meteorological Organization, in protest of Taiwan's membership. As a result, by the 1960s, China had virtually no representation in major intergovernmental organizations, while Taiwan acted as the de jure representative for all of China. This status quo shifted decisively during the 1970s, as the PRC came to be widely acknowledged as the de jure government of China and took Taiwan's place across many major institutions. Starting in 1971, Taiwan's membership in intergovernmental organizations declined sharply from 39 to 10, while China's membership rose from 1 to 21.[2]

---

[1] Among others, see Hsiung 1981; Chen 1983; Weng 1984; Chan 1989; Jacobson and Oksenberg 1990; Henckaerts 1996; Lanteigne 2005; Friedman 2006; Li 2006; Kent 2007; Tsang 2008; Guilloux 2009; Kieng-hong, Chow, and Kao 2010.

[2] Chan 1989, 14–18.

China–Taiwan competition over representation in international organizations was a distributive conflict with high stakes. Aside from the fruits of cooperation with other countries, the victorious country gained international status and prestige as the representative of all of China and undermined the opponent's claim to de jure international sovereignty.[3] Expulsion from major international organizations had clear material consequences: for example, Taiwan's non-membership in the International Monetary Fund (IMF) means it is unable to tap Fund resources in the event of a financial crisis, necessitating aggressive reserve accumulation for the purposes of self insurance. Taiwanese officials also point to the country's exclusion from many international economic institutions as a handicap as it competes with other regional economies such as South Korea and Singapore.[4] The transfer of Taiwan's seat at the United Nations Security Council to China brought along with it the ability to shape and, if necessary, veto, resolutions concerning disputes between the two countries.

However, China–Taiwan competition differs from previous cases analyzed in this book in one crucial respect: outside options were largely irrelevant as a source of bargaining leverage. This is for two reasons. First, the subject of contestation across institutional settings was about the mutually exclusive entry/exit of each country, particularly until Taiwan moderated its stance on joint membership in the mid-1980s. As such, bargaining leverage arising from outside options was generally moot – threatening to walk out is not a credible bargaining strategy when the topic of discussion is whether or not you should be shown the door.[5] Second, the paired nature of the competition mitigates the effect of general variation in outside options. If, within a specific policy area, a tendency toward institutional competition gives Taiwan attractive

---

[3] E.g., Kent 2007, 43.

[4] Discussions with officials at the Ministry of Economic Affairs and Ministry of Foreign Affairs, Taiwan, July 4–July 8, 2011.

[5] Recall that the relevance of outside options in the model presented in Chapter 2 stems from the fact that what is being contested is the distribution of benefits from an existing cooperative arrangement: outside options determine the range of partitions that are mutually acceptable in equilibrium. If outside options are attractive, highly skewed distributions are not sustainable, because the disadvantaged party would purse exit instead. In the case of China–Taiwan competition, what is being contested is not the distribution of benefits, but which country gets to participate in a cooperative arrangement. An unfavorable bargaining outcome results in expulsion from the institution, which is equivalent to exit. Hence, the attractiveness of exit places no meaningful constraints on the bargaining outcome.

outside options, these advantages should also be enjoyed by China. Any residual variation in outside options will be idiosyncratic and country specific.

What should we expect in examining this case study? It would be troubling if this case study exhibited variation consistent with the theory. Given the irrelevance of outside options, there should be no systematic tendency for competitive institutions to change more rapidly compared to uncompetitive institutions. For example, China should perform no better in its efforts to displace Taiwan in development organizations than it does in organizations such as the UN Security Council or the IMF. If competitive institutions exhibit a tendency to change promptly in China–Taiwan competition, it would strongly suggest that alternative mechanisms are at work: the tendency of such organizations toward change demonstrated in previous chapters may be due to alternative factors that covary with the attractiveness of outside options. Some plausible candidates may include variation in norms across policy areas, the willingness of powerful states to concede influence to rising powers in some policy areas but not others, or idiosyncratic factors such as organization leaders who were committed to equitable representation. Although there is no prima facie reason to believe these factors covary with outside options, it is useful to guard against this possibility not only by examining a wide range of institutions, but also by considering a case where the influence of outside options on bargaining is muted by construction.

Hence, China–Taiwan competition is a useful "placebo test," or control case, for the theoretical framework proposed in this book. From the perspective of causal inference, we can think of this as an instance where the treatment of interest (outside options) is not administered to the countries in question. This is a rare circumstance in international relations, where outside options in one form or another are ubiquitous. The case therefore allows us to examine institutional change while artificially suppressing the effect of this key independent variable across policy areas. Of course, ideally, we would prefer to have a much larger control group to moderate the idiosyncrasies of China–Taiwan competition. Unfortunately, the world as we know it does not offer many instances of existential, zero-sum contests over representation in international institutions.

China–Taiwan competition has several attractive features. First, it occurs simultaneously across a wide range of institutional settings, which allows for the examination of many policy areas; Second, it takes place between the same two countries across policy areas, obviating the need to control for country-specific factors that may affect bargaining outcomes;

Third, the stakes were considered extremely high, and the two countries treated the competition as a top diplomatic priority; Finally, diplomatic records concerning China–Taiwan competition are now generally available through the work of area experts and disclosures of relevant international institutions, providing an opportunity to examine the specific causal mechanisms that were at work.

What this chapter provides is one additional piece of evidence in support of the causal mechanisms articulated in this book. More specifically, there is no relationship between institutional change and the attractiveness of outside options in China–Taiwan competition, as expected. Careful examination of individual cases where institutional change did not occur, that is, those in which Taiwan successfully resisted displacement, show that unattractive outside options were not an important factor that accounted for maintenance of the status quo. Consistent with the premises of the theory, China's success in replacing Taiwan is not correlated with outside options or policy area competition.

OVERVIEW OF CHINA–TAIWAN COMPETITION

After the Japanese defeat and withdrawal from China at the end of World War II in 1945, internal conflict between communist and nationalist forces intensified. In 1949, the PRC was proclaimed, and by 1950, the nationalist forces of Chiang Kai-shek were relegated to control over Taiwan and the minor islands of Penghu, Kinmen and Matsu. However, the ROC remained the sole representative of China in major international organizations by virtue of having been widely recognized as the sovereign government of China up to that point.

The PRC government made numerous overtures to the United Nations in an attempt to displace the ROC as the sole representative government of China. However, these efforts were rebuffed as the Cold War intensified, particularly with the outbreak of the Korean War in 1950. The United States and its Western allies supported the ROC's status as the sole representative of China, and the PRC disengaged from international organizations as it became clear its diplomatic isolation was unlikely to be overturned.[6]

These conditions began to shift in the 1960s due to several factors. The Sino-Soviet split began to redefine the contours of Cold War rivalries,

---

[6] Kent 2007, chapter 1.

opening up the possibility of Chinese engagement with the West. The Cultural Revolution led to concern in the West that China's diplomatic isolation was leading to counterproductive radicalization. In the wake of the Cultural Revolution, China exhibited a greater willingness to engage with the international community. The Nixon administration initiated ping-pong diplomacy in 1971, and China's intensified efforts for international recognition bore fruit as an increasing number of countries shifted their diplomatic recognition.

Both China and Taiwan adopted uncompromising positions regarding the question of representation in international organizations. The United States in the 1970s advocated for a compromise, "Two China" solution, under which both China and Taiwan would receive representation in major institutions such as the United Nations.[7] However, this was steadfastly rejected by both China and Taiwan. Based on its "One China" principle, China insisted that co-existence with Taiwan, which it regarded as a renegade province, was unacceptable.[8] Chinese participation in international organizations was predicated first and foremost on the expulsion of Taiwan.[9] China took Taiwan's international legal status extremely seriously, backing up its claims with financial incentives and threats of retaliatory action. For example, after it had replaced Taiwan in the UN, China threatened to veto a UN Peace Keeping mission to Guatemala unless that country dropped its support for Taiwan.[10]

For its part, Taiwan rejected joint membership under its own *hanzei bu liangli* (the Chinese and the bandits would not co-exist) policy,[11] opting to pursue "total diplomacy" against China in a bid to maintain international legitimacy and recognition as the sole government of China.[12] Taiwan began to moderate its position in the late 1980s, as it began to adopt a more pragmatic course that sought separate representation in major international institutions. However, until that point, both countries pursued aggressive, zero-sum diplomacy to attain recognition as the sole representative of China.

THE OUTCOMES OF CHINA–TAIWAN COMPETITION

In 1971, the first year China displaced Taiwan in an intergovernmental organization, the Chinese economy was about four times larger,[13]

---

[7] Ibid., 47.   [8] Li 2006, 598–599.   [9] Kent 2007, 53.
[10] Chao and Hsu 2006, 49.   [11] Ibid., 47.   [12] Weng 1984, 465.
[13] World Bank, World Development Indicators, Real Historical Gross Domestic Product (GDP) and Growth Rates of GDP for Baseline Countries/Regions (in billions of 2005 dollars).

military spending forty times larger, and Composite Index of National Capability score eighteen times larger than respective figures for Taiwan.[14] Therefore, it is reasonable to consider adjustment in the direction of the PRC as institutional change reflective of underlying realities, and maintenance of Taiwanese membership an indication of path dependence.

The theoretical question of interest is whether China was able to achieve more rapid success in displacing Taiwan in organizations that are characterized by institutional competition and attractive outside options. If we observe this tendency, it would indicate the potential presence of some unaccounted for variable that may be responsible for making these institutions more malleable to change. For example, it may be that development lending is a field that attracts individuals disposed toward ideals such as equity and fairness, making these institutions more malleable to change when representation is incongruent with underlying economic capabilities. Alternatively, it may be that the United States resists change more aggressively in institutions such as the UN Security Council or IMF for reasons orthogonal to the theoretical framework proposed in this book. There may also be an element of coincidence, such as leaders more receptive to change being at the helm of particular institutions.

China–Taiwan competition is a useful case in evaluating my theory because it provides a unique opportunity to observe institutional change under conditions where the effect of outside options is suppressed. Alternative explanations for institutional change, such as those listed above, should apply in equal measure to institutional change in response to China–Taiwan competition. China–Taiwan competition takes place at the same time many of the distributive conflicts analyzed earlier in this book occurred. If development institutions exhibit greater malleability due to factors aside from my theory, we should observe China achieving more rapid success in displacing Taiwan in such institutions. If the United States is responsible for putting up greater resistance against change in institutions such as the UN Security Council and IMF, this should also prove challenging for China, particularly in institutions where the United States opposed Chinese membership. If individual leaders were responsible for supporting greater inclusiveness within their institutions, this should also allow for greater scope for Chinese inclusion.

---

[14] Singer, Bremer, and Stuckey 1972.

Table 9.1 lists all intergovernmental organizations that counted Taiwan among its membership in 1971 and subsequently switched to China or established some form of joint membership. As the table shows, no joint membership arrangements were accepted by either state until at least 1984, when Taiwan ceased participation but chose not to formally withdraw from Interpol in response to a downgrading of its status to a member of the PRC's delegation. A clearer acceptance of joint membership came in 1986, when both countries chose to participate in the Asian Development Bank (ADB) after Taiwan's formal designation was changed to "Taipei, China." This underscores the premise of this chapter, that the initial competition between China and Taiwan was zero sum, and neither country was willing to accept joint membership.

The table clearly illustrates that there is no relationship between the attractiveness of outside options and the tendency for institutions to make changes to accommodate China. One of the earliest institutions in which China secured membership was the UN Security Council, which, as discussed earlier, has established itself as the primarily source of legitimation for international interventions and has been characterized by path dependence of distributional outcomes. China did not displace Taiwan more quickly in development institutions, where institutional competition is expected to be fierce: although China's membership in UNDP came early in 1972, the World Bank IBRD and related institutions come toward the end of the list in 1980, and the ADB held out until 1986. In the IMF and World Bank, despite differences in outside options and bargaining outcomes articulated in earlier chapters, China displaced Taiwan simultaneously and largely in accordance with institutional rules.

Consistent with the premises outlined at the beginning of this chapter, there is no tendency for China to displace Taiwan in organizations characterized by policy area competition and attractive outside options. This should give us some confidence that these organizations were not more prone to change in general due to an omitted variable such as internal rules, norms, or the role of individuals. When the effect of outside options is muted by design, the relationship between competition and institutional change disappears.

How then did China go about displacing Taiwan across major international organizations? In the vast majority of cases, China replaced Taiwan through formal institutional procedures that governed the determination of credentials, that is, which party would be acknowledged as the de jure representative of a member country. In turn, China's success was driven primarily by a shift in international opinion, which allowed

TABLE 9.1 *Exit of Taiwan and Entry of China in Intergovernmental Organizations*[15]

Institution Name	Taiwan Exit	China Entry
United Nations (UN)	1971	1971
United Nations Security Council (UNSC)	1971	1971
International Civil Aviation Organization (ICAO)	1971	1971
International Labor Organization (ILO)	1971	1971
United Nations Educational, Scientific and Cultural Organization (UNESCO)	1971	1971
International Bureau of Education (IBE)	1971	1971
Intergovernmental Oceanographic Commission (IOC)	1971	1971
United Nations Development Programme (UNDP)	1971	1972
Intergovernmental Maritime Consultative Organization (IMCO)	1971	1973
UN High Commissioner for Refugees (UNHCR)	1971	1976
United Nations Children's Fund (UNICEF)	1971	1979
International Atomic Energy Agency (IAEA)	1971	1984
International Telecommunication Union (ITU)	1972	1972
Universal Postal Union (UPU)	1972	1972
World Meteorological Organization (WMO)	1972	1972
World Health Organization (WHO)	1972	1972
Asian Industrial Development Council (AIDC)	1972	1972
Asian and Pacific Council (ASPAC)	1973	1973
Permanent Court of Arbitration (PCA)	1973	1973
Asian-Pacific Postal Union (APPU)	1975	1975
International Hydrographic Organization (IHO)	1977	1977
International Monetary Fund (IMF)	1980	1980
International Bank for Reconstruction and Development (IBRD)	1980	1980
International Development Association (IDA)	1980	1980
International Finance Corporation (IFC)	1980	1980
International Committee of Military Medicine and Pharmacy (ICMMP)	1989	1990
International Criminal Police Organization (Interpol)	*	1984
Asian Development Bank (ADB)		1986
International Seed Testing Association (ISTA)		1989
International Office of Epizootics (OIE)		1992

*: Taiwan was never formally expelled or withdrawn from Interpol, but it ceased participation in most of the organization's activities in 1984.

the country[15] to secure majority support from member states across a wide range of institutions. Institutions with one-country-one-vote voting

---

[15] Note: Listed organizations are that counted Taiwan as a member in 1971 and China as a member in any subsequent year as of 2013. The organizations for which no date of Taiwanese exit is listed are those in which some form of joint membership has been

structures tended to respond to Chinese overtures more quickly, reflecting the numerical support the country enjoyed in the international community.

In the United Nations, the procedures that governed China–Taiwan competition were initially contested, as there were no provisions in the Charter regarding the determination of credentials. Prior to the outbreak of the Korean War in 1950, there appeared to be considerable momentum in favor of the PRC, and Secretary General Trygve Lie sought to transfer Chinese credentials to Beijing with a majority vote on the Security Council under the understanding that no veto would apply.[16] However, after the outbreak of the Korean War, support for the PRC in the organization deteriorated, and the General Assembly passed Resolution 396(V), which stated that:

> Whenever more than one authority claims to be the government entitled to represent a Member State in the United Nations … it should be considered by the General Assembly, or by the Interim Committee if the General Assembly is not in session … the attitude adopted by the General Assembly or its Interim Committee concerning any such question should be taken into account in other organs of the United Nations and in the specialized agencies …[17]

Subsequently, a numerical majority led by the United States and its allies in the General Assembly tabled the PRC's claim to the Chinese seat. In 1961, the bar for PRC membership was raised higher when the United States, Australia, Columbia, Italy, and Japan invoked Article 18 of the Charter, elevating the question of Chinese credentials to an "important question" necessitating a two-thirds majority of the General Assembly.[18]

Conditions began to shift in China's favor in the 1960s due to several factors. The Sino-Soviet split softened Western opposition to PRC membership in the UN. The Cultural Revolution raised concerns in Western capitals that Chinese diplomatic isolation was a potential threat to international peace as it contributed to radicalization.[19] Decolonization was rapidly swelling the ranks of developing countries, which were more sympathetic to the Chinese case, in the General Assembly. In 1970, a small majority of General Assembly members expressed support for the PRC over the ROC for the first time in history.[20]

---

established. Dates of exit and entry are from websites and direct contact with relevant organizations, foreign ministry publications of PRC and ROC, the *Yearbook of International Organizations*, and various secondary sources.

[16] Kent 2007, 37.   [17] U.N. General Assembly, Resolution 396(V), 12-14-1950.
[18] Kent 2007, 45.   [19] Ibid., 46–67.   [20] Ibid., 47.

By 1971, the United States was also softening its stance toward China, initiating ping-pong diplomacy and sending National Security Advisor Henry Kissinger to Beijing for negotiations. In August 1971, the United States shifted course in the UN, proposing a "Two China" solution that would allow both China and Taiwan to simultaneously secure representation in the organization, and seeking to maintain the two-thirds threshold governing the expulsion of Taiwan. As the minutes contained in the *Yearbook of the United Nations* notes:

> ... the United States representative [argued in favor of the 19-power proposal] ... that the People's Republic of China take over China's place as a permanent member of the Security Council and provided representation for both the People's Republic and the Republic of China in the General Assembly.[21]

Continuing US support for Taiwan not only reflected geopolitical concerns, but also popular and Congressional sentiment as well as the need to reassure other anti-communist allies of US reliability and commitment.[22] However, US diplomatic efforts failed spectacularly. For the first time, the General Assembly rejected a US-sponsored resolution to classify the credentials issue an "important question" on a 59 to 55 vote with fifteen abstentions.[23] This meant that subsequent resolutions on Chinese credentials could be passed with a simple majority. All related efforts by the United States and its allies to protect Taiwanese membership were rejected.

On October 25, 1971, the UN General Assembly adopted Resolution 2758 on a vote of 76 to 35 with seventeen abstentions.[24] Notably, several major countries, most prominently the United States, but also Japan, Brazil, Australia, Saudi Arabia, and South Africa, voted against the resolution. The text of the Resolution read as follows:

> THE GENERAL ASSEMBLY, *Recalling the principles of the Charter of the United Nations, Considering the restoration of the lawful rights of the People's Republic of China is essential both for the protection of the Charter of the United Nations and for the cause that the United Nations must serve under the Charter. Recognizing that the representatives of the Government of the People's Republic of China are the only lawful representatives of China to the United Nations and that the People's Republic of China is one of the five permanent members of the Security Council, Decides to restore all its rights to the People's Republic of China and to recognize the representatives of its Government as the only legitimate representatives of China to the United Nations, and to expel forthwith the*

---

[21] Yearbook of the United Nations 1971, 130.   [22] Poole 1974.
[23] Yearbook of the United Nations 1971, 133.   [24] Ibid., 132.

representatives of Chiang Kai-shek from the place which they unlawfully occupy at the United Nations and in all the organizations related to it.[25]

After the resolution passed, the General Assembly erupted into cheers and applause in what was described as an "unusually emotional display for the Assembly," while George Bush, Sr., the US Ambassador to the UN at the time, slumped into his seat "as if a great defeat of U.S. policy had just occurred."[26]

Following the resolution, U Thant, the Secretary General of the UN, transmitted the text of Resolution 2758 to executive heads of all UN-affiliated agencies, along with a reminder of General Assembly Resolution 396(V), which recommended that UN specialized agencies should take into account General Assembly decisions pertaining to the credentials of member states.[27] However, this was not a legally binding rule, and each specialized agency acted according to its own procedures and rules. Countries that opposed unitary Chinese membership, spearheaded by the United States, continued their diplomatic contest across specialized agencies. For example, the United States submitted a resolution to the International Labour Organization (ILO) in November 1971 that would postpone a decision on Chinese credentials.[28] This resolution was rejected overwhelmingly, reflecting the organization's one-country-one-vote voting rule and a division of opinion that closely mirrored that in the General Assembly.

On the other hand, US resistance proved more effective in institutions that did not operate strictly on one-country-one-vote principles. Responses to the Secretary General's letter concerning Chinese credentials are informative. One-country-one-vote agencies either moved to immediately expel Taiwan and seek Chinese membership[29] or did so during a general meeting of members taking place the following year.[30] On the other hand, the IMF and World Bank, which operated according to weighted voting rules that inflated the voting power of developed economies that opposed Chinese membership, replied tersely that the Secretary General's communication "had been brought to the attention of the Executive Directors" of the respective institutions.[31] No subsequent action was taken until nearly a decade later.

---

[25] Chen 1983, 57–58.   [26] Poole 1974, 6–9.
[27] Yearbook of the United Nations 1971, 133.   [28] Ibid., 133.
[29] The ILO, FAO, UNESCO, ICAO, IAEA, GATT.   [30] WHO, ITU, WMO.
[31] Yearbook of the United Nations 1971, 134–135.

China's failure to secure immediate expulsion of Taiwan from the Bretton Woods institutions was not due to lack of interest. In 1973, Chinese Minister of Foreign Affairs, Ji Pengfei, under direct approval of Mao Zedong, sent a formal notice to the heads of the IMF and World Bank requesting the expulsion of the "KMT counterrevolutionary clique."[32] World Bank President Robert McNamara responded to this cable by indicating that he would welcome an application of membership from the PRC, but he sidestepped the issue of Taiwan's representation. This reflected the US position at the time, which sought to support the inclusion of China in major international organizations, but not if it meant sacrificing Taiwan. United States opposition came from both the executive branch, which did not wish to see Taiwan isolated diplomatically, and Congress, which counted many supporters of Taiwan among its ranks. While the PRC made the expulsion of Taiwan a precondition for entering into membership discussions, representatives of the IMF and World Bank insisted that an application from the PRC must be forthcoming before the issue would be considered.[33] As Jacobson and Oksenberg note, "U.S. opposition effectively blocked [World Bank President] McNamara for several years from opening negotiations with China or attempting to bring the matter of Chinese representation to a vote."[34]

Another Chinese diplomatic push against Taiwan in the IMF came in 1976, when the institution announced that it would sell some of the gold originally deposited in its coffers by member states. Since the gold would be sold back at the original price of $35 per ounce, member states would be able to reap large profits by reselling at significantly higher prevailing market prices.[35] The PRC sought to take possession of the gold as the sole, legitimate representative of China. The IMF board split sharply between countries seeking to expel Taiwan from the Fund immediately and those who favored continued negotiations with China. However, unlike other UN special agencies, which had expelled Taiwan several years earlier, the weighted voting structure of the Fund produced a small majority in favor of continued negotiations.[36]

It was only in 1980, after resistance from the United States and Japan softened due to normalization of relations and the initiation of economic

---

[32] Jacobson and Oksenberg 1990, 63.   [33] Boughton 2001, 972–979.

[34] Jacobson and Oksenberg 1990, 64; See also Kapur, Lewis, and Webb 1997, 605, 1190.

[35] Boughton 2001, 973.

[36] The vote was 55 percent in favor of the Managing Directors' proposal to pursue continued negotiations, and 31 percent opposed (and implicitly supporting an immediate expulsion of Taiwan). (Ibid., 975).

reforms in China spearheaded by Deng Xiaoping, that China was able to achieve its objectives in the Bretton Woods institutions.[37] The decision was essentially simultaneous: the IMF recognized the PRC as the official representative of China on April 17, 1980, and the World Bank on May 15, 1980.[38]

As this exposition shows, the outcome of China–Taiwan competition largely reflected the internal rules of international institutions and how they translated the opinion of the international community at the time – a large majority in favor of China, but several large, advanced industrialized countries resisting – into voting outcomes. Consistent with the theoretical premises, there was no tendency for institutions situated in competitive policy areas to respond more swiftly to China's demands for institutional change.

CASE STUDY OF PATH DEPENDENT ORGANIZATIONS

In this subsection, I examine the institutions in which Taiwan has successfully retained membership over the long-term, either by keeping China out or through some form of joint membership. As of 2013, Taiwan was a member of thirty three international organizations. Of these, Taiwan has maintained continuous membership since 1971 in eight. They are the World Organization for Animal Health, Asian Productivity Organization, International Seed Testing Association, International Cotton Advisory Committee, ADB, Afro-Asian Rural Development Organization, Food and Fertilizer Technology Center for the Asian and Pacific Region (FFTC/ASPAC), and The World Vegetable Center. The organizations and dates of Taiwan's initial membership are listed in Table 9.2. Organizations in which joint membership has been mutually accepted are given in bold. How was Taiwan able to maintain membership in these organizations, despite being displaced by China in so many others? As I will show, Taiwan's maintenance of membership largely reflected idiosyncratic factors specific to each organization.

Development and Agricultural Organizations

The most obvious common thread among the organizations listed in Table 9.2 is that they are focused on some combination of economic development and agricultural research and aid. These are areas that

---

[37] Ibid., 976.   [38] Ibid., 978; World Bank 1980, 39.

TABLE 9.2 *Intergovernmental Organizations in which Taiwan has Retained Membership*

Organization Name	Year of Initial Membership
International Office of Epizootics / World Organization for Animal Health (OIE)	1954
Asian Productivity Organization (APO)	1961
International Seed Testing Association (ISTA)	1962
International Cotton Advisory Committee (ICAC)	1963
Asian Development Bank (ADB)	1966
Afro-Asian Rural Development Organization (AARDO)	1968
Food and Fertilizer Technology Center for the Asian and Pacific Region (FFTC/ASPAC)	1970
The World Vegetable Center (AVRDC)	1971

Note: Information from Taiwan Ministry of Foreign Affairs[39]; Bold indicates joint membership with China. The list includes international organizations in which Taiwan has maintained continuous membership since at least 1971.

Taiwan has prioritized in its foreign policy. As one of the "Asian Tigers," Taiwan is widely acknowledged as a development success story, and its success in agricultural development during 1950–1970 had made technical assistance in that area an important element of Taiwan's international cooperation.[40]

The international organizations in Table 9.2 are uniformly situated in policy areas with considerable competition. As discussed in earlier chapters, development organizations such as the ADB and Afro-Asian Rural Development Organization face extensive competition and attractive outside options. The primary functions of the International Cotton Advisory Committee are research, technical assistance, to serve as a discussion forum, and advocate for the cotton industry.[41] Similar functions are replicated by various multilateral associations, such as the International Cotton Association, Committee for International Co-operation between Cotton Associations, and regional organizations such as the African

[39] Ministry of Foreign Affairs (Republic of China), "IGOs in which we participate, Full Member," www.mofa.gov.tw/EnOfficial/NationalOrg/OrgList/?opno=3400817f-1a5b-443c-8969-174b5c7819b2.
[40] Lin 2012.
[41] "Overview." International Cotton Advisory Committee. www.icac.org/about/overview.

Cotton Association. It is therefore implausible that Taiwan was able to sustain membership in these organizations due to path dependence arising from unattractive outside options.

The most prominent organization listed in Table 9.2 is the ADB, a major regional development lending institution. An important factor that allowed Taiwan's maintenance of its membership in the ADB was support from Japan and the United States, which are the two leading members of the organization in terms of voting shares and also generally recognized as exerting the greatest informal influence over the organization's policies. By the mid-1980s, Japan and the United States saw Chinese attempts to displace Taiwan as having gone too far, resulting in diplomatic isolation for the island.[42] Hence, the two countries pushed back against Chinese demands that Taiwan be expelled from the ADB in a manner consistent with the United Nations and the Bretton Woods institutions.

The relatively slow pace of change at the ADB compared to other institutions reflected several factors unique to that institution, all orthogonal to policy area competition. These factors are outlined in a formal statement issued by the ADB summarizing the main arguments in favor of continued Taiwanese membership:

The Republic of China is a founding member of ADB since its establishment and actively participates in its activities and faithfully fulfills its obligations. The Chinese Communists, since the end of November 1982, have approached several ADB member countries including Japan and the United States to indicate interest in joining the ADB and to expel the ROC membership on the bank as in cases with the United Nations, World Bank and IMF. In light of the following considerations, the ADB should not yield to the request by the Chinese Communists and the ROC membership should remain unchanged: 1. The ADB is not a member of the UN family of organizations and is, therefore, not subject to any resolution adopted by the UN [...] 2. The ROC's subscription to the bank[...] [is] on the basis of the territory and population under the effective control of the ROC and its GNP, tax revenues and exports. This is totally different from the case of ROC's membership in the IMF or IBRD. 3. The ROC is a founding member [that has] always faithfully fulfilled its obligations. The charter of the ADB stipulates no provision for the expulsion of membership if the member has faithfully fulfilled its obligations [...] Furthermore, ADB, by its charter, is a non-political organization. Article 36 of its chapter specially prohibits political influence in the ADB's decision and policy. Only economic decisions should be relevant to the ADB's decision. In case political considerations are introduced in the operations of ADB and to violate the charter expel the ROC, the image of the ADB as a reputable international financial organization will be damaged.[43]

---

[42] Li 2006, 600–604.   [43] Chiu 1982, 230.

China ultimately accepted a compromise in which Taiwan maintained full membership as "Taipei, China," a precedent that for the first time broke the zero sum nature of competition between the two countries and paved the way for joint membership in a range of international institutions such as Asia Pacific Economic Cooperation (APEC) and the WTO.

Status of Members and Naming Issues

One quirk that has allowed Taiwan to retain its position in some organizations is how the status of members is defined. Three organizations, marked in bold in Table 9.2, are characterized by joint membership of China and Taiwan. China has occasionally conceded to joint membership under the condition that Taiwan is labeled in a way that conveys its status as a province or region of China, such as "Chinese Taipei," as in the case of the International Olympic Committee, or "Separate Customs Territory of Taiwan, Penghu, Kinmen and Matsu," in the case of the World Trade Organization. The bolded organizations have similarly adopted naming conventions that make Taiwanese membership palatable to China: "Taipei (Chinese)" for the World Organization for Animal Health, "Taipei China" for the ADB, and "Separate Customs Territory of Taiwan, Penghu, Kinmen and Matsu" for the International Seed Testing Association.

Some organizations have membership terms that make Taiwanese membership under these alternative labels acceptable to China. The ADB and the Asian Productivity Organization refer to "member economies" rather than "member states," and the ADB is careful to qualify that, "By making any designation of or reference to a particular territory or geographical area, or by using the term 'country' in the website, ADB does not intend to make any judgment as to the legal or other status of any territory or area. Boundaries, colors, denominations or any other information shown on maps do not imply, on the part of ADB, any judgment on the legal status of any territory, or any endorsement or acceptance of such boundaries, colors, denominations, or information."[44] Similarly, the International Seed Testing Association refers to "member laboratories" and "country/distinct economies."[45]

[44] "Members." Asian Development Bank. www.adb.org/about/members.
[45] "ISTA Member Laboratories," ISTA Online, http://seedtest.org/en/memberlaboratories .html.

By underplaying the status of members as sovereign states, these designations have mitigated the intractability of China–Taiwan competition in several of these organizations. China has also exhibited somewhat greater flexibility vis-à-vis organizations that already include non-state members, such as Hong Kong and the Cook Islands in the case of the ADB.[46] However, occasional accommodation on these grounds does not imply that China is automatically supportive of Taiwanese de facto membership in international organizations. Taiwan's disposition in Interpol is illustrative. Although Interpol has allowed joint participation by China and Taiwan, China convinced the organization to accept several tough conditions, including:

1. Taiwan had to accept a change of name from "Republic of China" to "Taiwan, China";
2. Taiwan could not use its national flag;
3. A demotion of the Taiwanese delegation, which would now be part of China's "national" delegation;
4. No formal voting rights.

Taiwan protested this downgrading of its membership by ceasing activities in Interpol, although it chose not to formally withdraw its membership.[47]

Research Organizations Headquartered in Taiwan

Two international organizations in the list were research centers established under the leadership of Taiwan in the early 1970s, and they continue to maintain their institutional headquarters in Taiwan. FFTC/ASPAC specializes in the collection and dissemination of research generated by agricultural centers in the Asia-Pacific region. The member states aside from Taiwan are Japan, South Korea, the Philippines, and Vietnam. The executive board largely consists of diplomatic officials of member states, who serve in their countries' cultural and interchange associations, de facto embassies in Taiwan.

The World Vegetable Center was founded by Taiwan, along with the Asian Development Bank, Japan, South Korea, the Philippines, Thailand, the United States, and Vietnam in 1971. The organization's mission is, "The alleviation of poverty and malnutrition in the developing world

[46] Chiu 1982, 250.   [47] Chang 1991.

through the increased production and consumption of nutritious and health-promoting vegetables."[48] The organization has an $18 million budget and a staff of about 300. It is headquartered in Shanhua, Taiwan.

Both of these organizations are small and clearly situated within competitive policy areas. There are many organizations that support research and technical assistance with a focus on agriculture, ranging in scope from large intergovernmental organizations such as the World Bank and International Fund for Agricultural Development (IFAD) to smaller agricultural research centers.[49] This is a point emphasized by both organizations as well. Both describe their missions by drawing comparisons to other organizations that perform similar functions. For example, the FFTC/ASPAC notes that, "While most agricultural research centers are specialized, and study a single crop or a single agro-ecological zone, FFTC offers practical technologies that are matched to the reality of the region's small-scale farmers, whose farm incomes are determined by total farm production."[50] The World Vegetable Center notes that "The Center is the only international agricultural research center headquartered in a Chinese-speaking country."[51]

For these institutions, the explanation for Taiwan's ability to retain membership is straightforward. These were organizations established through Taiwanese initiative and headquartered in Taiwan during the early 1970s when Chinese displacement was an increasing concern. As such, they are effectively Taiwanese outreach organizations open to international membership. Although both organizations perform meaningful functions, an important rationale for each is to increase the total number of international organizations in which Taiwan is a member. Since the institutions are small and characterized by easily duplicated functions, they have not come under heavy diplomatic contestation.

DISCUSSION

This chapter fundamentally differs from those that preceded it. If an association between the attractiveness of outside options and institutional change were uncovered in China–Taiwan competition, it would not

---

[48] "Quick Facts," The World Vegetable Center Website, http://avrdc.org/?page_id=569.
[49] For example, the Consortium of International Agricultural Research Centers coordinates the work of fifteen agricultural research centers located in various parts of the globe.
[50] "About Us," Food and Fertilizer Technology Center for the Asian and Pacific Region.
[51] "Quick Facts," The World Vegetable Center Website, http://avrdc.org/?page_id=569.

confirm the theory, but instead raise serious questions about its empirical validity. Because China–Taiwan competition took place under circumstances that suppressed bargaining leverage obtainable from outside options, the case serves as a useful test of the theoretical premises of this book. If unrecognized, omitted variables are responsible for the tendency of competitive institutions to respond more quickly to underlying realities than monopolistic ones, the effect of those omitted variables should be observable as the PRC sought to displace the ROC as the de jure government of China.

As this chapter shows, there was no tendency for institutions operating in competitive policy areas to respond more expediently to China's demands for change. The Bretton Woods institutions, which exhibit clear differences in the pace of distributive institutional change under normal conditions as demonstrated in previous chapters, approved China's displacement of Taiwan simultaneously. Several highly competitive institutions, such as development institutions, agricultural institutions, and laboratories, resisted Chinese demands by retaining Taiwan as a member. The pattern of observed change is largely consistent with the theoretical premise that the irrelevance of outside options will elevate the importance of formal, internal rules: relatively speaking, China struggled to achieve its objectives in weighted-voting institutions that gave greater authority to the United States and Japan.

As discussed earlier, the main limitation of the evidence presented in this chapter is that it is restricted to a single dyad and time period. The most empirically useful, zero-sum competition between China and Taiwan took place over the course of about fifteen years in the 1970s and early 1980s. While the case allows us to examine bargaining outcomes across a wide range of international institutions while holding constant the time period and countries concerned, it does not offer variation in time period and countries. This is a practical limitation imposed by the realities of world politics: there are no other instances of distributive conflict that occurred simultaneously across a wide range of international institutions and for which exit threats were rendered irrelevant.

However, it is useful to consider the conditions under which the evidence presented in this chapter would be problematic: not only must there be an omitted variable that systematically covaries with attractiveness of outside options, but that variable must also be systematically suppressed for China–Taiwan competition. If we consider the leading candidates for potential omitted variables, such as policy-area specific ideological variation, the role of specific individuals, or US policy prioritization, this does not appear highly plausible. To take a specific example, suppose one were to hypothesize that variation in institutional change is determined by US prioritization of certain policy areas over others: for example, the IMF and UN Security Council are more "important" and therefore the United States is less willing to concede to changes compared to development aid institutions. If such prioritization is a general feature of US foreign policy, it would surely come into play over a high-profile controversy such as the China credentials issue. However, as we saw, empirical outcomes are inconsistent with this explanation: for example, China achieved relatively rapid success in the UN Security Council, while the most successful instance of resistance by the United States came in the ADB, a regional development aid institution, where Taiwan has managed to hold onto its membership.

In sum, this chapter takes advantage of a unique empirical opportunity offered by the nature of contestation between China and Taiwan, which suppressed the utility of outside options in redistributive bargaining. The outcomes of China–Taiwan competition strongly suggest that the findings presented in the rest of the book cannot be attributed to omitted variables that make some institutions systematically more prone to change than others.

10

Conclusion

The governance of world politics has evolved dramatically over the past century. International institutions have moved from the fringe of international relations to a predominant mode of cooperation across a wide range of policy areas. Major organizations such as the United Nations (UN) Security Council and Internatioal Mometary Fund (IMF) play central roles in determining how contemporary international problems are addressed and resolved. This has given rise to recurrent conflicts over representation and informal control over international institutions, particularly as rising states seek to secure influence commensurate with their newfound power. Some institutions adapt flexibly to such demands, accommodating dissatisfied countries. Others fade as members reallocate their resources to alternatives. Yet others successfully resist change.

As this book illustrates, contestation over institutions is an increasingly crucial feature of international relations. Rather than seeking recognition through territorial acquisition and the subjugation of foreign populations through the use of force, countries increasingly vie for international prestige by seeking influence over international institutions.[1] In prior eras, many of the diplomatic contests described in the preceding chapters – over issues such as which states deserve great power status, who determines the course of economic relations and development, who controls new resources and technological innovations – were settled violently through militarized conflict. International institutions have become

---

[1] For an attempt to explicitly quantify one form of prestige in international organizations, see Hafner-Burton and Montgomery 2006.

crucial not only as facilitators of cooperation,[2] but also as moderators of shifts in the international balance of power.

This book has proposed and tested a theoretical framework to understand institutional change in international relations. I have argued that political institutions, much like firms in markets, are deeply influenced by the nature of their policy areas. Some policy issues are best managed through institutions that limit alternative policy solutions, such as concentration of functions in a single, universalistic institution. Such monopoly institutions are better able to survive even if they adopt rules, procedures, and norms that fail to reflect the realities of underlying economic or geopolitical power. Because dissatisfied states have no credible outside options, they are effectively trapped into grudging acceptance of distributive outcomes that seem biased and deeply unfair. On the other hand, competitive institutions are subject to policy area discipline: such institutions must accurately reflect underlying distributions of power or risk fading away as members pursue alternative modes of cooperation.

I examined the validity of this theory by exploiting various features of institutions that provide opportunities for causal inference and consideration of causal mechanisms. For the purpose of inference, the quasi-experiment created by key features of the IMF and World Bank was pivotal: common institutional rules, membership, and time periods allowed us to isolate the effect of policy are area variation on institutional change. I also examined how a large, exogenous shift in underlying economic power – Japan's dramatic rise after World War II – was accommodated across institutional contexts. Intelsat and the League of Nations / United Nations offered over-time variation in policy area characteristics as well as detailed diplomatic records that confirmed the validity of the proposed causal mechanisms. The Internet Corporation for Assigned Names and Numbers (ICANN) most clearly demonstrated how monopolistic institutions enable early members to secure asymmetrical advantages at the expense of new entrants. Conversely, an examination of competitive dynamics in development lending and regional integration projects illustrated the constraining effects of policy area discipline. Finally, features of China–Taiwan competition suppressed the effect of outside options on institutional change, allowing us to guard against the possibility that some unrecognized variable may be responsible for the findings observed in earlier chapters. The empirical evidence provides a wealth of support for the proposed theoretical framework.

---

[2] Keohane 1984; Axelrod and Keohane 1985; Keohane and Martin 1995.

In this concluding chapter, I will discuss several outstanding issues. First, I will revisit how the evidence presented in the book relates to alterative explanations for institutional change. Second, I will discuss the broader implications of the project, including what the theory tells us about how we should study institutions, suggestions for future research, and extensions to other institutional contexts. Finally, the closing section will assess the policy implications of the project in light of shifting contemporary geopolitical and economic realities.

ALTERNATIVE EXPLANATIONS FOR INSTITUTIONAL CHANGE

The theory proposed in this book has been validated by evidence where standard, power-based explanations of institutional change fall short. For sure, in many instances, powerful states get their way in international relations: the United States has succeeded in securing its preferred outcome over internet governance; the P5 of the UN Security Council are also among the most powerful states in the world. However, this book also illustrates the limitations of raw power. The United States has had to concede much more ground in institutions such as Intelsat and the World Bank than its policymakers preferred. Although the threat of exit by powerful states has been effective in facilitating change in some UN agencies, such as the International Fund for Agricultural Development (IFAD), it has been ineffectual in others, such as the United Nations Development Programme (UNDP). The League of Nations proved impervious to the demands of some of the most powerful states of the era. The flipside of US dominance of ICANN is the inability of some geopolitically and economically powerful states, such as China, the European Union (EU), and Japan to exercise influence over crucial aspects of internet governance. The United Kingdom and France remain on the P5 of the UN Security Council despite the exclusion of arguably more powerful states, such as Germany, India, and Japan.

To an important extent, the theory proposed in this book complements power-based theories by offering an explanation for *when and how* underlying power translates into influence over outcomes. Being a large geopolitical or economic power does not per se imply commensurate influence over international institutions. The theory offers a framework to map the ebb and flow of national capabilities onto representation and influence over the increasingly institutionalized governance architecture of world politics. Another way to think about the theory is that it offers a better way to conceptualize and measure power – when defined as influence over outcomes – according to policy areas and the preexisting configuration of political institutions.

The evidence presented in this book also illustrates some important limitations of the rational design approach toward international institutions. In many instances, the strategic setting of institutional renegotiation is fundamentally distinct from design. Consider an analogy with bargaining models of war. In theory, one could model contemporary conflicts between Iran and Iraq as part of a game that was initiated by the Treaty of Zuhab, which established current boundaries in 1639. To do so would ignore the fact that the current disputants are completely different actors – the nation states of Iran and Iraq as opposed to the Safavid and Ottoman Empires – operating under dramatically different realities that would not have been in any meaningful sense foreseeable by seventeenth century negotiators. In recognition of this reality, most contemporary bargaining models of war treat the status quo distribution of territory as exogenous.[3] The circumstances surrounding the renegotiation of major international institutions have become increasingly analogous. Contemporary debates over the renegotiation of institutions such as the UN Security Council and IMF feature radically different circumstances and many countries that were never present during the initial bargaining process.

The empirical studies in this book also illustrate how institutional designers often make mistakes. The asymmetrical initial structure of Intelsat was proposed by US policymakers who had misguided beliefs about the degree of network effects present in satellite telecommunications. The plethora of development institutions utilizing one-country-one-vote rules illustrates how policymakers often adopt suboptimal distributive arrangements for reasons orthogonal to the effective functioning of cooperation. The League of Nations clearly reflected numerous design flaws that the architects of the UN sought to remedy. This is not to challenge the utility of rational design theories: much like the theory proposed in this book, rational design offers an elegant explanation for a meaningful degree of observed variation in international politics. However, mistakes at the initial stages of bargaining create one more avenue through which status quo institutional structures may become effectively exogenous: institutional rules and distributional arrangements may become well established before participants acquire a full understanding

---

[3] For example, see Fearon 1994; Powell 1999; Reiter 2003.

of their interests and features of the strategic setting that affect bargaining outcomes. Initial bargains struck under conditions of limited information and uncertainty can become entrenched and difficult to overturn.

Importantly, the theory presented in this book offers an alternative explanation for the apparent congruence between institutional design features and underlying policy area realities – a key prediction of rational design theories. As I illustrated in Chapter 5, institutions that are designed poorly – for example, those that have rigid distributive rules in competitive policy areas – tend to wither as dissatisfied states exit or reallocate their contributions. As a consequence, surviving, successful institutions will generally be those with design features that conform to their policy areas. One potential danger is the conflation of this outcome, which essentially reflects an evolutionary process, with rational, anticipatory planning by institutional designers.[4] Another testable implication of my theory is that monopolistic institutions should be able to survive even with relatively poorly designed rules: the disutility from accepting suboptimal rules, much like the disutility from underrepresentation, may be outweighed by the high cost of exit.

This book also contributes important insights to the bounded rationality approach toward institutional change proposed by Jupille, Mattli and Snidal. As argued at the outset, the theory proposed in this book is complementary in important respects to the "use, select, change, create (USCC)" approach, which focuses on explaining how states utilize institutions to resolve policy problems within policy areas rather than variations in institutional change across policy areas. However, the book does challenge an important premise of their work, which is that rationalist accounts cannot offer a compelling explanation for variations in institutional persistence in change.

The evidence presented in the empirical chapters underscores the importance of paying attention to cross-policy-area variation in institutional change, as well as how variables that are treated as sequential in the USCC model oftentimes interact in interstate bargains. The *feasibility* of institutional selection and creation is often an important source of variation for institutional change. This is illustrated by the threats of exit by French and German officials vis-à-vis Intelsat, which allowed these countries to secure favorable institutional change. In contrast, the difficulty of creating credible institutional alternatives to the IMF has served as an important impediment to selection and change.

---

[4] For an earlier discussion of evolutionary processes in international relations, see Kahler 1999.

This raises an important potential threat to causal inference when thinking about USCC in terms of bounded rationality – the idea that policymakers satisfice by choosing from among the USCC strategies in descending order. "Use" of a current institution may be chosen not because actors satisfice, but because policy area characteristics preclude alternative arrangements. The evidence presented in this book strongly suggests that policymakers very frequently contemplate, threaten, and even carry out institutional selection and creation even in instances when "use" of status quo arrangements ultimately prevails. At least in cases like this, satisficing is not a compelling explanation for why the institutional status quo proves resilient.

Surely, in many instances, institutional change occurs for reasons that are not explicitly captured by my theoretical framework, such as the initiative of individual policy makers, the evolution of norms, incidental domestic political factors, or even happenstance. The theory presented in this book is not meant to displace other potential explanations for how institutions evolve and change. Such mechanisms are surely relevant and important for explaining residual variation that remains unaccounted for by the theory. If the task at hand is to provide a narrative of particular instances of institutional change or to account for specifics details, such as timing and precise outcomes, it would be foolhardy to omit the role of individuals or specific historical circumstances. The principal strength of the theory presented in this book is that it generates simple, easily testable, and generalizable predictions about institutional change that are consistent with observed variation across a wide range of policy areas.

BROADER IMPLICATIONS

This study has many additional implications that provide grounds for further research. I will first summarize several potential extensions in the field of international relations, and then discuss how the theory might be applied to the study of domestic political institutions.

Extensions in International Relations

The insights in this book could be fruitfully extended both theoretically and empirically to cover a wider range of issues and institutions in international relations. The formal model could incorporate additional features to more closely approximate real-life bargaining, for example, by incorporating incomplete information to model the possibility of failed challenges, variation in preference divergence or intensity, or coalition dynamics in the large-n case.[5] These changes will not affect the basic propositions of this book, which are based on the constraining effects of outside options on the bargaining range, but may generate additional predictions about factors that affect institutional change. From an empirical standpoint, much work remains to be done on institutional change, particularly in terms of less easily quantifiable measures such as influence over outcomes and ideational influence. Given the high priority placed on institutional renegotiation by government officials and policy experts in rising states, this issue will likely remain an important area of research well into the future.

Although I have focused primarily on institutional renegotiation in this book, the theory also has important implications for regime creation. One central insight of Fearon's seminal work on international bargaining over institutions is that long shadows of the future can counterintuitively hamper regime building by making states more willing to hold out for better deals upfront.[6] The relative stickiness of distributive outcomes in monopolistic institutions may have a similar effect. If states correctly anticipate that an institution will occupy a noncompetitive policy area, initial bargains may be more difficult to strike because states will view the outcome as longer lasting and therefore involving higher stakes. However, one interesting feature of institutions subject to strong network effects is that initial bargains can be forgone entirely. In the cases of Intelsat and ICANN, US policymakers attempted to unilaterally and rapidly establish institutions that other countries would be compelled to join on US terms. The rationale was that once these institutions were established, network effects would make it highly unattractive to abstain from participation, and unattractive outside options would give subsequent participants limited bargaining power. Hence, the initial establishment of highly monopolistic organizations may be more akin to standard setting in the private sector, in which institutions can be created not only through negotiated bargains but also from the promotion and rapid establishment of a standard around which other actors are forced to converge. If so, bargaining failure will be no impediment to institutional creation.

The theory also has important implications for a widely debated feature of international institutions: whether or not they extend the "afterglow" of prior conditions, particularly power distributions that

---

[5] Chaterjee et al. 1993; Acemoglu, Egorov, and Sonin 2007.   [6] Fearon 1998.

prevailed during earlier time periods.[7] The answer provided in this book is that the tendency of institutions to extend the afterglow of initial conditions varies by policy area. In competitive policy areas, such as development aid, trade agreements, and integration projects, institutions will flexibly reflect underlying distributions of power in real time, or alternative institutions that do so will proliferate and take their place. On the other hand, monopolistic institutions will be able to resist change and sustain initial conditions long after underlying realities have shifted. This means that underlying power shifts in the international system will feed through at different rates according to policy area. Understanding such tendencies will better inform our study of international power transitions and conflicts over global governance.

This book also provides guidelines for proper levels of analysis when studying international institutions. In policy areas where institutions are expected to exhibit path dependence due to the limited credibility of outside options, institutional reform will often occur for reasons aside from shifts in underlying power distributions. As the China–Taiwan case and efforts at UN Security Council reform illustrate, institutional change based on strict adherence to formal rules and procedures is one path available to states under such conditions. In such institutions, it makes sense to pay careful attention to the formal rules of cooperation and other influences that might facilitate change, such as normative factors. On the other hand, where institutions are expected to unproblematically reflect underlying power, a greater focus on national interests and capabilities is warranted. This is akin to the distinction Gourevitch draws between "strong" and "weak" institutions.[8] The theory therefore offers a novel framework through which to think about the strength of institutions and the conditions under which formal rules are likely to have a meaningful impact on cooperative outcomes.

Another promising area for future research is to consider other effects of institutional competition in international relations. Institutional competition has often been neglected by scholars of politics despite its increasing relevance for practitioners in some policy areas.[9] As I noted in Chapter 2, due to weak profit motives, international institutions are unlikely to face strong production and pricing incentives stemming from competition. However, employees in formal institutions do face various incentives and normative reasons to sustain and expand the scope of their

---

[7] Krasner 1976; Keohane 1984; Ikenberry 2000.   [8] Gourevitch 1999.
[9] Galvani and Morse 2004.

organizations.[10] This may contribute to various pathologies, particularly in international institutions on the losing end of competition. In the field of development aid, one clear consequence of competition is that recipient states, particularly middle income countries, have considerable leverage vis-à-vis aid agencies, reducing accountability and potentially diluting the effectiveness of programs. As described in Chapter 5, the evolution of UNDP from an aid agency to a fee-based consultancy that enables domestic governments to circumvent their own domestic rules and regulations is one manifestation of this. The examination of how institutional competition affects cooperation in other policy areas is a fruitful area for future research.

Extensions to Domestic Political Institutions

In this book, I have focused on explaining institutional change in international relations. This is a substantively important topic for reasons that should already be apparent. However, the theory could also be extended beyond the international realm to institutional arrangements characterized by analogous features at the domestic level. In Chapter 5, I considered redistributive conflict in regional integration projects, which can be thought of as proto-states. However, many other domestic political institutions are subject to intense contestation, much like the international institutions examined in this book. The effect of policy area competition on domestic institutional change remains underexplored.

Domestic political institutions differ from international institutions in one important respect: artificial monopolies, akin to what the founders of the League of Nations aspired to, are more feasible in domestic contexts where the rule of law is well established and enforced by governing authorities. Hence, monopoly institutions are more feasible in domestic politics even in the absence of policy area features that limit competition. However, there are certain conditions under which redistributive conflict in domestic politics will approach those described throughout this book.

First, in countries characterized by weak rule of law or government authority, competition and the threat of exit are more likely to be relevant as redistributive mechanisms. We can therefore expect that the dynamics described in this book will have greater explanatory power over redistributive domestic conflicts in developing countries and states undergoing

---

[10] Barnett and Finnemore 1999.

significant internal strife. Second, even among countries with strong governance, political institutions will not necessarily be shielded from competition. Some types of governing arrangements are more conducive to competition than others. Decentralization, if it allows greater autonomy for local governments to manage policy issues alongside the central government, can create opportunities for policy area competition. Bureaucratic politics can also lead to the creation of duplicative institutions overseeing the same policy issue: for example, the United States officially has sixteen agencies dedicated to the collection of intelligence.[11] Competition among domestic political institutions may be encouraged as a means to facilitate greater efficiency or accountability, as seen in the trend toward partial privatization of government functions across the globe and China's developmental model, which emphasizes innovation and competition at the local government level.[12]

Under such conditions, policy area effects similar to those described here are likely to be relevant for redistributive dynamics concerning issues such as patronage appointments in developing countries, committee assignments, and allocation of authority among bureaucratic agencies. The following, general conjecture follows from the theory outlined in this book: ceteris paribus, institutions that primarily pertain to activities that are easily replicable by other institutions or actors will be more prone to distributional fluidity among constituents (e.g., parties, regions, ethnic groups), versus those that engage heavily in activities subject to few outside options. The theory may be useful in generating new insights about domestic institutional change, such as processes of democratization: for example, democratization could be conceptualized as a redistributive response as economic growth places government functions under greater competition or citizens are better able to exercise outside options through personal or financial emigration.

IMPLICATIONS FOR THE WORLD ORDER: FROM BLOODSHED TO NEGOTIATION

What are the broader implications of this book for our understanding of the world order and contemporary international relations? Since the beginning of the twentieth century, international institutions have become

---

[11] "Members of the Intelligence Community," Office of the Director of National Intelligence. www.dni.gov/index.php/intelligence-community/members-of-the-ic.
[12] Naughton 1994; Weingast 1995

increasingly important as facilitators of cooperation and mediators of international disputes. As military conflict among great powers declined, bargaining over international institutions has emerged as an increasingly crucial mechanism through which power transitions are mediated and rising powers establish their influence over the international system. There are considerable reasons to believe this trend will continue well into the future.

It is widely recognized that international institutions have become an increasingly central element of contemporary international relations. Regardless of how they are defined, the number of international institutions has increased dramatically since the beginning of the twentieth century. The Union of International Associations compiles data on the number of intergovernmental organizations (IGOs), using a broad definition that includes bilateral and informal arrangements.[13] According to this broad definition, the number of IGOs has skyrocketed over the past century, particularly since the 1970s (Figure 10.1). The Correlates of War project uses a more narrow definition of international organizations, limiting the sample to formal organizations with at least three member states.[14] This data similarly shows that the number of international organizations has increased dramatically over the past century, particularly during the period since World War II (Figure 10.2).

International institutions are now actively involved in essentially every aspect of contemporary international relations, including security, economic issues, science and technology, the environment, and human rights. For sure, the importance of institutions varies by issue area. In economic affairs, international institutions such as the World Trade Organization (WTO) and IMF are widely recognized as playing increasingly central roles in the management of the world economy.[15] International institutions are also increasingly consequential in environmental affairs and

---

[13] The broad definition includes bilateral arrangements as well as institutions that have no formal secretariat. Here is the formal definition used by the Union of International Associations: "An IGO is an organization composed primarily of sovereign states, or of other intergovernmental organizations. IGOs are established by treaty or other agreement that acts as a charter creating the group. Examples include the United Nations, the World Bank, or the European Union." (Union of International Associations, "What is an Intergovernmental Organization (IGO)?" www.uia.org/faq/yb3).

[14] The formal criteria are as follows: (1) An IGO must consist of at least two members of the COW-defined state system; (2) An IGO must hold regular plenary sessions at least once every ten years; (3). An IGO must consist of at least three members of the COW-defined state system Pevehouse, Nordstrom, and Warnke 2004.

[15] Vreeland 2007; Goldstein 2008.

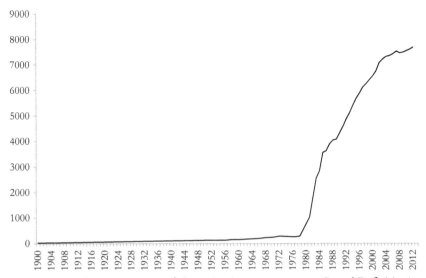

FIGURE 10.1 Intergovernmental Organizations, 1900–2013 (Broad Definition)
Source: Union of International Associations

human rights.[16] On the other hand, the role of international institutions in security issues remains relatively constrained by national interest and sovereignty concerns.[17] However, even in the realm of high politics, international organizations such as the North Atlantic Treaty Organization (NATO) and the UN Security Council are now routinely consulted by great powers prior to the use of force, an unthinkable development for the vast majority of human history.[18]

This proliferation and expansion of international institutions has been accompanied by a sharp decline in the traditionally preeminent means of resolving disputes among nations: violent conflict.[19] The number of wars among the Great Powers has gradually declined over time, and there has been no direct military confrontation between Great Powers for sixty years since the end of the Korean War in 1953 (Figure 10.3). This is by far the longest lull in direct Great Power conflict since the end of the fifteenth century.[20]

[16] Young 1989; Haas, Keohane, and Levy 1993; Risse-Kappen, Ropp, and Sikkink 1999; Moravcsik 2000.
[17] Jervis 1982; Mearsheimer 1994.
[18] Voeten 2001; Hurd 2002; Voeten 2005; Thompson 2006.   [19] Pinker 2012.
[20] A great power war is defined as a war in which at least one Great Power participated on each side of the conflict. Data on Great Power wars is from Levy 1989 for 1495–1815, and the Correlates of War Inter-State War Data (v4.0) thereafter (Sarkees and Wayman 2010), where "major powers" are used to define Great Powers (Correlates of War Project

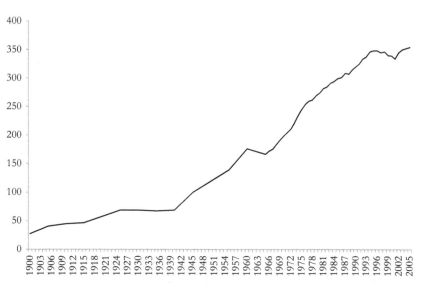

FIGURE 10.2 Intergovernmental Organizations, 1900–2005 (Narrow Definition)
Source: Pevehouse, Nordstrom, and Warnke 2004

Data on military personnel and expenditures also show visible declines over time, particularly since the end of World War II. Though military personnel and spending spiked during the two world wars, the overall trend is downward, and both figures are currently at historical lows (Figures 10.4, 10.5). For sure, this decline in interstate conflict has been accompanied by a rise in intrastate conflict since the end of World War II.[21] However, the importance of militarized conflict as a means of settling *interstate* disputes and determining the terms of the world order have clearly declined concurrently with the rise of international institutions.

This book does not address *why* military conflict has declined while international institutions have increased in importance. Some scholars have asserted a causal relationship between the two trends.[22] However, there are many other plausible reasons for why interstate conflict has declined in recent years: among others, the proliferation of nuclear weapons, which make it more costly to engage in direct conflict;[23] norms

2008). If India is considered a Great Power in the 1960s, the most recent Great Power war would be the 1962 Sino-Indian War.

[21] Fearon and Laitin 2003.

[22] Russett, Oneal, and Davis 1998; Russett and Oneal 2001; Oneal, Russett, and Berbaum 2003.

[23] Waltz 1990; Sagan and Waltz 2012.

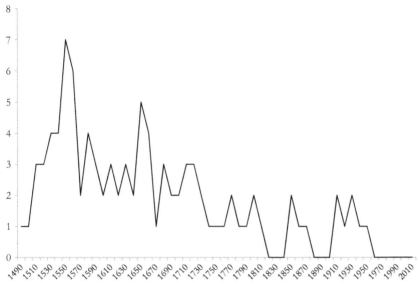

FIGURE 10.3 Great Power Wars by Decade, 1490–2010
Source: Levy 1989, Sarkees and Wayman 2010

against territorial revision;[24] the distribution of international power, which has been characterized by bipolarity and then hegemony;[25] the democratic peace and the spread of democracy among the most powerful states;[26] and economic interdependence.[27]

There are considerable reasons to believe these trends will continue and strengthen into the future. Notwithstanding arms reduction efforts from Cold War levels, it remains unlikely that nuclear weapons will be abandoned by major powers in the near future. As more countries develop economically and become more robust democracies, the democratic and liberal peace imply that the probability of interstate conflict will continue to decline. Projections of national geopolitical capabilities suggest that the world will either remain unipolar or evolve toward bipolarity with the growth of China over the coming decades. The proliferation and strengthening of international institutions, though not necessarily even across policy areas, shows no signs of abating.[28]

[24] Holsti 1991; Diehl and Goertz 2002.
[25] Waltz 1979; Keohane 1980; Gaddis 1986; Kindleberger 1986; Wohlforth 1999.
[26] Maoz and Russett 1993; Bueno de Mesquita et al. 1999; Russett and Oneal 2001.
[27] Oneal, Maoz, and Russett 1996.
[28] For sure, long-term forecasts of trends in international politics do not have an enviable track record: we should not be overconfident about our ability to predict the distant

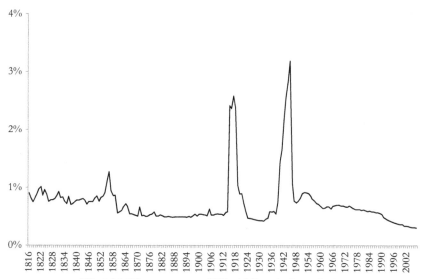

FIGURE 10.4 World Military personnel/World Population 1816–2007.
Source: Sarkees et al. 2010

For present purposes, what is important is not the cause but the *implications* of these trends. War has declined in importance as a means of challenging and determining the shape of the world order. Importantly, this does not imply that countries now share a common outlook about how international relations ought to be managed: what Robert Keohane describes as a state of "harmony."[29] Instead, questions that might have been settled on the battlefield are now increasingly determined through negotiations over which countries exercise control over influential international institutions.

Substantively, contestation over international institutions in many ways replicates the functions performed by military clashes in prior eras. Much as colonial possessions and acknowledgement as a Great Power were coveted in the nineteenth century, countries now seek greater

---

future. Some factors supportive of peace and the rise of institutions could prove temporary. Most obviously, the United States has been an important supporter of an international architecture based on cooperation through international institutions since the end of World War II. It is possible to imagine a world where, as US relative power declines, the risk of interstate conflict increases, and rising states seek to overturn the fundamental premises of the present international order, including its emphasis on international institutions. These events would not invalidate the insights contained in this book, which are drawn from over a century of history and data, but the ideas would hold less relevance insofar as the role of institutions in international politics declined.

[29] Keohane 1984.

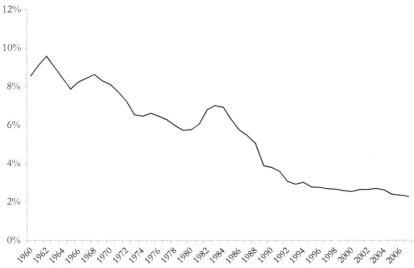

FIGURE 10.5 World Military Expenditures/World GDP 1960–2007.
Source: Sarkees et al. 2010; World Bank

representation and leadership positions in major international organizations as markers of international prestige and recognition. Of course, military force still remains an important element of international relations, and international institutions exercise, for the most part, far less authority than their domestic counterparts. However, it is clear that contestation over international institutions has become an increasingly critical feature of international relations.

An Illustration: US–Japan Competition over East Asia

One useful illustration of the increasing importance of international institutions as a focal point for international contestation is the evolution of US–Japan economic policy toward East Asia. In the early twentieth century, the United States and Japan clashed over varying visions about the future of the region. The US advocated for an open global system that would allow free access to the region's markets, and after the presidency of Woodrow Wilson, the country increasingly adopted the vocabulary of national sovereignty and self-determination.[30] In line with these

[30] Iriye, *Across the Pacific*, 137, 203–4.

principles, the United States set a date for the establishment of a fully autonomous Philippines and became a leading critic of Japanese prerogatives in the Chinese mainland.

The Japanese, on the other hand, defined their policy in strictly regionalist terms, seeking to establish what became known as the "Greater East Asian Co-Prosperity Sphere." Although Japanese rule in East Asia was characterized by aggression and brutality, Japanese writers and thinkers articulated a vision for East Asia in idealistic terms to match Wilson, emphasizing the mutuality and voluntary nature of the proposed cooperative system.[31] Japan saw its role as an East Asian leader guiding the region from the shackles of Western Imperialism.[32] Instead of imposing its will upon the East Asians, the Japanese ideology aimed to establish the "rule of righteousness,"[33] based on harmony and cooperation rather than exploitation.[34]

United States policy toward East Asia envisioned a cooperative *world order*, whereas the Japanese attempted to establish a system of competing regional blocs and a cooperative *East Asian order*. As Matsuoka Yosuke noted, "The world is to be divided into the great East Asia Zone, the European Zone (including Africa), the American Zone, and the Soviet Zone (including India and Iran)."[35] These competing and largely incompatible visions played an important role in moving the two countries toward hostility and ultimately war.

In the postwar period, the United States and Japan have been geopolitical allies, and the two economies have become deeply integrated. However, major philosophical differences remained in how the two countries approached regional issues in East Asia. These differences came to the forefront in the 1980s and 1990s at the height of Japan's rise to economic prominence. The economic debates in many ways echoed those of the 1930s. The United States continued to view East Asia from a global perspective, emphasizing the role of universalistic international organizations such as the WTO and IMF and espousing economic liberalization and free market capitalism. Japanese economic policymakers saw their country as an economic leader in East Asia, and Japan's developmental state model was heralded as potentially superior to the Western

---

[31] For example, see Miyazaki Masayoshi's arguments in *Toa Renmei*, Lebra-Chapman 1975, 4.

[32] E.g., Ibid., 6.   [33] Ibid., 7.

[34] See the arguments of Shinmei Masamichi's *Ideals of the East Asia Cooperative Body*, Ibid., 14–16.

[35] Iriye 1969, 209.

alternative. The notion of Japan leading a pack of "flying geese" in the region, an image first invoked by Kaname Akamatsu in the 1930s, was resurrected to describe the proposed path of regional development.[36] In their introduction to an influential volume on US–Japanese competition in East Asia, Jeffrey Frankel and Miles Kahler noted that:

"Although concern over conflict between Japan and the United States has centered on bilateral trade conflict and its possible spillovers into political and security collaboration, any move toward Japan-centered regionalism also threatens conflict with the United States. Fifty years ago, worsening conflict between the two countries was owed to Japan's expansionist policies in East and Southeast Asia. No one is predicting a reappearance of conflict of that intensity, but an array of models suggests that movement toward regional blocs could intensify international conflict between the United States and Japan."[37]

Analogously, in the wake of the Cold War, realist scholars such as Kenneth Waltz famously predicted that Japan would increase its military capabilities and perhaps acquire nuclear weapons as it reemerged as a Great Power and reasserted its authority over the region:

"Much in Japan's institutions and behavior supports the proposition that it will once again take its place among the great powers. In most of the century since winning its Chinese war in 1894–95, Japan has pressed for preeminence in Asia, if not beyond ... In recent years, the desire of Japan's leaders to play a militarily more assertive role has become apparent, a natural response to Japan's enhanced economic standing."[38]

Instead, as I illustrated in Chapter 4, Japan focused on international institutions as the primary avenues for promoting its newfound status and policy prescriptions for the international order. A crucial battleground for competing Japanese and American visions has been international economic institutions, in which Japan sought to achieve greater influence and recognition for its economic approach. Japan also sought to create regional institutions that it could dominate – most prominently the Asian Development Bank and Asian Monetary Fund – which would pose competition to universalistic institutions supported by the United States. Similarly, while Japan sought international status through imperialism and militarism in the late nineteenth and early twentieth centuries, the country has focused instead on achieving recognition through improved representation and stature in international institutions. UN Security

[36] Akamatsu 1935; Okita 1985; Kojima 2000. [37] Kahler and Frankel 1992, 8.
[38] Waltz 1993, 56, 65.

Council Reform has been one of the highest priorities of Japanese foreign policy in recent decades. Significant financial resources have been invested to support Japanese employees in international organizations. The promotions of Japanese nationals to leadership positions – exemplified by Sadako Ogata as the United Nations High Commissioner for Refugees and Koichiro Matsuura as the Director-General of the United Nations Educational, Scientific and Cultural Organization (UNESCO) – have been heralded as momentous foreign policy accomplishments.

Japan's experience reflects several features that may not necessarily hold for other rising states – a democratic government, strong geopolitical ties with the United States, and pacifist norms that emerged after the end of World War II. China's rise appears to be tracing a more traditional path, emphasizing a buildup of conventional military capabilities. However, China has also aggressively pursued a path similar to Japan vis-à-vis international institutions, seeking greater status and representation where it is perceived as lacking and proposing new institutions that reflect its interests.[39] It is also likely that China will prove more exceptional than Japan. Many other states that rose to prominence in the late twentieth century – Germany, Italy, and South Korea – and contemporary rising powers – India, Brazil, Indonesia, or a more politically integrated European Union – are more democratic and have heavily emphasized international institutions in their foreign policies. None have expanded their military capabilities in a manner comparable to China. It is difficult to predict how persistent traditional modes of international conflict will prove to be. However, there is no denying the increasing importance of bargaining over international institutions as a crucial mechanism for international contestation.

POLICY IMPLICATIONS

This book also has many important implications for policymaking. As noted earlier, redistributive institutional change is a top foreign policy priority for major states such as Brazil, China, Germany, India, and Japan, as well as many developing countries. These demands for change inevitably create tensions with states seeking to defend the status quo, such as the United States and Western European countries. The rapid growth of developing countries such as China and India will continue to

---

[39] Prominent examples include China's push for greater voting rights in the IMF and World Bank, aggressive challenging of US dominance over the internet architecture, and the creation of the Asian Infrastructure Investment Bank.

shift underlying power away from states advantaged by the status quo in major international institutions. Power transitions can be notoriously destabilizing for the international system, often producing geopolitical tensions[40] and economic turbulence.[41] How will institutional bargains play out amidst such shifts? Will existing international organizations successfully adjust? Will the international system fragment as dissatisfied states choose to opt out and establish competing institutions?

Several observations are in order. First, power transitions in policy areas with high costs of challenge are likely to prove the most problematic. In competitive policy areas with high costs of challenge, cooperation will likely fragment and move away from existing institutions. The proliferation of preferential trade agreements in response to gridlock at the WTO may be one manifestation of this.[42] On the other hand, in uncompetitive policy areas, international organizations will likely be sustainable despite glaring disparities in representation and influence. Nonetheless, such conditions are likely to foster resentment and potentially delegitimize cooperative arrangements over the long-term. Institutions that occupy such policy areas, such as the UN Security Council, IMF, and ICANN, will likely require the greatest degree of creative compromise and diplomatic initiative in coming years.

Institutional Design and Reform

One important policy implication that arises from this book is that institutional rules should be brought into greater conformity with underlying policy area characteristics. In policy areas where competition is fierce or likely, rules governing representation ought to be made flexible and responsive to underlying shifts in international power. Although the theory predicts that policy area discipline will eventually shift outcomes in this direction, arriving at greater flexibility through acrimonious contestation, the creation of duplicative institutions, and institutional failure is surely more wasteful of resources and goodwill than doing so through anticipatory planning. Institutions that facilitate cooperation in areas such as development aid, trade agreements, and regional integration should seek to adopt flexible, weighted voting rules. Protections for smaller members can be instituted by creating bicameral structures or supermajority rules that come into play over certain issues, as is the case in the EU and Intelsat in its later years as an intergovernmental organization.

---

[40] Organski 1968; Kennedy 1989; DiCicco and Levy 1999   [41] Kindleberger 1986
[42] Mansfield and Reinhardt 2003

The policy implications concerning noncompetitive institutions are more complicated. Privileged inception members of noncompetitive institutions occupy a position that allows them to exercise asymmetrical influence at the expense of new entrants. In such institutions, formal rules that make challenge more costly will tend to further advantage privileged members by reducing the likelihood of change driven by mechanisms aside from the threat of outside options. It follows that self-interested institutional designers of noncompetitive institutions should implement rules that maximize their own influence and limit the ability of dissatisfied states to challenge the status quo. However, such rules are also likely to exacerbate perceptions of inequity and injustice among newly rising states. The salient question is whether a superior position and control over noncompetitive institutions is sufficiently valuable to offset the cost of potential mistrust and chronic dissatisfaction among a subset of the international community.

This book also provides some guidelines for the creation of new institutions and how countries ought to respond to them. The theory predicts that the creation of alternative arrangements in monopolistic policy areas will only be effective if full displacement is possible. This is akin to private competition in markets subject to strong network effects, such as among word processing software or social networking platforms. In such markets, the simultaneous presence of competing platforms tends to be unstable: consumers have strong incentives to coordinate on a single product for the purposes of collaboration and exchange. Analogously, an alternative to ICANN or the IMF is more likely to ultimately succeed if it is unrestricted in scope: a universalistic alternative is far more credible than a regional one. This implies that regional institutions, such as the Chiang Mai Initiative, would be more credible as potential outside options if membership were made universal. Another implication is that a monopolistic institution may be vulnerable if an alternative can be proposed that replicates comparable functions along with some important, universal advantage lacking in the existing institution.

Policymakers in countries seeking institutional change in international relations may also find the material in this book useful. Countries like Brazil, Germany, India, and Japan make it more difficult to achieve UN Security Council reform by closely aligning their foreign policies with the UN system. Cultivating alternative sources of international legitimation, such as a Concert of Democracies,[43] ought to be a much higher foreign policy priority for these countries as they make the case for greater inclusiveness in the Security

---

[43] Ikenberry and Slaughter 2006.

Council. Although alternative institutions are unlikely to be anything more than second-best options for legitimation, their presence will narrow the scope for gross imbalances by giving some credibility to implicit threats of exit. It is also important to focus on remedying structural sources of imbalances in informal representation, an issue that has, to date, received limited diplomatic attention. An important reason why many non-Western countries exercise limited influence over international institutions is the location of institution headquarters, which rarely change after inception and skew heavily toward the United States and Western Europe. This makes it more difficult for policymakers in distant capitals to exercise influence and to convince nationals to take up positions as organization employees. This source of imbalance could potentially be remedied by negotiating for multiple-headquarter arrangements, which shift core institutional functions to various geographic locations across the globe. Such arrangements are increasingly common in the private sector: for example, multinational firms often divide main corporate functions across a large number of geographic hubs, and Accenture has no corporate headquarters and no executive office.[44] The fact that such arrangements are considered useful and practical for multinational corporations suggests that a comparable case could be made for international institutions, which similarly operate cross-nationally with a diverse workforce.

The Rise of China

A hotly contested contemporary foreign policy debate concerns whether China will attempt to establish itself as a major power through military force or peaceful integration and renegotiation of the existing world order.[45] The question is frequently mulled by policymakers on both sides of the Pacific. The United States has reinvigorated its East Asian alliances and reoriented its military forces toward the region while also seeking to encourage China's peaceful rise.[46] Japanese Prime Minister Shinzo Abe has remarked that, "There are concerns that China is attempting to change the status quo by force, rather than by rule of law. But if China

---

[44] For example, Phred Dvorak, "Why Multiple Headquarters Multiply: As Firms Expand Globally, More Feel the Need to Call More Than One City Home," *The Wall Street Journal*, November 19, 2007.

[45] Bijian 2005; Friedberg 2005; Kang 2007; Glaser 2011.

[46] For example, Margaret Talev, "Obama's Asia Pivot Puts U.S. Approach to China on New Path," *Bloomberg*, November 20, 2011; Jared A. Favole, "Obama, Meeting With Xi, Says US Welcome's China's 'Peaceful Rise'," *Dow Jones Newswires*, February 14, 2012.

opts to take that path, then it won't be able to emerge peacefully."[47] The theory developed in this book cannot predict China's trajectory, which will depend heavily on domestic political and geopolitical developments, but several observations are in order.

On balance, China is well placed to exercise influence over the world order without the need for a violent revision of the status quo. If China had failed to displace Taiwan in major international organizations starting in the 1970s, the prognosis would have been more troubling. As discussed in Chapters 8 and 9, in the 1960s, China exhibited some signs of attempting to challenge the international order, from which it was largely excluded, by mulling the creation of alternative institutions. Because Taiwan was an inception member in many major international organizations, Beijing's displacement of Taipei effectively transferred advantages – exemplified by P5 status on the UN Security Council – that would have been difficult to secure if the country had initiated membership from scratch. Some important imbalances do remain: China's voting share in the IMF of 3.8 percent is well below its 11.4 percent share of world gross domestic product (GDP),[48] and the number of Chinese nationals in international organizations lags behind other major countries.[49] However, on balance, it would appear that China has as much to lose from forcibly undermining the current architecture of international relations as it has to gain.

Another fascinating topic is China's emerging role as a creator of international institutions. One area where Chinese interests remain underrepresented is international economic institutions such as the IMF and World Bank. China has proposed the creation of new institutions such as the Asian Infrastructure Investment Bank (AIIB) and New Development Bank (NDB, initially called the BRICS Bank), which many observers have interpreted as an attempt to challenge the status quo order established by the United States and its allies.[50] The findings of this book allow us to analyze these initiatives

[47] Gerard Baker and George Nishiyama, "Abe Says Japan Ready to Counter China's Power," *Wall Street Journal*, October 26, 2013.

[48] Data as of November 2013. China's voting share is slated to rise to 6.1 percent after the implementation of quota reforms agreed to in 2010. See International Monetary Fund Finance Department, "Quota and Voting Shares Before and After Implementation of Reforms Agreed in 2008 and 2010," www.imf.org/external/np/sec/pr/2011/pdfs/quota_tbl.pdf.

[49] Union of International Associations 2010/2011.

[50] For example, see Ito 2015; "Should Washington Fear the AIIB?" *Foreign Affairs*, June 11, 2015; Robert Keatley, "China's AIIB Challenge: How Should America Respond?" *The National Interest*, April 18, 2015.

with considerable nuance.[51] Both the AIIB and NDB are essentially development aid institutions. As we saw repeatedly in the empirical chapters, development aid institutions already face formidable competition from numerous sources, including plenty of multilateral development banks akin to China's proposed institutions. A direct implication of this point is that China's proposed institutions will be subject to policy area discipline: if the institutions excessively overrerpresent Chinese interests, members will reallocate their resources and attention elsewhere, and the institutions will become nothing more than façades.

In contrast with the AIIB, which is explicitly focused on funding infrastructure development projects, one interesting feature of the NDB is a parallel treaty, the Treaty for the Establishment of a BRICS Contingent Reserve Arrangement (CRA), which was signed in 2015.[52] This is essentially a currency swap arrangement designed to address balance of payments difficulties, which could plausibly compete with the IMF. A Chinese multilateral initiative to compete against the IMF would plausibly represent a more direct challenge to the post–World War II international order, as the IMF has traditionally faced less competition and exhibited greater bias in favor of inception members as discussed in Chapters 3 and 4. However, as we saw with the Chiang Mai Initiative, policy area characteristics place significant limits on competition vis-à-vis the IMF. It is no coincidence that the CRA agreement is much more limited that the AIIB – it only covers five middle-income countries (Brazil, China, India, Russia, South Africa), compared to the much larger and diverse membership of the AIIB – and ties 70 percent of distributions to the presence of an IMF program.[53] A serious Chinese challenge to the IMF would require a willingness to delink from IMF conditionality – that is, accepting the costs of either lending unconditionally to countries in crisis or being implicated in imposing controversial conditions – and a dramatic expansion of membership in initiatives akin to the CRA. Such moves would signal that China is willing to bear considerable costs in order to create a credible, universalistic competitor to effectively replace the IMF. This would represent a far more serious attempt to challenge the US-established international order than the creation of institutions in policy areas already characterized by widespread competition.

---

[51] A more detailed treatment of this subject is available in Lipscy 2015.
[52] "Treaty for the Establishment of a BRICS Contingent Reserve Arrangement," BRICS Ministry of External Relations, July 15, 2015, http://brics.itamaraty.gov.br/media2/press-releases/220-treaty-for-the-establishment-of-a-brics-contingent-reserve-arrangement-for taleza-july-15.
[53] Ibid.

Bibliography

Abbott, Kenneth, and Duncan Snidal. 1998. Why States Act through Formal International Organizations. *Journal of Conflict Resolution* 42(1): 3–32.

Acemoglu, Daron, Georgy Egorov, and Konstantin Sonin. 2007. *Coalition Formation in Nondemocracies*. Working Paper, Cambridge: MIT.

Aizenmann, Joshua, and Jaewoo Lee. 2005. International Reserves: Precautionary vs. Mercantilist Views, Theory and Evidence. IMF Working Paper WP/05/198.

Akamatsu, Kaname. 1935. Waga Kuni Yomo Kogyohin No Susei. *Shogyo Keizai Ronso* 13: 129–212.

Aksoy, Deniz, and Jonathan Rodden. 2009. Getting into the Game: Legislative Bargaining, Distributive Politics, and EU Enlargement. *Public Finance and Management* 9(4): 613–43.

Amemiya, Takeshi. 1984. Tobit Models: A Survey. *Journal of Econometrics* 24(1–2): 3–61.

Amyx, Jennifer. 2002. Moving Beyond Bilateralism? Japan and the Asian Monetary Fund. *Pacific Economic Paper No. 331*.

2005. What Motivates Regional Financial Cooperation in East Asia Today? *Asia-Pacific Issues Paper No. 76*.

Annan, Kofi A. 2005. *In Larger Freedom: Towards Development, Security, and Human Rights for All*. New York: United Nations Publications.

Antonakakis, Nikolaos, Harald B. Badinger, and Wolf Reuter. 2014. From Rome to Lisbon and Beyond: Member States' Power, Efficiency, and Proportionality in the EU Council of Ministers. In *Department of Economics Working Paper Series No. 175*. Vienna University of Economics and Business.

Arab Monetary Fund. 2003. *The Lending Activity*. www.amf.org.ae/pages/page.aspx.

Arthur, W. Brian. 1994. *Increasing Returns and Path Dependence in the Economy*. Ann Arbor: University of Michigan Press.

Awanohara, Susumu. 1998. Asian Crisis Impact: Treasury's Change of Heart. *Capital Trends* 3(3).

Axelrod, Robert, and Robert Keohane. 1985. Achieving Cooperation under Anarchy: Strategies and Institutions. *World Politics* 38(1): 226–54.

Ayish, Muhammad I. 1992. International Communication in the 1990s: Implications for the Third World. *International Affairs* 68(July): 487–510.

Bain, Joe. 1956. *Barriers to New Competition: Their Character and Consequences in Manufacturing Industries.* Cambridge: Harvard University Press.

Banzhaf, J. F. III. 1965. Weighted Voting Doesn't Work: A Mathematical Analysis. *Rutgers Law Review* 19: 317–45.

Barnett, Michael N., and Martha Finnemore. 1999. The Politics, Power, and Pathologies of International Organizations. *International Organization* 53(4): 699–732.

Barro, Robert J., and Jong-Wha Lee. 2005. IMF Programs: Who Is Chosen and What Are the Effects? *NBER Working Paper No. 8951.*

Bauer, Veronika, Wolfgang Benedek, and Matthias C. Kettemann. 2008. *Internet Governance and the Information Society: Global Perspectives and European Dimensions.* Utrecht, The Netherlands: Eleven International Publishing.

Baumol, William J. 1982. Contestable Markets: An Uprising in the Theory of Industry Structure. *The American Economic Review* 72(1): 1–15.

Baumol, William J., John C. Panzar, and Robert D. Willig. 1982. *Contestable Markets and the Theory of Industry Structure.* New York: Harcourt.

Bayoumi, Tamim, and Barry Eichengreen. 1994. One Money or Many? Analyzing the Prospects for Monetary Unification in Various Parts of the World. *Princeton Studies in International Finance 76.*

Bennett, Andrew, Joseph Lepgold, and Danny Unger. 1994. Burden-Sharing in the Persian Gulf War. *International Organization* 48(1): 39–75.

Bijian, Zheng. 2005. China's "Peaceful Rise" To Great-Power Status. *Foreign Affairs* 84(5): 18–24.

Binder, Christina. 2006. Uniting for Peace Resolution (1950). In *Max Planck Encyclopedia of Public International Law.* New York, NY: Oxford University Press.

Binmore, Ken, Avner Shaked, and John Sutton. 1989. An Outside Option Experiment. *The Quarterly Journal of Economics* 104(November): 753–70.

Bird, Graham, and Dane Rowlands. 2001. IMF Lending: How Is It Affected by Economic, Political and Institutional Factors? *Journal of Policy Reform* 4(3): 243–70.

Bjarnason, Magnus. 2010. *The Political Economy of Joining the European Union.* Amsterdam, the Netherlands: Vossiuspers UvA.

Blake, Daniel J., and Autumn Lockwood Payton. 2009. Decision Making in International Organizations: An Interest Based Approach to Voting Rule Selection. Working Paper, Columbus, OH: Ohio State University.

Blaydes, Lisa. 2004. Rewarding Impatience: A Bargaining and Enforcement Model of OPEC. *International Organization* 58(Spring): 213–37.

Blomberg, Brock, and J. Lawrence Broz. 2007. *The Political Economy of IMF Voting Power and Quotas.* San Diego: University of California.

Blum, Yehuda Z. 1967. Indonesia's Return to the United Nations. *The International Comparative Law Quarterly* 16(2): 522–31.

1993. *Eroding the UN Charter.* Boston: Kluwer Academic Publishers.

Blustein, Paul. 2003. *The Chastening*. New York: PublicAffairs.

Boehmer, Charles, Erik Gartzke, and Timothy Nordstrom. 2004. Do Intergovernmental Organizations Promote Peace? *World Politics* 57(October): 1–38.

Boix, Carles. 2011. Democracy, Development, and the International System. *American Political Science Review* 105(4): 809–28.

Bosco, David L. 2009. *Five to Rule Them All: The UN Security Council and the Making of the Modern World*. Oxford: Oxford University Press.

Botcheva, Liliana, and Lisa Martin. 2001. Institutional Effects on State Behavior: Convergence and Divergence. *International Studies Quarterly* 45(1): 1–26.

Boughton, James M. 2001. *Silent Revolution: The International Monetary Fund 1979–1989*. Washington, D.C.: International Monetary Fund.

2012. *Tearing Down Walls: The International Monetary Fund 1990–1999*. Washington, D.C.: International Monetary Fund.

Bourantonis, Dimitris. 2004. *The History and Politics of UN Security Council Reform*. New York: Routledge.

2005. *Politics of UN Security Council Reform*. New York: Taylor & Francis.

Bravo, Karen E. 2005. Caricom, the Myth of Sovereignty, and Aspirational Economic Integration. *North Carolina Journal of International Law and Commercial Regulation* 31: 146–206.

Briggs, Herbert W. 1952. Chinese Representation in the United Nations. *International Organization* 6(2): 192–209.

Broz, Lawrence, and Michael Hawes. 2006. Congressional Politics of Financing the International Monetary Fund. *International Organization* 60(2): 367–99.

Buck, Susan J. 1998. *The Global Commons: An Introduction*. Washington, D.C.: Island Press.

Bueno de Mesquita, Bruce, James D. Morrow, Randolph M. Siverson, and Alastair Smith. 1999. An Institutional Explanation of the Democratic Peace. *American Political Science Review* 93(4): 791–807.

Burkman, Thomas W. 2008. *Japan and the League of Nations: Empire and World Order, 1914–1938*. Honolulu: University of Hawaii Press.

Burns, Josephine Joan. 1935. Conditions of Withdrawal from the League of Nations. *American Society of International Law* 29(1): 40–50.

Burton, Margaret E. 1975. *The Assembly of the League of Nations*. Chicago: University of Chicago Press.

Bush, Sarah. 2011. The Democracy Establishment. Ph.D. Dissertation, Princeton University.

Caballero, Ricardo J., Takeo Hoshi, and Anil K. Kashyap. 2008. Zombie Lending and Depressed Restructuring in Japan. *American Economic Review* 98(5): 1943–77.

Capannelli, Giovanni, Jong-Wha Lee, and Peter Petri. 2009. Developing Indicators for Regional Economic Integration and Cooperation. Asian Development Bank Working Paper Series on Regional Economic Integration No. 33.

Caporaso, James A., Gary Marks, Andrew Moravcsik, and Mark A. Pollack. 1997. Does the European Union Represent an N of 1? *ECSA Review* 10(3): 1–5.

Chan, Gerald. 1989. *China and International Organizations: Participation in Non-Governmental Organizations since 1971*. Oxford: Oxford University Press.

Chang, Cecilia S. 1991. *The Republic of China on Taiwan, 1949–1988.* New York: Institute of Asian Studies, St. John's University.

Chao, Chien-min, and Chih-chia Hsu. 2006. China Isolates Taiwan. In *China's Rise, Taiwan's Dilemmas and International Peace*, edited by Edward Friedman. New York: Routledge.

Chaterjee, K., B. Dutta, D. Ray, and K. Senguputa. 1993. A Non-Cooperative Theory of Coalitional Bargaining. *Review of Economic Studies* 60: 463–77.

Chen, Chi-Di. 1983. On Its Own: The Republic of China. *Asian Affairs* 10(3): 54–69.

Chiu, Hungdah. 1982. *Chinese Yearbook of International Law and Affairs.* Baltimore, MD: Occasional Paper/Reprints Series in Contemporary Asian Studies.

Claude Jr., Inis L. 1966. Collective Legitimization as a Political Function of the United Nations. *International Organization* 20(3): 367–79.

———. 1984. *Swords into Plowshares: The Problems and Progress of International Organization.* New York: Random House.

Cohen, Michael D., James G. March, and Johan P. Olsen. 1972. A Garbage Can Model of Organizational Choice. *Administrative Science Quarterly* 17(1): 1–25.

Communications Satellite Act. 1962. Sec. 102. 47 U.S.C. 701.

Copelovitch, Mark S. 2010. *IMF Loan Size and Conditionality Data, 1983–2003.* Madison: University of Wisconsin.

———. 2010. Master or Servant? Common Agency and the Political Economy of IMF Lending. *International Studies Quarterly* 54(1): 49–77.

Correlates of War Project. 2008. State System Membership List, V2008.1. Online, http://correlatesofwar.org.

Crawford, Susan B. 2004. The ICANN Experiment. *Cardozo Journal of International and Comparative Law* 12(409): 412.

Cronin, Bruce, and Ian Hurd. 2008. *The UN Security Council and the Politics of International Authority*: New York: Routledge.

Cukier, Kenneth Neil. 2005. Who Will Control the Internet? Washington Battles the World. *Foreign Affairs* 84(6).

David, Paul A. 1985. Clio and the Economics of Qwerty. *American Economic Review* 75: 332–37.

———. 1994. Why Are Institutions the 'Carriers of History'?: Path Dependence and the Evolution of Conventions, Organizations and Institutions. *Structural Change and Economic Dynamics* 5(2): 205–20.

de Beaufort Wijnholds, J. Onno, and Lars Sondergaard. 2007. Reserve Accumulation: Objective or by-Product? *European Central Bank Occasional Paper No. 73.*

De Vries, Margaret Garristen. 1987. *The International Monetary Fund, 1966–71: The System under Stress.* Washington, D.C.: International Monetary Fund.

Dedman, Martin. 2010. *The Origins and Development of the European Union 1945–2008: A History of European Integration.* London: Routledge.

Deegan, J., and E. W. Packel. 1978. A New Index of Power for Simple N-Person Games. *International Journal of Game Theory* 7: 113–23.

Deibert, Ronald, John Palfrey, Rafal Rohozinski, and Jonathan Zittrain. 2012. *Access Contested: Security, Identity, and Resistance in Asian Cyberspace.* Cambridge: MIT Press.

Demsetz, Harold. 1968. Why Regulate Utilities. *Journal of Law and Economics* 11(1): 55–65.

1982. Barriers to Entry. *American Economic Review* 72(1): 47–57.

Department of Commerce National Telecommunications Information Agency. 1998. *Statement of Policy on the Management of Internet Names and Addresses*. Washington, D.C.: Department of Commerce.

DiCicco, Jonathan M., and Jack S. Levy. 1999. Power Shifts and Problem Shifts: The Evolution of the Power Transition Research Program. *Journal of Conflict Resolution* 43(6): 675–704.

Diehl, Paul, and Gary Goertz. 2002. *Territorial Changes and International Conflict*. New York: Routledge.

Dooley, Michael P., David Folkerts-Landau, and Peter Garber. 2003. *An Essay on the Revived Bretton Woods System*. Cambridge, Mass., USA, National Bureau of Economic Research.

Dore, R.P. 1975. The Prestige Factor in International Affairs. *International Affairs* 51(2): 190–207.

Drazen, Allan. 2002. Conditionality and Ownership in IMF Lending: A Political Economy Approach. *IMF Staff Papers* 49: 36–67.

Dreher, Axel, and Nathan Jensen. 2007. Independent Actor or Agent? An Empirical Analysis of the Impact of U.S. Interests on International Monetary Fund Conditions. *The Journal of Law and Economics* 50(February): 105–24.

Dreher, Axel, and Roland Vaubel. 2004. The Causes and Consequences of IMF Conditionality. *Emerging Markets Finance and Trade* 40(3): 26–54.

Drezner, Daniel W. 2000. Bargaining, Enforcement, and Multilateral Sanctions: When Is Cooperation Counterproductive? *International Organization* 54(1): 73–102.

2004. The Global Governance of the Internet: Bringing the State Back In. *Political Science Quarterly* 119(3): 477–98.

2007. *All Politics Is Global: Explaining International Regulatory Regimes*. Princeton: Princeton University Press.

Dunbabi, J.P.D. 2014. *The Cold War: The Great Powers and Their Allies*. New York: Routledge.

Edwards, Don Agustin. 1929. Latin America and the League of Nations. *Journal of the Royal Institute of International Affairs* 8(2): 134–53.

Eichengreen, Barry. 2010. The Breakup of the Euro Area. In *Europe and the Euro*, edited by Alberto Alesina and Francesco Giavazzi. Chicago: University of Chicago Press.

Einhorn, Jessica. 2001. The World Bank's Mission Creep. *Foreign Affairs* 80(5): 22–35.

Emmerson, Donald. K. 1998. Americanizing Asia? *Foreign Affairs* 77(3): 46–56.

Fama, Eugene F., and Kenneth R. French. 1993. Common Risk Factors in the Returns on Stocks and Bonds. *Journal of Financial Economics* 33: 3–56.

Fearon, James D. 1994. Domestic Political Audiences and the Escalation of International Disputes. *American Political Science Review* 88: 577–92.

1998. Bargaining, Enforcement, and International Cooperation. *International Organization* 52(Spring): 269–305.

Fearon, James D., and David D. Laitin. 2003. Ethnicity, Insurgency, and Civil War. *American Political Science Review* 97(1): 75–90.

Feld, Harold. 2003. Structured to Fail: ICANN and the Privatization Experiment. In *Who Rules the Net?: Internet Governance and Jurisdiction*, edited by Adam D. Thierer and Clyde Wayne Crews. New York: The CATO Institute.

Felsenthal, Dan S., and Moshe Machover. 1997. The Weighted Voting Rule in the EU's Council of Ministers, 1958–95: Intentions and Outcomes. *Electoral Studies* 16(1): 33–47.

　1998. *The Measurement of Power: Theory and Practice, Problems, and Paradoxes.* Cheltenham: Edward Elgar.

Finnemore, Martha, and Kathryn Sikkink. 1998. International Norm Dynamics and Political Change. *International Organization* 52(4): 887–917.

Fleck, Robert K., and Christopher Kilby. 2006. World Bank Independence: A Model and Statistical Analysis of U.S. Influence. *Review of Development Economics* 10(2): 224–40.

Franda, Marcus F. 2001. *Governing the Internet: The Emergence of an International Regime.* Boulder: L. Rienner Publishers.

　2002. *Launching into Cyberspace: Internet Development and Politics in Five World Regions.* Boulder, CO: Lynne Rienner

Friedberg, Aaron L. 2005. The Future of U.S.–China Relations: Is Conflict Inevitable? *International Security* 30(2): 7–45.

Frieden, Jeffry A. 1999. Actors and Preferences. In *Strategic Choice and International Relations*, edited by David A. Lake and Robert Powell. Princeton: Princeton University Press.

Friedman, Edward. 2006. *China's Rise, Taiwan's Dilemmas and International Peace.* Routledge: New York.

Froomkin, Michael. 2000. Wrong Turn in Cyberspace: Using ICANN to Route around the APA and the Constitution. *Duke Law Journal* 50(1): 17–184.

Funding for United Nations Development Cooperation: Challenges and Options. 2005. New York: United Nations, Department of Economic and Social Affairs.

Gaddis, John Lewis. 1986. The Long Peace. *International Security* 10(Spring): 99–142.

Galvani, Flavia, and Stephen Morse. 2004. Institutional Sustainability: At What Price? UNDP and the New Cost-Sharing Model in Brazil. *Development in Practice* 14(3): 311–27.

Gartzke, Erik. 2010. *The Affinity of Nations: Similarity of State Voting Positions in the UNGA.* San Diego: University of California.

Gilligan, Michael J., and Leslie Johns. 2012. Formal Models of International Institutions. *Annual Review of Political Science* 15: 221–43.

Gilpin, Robert. 1981. *War and Change in World Politics.* New York: Cambridge University Press.

Glaser, Charles. 2011. Will China's Rise Lead to War? *Foreign Affairs* (March/April) 90(2): 80–91.

Glennon, Michael J. 2003. Why the Security Council Failed. *Foreign Affairs* (May/June) 82(3): 16–35.

Goldstein, Judith. 2008. *The Evolution of the Trade Regime: Politics, Law, and Economics of the GATT and the WTO*. Princeton: Princeton University Press.

Goldstone, Jack A. 1988. Initial Conditions, General Laws, Path Dependence, and Explanation in Historical Sociology. *American Journal of Science* 104(3): 829–45.

Goodrich, Leland M. 1947. From League of Nations to United Nations. *International Organization* 1(1): 9–11.

Gould, Erica. 2003. Money Talks: Supplementary Financiers and International Monetary Fund Conditionality. *International Organization* 57(3): 551–86.

Gourevitch, Peter Alexis. 1999. The Governance Problem in International Relations. In *Strategic Choice and International Relations*, edited by David A. Lake and Robert Powell. Princeton: Princeton University Press.

Greenspan, Alan. 2007. *The Age of Turbulence: Adventures in a New World*. New York: Penguin Press.

Grimes, William W. 2008. *Currency and Contest in East Asia: The Great Power Politics of Financial Regionalism*. Ithaca: Cornell University Press.

2011. The Asian Monetary Fund Reborn? Implications of Chiang Mai Initiative Multilateralization. *Asia Policy* 11(January): 79–104.

Gruber, Lloyd. 2000. *Ruling the World: Power Politics and the Rise of Supranational Institutions*. Princeton: Princeton University Press.

Guilloux, Alain. 2009. *Taiwan, Humanitarianism and Global Governance*. London: Routledge.

Haas, Ernst B. 1968. *The Uniting of Europe: Political, Social, and Economic Forces, 1950–1957*. Stanford: Stanford University Press.

Haas, Peter M., Robert O. Keohane, and Marc A. Levy. 1993. *Institutions for the Earth: Sources of Effective International Environmental Protection*. Cambridge: MIT Press.

Hafner-Burton, Emilie M., and Alexander Montgomery. 2006. Power Positions: International Organizations, Social Networks, and Conflict. *Journal of Conflict Resolution* 50(1): 3–27.

Haggard, Stephan. 1985. The Politics of Adjustment: Lessons from the IMF's Extended Fund Facility. *International Organization* 39(Summer): 505–34.

1990. *Pathways from the Periphery: The Politics of Growth in the Newly Industrializing Countries*. Ithaca: Cornell University Press.

Haggard, Stephan, and Robert R. Kaufman. 1992. *The Politics of Economic Adjustment: International Constraints, Distributive Conflicts and the State*. Princeton: Princeton University Press.

Hahn, Robert W., and Randall S. Kroszner. 1990. Lost in Space: U.S. International Satellite Communications Policy. *Cato Review of Business and Government* 13(2): 57–66.

Hawkins, Darren G., David A. Lake, Daniel L. Nielson, and Michael J. Tierney. 2006. *Delegation and Agency in International Organizations*. Cambridge: Cambridge University Press.

Henckaerts, Jean-Marie. 1996. *The International Status of Taiwan in the New World Order*. London: Kluwer Law International.

Henning, C. Randall. 2002. *East Asian Financial Cooperation*. Washington, D.C.: Peterson Institute for International Economics.

Herrero, M. 1985. *A Strategic Bargaining Approach to Market Institutions.* Ph.D. Thesis, London: London University.

Hicks, J.R. 1935. The Theory of Monopoly. *Econometrica* 3(1): 1–20.

Higgins, Rosalyn. 1970. The Place of International Law in the Settlement of Disputes by the Security Council. *The American Journal of International Law* 64(1): 1–18.

Hilderbrand, Robert C. 1990. *Dumbarton Oaks: The Origins of the United Nations.* Chapel Hill: University of North Carolina.

Hills, Jill. 1994. Dependency Theory and Its Relevance Today: International Institutions in Telecommunications and Structural Power. *Review of International Studies* 20(2): 169–186.

   2007. *Telecommunications and Empire (History of Communication).* Urbana, IL: University of Illinois Press.

Hirschman, Albert O. 1970. *Exit, Voice, and Loyalty: Responses to Decline in Firms, Organizations, and States.* Cambridge: Harvard University Press.

Holsti, Kalevi J. 1991. *Peace and War: Armed Conflicts and International Order: 1648–1989.* Cambridge: Cambridge University Press.

Horsefield, Keith J. 1969. *The International Monetary Fund, 1945–1965: Twenty Years of International Monetary Cooperation.* Washington, D.C.: International Monetary Fund.

Housden, Martyn. 2012. *The League of Nations and the Organisation of Peace.* Harlow, United Kingdom: Pearson.

House of Commons Deliberation (United Kingdom). 1984. Greenland (Withdrawal from EEC). HC Deb 20 July, vol. 64, cc671–83.

Howard-Ellis, C. 1928. *The Origin, Structure, & Working of the League of Nations.* New York: Houghton Mifflin Company.

Hsiung, James Chieh. 1981. *Contemporary Republic of China: The Taiwan Experience, 1950–1980.* New York: Praeger.

Hurd, Ian. 2002. Legitimacy, Power, and the Symbolic Life of the UN Security Council. *Global Governance* 8(1): 35–51.

   2008. *After Anarchy: Legitimacy and Power in the United Nations Security Council.* Princeton: Princeton University Press.

Hutchinson, Michael. 2001. A Cure Worse Than the Disease? Currency Crises and the Output Costs of IMF-Supported Stabilization Programs. *NBER Working Paper No. 8305.*

Ikenberry, John G. 2000. *After Victory: Institutions, Strategic Restraint, and the Rebuilding of Order after Major Wars.* Princeton: Princeton University Press.

   2001. *After Victory.* Princeton: Princeton University Press.

Ikenberry, John G., and Anne-Marie Slaughter. 2006. *Forging a World of Liberty under Law: U.S. National Security in the 21st Century.* Princeton: The Woodrow Wilson School of Public and International Affairs, Princeton University.

Imber, Mark F. 1989. *The USA, ILO, UNESCO, and IAEA.* New York: St. Martin's Press.

International Monetary Fund. 2013. *Financial Organization and Operations of the IMF,* 57. Washington, D.C.: International Monetary Fund.

2013. *Stocktaking the Fund's Engagement with Regional Financing Arrangements.* Washington, D.C.: International Monetary Fund.

Internet Corporation for Assigned Names and Numbers. 2014. Bylaws for Internet Corporation for Assigned Names and Numbers. www.icann.org/resources/pages/governance/bylaws-en.

Iriye, Akira. 1969. *Across the Pacific.* New York: Harbinger Books.

Ito, Takatoshi. 2015. The Future of the Asian Infrastructure Investment Bank: Concerns for Transparency and Governance. In *Center on Japanese Economy and Business Occasional Paper Series.* New York, NY: Columbia University.

Jacobson, Harold K., and Michel Oksenberg. 1990. *China's Participation in the IMF, the World Bank, and GATT: Toward a Global Economic Order.* Ann Arbor: University of Michigan Press.

Jervis, Robert. 1982. Security Regimes. *International Organization* 36(2): 357–78.

Johns, Leslie. 2007. A Servant of Two Masters: Communication and the Selection of International Bureaucrats. *International Organization* 61(Spring): 245–75.

Johnson, Chalmers A. 1982. *MITI and the Japanese Miracle: The Growth of Industrial Policy, 1925–1975.* Stanford: Stanford University Press.

Johnson, R. J. 1978. On the Measurement of Power: Some Reactions to Laver. *Environment and Planning* 10: 907–14.

Jupille, Joseph, Walter Mattli, and Duncan Snidal. 2013. *Institutional Choice and Global Commerce.* Cambridge: Cambridge University Press.

Kahler, Miles. 1993. Bargaining with the IMF: Two-Level Strategies and Developing Countries. In *Double-Edged Diplomacy: International Bargaining and Domestic Politics*, edited by Peter Evans, Harold K. Jacobson and Robert D. Putnam, 363–94. Berkeley: University of California Press.

1999. Evolution, Choice, and International Change. In *Strategic Choice and International Relations*, edited by David A. Lake and Robert Powell, 165–96. Princeton: Princeton University Press.

Kahler, Miles, and Jeffrey Frankel. 1992. Introduction. In *Regionalism and Rivalry: Japan and the United States in Pacific Asia*, edited by Miles Kahler and Jeffrey Frankel. Chicago: University of Chicago Press.

Kang, David C. 2003. Hierarchy and Stability in Asian International Relations. In *International Relations Theory and the Asia-Pacific*, edited by G. John Ikenberry and Michael Mastanduno. New York: Columbia University Press.

2007. *China Rising: Peace, Power, and Order in East Asia.* New York: Columbia University Press.

Kapur, Devesh, John P. Lewis, and Richard Charles Webb. 1997. *The World Bank: Its First Half Century*: Washington, D.C.: Brookings Institution Press.

Katada, Saori. 2004. Japan's Counter-Weight Strategy: U.S.-Japan Cooperation and Competition in International Finance. In *Beyond Bilateralism: U.S.-Japan Relations in the New Asia Pacific*, edited by Ellis S. Krauss and T.J. Pempel, 176–97. Stanford: Stanford University Press.

Katkin, Kenneth. 2005. Communication Breakdown?: The Future of Global Connectivity after the Privatization of Intelsat. *International Journal of Communications Law & Policy* 10.

Katz, Michael L., and Carl Shapiro. 1985. Network Externalities, Competition, and Compatibility. *The American Economic Review* 75(3): 424–40.

Kelsen, Hans. 1948. Withdrawal from the United Nations. *The Western Political Quarterly* 1(1): 29–43.

Kennedy, Paul. 1989. *The Rise and Fall of the Great Powers*: New York: Vintage.

Kent, Ann. 2007. *Beyond Compliance: China, International Organizations, and Global Security*. Stanford: Stanford University Press.

Keohane, Robert. 1980. The Theory of Hegemonic Stability and Changes in International Economic Regime. In *Changes in the International System*, edited by Ole Holsti, Randolph Siverson and Alexander George. New York: Westview Press.

Keohane, Robert. 1984. *After Hegemony: Cooperation and Discord in the World Political Economy*. Princeton: Princeton University Press.

Keohane, Robert, and Lisa Martin. 1995. The Promise of Institutionalist Theory. *International Security* 20(1): 39–51.

Kieng-hong, Peter, W. Emily Chow, and Shawn S. F. Kao. 2010. *International Governance, Regimes, and Globalization: Case Studies from Beijing and Taipei*. Plymouth, UK: Lexington Books.

Kijima, Rie. 2010. Why Participate? Cross-National Assessments and Foreign Aid to Education. In *The Impact of International Achievement Studies on National Education Policymaking*, edited by Alexander W. Wiseman. Bradford, UK: Emerald Group Publishing.

Kindleberger, Charles P. 1986. *The World in Depression 1929–1939*. Berkeley: University of California Press.

2000. *Manias, Panics, and Crashes: A History of Fianncial Crises*. New York: John Wiley & Sons.

King, Gary, James Honaker, Anne Joseph, and Kenneth Scheve. 2001. Analyzing Incomplete Political Science Data: An Alternative Algorithm for Multiple Imputation. *American Political Science Review* 95(1): 49–69.

King, Gary, Robert Keohane, and Sidney Verba. 1994. *Designing Social Inquiry: Scientific Inference in Qualitative Research*. Princeton: Princeton University Press.

King, Gary, Jennifer Pan, and Margaret E. Roberts. 2013. How Censorship in China Allows Government Criticism but Silences Collective Expression. *American Political Science Review* 107(2): 326–43.

Kirsch, Werner. 2013. On Penrose's Square-Root Law and Beyond. In *Power, Voting, and Voting Power: 30 Years After*, edited by M.J. Holler and H. Nurmi. Berlin: Springer-Verlag.

Klein, Hans. 2004. Working with the Resources at Hand: Constraints on Internet Institutional Design. *Continuum: Journal of Media & Cultural Studies* 9(3): 398–405.

Klingebiel, Stephan. 1999. *Effectiveness and Reform of the United Nations Development Programme (UNDP)*. New York: Taylor & Francis.

Koczy, Laszlo A. 2012. Beyond Lisbon: Demographic Trends and Voting Power in the European Union Council of Ministers. *Mathematical Social Sciences* 63: 152–58.

Kojima, Kiyoshi. 2000. The "Flying Geese" Model of Asian Economic Development: Origin, Theoretical Extensions, and Regional Policy Implications. *Journal of Asian Economics* 11: 375–401.

Koremenos, Barbara. 2001. Loosening the Ties That Bind: A Learning Model of Agreement Flexibility. *International Organization* 55(2): 289–325.

2005. Contracting around International Uncertainty. *American Political Science Review* 99: 549–65.

Koremenos, Barbara, Charles Lipson, and Duncan Snidal. 2001. The Rational Design of International Institutions. *International Organization* 55(4): 761–99.

Krasner, Stephen D. 1976. State Power and the Structure of International Trade. *World Politics* 28(April): 317–47.

1983. *International Regimes*. Ithaca: Cornell University Press.

1991. Global Communications and National Power: Life on the Pareto Frontier. *World Politics* 43(3): 336–66.

Kreps, David M., and Robert Wilson. 1982. Reputation and Imperfect Information. *Journal of Economic Theory* 27(2): 253–79.

Krishna, V., and Serrano R. 1996. Multilateral Bargaining. *Review of Economic Studies* 63: 61–80.

Kuziemko, Ilyana, and Eric Werker. 2006. How Much Is a Seat on the Security Council Worth? Foreign Aid and Bribery at the United Nations. *Journal of Political Economy* 114: 905–30.

Lake, David A. 1996. Anarchy, Hierarchy, and the Variety of International Relations. *International Organization* 50(Winter): 1–34.

2001. Beyond Anarchy: The Importance of Security Institutions. *International Security* 26(1): 129–60.

2009. *Hierarchy in International Relations*. Ithaca: Cornell University Press.

Lake, David A., and Robert Powell. 1999. *Strategic Choice and International Relations*. Princeton: Princeton University Press.

Lanteigne, Marc. 2005. *China and International Institutions: Alternative Paths to Global Power*. New York: Routledge.

League of Nations Photo Archive. 2002. Geneva, Switzerland: League of Nations Archives.

Lebow, Richard Ned. 2008. *A Cultural Theory of International Relations*. Cambridge, UK: Cambridge University Press.

Lebra-Chapman, Joyce. 1975. *Japan's Greater East Asia Co-Prosperity Sphere in World War II*. Oxford: Oxford University Press.

Lee, Yong Wook. 2006. Japan and the Asian Monetary Fund: An Identity-Intention Approach. *International Studies Quarterly* 50: 339–66.

Leonard, Dick. 2006. A New Deal for Greenland and the EU? *European Voice*.

Leonard, Thomas M. 2011. *The History of Honduras*. Santa Barbara, CA: ABC-CLIO.

Levermore, Charles Herbert 1922. *Yearbook of the League of Nations, Volume 2*. New York: Brooklyn Daily Eagle.

Levy, Jack S. 1989. *Great Power Wars, 1495–1815*. New Brunswick, NJ and Houston, TX: Jack S. Levy and T. Clifton Morgan [producers].

Levy, Steven A. 1975. INTELSAT: Technology, Politics and the Transformation of a Regime. *International Organization* 29(3): 655–80.

Li, Chien-pin. 2006. Taiwan's Participation in Inter-Governmental Organizations: An Overview of Its Initiatives. *Asian Survey* 46(4): 597–614.

Liebowitz, Stan J., and Stephen E. Margolis. 1995. Policy and Path Dependence: From Qwerty to Windows 95. *Regulation* 18(3): 33–41.

Lim, Daniel Yew Mao, and James R. Vreeland. 2013. Regional Organizations and International Politics: Japanese Influence over the Asian Development Bank and the UN Security Council. *World Politics* 65(1): 34–72.

Lin, James. 2012. *International Development Organizations and Agricultural Development in Taiwan, 1945–1975*. Berkeley, CA: University of California.

Lipscy, Phillip Y. 2015. Who's Afraid of the AIIB: Why the United States Should Support China's Asian Infrastructure Investment Bank. *Foreign Affairs*.

2003. Japan's Asian Monetary Fund Proposal. *Stanford Journal of East Asian Affairs* 3(1): 93–104.

Livingstone, Frances. 1965. Withdrawal from the United Nations: Indonesia. *The International and Comparative Law Quarterly* 14(2): 637–46.

Lodge, Henry Cabot. 1919. Henry Cabot Lodge: Reservations with Regard to the Versailles Treaty. In *Chicago Daily News Almanac and Year Book*, edited by George Edward Plumbe, James Langland, and Claude Othello Pike. Chicago: Chicago Daily News: 716–17.

Lombaerde, Philippe De. 2006. *Assessment and Measurement of Regional Integration*. New York: Routledge.

Lu, David J. 2002. *Agony of Choice: Matsuoka Yosuke and the Rise and Fall of the Japanese Empire, 1880–1946*. Lanham: Lexington Books.

Magee, Giovanni, and Massimo Morelli. 2003. Self Enforcing Voting in International Organizations. *NBER Working Paper No. 10102*.

Mahoney, James, and Kathleen Thelen. 2009. *Explaining Institutional Change: Ambiguity, Agency, and Power*. Cambridge: Cambridge University Press.

Malkiel, Burton G. 2003. The Efficient Market Hypothesis and Its Critics. *Journal of Economic Perspectives* 17(1): 59–82.

Malkiel, Burton G., and Eugene F. Fama. 1970. Efficient Capital Markets: A Review of Theory and Empirical Work. *The Journal of Finance* 25(2): 383–417.

Malone, David. 2004. *The UN Security Council: From the Cold War to the 21st Century*. Boulder, CO: Lynne Rienner.

Mansfield, Edward D., and Eric Reinhardt. 2003. Multilateral Determinants of Regionalism: The Effects of GATT/WTO on the Formation of Preferential Trading Arrangements. *International Organization* 57(Fall): 829–62.

Maoz, Zeev, and Bruce Russett. 1993. Normative and Structural Causes of Democratic Peace. *American Political Science Review* 87(3): 624–38.

Martin, Lisa. 1992. Interests, Power, and Multilateralism. *International Organization* 46(4): 765–92.

1997. An Institutionalist View: International Institutions and State Strategies. *Working Paper*. Cambridge: Harvard University.

Martin, Lisa, and Beth Simmons. 1998. Theories and Empirical Studies of International Institutions. *International Organization* 52(4): 729–57.

Mattli, Walter. 1999. *The Logic of Regional Integration: Europe and Beyond*. Cambridge: Cambridge University Press.

McCormick, Patricia. 2008. The Privatization of Intelsat: The Transition from an Intergovernmental Organization to Private Equity Ownership. In *Telecommunications Research Trends*, edited by Hans F. Ulrich and Ernst P. Lehrmann. New York: Nova Science Publishers.

McDowell, Jonathan. 2013. *Master Orbital Launch Log*. Cambridge, MA: Harvard University.

Mearsheimer, John J. 1994. The False Promise of International Institutions. *International Security* 19(3): 5–49.

Miller, Andrew R., and Nives Dolsak. 2007. Issue Linkages in International Environmental Policy: The International Whaling Commission and Japanese Development Aid. *Global Environmental Politics* 7(1): 69–96.

Milner, Helen V. 2006. The Digital Divide: The Role of Domestic Political Institutions in the Spread of the Internet. *Comparative Political Studies* 39(2): 176–99.

Minford, Patrick, Vidya Mahambare, and Eric Nowell. 2005. *Should Britain Leave the EU?: An Economic Analysis of a Troubled Relationship*: Northampton, MA: Edward Elgar Publishing.

Ministry of Foreign Affairs (Japan). 2011. *Nihon Gaiko Bunsho: Nichu Sensou (Japanese Dipomatic Documents, Sino-Japanese War)*. Tokyo Japan: Rokuichi Shobo.

Mitchell, Ronald B. 2006. Problem Structure, Institutional Design, and the Relative Effectiveness of International Environmental Agreements. *Global Environmental Politics* 6(3): 72–89.

Moe, Terry. 1989. The Politics of Bureaucratic Structure. In *Can the Government Govern?*, edited by John E. Chubb and Paul E. Peterson. Washington, D.C.: The Brookings Institution.

Moravcsik, Andrew. 1998. *The Choice for Europe: Social Purpose & State Power from Messina to Maastricht*. Ithaca: Cornell University Press.

———. 2000. The Origins of Human Rights Regimes: Democratic Delegation in Postwar Europe. *International Organization* 54(2): 217–52.

Morris, Stephen D., and John Passé-Smith. 2001. What a Difference a Crisis Makes: NAFTA, Mexico, and the United States. *Latin American Perspectives* 28(3): 124–49.

Mueller, Milton, John Mathiason, and Hans Klein. 2007. The Internet and Global Governance: Principles and Norms for a New Regime. *Global Governance* 13(2): 237–54.

Mukherjee, Bumba, and David A. Singer. 2010. International Institutions and Domestic Compensation: The IMF and the Politics of Capital Account Liberalization. *American Journal of Political Science* 54(1): 45–60.

Mukherji, Indra Nath. 2005. The Bangkok Agreement: A Negative List Approach to Trade Liberalization in Asia and the Pacific. *Asia-Pacific Trade and Investment Review* 1(2): 55–68.

Mundell, Robert A. 1961. A Theory of Optimum Currency Areas. *American Economic Review* 51(4): 657–65.

Muthoo, Abhinay. 1999. *Bargaining Theory with Applications*. Cambridge: Cambridge University Press.

Myers, Denise P. 1935. *Handbook of the League of Nations*. Medford, MA: World Peace Foundation.

Naughton, Barry. 1994. Chinese Institutional Innovation and Privatization from Below. *The American Economic Review* 84(2): 266–70.

Nelson, Rebecca M., and Martin A. Weiss. 2015. IMF Reforms: Issues for Congress. Washington, D.C.: Congressional Research Service.

NHK (Nihon Hosou Kyokai). 2011. Nihon Wa Naze Senso He to Mukatta No Ka: Gaiko Haisen Koritsu He No Michi (Why Did Japan Head towards War?: The Path towards Diplomatic Defeat and Isolation).

Nicholls, Shelton, Anthony Birchwood, Philip Colthrust, and Earl Boodoo. 2000. The State of and Prospects for the Deepening and Widening of Caribbean Integration. *The World Economy* 23(9): 1161–94.

Nixon, F.G. 1970. A Progress Report on the Move toward Definitive Agreements. *The University of Toronto Law Journal* 20(3): 380–85.

North-South Monitor. 1985. *Third World Quarterly* 7(4): 1009–64.

North, W. Haven, Fuat Andic, Duduzile Chandiwana, Peider Könz, and Ralf Maurer. 1996. *Building Development Partnership through Co-Financing*. New York: Office of Strategic Planning, UNDP.

Nye, Joseph S. 1968. Comparative Regional Integration: Concept and Measurement. *International Organization* 22(4): 855–80.

O'Mahony, Mary, and Marcel P. Timmer. 2009. Output, Input and Productivity Measures at the Industry Level: The EU Klems Database. *Economic Journal* 119(538): F374–F403.

Oatley, Thomas, and Jason Yackee. 2004. American Interests and IMF Lending. *International Politics* 41(3): 415–29.

Oatley, Thomas, and Robert Nabors. 1998. Redistributive Cooperation: Market Failures and Wealth Transfers in the Creation of the Basle Accord. *International Organization* 52(Winter): 35–54.

Ogata, Sadako. 1989. Shifting Power Relations in Multilateral Development Banks. *The Journal of International Studies* 22: 1–25.

Okita, Saburo. 1985. Special Presentation: Prospect of Pacific Economies. In *Pacific Cooperation: Issues and Opportunities: Report of the Fourth Pacific Economic Cooperation Conference*, 18–29, edited by Korea Development Institute. Seoul, Korea: Korea Development Institute.

Oneal, John R., Bruce Russett, and Michael L. Berbaum. 2003. Causes of Peace: Democracy, Interdependence, and International Organizations. *International Studies Quarterly* 47(3): 371–93.

Oneal, John R., Zeev Maoz, and Bruce Russett. 1996. The Liberal Peace: Interdependence, Democracy, and International Conflict: 1950–1985. *Journal of Peace Research* 33(1): 11–28.

Organski, A. F. K. 1968. *World Politics*. New York: Knopf.

Osborne, M., and Ariel Rubinstein. 1990. *Bargaining and Markets*. San Diego: Academic Press.

Oye, Kenneth A. 1985. Explaining Cooperation under Anarchy: Hypotheses and Strategies. *World Politics* 38(1): 1–24.

Pak, Chi Young. 2000. *Korea and the United Nations*. The Hague, Netherlands: Martinus Nijhoff Publishers.

Paul, T.V., Deborah Welch Larson, and William C. Wohlforth. 2014. *Status in World Politics*. New York: Cambridge University Press.

Penrose, L.S. 1946. The Elementary Statistics of Majority Voting. *Journal of the Royal Statistical Society* 109: 53–57.

Peters, B. Guy, Jon Pierre, and Desmond S. King. 2005. The Politics of Path Dependency: Political Conflict in Historical Institutionalism. *Journal of Politics* 67(4): 1275–300.

Pevehouse, Jon C., Timothy Nordstrom, and Kevin Warnke. 2004. The COW-2 International Organizations Dataset Version 2.0. *Conflict Management and Peace Science* 21(2): 101–19.

Phoebus, Athanassiou. 2009. Withdrawal and Expulsion from the EU and EMU. *European Central Bank Legal Working Paper Series* 10.

Pierson, Paul. 1996. The Path to European Union: An Historical Institutionalist Account. *Comparative Political Studies* 29(2): 123–64.

2000. Increasing Returns, Path Dependence, and the Study of Politics. *The American Political Science Review* 94(2): 251–67.

Pinker, Steven. 2012. *The Better Angels of Our Nature: Why Violence Has Declined*. New York: Penguin Books.

Pollack, Mark A. 2005. Theorizing the European Union. *Annual Review of Political Science* 8: 357–98.

Poole, Peter A. 1974. *China Enters the United Nations: A New Era Begins for the World Organization*. New York: World Focus Books.

Posner, Daniel N. 2004. The Political Salience of Cultural Difference: Why Chewas and Tumbukas Are Allies in Zambia and Adversaries in Malawi. *American Political Science Review* 98(4): 529–45.

Powell, Robert. 1994. Anarchy in International Relations Theory: The Neorealist-Neoliberal Debate. *International Organization* 48(2): 313–44.

1999. *In the Shadow of Power: States and Strategies in International Politics*. Princeton: Princeton University Press.

Prestowitz, Clyde V. 1988. *Trading Places: How We Allowed Japan to Take the Lead*: New York: Basic Books.

Privatization of Intelsat. 2001. *The American Journal of International Law* 95(4): 894–95.

Rapkin, David P., Joseph U. Elston, and Jonathan R. Strand. 1997. Institutional Adjustment to Changed Power Distributions: Japan and the United States in the IMF. *Global Governance* 3(171–95).

Reiter, Dan. 2003. Exploring the Bargaining Model of War. *Perspectives on Politics* 1(1): 27–43.

Remmer, Karen. 1986. The Politics of Economic Stabilization: IMF Standby Programs in Latin America, 1954–1984. *Comparative Politics* 19(1): 1–24.

Risse-Kappen, Thomas, Stephen C. Ropp, and Kathryn Sikkink. 1999. *The Power of Human Rights: International Norms and Domestic Change*. Cambridge: Cambridge University Press.

Rodden, Jonathan. 2002. Strength in Numbers: Representation and Redistribution in the European Union. *European Union Politics* 3(2): 151–75.

Rodrik, Daniel. 2008. *The Real Exchange Rate and Economic Growth*. Cambridge, MA: Harvard University.

　1994. Getting Interventions Right: How South Korea and Taiwan Grew Rich. *NBER Working Paper No. 4964*.

Rosendorff, B. Peter, and Helen V. Milner. 2001. The Optimal Design of International Trade Institutions: Uncertainty and Escape. *International Organization* 55(4): 829–58.

Rowen, Henry. 1998. The Political and Social Foundations of the Rise of East Asia: An Overview. In *Behind East Asian Growth*, edited by Henry Rowen. New York: Routledge.

Rubin, Robert. 2004. *In an Uncertain World: Tough Choices from Wall Street to Washington*. New York: Random House.

Rubinstein, Ariel. 1982. Perfect Equilibrium in a Bargaining Model. *Econometrica* 50(1): 97–109.

Russett, Bruce, and John R. Oneal. 2001. *Triangulating Peace: Democracy, Interdependence, and International Organizations*. New York: W.W. Norton.

Russett, Bruce, John R. Oneal, and David Davis. 1998. The Third Leg of the Kantian Tripod for Peace: International Organizations and Militarized Disputes, 1950–1985. *International Organization* 52(3): 441–67.

Sagan, Scott D., and Kenneth N. Waltz. 2012. *The Spread of Nuclear Weapons: An Enduring Debate*. New York: W. W. Norton & Company.

Sakakibara, Eisuke. 2000. *Nihon to Sekai Ga Furueta Hi [The Day That Rocked Japan and the World]*. Tokyo, Japan: Chuo Koron Shinsha.

　2001. The Asian Monetary Fund: Where Do We Go from Here? Kuala Lumpur, Malaysia: Paper presented at the International Conference on Globalization.

Sandler, Todd. 1993. The Economic Theory of Alliances: A Survey. *The Journal of Conflict Resolution* 37(3): 446–83.

Sarkees, Meredith Reid, and Frank Wayman. 2010. *Resort to War: 1816–2007*. Washington, D.C.: CQ Press.

Satoh, Yukio. 2001. Step by Step toward Permanent Membership: Japan's Strategy for Security Council Reform. *Gaiko Forum: Japanese Perspectives on Foreign Affairs* 1(2).

Schneider, Christina J. 2009. *Conflict, Negotiation, and European Union Enlargement*. New York: Cambridge University Press.

Schwelb, Egon. 1967. Withdrawal from the United Nations. *The American Journal of International Law* 61(3): 661–72.

Scott, George. 1974. *The Rise and Fall of the League of Nations*. London: Macmillan.

Sebesta, Lorenza. 1997. The Good, the Bad, the Ugly: U.S.-European Relations and the Decision to Build a European Launch Vehicle. In *Beyond the Ionosphere: The Development of Satellite Communications*, edited by Andrew J. Butrica. Washington, D.C.: NASA History Series.

Selten, Reinhard. 1978. The Chain Store Paradox. *Theory and Decision* 9(2): 127–59.

Shambaugh, Jay. 2004. The Effect of Fixed Exchange Rates on Monetary Policy. *Quarterly Journal of Economics* 119(1): 301–52.

Shanks, Cheryl, Harold K. Jacobson, and Jeffrey H. Kaplan. 1996. Inertia and Change in the Constellation of International Governmental Organizations. *International Organization* 50(4): 593–627.

Shapley, L.S., and Martin Shubik. 1954. A Method for Evaluating the Distribution of Power in a Committee System. *American Political Science Review* 48(3): 787–92.

Simmons, Beth. 2001. The International Politics of Harmonization: The Case of Capital Market Regulation. *International Organization* 55(3): 589–620.

Singer, J. David, Stuart Bremer, and John Stuckey. 1972. Capability Distribution, Uncertainty, and Major Power War, 1820–1965. In *Peace, War, and Numbers*, edited by Bruce Russett. Beverly Hills: Sage.

Spencer, Richard Carleton. 1930. *The Relationship between the Assembly and the Council of the League of Nations*. Urbana, Ill: University of Illinois.

Stigler, George. 1968. *The Organization of Industry*. Chicago: University of Chicago Press.

Stiglitz, Joseph. 2002. *Globalization and Its Discontents*. New York: W.W. Norton & Co.

Stone, Randall W. 2002. *Lending Credibility: The International Monetary Fund and the Post-Communist Transition*. Princeton: Princeton University Press.

    2004. The Political Economy of IMF Lending in Africa. *American Political Science Review* 98(4): 577–91.

    2008. The Scope of IMF Conditionality. *International Organization* 62(4): 589–620.

    2011. *Controlling Institutions: International Organizations and the Global Economy*. Cambridge: Cambridge University Press.

Suh, Sang-Chul, and Quan Wen. 2003. Multi-Agent Bilateral Bargaining and the Nash Bargaining Solution. Vanderbilt University, Department of Economics Working Papers, 306.

Sutton, John. 1986. Non-Cooperative Bargaining Theory: An Introduction. *The Review of Economic Studies* 53(5): 709–24.

Swaine, Michael D. 2013. Chinese Views on Cybersecurity in Foreign Relations. *China Leadership Monitor* 42.

Swiss Federal Council. 2006. *Europe 2006 Report*. Bern, Switzerland.

Talbot, Ross B. 1980. The International Fund for Agricultural Development. *Political Science Quarterly* 95(2): 261–76.

Taylor, Alastair M. 1965. Sukarno: First United Nations Drop-Out. *International Journal* 20(2): 206–13.

Taylor, Travis S. 2009. First Steps to the Moon, First Global Broadcast. Intelsat Official Blog: blog.intelsat.com/2009/07/first-steps-on-moon-first-global.html

Thacker, Strom C. 1999. The High Politics of IMF Lending. *World Politics* 52: 38–75.

The George Washington University National Security Archive. 1964. Indonesia: Sukarno's Confrontation with Malaysia: January–November 1964. www2 .gwu.edu/~nsarchiv/NSAEBB/NSAEBB52/doc1.pdf.

1965. Sukarno's Confrontation with the United States: December 1964– September 1965. www2.gwu.edu/~nsarchiv/NSAEBB/NSAEBB52/doc189.pdf.

Thelen, Kathleen. 2004. *How Institutions Evolve: The Political Economy of Skills in Germany, Britain, the United States, and Japan.* Cambridge: Cambridge University Press.

Thierer, Adam D., and Clyde Wayne Crews. 2003. *Who Rules the Net?: Internet Governance and Jurisdiction.* New York: The CATO Institute.

Thompson, Alexander. 2005. *The Rational Choice of International Institutions: Uncertainty and Flexibility in the Climate Regime.* Paper presented at the annual meeting of the American Political Science Association, September 1–4, Washington, D.C.

2006. Coercion through IOs: The Security Council and the Logic of Information Transmission. *International Organization* 60(Winter): 1–34.

Thussu, Daya Kishan. 2001. Lost in Space. *Foreign Policy* 124: 70–71.

Tierney, Michael J., Daniel L. Nielson, Darren G. Hawkins, J. Timmons Roberts, Michael G. Findley, Ryan M. Powers, Bradley Parks, Sven E. Wilson, and Robert L. Hicks. 2011. More Dollars Than Sense: Refining Our Knowledge of Development Finance Using AidData. *World Development* 39(11): 1891–906.

Timmer, Marcel P., and Gaaitzen J. de Vries. 2009. Structural Change and Growth Accelerations in Asia and Latin America: A New Sectoral Data Set. *Cliometrica* 3(2): 165–90.

Tirole, Jean. 1988. *The Theory of Industrial Organization.* Cambridge: MIT Press.

Tobin, James. 1958. Estimation for Relationships with Limited Dependent Variables. *Econometrica* 26(1): 24–36.

Tomuschat, Christian. 1995. *The United Nations at Age Fifty: A Legal Perspective.* Boston, MA: Springer.

Trooboff, Peter D. 1968. INTELSAT: Approaches to the Renegotiation. *Harvard Law Review* 9(1): 1–84.

Tsang, Steve. 2008. *Taiwan and the International Community.* New York: Peter Lang.

US Department of State. 1964. *International Telecommunications Satellite Consortium: Agreement between the United States of America and Other Governments.* Washington D.C.: U.S. Department of State.

US Department of State. 1984. U.S./UNESCO Policy Review. 27 February.

2010/2011. *Who's Who in International Organizations.* New Providence, NJ: De Gruyter.

2014. *Statistics, Visualizations and Patterns, Yearbook of International Organizations.* New York: Union of International Associations & Brill.

Union of International Associations. 2005. Statistics, Visualizations and Patterns, Yearbook of International Organizations. Union of International Associations & Brill.

van Ginneken, Anique H. M. 2006. *Historical Dictionary of the League of Nations.* Lanham: The Scarecrow Press.

Van Rijckeghem, Caroline, and Beatrice Weder. 2000. Spillovers through Banking Centers: A Panel Data Analysis. *IMF Working Paper WP/00/88*.

Voeten, Erik. 2001. Outside Options and the Logic of Security Council Action. *American Political Science Review* 95(4): 845–58.

　　2005. The Political Origins of the UN Security Council's Ability to Legitimize the Use of Force. *International Organization* 59(3): 527–57.

　　2008. Why No UN Security Council Reform? Lessons for and from Institutionalist Theory. In *Multilateralism and Security Institutions in an Era of Globalization*, edited by Dimitris Bourantonis, Kostas Ifantis and Panayotis Tsakonas, 288–305. New York: Routledge.

Vogel, Ezra. 1979. *Japan as Number One: Lessons for America*. Cambridge: Harvard University Press.

Vreeland, James R. 2003. *The IMF and Economic Development*. Cambridge: Cambridge University Press.

　　2007. *The International Monetary Fund: Politics of Conditional Lending*. New York, NY: Routledge.

Wade, Robert. 1996. Japan, the World Bank, and the Art of Paradigm Maintenance: The East Asian Miracle in Political Perspective. *New Left Review* 217 (May–June): 3–36.

Waltz, Kenneth N. 1979. *Theory of International Politics*. New York: McGraw-Hill.

　　1990. Nuclear Myths and Political Realities. *American Political Science Review* 84(3): 731–45.

　　1993. The Emerging Structure of International Politics. *International Security* 18(2): 44–79.

Weingast, Barry R. 1995. The Economic Role of Political Institutions: Market-Preserving Federalism and Economic Development. *Journal of Law, Economics, and Organization* 11(1): 1–31.

Weiss, Jessica Chen. 2013. Authoritarian Signalling, Mass Audiences and Nationalist Protest in China. *International Organization* 67(1): 1–35.

Weiss, Thomas G., David P. Forsythe, Roger A. Coate, and Kelly-Kate Pease. 2013. *The United Nations and Changing World Politics*. Boulder, CO: Westview Press.

Wells, H.G. 1914. *The War That Will End War*. London: Frank & Cecil Palmer.

Wendt, Alexander. 1999. *Social Theory of International Politics*. Cambridge: Cambridge University Press.

Weng, Byron S. J. 1984. Taiwan's International Status Today. *The China Quarterly* 99(September): 462–80.

Whalen, David J. 2010. Communications Satellites: Making the Global Village Possible. Washington, D.C.: NASA.

Widenor, William C. 1980. *Henry Cabot Lodge and the Search for an American Foreign Policy*. Berkeley, CA: University of California Press.

Williamson, John. 1983. *IMF Conditionality*. Washington, D.C: Institute for International Economics.

Williamson, Oliver E. 1971. The Vertical Integration of Production: Market Failure Considerations. *American Economic Review* 61(2): 112–23.

Wilson, David. 1971. Space Business: The History of INTELSAT. In *Yearbook of World Affairs* 25: 72.

Wohlforth, William C. 1999. The Stability of a Unipolar World. *International Security* 24(1): 5–41.

World Bank. 1980. *World Bank Annual Report*. Washington, D.C.: World Bank.
  1993. *The East Asian Miracle: Economic Growth and Public Policy*. Oxford: Oxford University Press.

Yasumoto, Dennis T. 1983. *Japan and the Asian Development Bank*. New York: Praeger Publishers.

Yearbook of the United Nations. 1971. New York: United Nations.

Young, Oran R. 1989. *International Cooperation: Building Regimes for Natural Resources and the Environment*. Ithaca: Cornell University Press.

Index

f refers to figure caption and t refers to table caption

CPSIA information can be obtained
at www.ICGtesting.com
Printed in the USA
LVHW01s1920060618
579821LV00014B/244/P